MW00570502

An Introduction to Teaching

An Introduction to Teaching

A Question of Commitment

Ralph E. Martin, Jr.
Ohio University

■ *George H. Wood*
Ohio University

■ *Edward W. Stevens, Jr.*
Ohio University

Allyn and Bacon, Inc.
Boston   London   Sydney   Toronto

Library of Congress Cataloging-in-Publication Data
Martin, Ralph E., 1951–
    An introduction to teaching.

    Bibliography: p.
    Includes index.
        1. Teaching—Vocational guidance.   I. Wood, George H.
II. Stevens, Edward, 1938–   .   III. Title.
LB1775.M4334 1988   371.1′02   87-31888
ISBN 0-205-11375-3

Series Editor: Susanne E. Canavan
Developmental Editor: Elizabeth Brooks
Cover Administrator: Linda Dickinson
Editorial-Production Service: Editing, Design & Production, Inc.

Printed in the United States of America.
10 9 8 7 6 5 4   93 92 91 90

Photo credits
H. Armstrong Roberts: pp. 8, 14, 23, 32, 47, 91 (top), 92, 98, 101, 119, 127, 136, 150, 186, 229, 302, 313, 318, 324, 347, 351, 381, 382, 400, 411 (bottom), 413; Freda Leinwand: pp. 87, 91 (bottom), 169, 411 (top); Mike Penney: pp. 42, 68, 163, 196, 203, 220, 227, 287, 296, 346, 360.

To our first teachers—our parents.

Brief Contents

I: LOOKING AT TEACHING   1

CHAPTER 1: LOOKING IN CLASSROOMS   3

CHAPTER 2: WHO ARE TEACHERS AND WHY DO THEY TEACH?   29

CHAPTER 3: THE CURRENT CONTEXT FOR SCHOOLING   53

CHAPTER 4: LEARNING ABOUT TEACHING   85

II: WORKING WITH STUDENTS   109

CHAPTER 5: STUDENTS   111

CHAPTER 6: COMMUNICATING WITH STUDENTS   143

CHAPTER 7: CLASSROOM ATMOSPHERE   185

III: THE SCHOOL AND THE TEACHER   215

CHAPTER 8: SCHOOL ORGANIZATION AND THE ROLE OF THE TEACHER   217

CHAPTER 9: CONTEXTS FOR TEACHING: PERSPECTIVES BEFORE THE TWENTIETH CENTURY   245

CHAPTER 10: NEW CONTEXTS FOR BEING A TEACHER: THE TWENTIETH CENTURY   275

IV: THE SCIENCE AND ART OF TEACHING   309

CHAPTER 11: TEACHERS AND PLANNING   311

CHAPTER 12: TEACHERS AND TEACHING   341

CHAPTER 13: CAN YOU TEACH?   375

Contents

Preface   xv

I LOOKING AT TEACHING   1

1 LOOKING IN CLASSROOMS   3
   INTRODUCTION   3
   LOOKING AT TEACHERS   4
     A Scenario: The Classroom Report
     Thinking About Teaching
     Looking in Classrooms
     What Is the Quality of Teacher-Student Relationships?
   BECOMING THE BEST   20
     Avoiding the Handicaps of Teaching
     Bringing Out the Best in Yourself and Others
   CHAPTER SUMMARY   25
   FOR DISCUSSION   25
   IN THE SCHOOL/IN THE CLASSROOM   26
   SUGGESTED READINGS   27
   CHAPTER REFERENCES   28

2 WHO ARE TEACHERS AND WHY DO THEY TEACH?   29
   A SCENARIO   29
   INTRODUCTION   31
   TEACHERS   31
     Who Are Teachers?
     How Good Are Our Teachers?
   WHY TEACH?   39
     Not for the Pay
     The Joy of Teaching
   CHAPTER SUMMARY   46
   FOR DISCUSSION   48
   IN THE SCHOOL/IN THE CLASSROOM   49
   SUGGESTED READINGS   49
   CHAPTER REFERENCES   50

3 THE CURRENT CONTEXT FOR SCHOOLING   53
   A SCENARIO   53
   INTRODUCTION   54

THE NEW CONCERN FOR PUBLIC EDUCATION   54
  The Continuing Debate
THE MULTIPLE ROLES OF PUBLIC SCHOOLING   67
  Solving the Problems of Democracy
  Solving the Personal Problems of Students
  Social or Academic Skills?
THE CONTEXTUAL CHALLENGE TO EDUCATORS   75
  Schooling and Instrumental Reason
EDUCATORS AND THE SEARCH FOR PURPOSE   77
  Creating a User-Friendly Environment
CHAPTER SUMMARY   80
FOR DISCUSSION   81
IN THE SCHOOL/IN THE CLASSROOM   81
SUGGESTED READINGS   82
CHAPTER REFERENCES   83

4 LEARNING ABOUT TEACHING   85
A SCENARIO   85
BECOMING A TEACHER   86
  Is a Teacher Born or Prepared?
  Your Personal Responsibility
  Accepting the Tasks
MAKING DECISIONS   95
  Personal Expectations
  Specialized Knowledge
  Professional Knowledge
REFLECTING ON TEACHING   97
  What It Means to Reflect
  Prerequisites for Reflection
  How to Reflect
MEETING CHALLENGES   104
  Society's Challenge
CHAPTER SUMMARY   104
FOR DISCUSSION   105
IN THE SCHOOL/IN THE CLASSROOM   106
SUGGESTED READINGS   106
CHAPTER REFERENCES   107

II WORKING WITH STUDENTS   109

5 STUDENTS   111
SCENARIO: REACTION TO TEACHERS   111
  Reaction to Administrators
INTRODUCTION   113

STUDENT ACADEMIC PERFORMANCE   114
    Falling Test Scores
    Dropping Out or Staying In?
    Teacher Perceptions
YOUTH CULTURE   120
    The Family
    Peer Pressures
    The Media
THE HURRIED CHILD   130
    The Social Construction of Childhood
    The Disappearance of Childhood
THE CHALLENGE FOR THE TEACHER   135
    The Hope
CHAPTER SUMMARY   138
FOR DISCUSSION   139
IN THE SCHOOL/IN THE CLASSROOM   139
SUGGESTED READINGS   140
CHAPTER REFERENCES   141

6 COMMUNICATING WITH STUDENTS   143
  A SCENARIO   144
  INTRODUCTION
  BARRIERS TO EFFECTIVE CLASSROOM
  COMMUNICATION   145
    Teachers' Verbal and Nonverbal Messages to Students
    Communicating Expectations and Stereotypes
  CHANNELS OF EFFECTIVE COMMUNICATION   161
    Classroom Communication Skills
    Human Relations Skills
    Positive Expectations
    Overcoming Stereotypes
  CHAPTER SUMMARY   176
  FOR DISCUSSION   177
  IN THE SCHOOL/IN THE CLASSROOM   178
  SUGGESTED READINGS   179
  CHAPTER REFERENCES   179

7 CLASSROOM ATMOSPHERE   183
  A SCENARIO   184
  INTRODUCTION   184
  DISCIPLINE IN SCHOOLS—IMAGE VS. REALITY   185
    Perceptions of Discipline in the Schools
  CLASSROOM MANAGEMENT   192
    Behavior Modification

Advantages and Disadvantages to Behavior
Modification Strategies
CLASSROOM ATMOSPHERE   197
Comprehensive Classroom Management and
Atmosphere
Advantages and Disadvantages to Comprehensive
Classroom Management and Atmosphere
BARRIERS TO DEVELOPING SELF-DISCIPLINE   207
Corporal Punishment
Suspension
Arbitrary Rules
CHAPTER SUMMARY   209
FOR DISCUSSION   210
IN THE SCHOOL/IN THE CLASSROOM   211
SUGGESTED READINGS   211
CHAPTER REFERENCES   212

III THE SCHOOL AND THE TEACHER   215

8 SCHOOL ORGANIZATION AND THE ROLE OF THE
   TEACHER   217
   A SCENARIO   217
   INTRODUCTION   219
   SIMILARITIES IN SCHOOLS ACROSS THE NATION   221
   Organizational Structure
   Funding and Governance
   Academic Programs
   Male Dominance in Leadership Roles
   SOURCES OF DIFFERENCES IN SCHOOLS   228
   Two Schools and Their Communities
   Metaphorical Representations of Schools
   THE COMPLEX ROLES OF THE TEACHER   234
   Role Definition
   Teachers and Roles
   CHAPTER SUMMARY   239
   FOR DISCUSSION   241
   IN THE SCHOOL/IN THE CLASSROOM   242
   SUGGESTED READINGS   243
   CHAPTER REFERENCES   243

9 CONTEXTS FOR TEACHING: PERSPECTIVES BEFORE
   THE TWENTIETH CENTURY   245
   A SCENARIO: A MATTER OF VALUE   245
   INTRODUCTION   246

COLONIAL PRECEDENTS   247
AN EMERGING NATION   250
BASIC EDUCATION   251
SCIENCE AND MENTAL DEVELOPMENT   252
BEING A GOOD TEACHER   255
  Establishing a Teaching Force
EXPANDING THE SYSTEM OF PUBLIC EDUCATION   263
  Patterns of Enrollment
  A Science of Pedagogy
  Reform in Psychology and Curriculum
CHAPTER SUMMARY   271
FOR DISCUSSION   271
IN THE SCHOOL/IN THE CLASSROOM   272
SUGGESTED READINGS   273
CHAPTER REFERENCES   273

10 NEW CONTEXTS FOR BEING A TEACHER: THE
   TWENTIETH CENTURY   275
   A SCENARIO: COMPETING AGENDAS   275
   THE EARLY TWENTIETH CENTURY AND ITS LEGACY   277
     Managing the School
     Classifying Students: The Standardized Test
     A New Structure and New Expectations for the Secondary
     School
   TEACHER PREPARATION AND
   CURRICULUM REFORM: THE FIRST PHASE   289
     Preparing Teachers: A New Approach
     Discontent and Progressivism
   REACTIONS TO PROGRESSIVISM   296
   EQUAL OPPORTUNITY   300
   CHAPTER SUMMARY   305
   FOR DISCUSSION   305
   IN THE SCHOOL/IN THE CLASSROOM   306
   SUGGESTED READINGS   306
   CHAPTER REFERENCES   307

IV THE SCIENCE AND ART OF TEACHING   309

11 TEACHERS AND PLANNING   311
   A SCENARIO   311
   INTRODUCTION   312
   WHY DO TEACHERS PLAN?   312
     Why are Plans Important?
     What Are the Reasons for Planning?

What Are the Benefits of Planning?
HOW DO TEACHERS PLAN?   315
What Types of Planning Must Teachers Do?
A Planning Approach
PLANNING LESSONS   320
Level 1: Pre-Lesson Planning
Level 2: Daily Lesson Planning and Teaching
Level 3: Post-Lesson Planning
CHAPTER SUMMARY   336
FOR DISCUSSION   337
IN THE SCHOOL/IN THE CLASSROOM   337
SUGGESTED READINGS   338
CHAPTER REFERENCES   339

12 TEACHERS AND TEACHING   341
INTRODUCTION   341
A CLASSROOM SCENARIO   341
HOW DO TEACHERS TEACH?   344
What Types of Teaching Approaches Do
Teachers Use?
USING QUESTIONS TO TEACH   352
Why Are Questions Important?
What Does the Research Say About
Teacher Questioning?
Summary on Questions
GENERAL METHODS OF TEACHING   365
CHAPTER SUMMARY   365
FOR DISCUSSION   368
IN THE SCHOOL/IN THE CLASSROOM   369
SUGGESTED READINGS   371
CHAPTER REFERENCES   372

13 CAN YOU TEACH?   375
A SCENARIO   375
INTRODUCTION   376
WHO ARE YOU?   377
Teacher Roles
The Context of Teaching
Your Personality
What Types of Content Do You Favor?
What Do You Really Believe About Teaching?
CAN YOU TEACH?   395
Student Differences
Student Learning Styles

What Is Your Philosophy of Education?
Developing Your Philosophy
Inventory and Prescription
Are You Up to the Challenge?
What If I Don't Want to Teach?
A CLOSING COMMENT   **412**
CHAPTER REFERENCES   **414**

INDEX   **415**

Preface

Exciting, depressing, fulfilling, tedious, demanding, stimulating—all these words, among others, can describe teaching. What does it mean to be a teacher? Why do persons offer different impressions and definitions of teaching? What are students like? What conditions enhance or detract from teaching? What do I need to know to teach? Students in introductory education courses ask questions like these. In fact, these questions persist for professional teachers throughout their careers. Like you they are intelligent, concerned about their futures, and want to do something worthwhile. Like you they expect realistic answers to their questions and know that not all questions have simple answers. Actually, some questions have no definitive answers at all.

An Introduction to Teaching: A Question of Commitment provides an *introduction* to teaching. We don't claim to cover all you need to know about teaching, nor to offer the final word. In fact we don't like those kinds of texts. Using our nearly fifty years of experience as teachers, we introduce you to a series of topics of concern in order to help you start experiencing teaching.

We don't try to recruit you into a profession for which you may not be suited. We do encourage you to think carefully, broadly, and deeply, however, about what it means to teach. If you wish to experience teaching before you make your decision, then our book is written for you. If you *do* decide to teach, then we encourage you to make a professional commitment toward becoming an effective teacher.

Effective teaching requires considerable effort and thought. We encourage you to identify and to shape your *own* attitudes toward effective teaching in a number of ways. First, the chapters contain several important features that require your thoughtful attention. Realistic scenarios help you focus on the issues that follow and to match them with your own experiences. Exercises titled "For Reflection" cause you to closely examine your beliefs and to take positions on the major concepts presented. "Research Notes" and "Suggested Readings" supplement the chapters by suggesting additional sources for study. The "Focus" sections add depth and provide perspective through firsthand accounts of the issues as seen by other authors. "For Discussion" questions are designed to delve more deeply into the issues, and "In the School/In the Classroom" exercises suggest learning opportunities for you in schools with teachers and pupils.

An Introduction to Teaching is divided into four sections. The first, "Looking at Teaching," explores the classroom roles of teachers and examines who teachers are as well as their reasons for deciding to teach. This section also probes into the current conditions affecting schools and outlines a developmental process for becoming a teacher. Section II, "Working with Students," focuses on the techniques for successfully communicating with students and reasons for why some classrooms are successful and others are not. The three chapters in Section III, "The School and the Teacher," examine the ways in which modern schools became what they are today. One chapter focuses on the ways teachers function in today's school organizations. The other two chapters document the social, historical, and philosophical contexts for teaching before and during the twentieth century. "The Science and Art of Teaching," Section IV, moves beyond learning *about* teaching and into the action of teaching. Two chapters are devoted to introductory planning and teaching techniques. The last chapter of this section pulls together the entire book by providing exercises to help you to crystallize your beliefs and to sharpen your expectations. The book ends with the question, "Can you teach?" We realize that not everyone is suited for teaching and believe that each prospective teacher must honestly face this question.

We wrote this book because we care about the field of teaching, its reputation, and its future as a trusted, valued profession. You deserve an accurate look at teaching and the opportunity to acquire firsthand experiences that will help you decide for yourself about a career in teaching. Most of all we care about the children you may teach. This book helps us to reach those who will teach our next generation of leaders, defenders, manufacturers, teachers, healers, and so on—the children of our friends, neighbors, and, perhaps, our own children.

No book is written alone. We had much help, but any errors or oversights are our responsibility. To those we counted on for various types of assistance we offer our thanks and express our gratitude for their hours of help: Patrice Ahmad, Melissa Brown, Anne Ireton, Jane Muniak, Debra Rader, Renee Riddle, Lillian Sands, Nell Ann Sands, and Carleen Woodruff.

In addition we thank the following reviewers who contributed to the development of this book:

Kathleen Amershek
University of Maryland

Sandra D'Amico
University of Florida

Daniel Collins
Central University of Iowa

David David
Texas A&M University

Jesus Garcia
Texas A&M University

Herbert Hite
Western Washington College

Jerald Hunt
Millikin University

David Larkin
Bemidji State University

G. T. Miedl
Central State University

Annabelle Raiche
College of St. Catherine

Susan Sears
Ohio State University

John P. Strouse
Ball State University

Finally we thank Marilyn, Marcia, and Claudette, who supported us with encouragement and tolerated our frustrations. Jennifer, Jessica, Jonathan, Michael, John, Megan, and Sean provided constant inspiration.

R. E. M.
G. H. W.
E. W. S.

An Introduction to Teaching

I

Looking at Teaching

We begin this book with an overview of the career you are considering as a profession—teaching. For one reason or another, you may have already decided to become a teacher. But that is only the first of many decisions you now face. For example, you face choices in terms of the grade level you would like to teach, where you want to work, and how you will actually prepare for the profession of teaching. This text is designed to help you confront these and other choices you will make throughout your career.

You probably have not yet begun to explore many of these issues. Just starting your preparation, you are like someone learning to swim; anxious to dive in, but wanting some instruction at the beginning to avoid mistakes. As you think about teaching you probably have some notion that you will like it and will be able to do it. But where do you get started, how do you get to know what the issues are?

To help you get started, think about the following questions:

Why do I want to teach school?
What do I need to know in order to become a good teacher?

Although your answers to these questions may change over time, we believe they are a good place for you to start. Keep them in mind as you read this text and attend class.

Speaking of starting, we start this book with a broad look at teaching. This means starting with a chapter that introduces you to the issues in the field of education that we will be exploring. Chapter 2 looks at the people who work in schools—teachers. We examine who they are and what teaching is like as seen through the eyes of experienced professionals. Chapter 3 focuses on current debates over the role of public education. We want to introduce you to some of the issues you will have to face as a teacher in American public schools. Chapter 4 sets forth the agenda for the rest of the text. Not only does it outline the issues to be covered, but it also challenges you to make some personal commitments in terms of your own preparation to teach.

The authors of this book have enjoyed over 50 years of teaching experience at the public school and university levels. We hope that in the pages that follow we will be able to share with you some of the lessons we have learned. Most importantly, we hope to help you get off to a good start in one of the most demanding, and rewarding, professions today—teaching.

1

Looking in Classrooms

INTRODUCTION

■   "Are you kidding? Leave teaching? This is the most important job
    in the world!"

   "What! Are you crazy? Of course, I'd take it [a different job]. I'd do
    anything to get out of this place. Want some advice? Go into
    business, or computers—that's where the money is."

   "Don't pay attention to that stuff [courses on teaching]. That's all
    theory and doesn't work. You want to learn about teaching?
    Just watch me. It's the classroom; that's where you really learn
    about teaching."

   "What could you possibly hope to learn from me? I can't imagine
    you want to observe any of *my* classes! I don't do anything
    special."

Do any of these remarks sound familiar to you? These are
remarks we have heard from teachers, either directly from them or
indirectly through our own students. Now who is right? Who is wrong?
Actually these questions are not important because all of the teachers
who spoke these remarks are correct, at least partially, simply because
these are their beliefs. One teacher is delighted with his profession and
would do little else. Another teacher is disenchanted and desires
something else, yet chooses to stay and perhaps feels trapped. On the
topic of learning about teaching, one teacher credits the classroom as
the place to learn about teaching, while another teacher depreciates
her teaching because she suspects that an observer will find little of
value. Why do these people, all of them teachers, feel differently about
teaching?

Feelings are based on perceptions, and perceptions are based on
experiences. For example, most of us have fundamental perceptions
about teaching. Our own perceptions are built on our own experiences—usually from how we remember our teachers when we were
students. Perceptions accumulate and develop into beliefs that help to
guide how we respond to what we see. So, our beliefs about teaching

are based on what we have experienced. These beliefs affect how we judge what we see and hear when we look in classrooms. Our beliefs also influence our expectations and affect how we treat those around us.

What is not so simple to figure out is why we believe what we do about teaching. The purpose of this book is to help you look into teaching and sort out your beliefs—to know fully why you believe as you do. We hope your beliefs are challenged, stimulated, and perhaps revised. Later chapters will focus on specific aspects of teaching. In this chapter we will look briefly into a few classrooms. Through the eyes of prospective teachers, people like you, we will see different types of teaching and teachers. Your primary mission will be to judge for yourself whether or not you wish to teach and to set goals for yourself if you do decide to teach.

LOOKING AT TEACHERS

☐ A Scenario: The Classroom Report

Several prospective teachers have been sent to local schools to observe and identify the issues important to teaching. After a period of time devoted to investigating teaching, these university students reported back to their seminar to exchange experiences and viewpoints. All have sharpened their perceptions about teaching; all have perspectives influenced by the rich variety of experiences they have gained. Their mission was to (1) shadow a teacher and find out what he or she does, (2) take in every detail, and (3) ask questions to find out how the teacher regards the profession of teaching and the role of teacher. The instructor starts:

"Well, was it a good two weeks?" Sounds varying from enthusiastic yesses to grunts and groans circle the seminar table. The students have many different opinions. "Let's begin by looking at your teachers. What did they do and how do they feel about teaching? Amanda?"

"I think my teacher is terrific. She does incredible things considering the school. There is absolutely no enthusiasm in the school, from the other teachers and most of the students, I mean. The place is run down and the rooms are shabby. But my teacher made an extra effort to buy or make educational things to help make the room attractive and a good place to learn. She knows her stuff too. She told me that she spent part of one summer learning a new approach to teaching in which she arranges the room in special groups, real close to her, and points to charts with students taking turns responding as she snaps her fingers. She expects her students to do a lot of repetition. At first it seemed rather mechanical and kind of insensitive. But the students appreciate the structure and they know what they are supposed to do. She doesn't have problems and the students like her a lot. Everything is quick-paced and the students learn a lot. This routine is followed for reading, math, spelling, and language arts. Parents seemed happy about it, she said. Yet, there is something I still don't understand. The teacher said she didn't know if the kids were reading any better and she wondered if she was overdoing it with pretests, worksheets, and post-tests. But, she didn't seem to have any time to do many creative things. There wasn't any room for spontaneity; she didn't seem to have any flexibility. Yet, I believe she is a good teacher."

"That sounds cold!" Willis had been to an inner-city school in a strong, integrated neighborhood supportive of its schools. "That teacher can't be that good. Look at the way she expected those kids to behave—like puppets. Jerking them around with her snapping fingers. The claim of no room for creativity is an excuse for the easy way out. My teacher is creative and not afraid to show it. She told me that the parents wouldn't stand for something that standard. My teacher was always on the move, going from student to student and group to group. It's amazing how she keeps track of what goes on, but she seems to somehow. Students read all kinds of books and do a lot of art, social studies, and science too. She likes the kids and shows it. Her class wasn't some type of assembly line. But, she had organization. She used different-colored folders for everything. Checklists and written reports just about covered everything, too. I don't know how she does it. I mean I don't know how she keeps track of everything. So I asked like you told us to and I couldn't believe what I heard. That lady said she wasn't sure either. Can you imagine that? She has 15 years of experience and feels like she sometimes doesn't know what's going on. But she does. Why does she say she doesn't? I just wish the kids would appreciate her more."

Jon joined in: "Well, all I know is that I can't keep up with what you're saying, Willis. My teacher meant business and you could tell. He kept an orderly shop and believed that anything worth doing should be done in school. That's what the time was for, he said. No homework for the students and no homework for him. Besides, he said the students wouldn't do it anyway. That's the way it was. Keep it simple, he advised. And it must work because he didn't have any problems. The kids did what he expected. He said that the school was a place for him to do his business; it was no place for frills, so you wouldn't catch him after school or doing other stuff. To teach—that was his job. I don't know if I could do things the same way, but it sure worked for him. 'Keep 'em busy' was his motto—in school that is. He went by the book and used the curriculum guide like it was law. The principal was proud that the guide received state approval last year. 'It meets all the minimum standards,' he said. This point seemed important—meeting minimum standards. But that's all the teacher taught even when he had plenty of time to do extra things. The minimum was the maximum. Does that mean the kids got a minimum education? Or does it mean that that was the maximum they believed the kids could learn?"

"Gosh, I feel kinda cheated," mumbled Maria. After some encouragement she continued tentatively with obvious embarrassment for her teacher. "Well, I'm not sure why, but my teacher had lots of problems. Maybe it was the school, the kids, the parents, or the neighborhood. I don't know. The students didn't seem to want to do anything. They were actually abusive and the teacher couldn't do anything. It seemed like the kids controlled him. My teacher felt terrible most days; he didn't have enough books and materials, and he kept apologizing because he felt I was wasting my time. I was supposed to be observing teaching, but what I saw was a school like a run-down fortress with a bunch of 'animals'—that's what the teachers called them—running around inside doing terrible things to each other and using the school for their own business. I was afraid to go there. When my teacher asked me how I felt and I told him that, he surprised me by saying he was afraid too. I don't know if I can handle being a teacher if that's what it's like. But my teacher did try," Maria added in defense. "He told me about a few students he had over the years who made something of themselves—that made him feel proud. So I guess that's why he stuck it out."

"Well, my teacher didn't have those kinds of problems." Now it was Joshua's turn. "But she was frustrated just the same. I couldn't believe all the stuff she had to put up with, and it didn't come from just the students either. She was always being interrupted by announcements, or knocks at the door from all kinds of people wanting this or that. Paperwork! I don't know how many different forms my teacher had to fill out and they all seemed to ask for the same information, but in a different order. Barf! Couldn't somebody else do that stuff? Of course, it was the beginning of the school year and the new materials hadn't arrived and probably wouldn't, according to my teacher, until after Christmas. They were needed for the new text that was adopted over the objections of the teachers in the school and of course they didn't get a copy of the new text until after the first week of school. What a mess! Who's responsible? And who gets blamed when kids aren't learning?"

"My teacher had textbooks, but she didn't use them and didn't need them." Tina had picked up on the text issue. "She was probably the best teacher I have ever seen. Boy! I wish I had teachers like her when I was in school. A woman physics teacher is hard to find and this lady knew her stuff. She expected her students to work hard, but have fun, too. How many of you took physics in school? I thought so. Not many do. But, this lady's classes were filled. The things she did were totally remarkable. No wonder so many students were eager to get into her classes. I was surprised how much you can learn from simple things, and she seemed to have a million ideas. They didn't need books, except for references, because they were always doing things—real experiments. Guess what she said when I asked her about not having any books? 'Books are crutches,' she said. 'They are only needed by the weak or feeble.' She believes teachers must know their subjects and that students learn best by doing, and she stuck to her ideas, too. I bet you guys think she is a young scientist." The nodding heads confirmed Tina's suspicion. "Well, you're wrong. She's a 56-year-old grandmother who has been teaching for 23 years! She won't quit even though it is a tough school and she could retire if she wanted to. The drugs and vandalism don't bother her. She reaches whoever she can and I have a feeling she is about the only positive experience most kids ever find in the school where I was. Well the other teachers are okay too, I guess. After all, this lady is a hard act to follow."

"I'll say." Herbie took his turn at bringing the first round of the seminar to a close. "My teacher was starting his first year at the school. And even though he had already taught for 4 years he was panicked about the first evaluation the principal would be doing soon. This is a special magnet school and it prided itself in having the best teachers it could attract. My teacher worked hard to impress the administrators because the school had a good reputation and the students were pretty easy to work with. He told me if he didn't produce he could be transferred back to his old school anytime during the year. So, I guess he was real uptight about it. Personally I think he was selling out. When we talked he had great ideas about teaching and the things he would like to do. But he thought he had to teach the way the principal expected if he wanted to stay, so he followed someone else's ideas and seemed always to give in. Something seemed to be missing—you know, that special spark. He seemed more concerned about fitting in instead of doing a good job of teaching. I actually believe he was more concerned about himself and making a good impression than he was concerned about his students. I just wish he didn't have so many doubts about himself. He had a lot of impressive ideas and I believe he could be fantastic if he would cut himself loose from someone else's expectations."

How are these scenes related to teaching?

Now it was time to sort out the prospective teachers' ideas. They had several personal snapshots of teachers, schools, and teaching. Left to themselves, their vision of education would be no greater than their independent snapshots. These independent snapshots would provide only a limited view of teaching that seems tremendously myopic and indicative of simplistic conceptions about teaching. But, simply coming together and exchanging experiences and ideas added extra snapshots to their photo album of teaching. In time this album would be filled and provide rich memories useful to their personal decision making; all would have expanded conceptions about teaching—that was the real goal—and thereby expand their perceptions and form realistic expectations.

Notes had been taken and were sorted out after some follow-up questions. The issues we would explore in our education seminar were listed before us and would provide the framework for our thinking about teaching.

☐ Thinking About Teaching

What are some characteristics the teachers in the scenario had in common? As a beginning, most of the instruction occurred as a consequence of direct teacher influence. For the most part classroom routines were established and student movements were directed, in some instances very precisely. Teaching materials, often a standard

"Oh, that's the faculty lounge."

Phi Delta Kappan, May 1984, p. 614.

text, were a constant and activity was business-like with noted exceptions. At times students may have been uncertain what to do and off-task behavior did occur.

All teachers had an image of their competence and confidence. Sometimes this was overtly communicated; other times the student observers had to speculate. Still, for the most part teachers' positive self-images—confident beliefs in their skills and ideas—were the exception rather than the rule. Why is this? How is it possible for specially prepared, experienced persons to discredit their beliefs or to be uncertain? Questions such as these may be answered by looking closely at what teachers do in their classrooms.

FOR REFLECTION 1.1   Thinking About Your Teachers

Think about the teachers you have had—the good, the best, the mediocre, and the worst. Think carefully about them. Identify what they did and speculate about how they perceived their role as teachers. Compare the characteristics of your best and worst teachers in this exercise and answer the follow-up questions.

My BEST teacher: My WORST teacher:

1.   1.
2.   2.
3.   3.
4.   4.
5.   5.
6.   6.
7.   7.
8.   8.
9.   9.
10.   10.

How did your best and worst teachers seem to perceive their role as teachers? How were these roles similar and how were they different?

Think about the level of self-confidence of your teachers, particularly your best and worst. How self-confident do you believe each was?

If your answers to the question above vary, speculate about the reasons for these differences.

What did each of these teachers expect from you? Why?

How did your classmates feel about each of these teachers? Is there a difference? Why?

What type of impact did each of these teachers make on you?

Why do you believe you might want to teach?

☐ **Looking in Classrooms**

What to Look For?
If we believe some things about teaching can be learned by looking in classrooms and observing teaching, what should we look for and how should we evaluate what we think we see? Three broad, fundamental questions can help us focus on these issues: (1) What do teachers expect? (2) What is the classroom environment like? and (3) What is the quality of teacher-student relationships? Let us consider these questions as we begin to look in classrooms.

What Do Teachers Expect?

Children begin to learn long before they enter any formal school. During their early years they form interests and begin to develop skills that help prepare them for academic achievement in school. Some family practices, like offering encouragement, lending motivation, and providing a wide range of experiences, help children to acquire information and to learn how to process it. Children demonstrate preferences for certain styles of learning at an early age. These can be encouraged or discouraged by parental expectations. In school, teacher expectations can influence how children perceive their abilities to learn. Teacher expectations can also influence student achievement.

Teacher expectations can be defined as "the inferences that teachers make about the future academic achievement of students and about the types of classroom assignments that students need, given their abilities."[1] Teachers base their expectations on several perceptions. When their expectations tend to be fulfilled, teachers are apt to place confidence in their perceptions and rely heavily on them for future class decision making.

In its simplest form learning may be described as a change in behavior. At the center of this process is a chain of communication between teachers and students and the influence that teacher communication exerts on student behavior. Jere Brophy and Thomas Good have proposed a model for thinking about the possibilities of teacher influence exerted through what they expect of students. The model has five steps[2]:

1. The teacher has particular perceptions of each student and expects specific behavior and particular levels of achievement from each student.
2. Because the teacher has different expectations for the students, the teacher's behavior is affected when he or she interacts with each student for whom expectations have been formed.
3. Students perceive that they receive different treatment from the teacher. This different treatment tells them what the teacher expects and can affect their self-concepts, achievement, motivation, and aspirations.
4. If this treatment is consistent and continues long enough, and if students do not behave in ways that resist or change the teacher's expectations, then the expectations can be responsible for shaping the student's achievement and classroom behavior. Students who are perceived as being high achievers can be taught in ways that influence them to achieve at high levels. Meanwhile, students for whom teachers hold low ex-

pectations may be treated in ways that encourage their achievement levels to decline.

5. Given time and consistent treatment, students' achievement and behavior can increasingly conform to what teachers expect.

When used to describe the interactions of teachers and students, consistency, time, and lack of resistance are key assumptions of this model. But many other factors are a part of this model and come from the larger classroom environment. What can we observe about the classroom and its inhabitants when we look in classrooms?

What Is the Classroom Environment Like?
Expectations carry an emotional tone. What is an example of the emotional tone of the classroom environment? John Goodlad gives us a glimpse:

> The emotional tone is neither harsh and punitive nor warm and joyful; it might be described most accurately as flat. . . . [T]he classes in our sample, at all levels tended not to be marked with exuberance, joy, laughter, abrasiveness, praise and corrective support of individual student performance, punitive teacher behavior, or high interpersonal tension. . . . All of those characteristics we commonly regard as positive elements in classrooms were more to be observed at the early elementary level. A decline set in by the upper elementary grades and continued through the secondary years, with a sharp drop at the junior high level. . . . [T]here may be something self-protective for teachers in maintaining classroom control and a relatively flat emotional tone.[3]

Let us assume Goodlad is correct. He asserts that the flat emotional tone of many classrooms helps teachers protect themselves— it helps them to maintain classroom control. What does classroom control possibly mean for the students?

Control implies something about how teachers treat their students. Take a look at Research Notes 1.1 to see some of the ways teachers may treat students differently. The contrast is distinct and perhaps startling. It seems that those who more often need encouragement, reinforcement, and feedback about their progress are given perhaps less than they need to perform according to their ability. It also seems that slower students are actually encouraged not to respond and not to volunteer. Overall, classroom instruction seems to favor the more able students and is marked by a positive emotional climate only during the earlier years of school. It seems that current dominant teaching practices may be designed to discourage students from taking risks—all at a time when some argue that students are strongly motivated to take risks.[4]

The type of classroom environment can influence students' attitudes and learning.

What are the consequences of this apparent incongruity? The consequences appear to bend toward students' becoming more passive to reduce the risk of public failure.[5] Perhaps this makes sense. After all, who wants to call attention to his or her shortcomings and failures?

Teachers can behave just as differently toward groups of students as they do with individuals. Studies done in first-grade classrooms show that student group placement may "represent an expectation effect that influences student achievement directly (by exposing students to poor or good reading models) or indirectly (by decreasing or increasing motivation)."[6] Once formed, these groups tend to remain as students are passed along to the next grade; teachers make referrals to the next teacher. Combine this possibility with the fact that teachers have been observed tending to perform twice as many managerial acts with low-achievement groups instead of focusing on instruction as they do with high-achievement groups. This results in the possibility of compounded negative effects linked with expectations. These negative effects can continue to build for years.[7]

RESEARCH NOTES 1.1 How Do Teacher Expectations Affect the Way They Treat Students?

Thomas Good and Rhona Weinstein report the following differences observed in the ways teachers treat students whom they perceive as MORE and LESS capable:

Students believed to be MORE capable have:	Students believed to be LESS capable have:
More opportunities for class performance on meaningful tasks	Less opportunities for class performance on meaningful tasks
More opportunities to think	Most work aimed at practice; students have less opportunity to think
More assignments that stress higher levels of thinking	Less choice among assignments; tasks emphasizing more drills
Fewer interruptions and more autonomy while learning	Frequent teacher interruptions and less autonomy
More opportunity for self-evaluation	Less opportunity for self-evaluation
More honest feedback from the teacher	Less honest feedback; feedback received is more gratuitous
More respect shown by the teacher	Less respect shown by the teacher

This list is adapted from Thomas L. Good and Rhona S. Weinstein's chapter, "Teacher Expectations: A Framework for Exploring Classrooms" in Karen Zumwalt, ed., *Improving Teaching* (Alexandria, Va.: Association for Supervision and Curriculum Development, 1986), p. 72.

☐ What Is the Quality of Teacher-Student Relationships?

One measure of the quality of teacher and student relationships concerns the locus of responsibility for learning and evaluation. Who decides and who controls? Marshall and Weinstein argue that the amount of responsibility students have for their own learning and evaluation may affect their susceptibility to their teachers' expectations.[8] It seems that teachers give more opportunities to high achievers for making choices than they give to low achievers. On the other hand, teachers tend to structure the learning and evaluation of low achievers more by giving them a greater number of directions and making evaluation decisions for them. What is implied for each type of learner? What are the effects?

Implications for success favor the high achiever and the outlook is dimmer for low achievers. When the teacher is the evaluator and students must depend on the teacher, their performance is more susceptible to the teacher's expectations. Conversely, an encouraging teacher—one who motivates and holds students responsible for their own performance and gives them a role in evaluating it—may find that learning becomes more realistic as students' understanding becomes elevated.

Classrooms are busy places. Their environments are complex and reflect the subtle differences of their occupants. The responsibilities placed on teachers are enormous, for they must constantly perceive, interpret, decide, and act. Teachers who develop ways to observe the happenings of their classroom environments accurately and who are willing to interpret from multiple points of view seem likely to offer fair yet rigorous expectations to all students. All of this appears to come to a fundamental distinction. Some teachers believe they make a difference and will influence student learning. These teachers will see student failure as a signal for more learning. They will sharpen their perceptions to find out the cause of failure and provide more opportunities for learning. Good teachers will not allow themselves to become occupied with assigning blame for failure. They assume a portion of the responsibility and try to bring out the best in the learner. At the same time these teachers see the human limitations of this arrangement and realize they must be met at least part of the way by willing learners.

Conditions that render pupils as unwilling learners and that fall beyond the scope of the classroom require different levels and types of teacher intervention. Big problems require different solutions, and although they may complicate what teachers can do in their own classrooms, there are several things individual teachers can do to work toward getting the most fulfillment from their profession by making a difference in students' lives.

Bringing out the best in learners requires that teachers attempt to offer the best of themselves. Before they can do this, teachers must attend to several things first, and this takes time. Teachers try to learn from other teachers; they gain feedback about their own teaching, compare, and judge for themselves. Teachers also take time to talk with students to find out how they perceive school. And, perhaps above all else, teachers take the time to think—to reflect—about what they do. These are some of the things experienced teachers may do. But what about you and others like you? How can persons who are in the process of becoming teachers work toward their highest potential and become their best?

FOCUS 1.1 "I Have the Best Job in the World"

That's how Marie Krafsky might put it. Watch her—or the countless teachers like her—in action, and you might add that she does the best job in the world as well.

by
Tony Scherman

Marie Krafsky now teaches sixth grade at Thomas Jefferson School in Edison, N.J. A teacher. Think back. Did a good one ever change your life? Marie has changed people's lives: On the day I see her, for instance, sixth grader Jessie tells her that her brother, a college student, plans a history career because of Marie's inspiration.

At 45, Marie Krafsky is good, and she knows it—she's a master inventor and improviser of learning techniques: "My bag of tricks," she calls them. Winner of system-wide teaching awards in the large Edison district, where she's spent 21 years. Dedicated traveler, along with her husband, Mel. And last—but certainly not least—lifelong Brooklyn Dodgers fan.

Still she says, "I'm nothing special—at least I hope not. I think I represent the majority of people in my profession. But sometimes I feel like a stranger in the world. I try to fight these windmills—teachers who are negative, and you see what they're doing to kids; parents who are negative, and you can't change them; people who tell you your job and know nothing about it. I'm a teacher, every day. I work with kids who can't understand something yet. My job is to make them understand."

All across the country, the scene reenacts itself: A teacher faces a roomful of young people who need attention, discipline and love. If the teacher's like Marie, odds are that the kids will have a pretty good day.

Marie usually does, even if this one, a sunny Wednesday not long ago, starts a bit early.

6:30 a.m.: I'm exhausted. I was out until 2 a.m. at a play. When you're teaching tired, you have to psych yourself to try harder, not to get impatient.

9:00 a.m.: Prep period for the day's classwork. A math test to copy, math papers to grade, and a visit to my refuge: the unofficial hangout, "Frank's Place." Last year, Frank the janitor invited me in for a cup of coffee. Pretty soon a group of us just gravitated back there. We'll bring in bagels, a cake, hard rolls. It's the therapy room, the party room.

10:00 a.m.: My math group comes in. The best thing about teaching is to watch that little light turn on—that "I got it!"—when they suddenly understand something that they didn't before. [That happens in a big way this morning—the entire class passes the test and 18 of 21 kids ask to take a second test for extra credit.]

Part of it's the approach. I always invent games to make the concepts more vivid. And I'm always asking "Why?" I'll help them, but they have to make their own discoveries. One day, just as I worked up to a big "Why?" Tommy, a little boy sitting at the back, smacked his forehead and said, "I can't believe it! There she goes with that 'Why?' "

And we'll have math contests. The other day, another Tommy was up at the board trying to divide a fraction. He froze. His team is shouting, "C'mon, Tommy, c'mon!" Now, teachers are strong actors and actresses, and it helps to provide an element of surprise. I grab Tommy by the waist and flip him upside down. Hanging there, he shouts, "I got it!" Invert and multiply—he won't ever forget how to divide fractions.

10:50 a.m.: My reading class, which comes in next, is the slowest group of sixth-grade readers. So, for the first class of the year, I diagram a football play on the board, and ask them what it is. All sorts of responses: tic-tac-toe without the grid, a seating chart. One boy—that was great—said it was hugs and kisses. If someone guesses, of all things, that it's a football play, I say, "What would I be doing with a football play on the blackboard?" In the end, I tell them it really is a football play. And that there are two things they have to learn in this classroom: Expect the unexpected, and don't let me change your mind if you know you're right.

Today three of the kids have to go "testify" about some boys' bathroom hi-jinks—they saw someone break a toilet seat. One of the three, let's call him Freddie, is a special person, fantastic kid. His father and brother both are on drugs and alcohol. He lives with his mother. He's the kind of child who just can't say "I like you." It's inside, but it won't come out.

I went to war over him. Special services wanted to classify him as "emotionally disturbed." I told them: "You don't go putting labels all over a child because he's got a few problems." I won—he stayed. He earned an A in reading. He came up to me and said it was his first A ever.

Think about it: a kid that's been in school for six years, and he never got an A. If it were you, wouldn't it turn you off to school?

Today he asks to correct a spelling test. He's just spent a day on suspension—he wrote a dirty word on the computer! Now he's saying, "I want to be part of this class, even if I sometimes push myself out."

Freddie once wrote a story that I'll always remember. A Christmas tree was too small. A fairy came and said, "If you try hard you'll get big and be picked for Christmas." The tree tried and tried. Nothing. Then, on Christmas Eve, the tree woke up and it had suddenly grown. It still wasn't as big as the others, but it went to the fairy and told her, "You did this for me. I wish I could hug you, but I can't."

12:30 p.m.: Marie goes off to Frank's room. One day a very small boy happened past the teachers' lair, peered in and shrieked, "Look! The teachers are eating!" "What did he think," laughs Marie. "We get greased and oiled?"

In the hall before class, sixth-grade live wire Andy spots Marie and shouts, "There she is!" What's up? Nothing. He's just pleased to see her.

1:15 p.m.: The kids race in for social studies. It's oral report time, today on the Crusades. A pretty Indian girl named Kamala goes first. "Holly," she keeps saying for "Holy." Repeated corrrections from classmates. One finally says, "Hey give her a break."

Kamala's report, say her critics, "doesn't sound like her." She cheerfully confesses she cribbed it from the encyclopedia. "Did you learn anything?" Marie asks gently. She refuses to be too hard on Kamala, who only began to speak English recently. ("I can't fault her for a language barrier. She tried hard, and she's improving.")

"What city did the Turks invade?" asks Marie. Hands shoot up: "Rome." "Madrid." "Vatican City?" "Lebanon?" "Bethlehem?" After repeated hints, Marie finally has to tell them: "Jerusalem."

Reports are tough for them. At the beginning of the year everyone was all concerned about length: "Mrs. Krafsky, how long should I write?" "Till you're finished." I had them write a Footstep Report: take their shoes off, trace their feet, and write, "A Day in the Life of a Cave Person." It could only be as long as their two feet. Very tough, writing a good short report. They went nuts: "Can I put boots on?" Can I borrow my father's feet?" "But I have little feet!" "Tough," I said, "write a little report."

2:00 p.m.: The second social studies class "visits" Arcade Island, a remote spot, imagined in great geographic detail, where the class has been shipwrecked. For each visit they have to think up and solve a new set of problems. Today they must communicate with a native who speaks no English.

A boy named Li Chun fits the bill nicely—he pleasantly rattles on in Chinese as the puzzled visitors try to get through to him. Frustrated, they invent a new character, a grizzled longtime castaway who still remembers a few scraps of English. Andy will play him.

The veteran castaway has a plan for escape from the island. "Home!" chortles Andy in his pidgin-English. "Boat!" He races out into the hall, followed by one or two henchmen. Marie, wondering but game, lets them go. Andy charges back, wheeling a jumbo garbage can. "Boat!" Leaping inside, he disappears—until the garbage can tips, disgorging its kicking contents onto the floor. The class erupts, and Marie comes over, a bit concerned: "Are you all right?" Andy looks up. "Of course I'm all right; I'm role playing!"

> Manir, the castaways' president, is impressed with the boat. He scratches his head: "You mean we could've gotten off this crazy island six months ago?"
>
> The bell rings. The first buses are already rolling in.
>
> *I keep looking for something new, for fresh methods, for learning games. Arcade Island is all about taking a problem and having the kids find possible solutions. There's usually more than one solution, and hopefully they learn to be comfortable with that. When I was a kid in the '50s, we could make decisions. And we could imagine. Kids today don't have that. Take away their computers, and they have nothing to do. They haven't been taught to think. These poor kids—getting them to think is the most difficult job in the world.*
>
> *3:15 p.m.: At the end of the day you're exhausted. Today hasn't been bad, but there are times, after everyone's on their buses and gone, when it's hard to walk down that hall and get in your car. But you've just got to face being wiped out at day's end. Especially if you're funny like me, and won't leave a problem alone or back away from a confrontation. The day I become intimidated—by a principal, an administrator, a superintendent, a parent, a child—that's when I'll pack it in.*
>
> *In my house there are two sculptures and a bas-relief of Don Quixote. He failed. Sometimes I do, too. But he kept trying. So do I.*
>
> ---
>
> From *Family Weekly,* September 9, 1984, pp. 4–7.

BECOMING THE BEST

■ We have just offered you a challenge to work toward becoming the best teacher possible, if you decide to become a teacher. In the least, you owe it to yourself and to the students whose lives you will influence. Commitment to becoming the best will affect some of your expectations, particularly your personal expectations. You will expect more of yourself and others. Some factors appear to handicap many teachers today. You will have to overcome these handicaps and just knowing about them is the first step toward overcoming them.

☐ **Avoiding the Handicaps of Teaching**

Douglas Heath identifies four handicaps inherent in teaching.[9] He argues that these handicaps affect many teachers and get in the way of their professional growth.

The first handicap concerns educational philosophy. The handicap consists of not having a clear view about what students are expected to do. In this case the teachers' goals become whatever the textbook contains. One way to overcome this handicap is to form priorities and develop clear expectations by thinking through what student outcomes you believe are most important. Think about the students' futures and develop instructional goals designed to move the students forward in their lives.

A second handicap concerns not knowing how to select or design teaching strategies to achieve the instructional goals. Clearing up the first handicap helps to decide how to avoid the second handicap by uncovering the teaching options available to you.

Handicap number three involves how teachers tend to think. A great many teachers tend not to be reflective about their teaching. They do not give much thought to the effects of what they do. To overcome this handicap time must be devoted to thinking frequently about (1) what you want to accomplish as you teach, (2) how well the means you have selected for your teaching actually help you to accomplish these goals, and (3) the condition of the relationships among students and between students and you. Reflective thinking provides opportunities to make professional decisions systematically and to work toward establishing a climate necessary for fulfilling your goals. This topic is explored in detail in Chapter 4, Learning About Teaching.

The fourth handicap concerns your willingness to take risks. Heath reports that both new and experienced teachers wish they were more adventurous and that teaching was intellectually more exciting. Yet a majority of teachers do not take risks. These teachers are comfortable with what they do, they may fear making mistakes by trying something new, or they do not feel confident enough to share their feelings of uncertainty with others. Teachers often are isolated and have no dependable means of support. "To grow is to risk, to try the untried and uncertain."[10] Risk taking requires the desire to take chances and the interpersonal openness to listen and work with students. Avoiding the three above-mentioned handicaps can help you feel more confident in taking risks.

☐ Bringing Out the Best in Yourself and Others

Becoming the best requires that you take risks. For those of you confident enough to take the risks, the result is often getting more than you expect. Problems can be one liability in taking risks, but the dividends can far exceed the liabilities. If the risks you take are unselfish and if they are directed toward helping others to do their best, chances are good that you will succeed.

Bringing out the best in others is one responsibility of teaching. We offer some suggestions you may wish to try while working with others as you explore teaching.[11]

Expect the best and let others know it. Treat them accordingly and watch the results. Study your own needs as well as those of your peers or pupils. Get to know them and limit your assumptions. Pep talks do little good if you misassume what will motivate others. Take the time to find out.

Set high standards for yourself and for others. Then be certain to create an environment where everyone is free to take risks without fear of failure. Fear can be fatal and can lead to low achievement and low self-confidence. As you, your peers, and your pupils work toward high standards, be certain to use appropriate role models to provide encouragement. Also, take the time to recognize the achievements of others and applaud their successes.

Finally, place a premium on collaboration. An esprit de corps makes everyone feel better about taking risks and provides support for continued encouragement when anyone experiences temporary setbacks.

"What did I learn today? My mother will want to know."

Phi Delta Kappan, October 1982, p. 144.

Risk-taking is rewarding.

FOR REFLECTION 1.2   Expecting Your Best

Giving your best assumes that you expect the best—of yourself and others. Your expectations are based on what you believe about yourself, others, and teaching. Your collection of beliefs helps form the framework of a philosophy that becomes your philosophy of life, learning, and teaching. It is important to clarify your beliefs and to consider how your mind-set influences your decisions. Take notice of your underlying assumptions and expectations as you invest a few moments in answering the following questions. Review this experience periodically to detect any changes in your beliefs.

1. What is the purpose and function of schools?

2. What is the purpose of teachers?

3. How should teachers teach?

4. What are your personal strengths that might help you become a teacher?

5. What personal qualities do you have that might limit your ability to teach?

6. How can you capitalize on your strengths and overcome your limitations?

7. Set several personal development goals for yourself that could be met by your participation in this course. What are they? How will you accomplish them?

CHAPTER SUMMARY

■ What you believe about teaching affects how you choose to prepare for it. Your perceptions influence your expectations, and your expectations can affect how you interact with others—your peers, classroom teachers, school administrators, and students. Your challenge is to learn all that you can about teaching so that you continue to collect snapshots that portray teaching accurately and fairly. Your mission as a teacher, should you choose to become one, is to broaden your perspective, set clear goals for yourself, and work toward accomplishing those goals— all while having the responsibility for bringing out the best in others while offering your best. The next chapter helps you take a closer look at teachers before turning your attention to the current milieu of teaching.

FOR DISCUSSION

1. Think about the grade level or subject(s) that you are interested in teaching. What are the ten most important skills, attitudes, or values that you think a teacher needs to instruct pupils effectively? (You might keep this list and compare it with your answers when you come to the end of this book.)

2. Let us assume that you read this book, completed this education course, and decided not to teach. How might your brief experiences with teaching be beneficial? Harmful?

3. What would you think about schools and teachers if you learned that:
   a. Twenty-three million Americans are functionally illiterate, including 13% of all 17-year-olds and perhaps up to 40% of minority youth?
   b. Pupils' average achievement scores on most standardized tests have declined for 25 years, with critical declines in science and mathematics during more recent years? (There seems to be an increase in test scores now, but it is too soon to see if this trend has reversed or merely reached a plateau.)
   c. Nearly 40% of 17-year-olds cannot draw inferences from what they read; 80% cannot write persuasive essays, and 67% cannot solve math problems that require several steps?
   d. More than half of the gifted students in schools do not function at their level of tested abilities?

e. Fifty percent of first-year college students cannot think abstractly enough to function well in an environment of higher education?

4. Think carefully about all the responsibilities that teachers have. What do teachers do? Compile a comprehensive list, examine it carefully, and consider if you are willing to do all that teachers are expected to do.

5. What types of expectations do you believe Marie Krafsky (Focus 1.1) had for her students? How do you believe these expectations affected her teaching?

6. Expectations influence the decisions we make. What do you expect from a career in teaching?

IN THE SCHOOL/IN THE CLASSROOM

1. Visit several *different* teachers with two or three classmates. After observing the teachers' similarities and differences, speculate about the expectations they have for their students. How do they treat different students?

2. Rank-order the teachers according to your preferences by answering the following questions:

   a. As a pupil, I would prefer to be in this class:
   _____ Why? _____

   b. I believe I would learn the most in this class:
   _____ Why? _____

   c. I think this teacher would be least likely to criticize me:
   _____ Why? _____

   Compare your rankings with the other observers. (Be certain you are comparing rankings for the same teachers.) Identify, compare, and discuss the teaching characteristics that contributed to your rankings. If your classmates feel differently about the teachers, try to identify teacher characteristics that attracted some of your classmates and repelled others.

3. Should schools hire teachers with the same characteristics? Why?

4. What function do you think the expectations of the persons who hire teachers have on employer-interviewer relations?

5. To what degree do you think employer expectations influence the decisions to hire or pass over a teacher candidate?

SUGGESTED READINGS

Cusick, Philip. *Inside High School*. New York: Holt, Rinehart and Winston, 1973. This book is written for those considering a career in American schools. Cusick provides a realistic description of what goes on inside a high school. His focus is on students' behaviors and how their behaviors affect themselves, teachers, school administrators, and the school organization.

Duke, Daniel. *Teaching—The Imperiled Profession*. Albany, N.Y.: State University of New York Press, 1984. Professor Duke provides a candid response to his book's central question: "Is there reason to believe that teaching as a profession is any less viable today than in the past?"

Good, Thomas, Bruce Biddle and Jere Brophy. *Teachers Make a Difference*. New York: Holt, Rinehart and Winston, 1975. Without heavy reliance on statistics, the authors supply ample research findings to provide information to those who want to know about the effects of schools and teachers on students.

Jackson, Philip. *Life in Classrooms*. New York: Holt, Rinehart and Winston, 1968. This book focuses almost exclusively on the elementary school. Jackson believes that children develop adaptive strategies to the facts of institutional life early, during the formative years; yet, although surely different, there are basic similarities with life in high school and college classrooms. The main goal of this book is to awaken concern over elements of school life that receive less attention than deserved.

Kohl, Herbert. *Growing Minds: On Becoming a Teacher*. New York: Harper & Row, 1984. Kohl is a prolific writer and his sensitivity to his students provides a realistic foundation for thinking about becoming a teacher. Personal accounts take you into Kohl's classrooms where he shares his ideas and techniques with you as he focuses his attention on helping his students to grow—to become their best.

Zumwalt, Karen. *Improving Teaching*. Alexandria, Va.: Association for Supervision and Curriculum Development, 1986. This edited collection of contributed chapters can help you to see the issues and flaws of teaching. Numerous ideas are offered for improving teaching and two of the chapters influenced this chapter: Heath's chapter on developing teachers and Good and Weinstein's chapter on teacher expectations.

CHAPTER REFERENCES

1. Thomas L. Good and Rhona S. Weinstein, "Teacher Expectations: A Framework for Exploring Classrooms," in *Improving Teaching,* ed. Karen Zumwalt (Alexandria, Va.: Association for Supervision and Curriculum Development, 1986), pp. 63–64.
2. Jere E. Brophy and Thomas L. Good, "Teachers' Communication of Differential Expectations for Children's Classroom Performance: Some Behavioral Data," *Journal of Educational Psychology* 61 (1970): 365–374.
3. John Goodlad, *A Place Called School: Prospects for the Future* (New York: McGraw-Hill, 1984), pp. 108, 112.
4. W. Doyle, "Classroom Tasks and Students' Abilities," in *Research on Teaching: Concepts, Findings and Implications,* ed. Penelope Peterson and Herbert Walberg (Berkeley, Calif.: McCutchan, 1979), pp. 183–209.
5. Good and Weinstein, "Teacher Expectations," p. 66.
6. Ibid., p. 67.
7. D. Eder, "Ability Grouping as a Self-Fulfilling Prophecy: A Microanalysis of Teacher-Student Interaction," *Sociology of Education* 54 (1981): 151–162.
8. H. H. Marshall and R. S. Weinstein, "Classrooms Where Students Perceive High and Low Amounts of Differential Teacher Treatment" (Paper presented at the Annual Meeting of the American Educational Research Association, New Orleans, 1984).
9. Douglas H. Heath, "Developing Teachers, Not Just Techniques," in *Improving Teaching,* ed. Karen Zumwalt (Alexandria, Va.: Association for Supervision and Curriculum Development, 1986), pp. 1–14.
10. Ibid., p. 4
11. Alan Loy McGinnis, *Bringing Out the Best in People* (Minneapolis, Minn.: Augsburg Publishing House, 1985).

2

Who Are Teachers and Why Do They Teach?

■ "Now this. Twenty years I've given to this city and school district and now they want to give me a test, an objective-style paper and pencil test, to see if I'm good enough to keep teaching here!" Lois Applebaum fumed as she reread the memo from the Middleburg School Board mandating the testing.

"Did you see this, Jayne? And I quote, 'All teachers of Middleburg Public Schools will be tested on May 13 for the purpose of evaluating their competence and continued employment.' So, we are all to parade in and on the basis of their little test have our future decided!"

Jayne Comminski was slow to respond. Obviously Lois, the head of the Math Department, was upset. And being a first-year teacher Jayne was never quite sure of where she stood with the faculty.

But Lois was insistent. "Well, Jayne, what about it? Here you are, fresh with your college degree you spent four years earning and now you need to prove your competence on a written test. How do you feel about this?"

"I'm not totally sure," Jayne started tentatively. "But there is a lot of public concern about the quality of public school teaching today. Something needs to be done and maybe this is a step in the right direction. Maybe if we take this examination and prove to the public we do read, write, and compute well and know a great deal about teaching we can begin to regain some public support. And maybe," Jayne paused, "maybe those who cannot pass the exam just don't belong in teaching anyway."

"But a test, a paper and pencil test, what does that tell us about teaching? Look, fifteen years ago I went through the tenuring process and was rated as a good enough teacher to be granted tenure. Every year I am supposed to be evaluated by an administrator. Why do we now turn to a written test?" Lois retorted.

Now it was Jayne's turn to vent a little steam. "Yes, but I always hear us complain about how meaningless those administrative evaluations are—'Those administrators aren't qualified to evaluate me.' Well then, who is? And as for the overreliance on a paper and pencil test—what does that say about our work as teachers when we rely on similar measures to evaluate students?"

Lois had to admit Jayne did have a point. Indeed, there were teachers, both experienced and new, who didn't quite seem to do the job. And teachers do rely a great deal on testing yet seem loath to be tested themselves. But Jayne understood Lois's points as well. What had happened to the supposedly careful, ongoing evaluation of teachers that was to occur both before and after the granting of tenure? And a one-shot testing experience did not seem to be the best way to carefully examine the competence of a teacher in the classroom.

"One more thing." It was Lois breaking the long contemplative silence that had settled between them. "Certainly there should be concern over the quality of the teaching. But with all this debate over standards for teachers as well as students, it seems like no one wants to get to the real heart of the matter. You know, we also need to talk about the conditions of schooling, the conditions under which teachers work and students learn."

"I'm following you," Jayne nodded, "go on."

"For example, look at the number of students we have to deal with every day, and we are expected to give them all special, individual attention. And consider our rate of pay, it doesn't even begin to compare with other jobs requiring a college degree—or in some cases just a high school diploma. The working conditions of teachers is another issue. Often there are not enough books or even desks, there is a lack of other supplies, and we are expected to be teacher, janitor, and police officers all in one."

"You know, this reminds me of a discussion we had in an education class," Jayne interrupted. "The issue was how much do we in American society actually value children? The professor used a simple example to demonstrate this. He talked about how, if he hired a babysitter to watch his child, he usually only paid about two dollars an hour. But to mow his lawn he was willing to pay the same person ten dollars for a 1-hour job. His point was that we don't spend money for the welfare of children and I guess that applies to the schools as well."

"Sure it does," Lois rejoined. "Before we get too all-fired-up about raising standards for teachers we better decide that as a society we are willing to invest the money needed to make schools a good place to work and learn. If we are unwilling to make that commitment then we will have a hard time attracting to teaching the individuals who will meet all these new, increased standards."

The bell rang, interrupting the two teachers' hurried lunch. Their allotted 30 minutes to gulp down their lunch was over; Jayne was off to supervise the playground, and Lois to patrol the girls' restrooms on the second floor. They left behind stacks of partially graded papers that would have to be taken home that night.

INTRODUCTION

■ The problems and questions that Lois and Jayne discussed are those both experienced and novice teachers face. How do they meet all the demands of their jobs? And what about colleagues who do not meet our expectations of a good teacher?

Likewise, the district for which they work is not at all unusual in its response to the issue of teacher competence. Faced with increasing public concern over the quality of schooling, more and more attention has focused on the quality of teachers. Many states either now require or are considering the submission of standardized test results (such as the National Teachers Examination) before certification. Local school districts are similarly requiring such scores before they will consider a candidate for employment. Some states have gone so far as to require teachers already in the classroom to be tested in order to maintain or renew their state certification.

But as Lois pointed out, much of the new rush to do testing only treats the symptoms and not the disease. What can we legitimately expect of teachers, given the often unfortunate conditions under which they labor? With too many students, too little time, too few materials, and not enough pay, teachers face an almost impossible task. This is not to say that teachers always fail in their mission. In fact, even against these odds many teachers are very successful and their good work should be seen as nothing short of miraculous.

In this chapter we look at teachers—who they are and why they teach. Our look at teachers and teaching will follow two paths. First, we will see who teachers are and explore the issue that has received so much attention in the media recently—the quality of the current and future teaching corps. Then we turn our attention to why teachers go into teaching and what teaching has to offer as a career.

TEACHERS

□ Who Are Teachers?

Recent statistics tell us that the teaching corps today is predominantly female, white, and under the age of 40 with 15 years or less of full-time

Teaching is a commitment to children.

teaching experience.[1] Of course these are just averages and do not tell us enough about particular grade levels to be really informative. So let's look a bit closer at the particulars.

Gender
By far and away, the majority of elementary school teachers are women. Eighty-five percent of teachers in grades K to 6 are women. At the secondary level, men outnumber women by 54% to 46%. However, the trend at the secondary level is to more female teachers, which means for the foreseeable future teaching will be a primarily female-dominated field.

Race

The teaching population is currently nearly 86% white. This varies only slightly between grade levels, with 90% of secondary teachers being white and 83% of elementary teachers being white as well. Fewer than 10% of our teachers are black (11.4% at the elementary level, 7.4% at the secondary level), and other ethnic or racial groups make up 5% of the teaching corps.

These figures are of concern to many educators as our minority population in schools continues to grow. The birth rates of blacks and Mexican-Americans is such that they will be a larger part of our population in the future. Furthermore, currently over 16% of public secondary schools and 18% of elementary schools have student bodies with over a 50% minority population.

Age and Experience

Elementary school teachers are similar in age but have less experience than do their secondary school counterparts. Nearly 57% of all teachers are under the age of 40, while 85% of all teachers are under 50 (and 16% are under age 30). Sixty-one percent of elementary teachers have more than 10 years experience and 67% of secondary teachers have the same. Many demographers project a rapid change toward youthfulness in the teaching population as retirements take more and more senior staff members.

Although the above figures tell you a bit about who teaches, that is, who you will work with, they don't tell you how well they teach. This issue has dominated recent debate about schools and we think you should be apprised of it now.

☐ How Good Are Our Teachers?

September 24, 1984, the cover of *Newsweek* magazine confronted millions of Americans with a simple headline: "Why Teachers Fail." Accompanied by a drawing of a teacher wearing a dunce cap, the claim being made was not hard to miss—teachers are not very smart folks. *Newsweek,* however, was far from alone in this charge. In fact its cover seems almost a copy from the March 14, 1983, cover of *U.S. News and World Report*. There a teacher was shown in a dunce cap (this time a picture) with the question, "What's Wrong With Our Teachers?" These magazine covers reflected the growing national concern over public education.

Academic Ability of Teachers

What do we actually know about the academic ability of teachers? Before surveying the literature we need to raise one important proviso.

While academic ability is certainly an important characteristic of a good teacher, it is only one of the many attributes a teacher needs. As Daniel Duke points out, factors related to teacher effectiveness include "verbal ability, the quality of their preparation, their job experience, and their expectations for students."[2] We often see stories pop up in the popular press designed to impress us with the weaknesses of school teachers, featuring for example, the claim that a musical genius like Beethoven would not be able to teach music today in the public school. The implication is that this musical genius would not be able to share his gifts with young students because of unfair or irrational teacher licensing requirements. But genius or not, would we really want this often temperamental, partially deaf individual attempting to meet the diverse needs of children in classrooms?

When we talk about the academic capabilities of our current teaching force, the first thing we have to admit is that we do not know much. While we are bombarded almost daily with reports in the media about the ineptness of teachers, there is little data beyond anecdotal stories.

There have, however, been disturbing signs on the horizon. When teachers were tested on academic skills, an alarming rate of failure, sometimes up to 30%, has been reported. More importantly, a variety of studies seems to suggest that the best and brightest of our teachers are the most likely to leave the classroom.

In the only study of its kind to track such phenomena, Vance and Schlechty found that with regard to scores on tests of academic ability, those teachers "who score highest leave teaching in the greatest numbers and . . . those who score lowest are most likely to stay in the classroom."[3] This does not mean that all good teachers leave, or even that those who leave are good. It does mean, however, that for some reason teaching is perhaps less attractive to the academically able, which is a genuine cause for concern.

Are we losing our best and brightest teachers? The answer is at best unclear—especially because most reports are only concerned with academic ability and pay little attention to classroom performance. But before we leave this issue it is important to note that public perception of teacher competence is often higher than the popular media would lead us to believe. For example, in the 1986 Gallup Poll of public attitudes about public schools, "teachers' lack of interest" (the most frequently mentioned teacher issue) was cited by only 4% of those questioned as the biggest problems faced by their local school. On the other hand, only 41% of those responding to a question on the "grade deserved by teachers in the public schools in this community" gave teachers a grade of A or B (11% and 30% respectively, with 28% giving a grade of C).[4] To confuse the issue further, when John Goodlad asked teachers, parents, and students to rank-order the problems of their particular school, "poor teachers and teaching" ranked as a "minor problem" or "not a problem" at nearly all grade levels.[5]

What is to be made of these differing statements? We can hazard two tentative guesses. First, given that teachers are the most numerous of public school employees, they are most often held to blame when there appear to be problems with the school. Second, it is easy to criticize the teachers in the school across town, but people are largely satisfied with the teacher in their child's classroom. When it comes to new recruits to the teaching field, the public is similarly satisfied. In the same Gallup Poll cited above, only 6% of public school parents saw the "difficulty in getting new teachers" as the biggest problem their school district faced.[6] And yet there is a reportedly great concern with the caliber of future teachers. We now turn our attention to those coming into the field, you and your colleagues.

The Future Teaching Corps

WHO GOES INTO TEACHING?   While we have looked at who teachers are, it is also important to consider who teachers will be. The answer to that question is simple—look around at your classmates and you will see the individuals with whom you may be spending the next 10 to 20 years of your life. As you look around, reflect on the following statements that have been made about you and your peers:

> Too many teachers are being drawn from the bottom quarter of graduating high school and college students.[7]
> Most teaching recruits are now drawn from the bottom group of SAT scorers; most of the few top scorers who are recruited to education leave the profession quickly.[8]
> The real crisis in teaching today is in who is entering the profession. And if we don't do something about that now, it will hurt America's competitive standing in the future.[9]

Not very encouraging words.

The numbers behind these words are confusing. For example, the SAT scores of students intending to major in education rank 26th out of 29 fields. Reflecting on these statistics, Linda Darling-Hammond has said:

> Although these measures of academic ability do not fully predict teaching performance, it is clear that the teaching profession is

attracting and retaining fewer academically able young people than it has in the past.[10]

On the other hand, a variety of studies point out that education majors do just as well in their academic performance as do their peers in other fields. And the SAT scores mentioned above are misleading. They are based on what those students taking the SAT project their major to be. Often students who intend to teach English, math, science, or history indicate those areas as majors rather than education. Thus, these scores may reflect a poorer showing by education majors than is the case. In fact, many of our colleges report a noticeable improvement in the ability of their students over the past 5 years, which is a promising trend.

Hopefully, you are one of those bright, committed individuals who are entering education today. The next issue that must be faced is the quality of your preparation. Teacher education programs have received as much criticism, some of it well deserved. But drastic changes have occurred in the past few years that will improve the teacher education programs and the preparation of future teachers.

THE QUALITY OF TEACHER EDUCATION   What is the public perception of teacher preparation? *Newsweek* magazine has said that "teacher training is perhaps the biggest running joke in higher education."[11] Only 49% of teachers themselves, when asked to grade their teacher education training, would give their preparation programs an A or B grade.[12] Or, as Albert Shanker, President of the American Federation of Teachers has put it:

> Education is the only professional field where after people graduate they say they could have been better off without the training.[13]

What are the major concerns about teacher education? Basically, they fall into three categories: admissions, course work, and graduation requirements. As for admissions, most colleges and schools of education are willing to accept any student with a 2.0 (C) grade average. In fact, in a recent report that surveyed teacher education programs it was found that rarely does anyone who applies for admission to teacher education get rejected.[14] To counter this trend the National Council for Accreditation of Teacher Education (NCATE), which approves teacher education programs throughout the country, is revising its standards to include a minimum 2.5 grade point average and a standardized test of basic skills for admission to teacher education. Additionally, many universities have voluntarily raised admission requirements.

As for curriculum, the complaint is often made that future teachers spend too much time studying pedagogy and not enough time studying in the academic disciplines. Of course, these arguments are often overstated for effect. Many education courses, especially methods courses, are offered by academic departments, not education faculty. In fact, more often than not, less than 25% of a prospective teacher's course work is controlled by education faculty. Yet the perception that teacher education is not rigorous enough persists.

In the face of this growing criticism a number of alternatives has been proposed. One such alternative is making teacher preparation a five-year program, with students taking an academic major and then moving on to teacher preparation. Recently, many programs require more direct, hands-on experience linked with teacher education courses. And many faculty in teacher education are working to strengthen their course offerings and requirements. This book, in fact, grew out of the authors' desire to put more "meat" into teacher education courses.

Of course, strengthening admission requirements and adding more rigor to courses will not alter the quality of teacher education candidates alone. Who is allowed to graduate from these programs is the third component of any serious attempt to upgrade teacher education. Currently, few schools require any sort of certification test and few states require anything of candidates for teaching certification other than a diploma. However, this is also changing as more and more states and universities require successful completion of some form of standardized test and demonstration of teaching ability before being recommended for certification.

One last note here about an often overlooked area in teacher preparation: the faculty in teacher education programs. More and more we see universities that have no interest in "dirtying" their hands in the practical work of teacher education. Indeed, since universities are rated on the amount of research that faculty members produce rather than the quality of the teachers they turn out, there is little incentive to focus on teacher preparation. Additionally, in many institutions faculty members have little or no recent experience in teaching (for example, a survey of the Stanford and Berkeley education programs revealed that 70% of the faculty had never taught in public schools).[15] Clearly there is a need to reward faculty who are concerned with public schools and are active in the field of teacher education.

Will all these recommendations for reform actually make any difference? There is much concern over the use of standardized tests for admission and graduation. Many educators argue that they are not good measures of academic or teaching ability. (An interesting aside here: While teachers object to being tested themselves, they often rely on the very same types of tests to evaluate their students.) Yet, on the other hand, it does seem only fair that the public be assured that their teachers can read, write, compute, and speak competently. There is no doubt teachers should be well-versed in their subject matters, requiring more courses in the academic disciplines. But, on the other hand, should this be done at the expense of the very courses that attempt to build the skills, attitudes, and behaviors needed to get this academic content across to students?

While it is too early to predict, the attention now given to teacher preparation offers the potential of paying high dividends. If more academically gifted students enter a curriculum that is rigorous in terms of both academics and field work/practical work in school classrooms with high expectations for graduates, we cannot help but do better. Indeed, we believe that there is great potential in both the current teaching corps and teacher education students. Not only does the renewed attention in teaching justify this optimism, but the reasons teachers give for entering teaching are also promising. Why teachers enter teaching, and some of the changes in the conditions of teaching, are the concerns of the next section.

RESEARCH NOTES 2.1   Reasons for Originally Becoming a Teacher

Reason	1971	1976	1981
Desire to work with young people	71.8%	71.4%	69.6%
Interest in subject-matter field	34.5	38.3	44.1
Value or significance of education in society	37.1	34.3	40.2
Influence of a teacher in elementary or secondary schools	17.9	20.6	25.4
Long summer vacation	14.4	19.1	21.5
Influence of family	20.5	18.4	21.5
Job security	16.2	17.4	20.6
Never really considered anything else	17.4	17.4	20.3
Opportunity for a lifetime of self-growth	21.4	17.4	13.1

From National Education Association, *Status of the American School Teacher, 1980–81* (Washington, D.C.: National Education Association, 1982), p. 72.

WHY TEACH?

☐ **Not for the Pay**

We turn first to the extrinsic rewards of teaching. With the exception of job security and the long summer break, few if any teachers choose teaching because of the rewards of pay or benefits. And rightfully so.

Teacher Pay and Job Advancement
Simply put, teachers do not go into teaching for the pay. The average pay for teachers today is just over $23,000. It is important to remember that the average years of experience of teachers is 15 years and over half of all teachers hold a master's degree or higher. Thus, this salary figure reflects the salary earned by teachers after years of service and additional education. Starting salaries are much lower, averaging around $15,000. Not much compared with starting salaries in engineering ($22,500), accounting ($17,000), computer sciences ($21,000), or sales-marketing ($17,000). Perhaps even more importantly, teacher salaries over the past 20 years, while increasing in dollar terms, have actually been decreasing given the pressures of inflation.

One of the ways compensation problems are resolved in many public and private occupations is through job advancement. While beginning pay and authority may be limited, there is always the potential to advance to positions of greater remuneration and status. However, with teaching that is not the case. The job of classroom teacher carries with it all the rights and privileges available from the first day on the

FOR REFLECTION 2.1   Why Become a Teacher?

On your own, make a list of the reasons you have for becoming a teacher. List as many as you can and list them in order of importance. With classmates, compile a master list of all the reasons you have given. Again, rank-order them from most to least important.
   Now, reflect upon the following questions:
1. How is your personal list different from the class list? What does this tell you about your choice to teach?
2. How is the class list similar to and different than the list in Research Notes 2.1 of the text? How do you explain this difference between future teachers and practice teachers?
3. Which of your reasons do you feel is most likely to lead to your future success as a teacher? Which will be the greatest sources of disappointment?

job. Pay is based, for the most part, on longevity and additional school-ing, and is usually not linked to performance. The only way "up" avail-able to most teachers is to *leave* the classroom and become an administrator—taking them away from children and subject field.

There has recently been interest in changing the condition of pay and advancement for teachers. Primarily, this consists of creating career ladders for teachers and improving pay overall. However, for now one of the major frustrations teachers face is the lack of adequate pay. In fact, nine teachers in ten feel that their salaries are too low and the same percentage contend that low pay is the major reason for leaving the classroom. Clearly something must be done.

Time Off and Job Security

Some of the concern with salary needs to be tempered with the fact that most teachers work a 9-month year. Extended time off (without pay) is available around the Christmas holiday season (usually 2 weeks), Thanksgiving (4 to 5 days), and a week-long "spring break." One of the fringe benefits most frequently cited by teachers as a reason for entering teaching is the nearly 3-month-long summer vacation. This time is used by teachers to earn additional income either in or outside of education, obtain additional education, travel, be with their family, and just plain relax.

Teaching also offers a fair amount of job security. Even with the reduction in the age-group attending schools, teaching is not subject to the whims of the business market. Whereas industries or stores often close, schools seldom close except to consolidate. In fact, for the first time in a decade we seem to be facing a serious shortage of teachers. In a variety of areas such as math, science, computer science, bilingual education, and special education there is already a shortage of teachers nationwide. The only field experiencing a considerable surplus of teachers at this time is physical education. All indications are that this trend will only accelerate, leading to more and more jobs for teachers.[16] As we often tell our students, there are plenty of jobs for good teachers who are willing to be flexible and to go where the jobs are.

☐ The Joy of Teaching

What really attracts most teachers to the field? The answer is the intrinsic rewards, the joys of teaching. For example, comments like these most accurately reflect the reasons most of us go into teaching:

> Why, then, do so many teachers remain in the classroom? Because, they say, there are priceless rewards such as the moment

© 1985 *Washington Post Writers Group,* reprinted with permission.

when a child suddenly understands a math problem or discovers the joy of Shakespeare's plays.

Explains California industrial-arts teacher Ernest Smith: "It's a great feeling to meet a former student who says: 'You gave me a tough time, but now my life is better.'"

For some individuals, these rewards were sufficiently attractive to lure them from higher-paying jobs in private industry. Wynetta McNeil, 31, left previous positions in finance and consulting to teach math and social sciences in Atlanta. She says: "I found that my skills were strong as a motivator. A lot of kids I work with have the talents that just have to be tapped. When I see a little light bulb click on over their heads, I feel satisfied."

Melissa Lane, 16, a junior at North Hollywood High School, says good teachers are easy to identify: "They are excited about the subjects they teach. They're available at lunchtime if you need them. They always have plans and projects."[17]

The Desire to Work with Young People

More than anything else, teachers teach because they like kids—at least that's why they started in the field. Teachers under 30 years of age gave this response in even higher percentages (78.6%) than did all teachers. When asked why they *presently* teach, 69% of all teachers still give this as a reason with the under 30 age-group more likely than any other to select it.[18]

By far, the greatest satisfaction to be found in teaching comes from the students. Teachers talk about the excitement in a child's eyes when he or she discovers a new insight or sees something he or she made enjoyed by another; helping a student expand the mind's horizons through a book that would not have otherwise been read; watching a student develop real pride in the ability to write, speak, act, paint, compute, sing, or do any one of a million tasks well and with grace. This is what teaching is really about, this is why so many stay at it.

Schools are the places to be for those who enjoy youth, are willing to suffer through the frustrations of growing up again and again, are able to patiently explain and reexplain, and have a genuine concern about a child's growth. Listen to the way teachers who enjoy their work talk about it:

> You work with kids. That's what you do. And school is a place that will allow you to do that. [Elementary teacher]
>
> I'm with my children all day long. I watch them change by the moment. Some days they'll tell me all of their secrets. Other days they withdraw into their own little shells. Whatever they do, I'm there to see and hear it, and I take it all to heart. [Elementary teacher]
>
> It is the subject matter and the kids. I love the subject matter and naturally you need an audience for that. The kids are the audience and they are important to me. I can't teach my subject matter without touching the kids in some way. [Secondary teacher][19]

And then there is the unabashed joy of Viola A. Schuler's story of Darrell in "Teacher, I Can Read!" (Focus 2.1).

Working with children is the best reason for entering the profession.

FOCUS 2.1 "Teacher, I Can Read!"

by Viola A. Schuler

Darrell had a face only a mother could love. Some would say he was downright homely. At first he was quite offensive to us because of his residual bed-wetting smell and his always-dripping nose. But his body was wiry and strong, and he appeared to be a happy child.

Darrell came to my class that fall with high hopes for learning. His excitement about going to school was almost impossible to throttle. After the first week I knew he would wrap himself around my heart. I also realized that he and I were in for the biggest struggle of his young life: learning to read.

Darrell's family had a troubled history. His father had abandoned the family when Darrell was quite young. His mother held a part-time job and saw to it that Darrell and his preschool-age brother were awake by 6:30 every morning in order to be at the local day-care center by 7 a.m.

It was late October before Darrell became accustomed to a full day of school. He was an afternoon learner who yawned continually until nearly 11 every morning. He was also unfailingly forgetful. It was to be a year of lost coats, boots, mittens, library books, and notes to his mother.

Though at first the students had been tempted to shun Darrell because of his offensive smell and peculiar mannerisms, it wasn't long before they surrendered, just as I had, to his big eyes, his soft voice, and his warm smile.

Our classroom was cavernous, with a 13-foot ceiling. The bright yellow walls accentuated the rudimentary artwork that adorned them. A soft checkerboard rug lay in the front of the room near the chalkboard, and it was here that I conducted the daily phonics lessons. This was the first opportunity for the first-graders to open their minds, and the differences in their learning pace was readily apparent.

Darrell, however, was in serious trouble. He could neither recognize the letters of the alphabet nor recall any of their sounds. I knew I had to separate the children into reading groups before the faster ones drained the eagerness from the slower, but I worried that Darrell's ego would be damaged by the awareness that every other child in the room had begun to read.

He could not seem to connect the sounds to the written word. This particular miracle of the mind—listening to sounds and blending them together to produce words—was a gift that eluded him. So much for phonics, I thought; lots of people have learned to read without ever knowing the sounds of the letters. At the time, I was more concerned about Darrell's emotional state. I feared the struggle would sap his enthusiasm for learning.

Darrell did make progress. But, with the other children moving ahead so rapidly, it seemed a small consolation.

Each day after his reading group had finished, he would race to the back of the room. There on a table were salt, sand, finger paints, and sometimes an individual portion of chocolate pudding, tools intended to help the students learn to read. Darrell would glide his finger through the salt or the pudding, tracing the letters of all the words he had missed that day. He repeated the words over and over as his index finger, Band-Aid and all, helped to send messages to his brain. Chocolate pudding was his favorite teaching tool; being able to stop occasionally and lick the treat from his hand seemed to lessen the burden of the job. Learning to read was undeniably hard work for Darrell, but he attacked it with an inexhaustible energy that earned my admiration.

As we gradually moved away from phonics, I learned that Darrell was vitally interested in horses and dinosaurs. He would invent endless stories about them, which he dictated to me eagerly. He began to read his own words aloud as I slowly moved my hand to direct his eyes across the page. His storytelling expertise quickly developed. I was amazed at the confidence with which this young author worked his audience. Why had I ever worried that his self-esteem would wither?

When spring finally arrived, it brought with it a new source of excitement for the class: they were reading their first library books. Darrell, however, was still only a spectator, longingly watching his friends zip through books.

At last I decided that the time was ripe for him to tackle his first book. After recess one morning, Darrell's reading group was pleasantly surprised to find that they had glossy new books waiting for them at the reading table. They were privileged to be the first to crease back the covers.

Darrell was the first to reach the table. I watched as he flipped through the new pages with anticipation. With his tongue twisted, his mouth moved silently. His eyes shone. It was an important moment for him.

He grew quiet. I wondered if he was being generous, allowing the others to read first, or if he was being cautious, afraid of being outdone yet again. As the other children read, he seemed to absorb every word like a thirsty paper towel. He held the book to his nose to smell the fresh ink on its pages. At last it was his turn. The others had all been successful. Could he do the same?

Gradually and deliberately, but with unexpected confidence, Darrell started to read, one word at a time. Then the words began to flow more quickly and more smoothly. He held the book tightly, his palms clammy. His face radiated happiness. There was no stopping him. Soon, every child in the room was listening. My teacher's guide began to blur as the children let out a long and resounding cheer.

Just once he lifted his gleaming eyes from the page to look at me. His voice shook with excitement as he said proudly, "Teacher, I can read!"

Excerpts taken from *Phi Delta Kappan*, January 1985, pp. 368–369.

Why do most good teachers and educators keep going back, day after day, regardless of the frustrations or negative publicity? Because their lives are devoted to the education of the young. They draw their strength from their interaction with children, the daily excitement of growing learners. Even on the toughest days, the days when nothing seems to go right, it often only takes the smile of one child to make it all worthwhile.

Interest in Subject Matter

Nearly 45% of all teachers currently teaching say that their interest in a particular subject area helped draw them into teaching. As we would expect, this is a reason given more frequently by junior high or senior high teachers (56.6% and 65.7%, respectively) than by elementary teachers (26.7%).[20] However, for all teachers, an interest in the life of the mind, of ideas, books, and so on plays a central part in bringing them back to the classroom.

Indeed, schools are probably one of the few areas in our society concerned primarily with the development and transmission of knowledge. Where else in our society could you dress up like Thomas Jefferson to discuss with high school juniors the drafting of the Declaration of Independence? Or take a group of seven-year-olds out stomping around in a pond to gather samples of the life cycles of a frog? Or act out the intricacies of a Shakespearean play, excavate a mock-up of Egyptian ruins, construct mathematical models, and on and on. It is indeed a place to nurture one's love for a field and we can all recall teachers who did this in our own experience. Their rooms were alive with the tools of their trade, as well as our own products drawn out by these special individuals.

There is a danger in all this, of course. How often have we heard someone say that they teach "math," "science," "first grade," "physical education," when asked what they do? In fact, we all teach children. As a secondary level math teacher puts it: "If someone told me that my job is just to teach math, I would quit. I couldn't stand to see myself as someone who teaches skills and nothing else. I have to feel I am doing something more lasting."[21] Good teachers never forget that good teaching and learning are inseparable; one does not exist without the other. No matter how much we may love our subject matter if we can't communicate it to our students we really are not teaching.

So schools can give one the best of both worlds: an opportunity to immerse ourselves in material we enjoy and to share that enjoyment with young people. This situation virtually no other field can offer.

Diversity and Variety

Though not often mentioned in surveys, teaching offers another very important benefit—diversity and variety. If ever there was an occupation about which the saying "no day is the same" was true, it would have to be teaching. To some, this diversity is an annoyance and they try to structure their teaching to insure order, conformity, and a false sense of discipline. But what this overlooks is the very nature of subject matter and the learners.

Subject matter is never static. One indicator of this is the constant pressure on publishers to update textbooks. As teachers know more about content and learning, they want to try new methods of presentation and organization. More importantly, the conditions of children's day-to-day lives are constantly changing. Thus, subject matter makes new and different connections with students from year to year demanding constant revision, research, and updating of lesson plans.

Students vary as well. They all come with special demands, their own private joys and cares. Thus, life in the classroom can rapidly become a three-ring circus as a teacher juggles these competing demands—which, when skillfully done, is just as exciting as the circuses of our childhood.

Finally, teaching itself is something at which you can become progressively better. Too often students in teacher preparation programs believe that by simply completing the prescribed curriculum they will become the best teacher possible. This is not the case. After gaining classroom experience, many teachers benefit from programs of self-renewal, either in their districts or a university setting. Unlike many repetitious jobs, teaching constantly changes, offering a new challenge almost every day.

CHAPTER SUMMARY

■ As you read this chapter, you should have thought about your own reasons for teaching. Behind many reasons teachers give for teaching is a belief that they are performing a vital public service. It is a field with a mission tied to the welfare of the nation. Children are, without a doubt, our most valuable national treasure. Those who choose to work with them are committing themselves to the enhancement of that treasure.

We have tried to present both sides of teaching, both the frustrations and the joys. It is important that you know as much as possible about those you will work with in the field and the conditions of your work. With that in mind, we reviewed the quality of the current teaching corps, the outlook for future teachers, and the extrinsic and intrinsic rewards of teaching.

Working with colleagues can make the difference between success or failure.

In the face of all this you should remember that no other occupational group in our society takes on such a monumental task. Entrusted to teachers is the future. Much of what they do will be reflected in the quality of life in the future. As the first teacher in space, Christa McAuliffe so eloquently put it, "I touch the future; I teach."

Perhaps this is why the debates over education are so vociferous and heated—so much is at stake. It is this responsibility that makes teaching both difficult and rewarding. Again, from a teacher:

> When you realize what you say in the classroom—even though you think no one is listening—has an effect on your students, you realize that you are a role model, even if you don't see yourself that way. The kids take what I have to say, think about it, and make decisions based on it. I have that kind of influence; . . . it's scary but it makes me feel good. It's a big responsibility.[22]

It is an occupation that is designed to meet future personal as well as social goals. Teachers are obligated to help each of their students, help them think, live, and grow. While often teachers never know the consequences, they judge every action with an eye to the future:

> I like to see them when they come back, so I can see how they're doing, how they're turning out. I love to watch them grow. It's terrific. It's true with any age group—you can see the growth and development. Let's hope it continues. . . . They're all individuals and they bubble about certain things. Some of them, my God, are so brave.[23]

FOR DISCUSSION

1. It is easy to say that teachers' salaries should be raised. But should teachers be expected to work a longer school day or year in return for higher pay? Take on more responsibilities?

2. Your instructor can provide you with a sample pay scale for teachers. What does the pay scale reward? What goes unrewarded? How would you change the scale to generate an alternative set of rewards?

3. Much has been said about the academic quality of teacher education majors. Additionally, there has been concern about the quality of their preparation for teaching. In response to this, should teacher training be expanded to 5, or even 6, years as opposed to the current 4? What should be done with the extra time?

4. List your reasons for becoming a teacher. Which of these do you think is the most realistic? Which are most likely to lead to frustration? Based on this, how likely are you to remain in teaching?

5. List the various activities with students you have been engaged in as an adult. This might include being a camp counselor or similar youth work. What did you gain from each of these experiences in terms of understanding children or skills you have been developing? How will these enhance your development as a teacher? What further experiences working with children do you believe you need?

IN THE SCHOOL/IN THE CLASSROOM

1. Poll teachers working in the type of teaching position you hope to hold using the following questions:
   a. Why did you first enter teaching?
   b. Why are you still in teaching?
   c. What are your greatest frustrations in teaching?
   d. If you had to do it over again, would you still choose teaching as a career?
   e. How long do you plan to remain in teaching?
   Compare the answers you get on questions *a* and *b* with those of your classmates. Are they similar to or different than the figures cited in the text? Why? How, if at all, does this information affect your decision to become a teacher?

2. Follow a teacher through several normal days. Record what he or she does in terms of interaction with students, with adults, and basic record keeping. Take your observations and compute the percentage of the teacher's time spent in each activity. Now compare that use of time to the reasons teachers give for entering teaching. Do you see any particular potential for frustration or reward? Further, how predictable did you find their day to be? What do you most enjoy about the day? Least enjoy? How does this affect your decision to become a teacher?

SUGGESTED READINGS

Conroy, Pat. *The Water is Wide*. Boston: Houghton Mifflin, 1972. The basis for the movie *Conrack,* this readable book follows first-year teacher Pat Carnoy to the South Carolina coastal islands. Here he not only teaches but learns—about friendship, life, himself. A moving account of one teacher's work to improve the lives of children.

Kohl, Herbert. *36 Children*. New York: Signet, 1967. Another first-person account of life in the classroom. Kohl carefully portrays his students and himself as the real joy of teaching and watching children learn shines through each page.

Lieberman, Ann, and Lynne Miller. *Teachers, Their World, and Their Work*. Alexandria, Va.: Association for Supervision and Curriculum Development, 1984. This volume surveys the research on the working conditions faced by many teachers. After looking at what teachers and administrators say about their work the authors present a variety of proposals for reform.

Ryan, Kevin, Katherine K. Newman, Gerald Mager, Jane Applegate, Thomas Lasley, Flora Randall, and John Johnston. *Biting the Apple.* New York: Longman, 1980. Interviews with 13 teachers in their first year of work fill this book. The problems, successes, and unexpected events these novice teachers faced gives an insight into the life of the beginning teacher.

CHAPTER REFERENCES

1. Demographic statistics in this section come primarily from *E. D. Tabs: The 1985 Public School Survey Early Tabulations* (Washington, D.C.: U.S. Department of Education, 1986).
2. Daniel L. Duke, *Teaching: The Imperiled Profession* (Albany, N.Y.: State University of New York Press, 1984), p. 14.
3. Victor S. Vance and Phillip C. Schlechty, "The Distribution of Academic Ability in the Teaching Force: Policy Implications," *Phi Delta Kappan,* September 1982, p. 22.
4. Alec M. Gallup, "The 18th Annual Gallup Poll of the Public's Attitudes Toward the Public School," *Phi Delta Kappan,* September 1986, pp. 43–59.
5. John Goodlad, *A Place Called School* (New York: McGraw-Hill, 1984), pp. 72–74.
6. Gallup, "The 18th Annual Gallup Poll," 43–59.
7. National Commission on Excellence in Education, *A Nation At Risk* (Washington, D.C.: U.S. Department of Education, 1983), p. 22.
8. Linda Darling-Hammond, *Beyond the Commission Reports: The Coming Crisis in Teaching* (Santa Monica, Calif.: The Rand Corporation, 1984), p. 14.
9. Emily Feistritzer, quoted in "What's Wrong With Our Teachers," *U.S. News and World Report,* March 14, 1983, p. 37.
10. Darling-Hammond, *Beyond the Commission Reports,* p. 3.
11. "Why Teachers Fail," *Newsweek,* September 24, 1984, p. 64.
12. Alec Gallup, "The Gallup Poll of Teachers' Attitudes Toward the Public School," *Phi Delta Kappan,* October 1984, p. 100.
13. Albert Shanker, quoted in "Why Teachers Fail," p. 65.
14. C. Emily Feistritzer, *The Making of a Teacher* (Washington, D.C.: National Center for Education Information, 1984), p. 6.
15. "Teachers Get No Respect," *Newsweek,* September 24, 1984, p. 70.
16. "Teacher Supply and Demand by Field and Region," *Education Week,* April 24, 1985, pp. 12–13.
17. "What's Wrong With Our Teachers?" *U.S. News and World Report,* March 14, 1983, p. 40.
18. National Education Association, *The Status of the American School Teacher* (Washington, D.C.: National Education Association, 1982), pp. 71–73.

19. Ann Lieberman and Lynn Miller, *Teachers, Their World, and Their Work: Implications For School Improvement* (Alexandria, Va.: Association for Supervision and Curriculum Development, 1984), pp. 9, 10.
20. National Education Association, *The Status of the American School Teacher,* pp. 71–73.
21. Lieberman and Miller, *Teachers, Their World, and Their Work,* p. 10.
22. Ibid., pp. 10–11.
23. Ibid., p. 11.

3

The Current Context for Schooling

A SCENARIO

■ Three-thirty Friday afternoon. Steve Wilson is finishing another week at Hillsboro Elementary School. Usually, he goes out with friends for a couple of hours at the end of the week, but today he begged off. Too tired to enjoy his friends, he slumps down in his chair behind his desk and thinks about his week, and the causes of his exhaustion.

"I'm asked to do so much besides teach anymore," he thinks to himself. "I remember when I first started teaching, nearly twenty years ago, there were so many things we took for granted. All our students looked the same and seemed to come from the same family background. Their parents were together and all had jobs—that only applies to a small majority of my students this year."

He thought about all the ways the changes in his students affected his job. They came with such diverse backgrounds, often needing the personal attention they couldn't get at home. The strain on families who had lost jobs often showed up in the classroom as well. Students just seemed to come to him with more personal needs all the time.

Then there are the social tasks. "I wonder what we'll have an assembly for next," Steve mused. "Let's see, in the past month alone we've dealt with protective skills so kids won't get kidnapped or the like, alcohol and drug abuse, and, oh yeah, the sign-up meeting for youth basketball. It sure would be nice to have a week without an assembly. . . ."

What really bothered Steve was not the fact that his school, like others, was trying to meet needs that were not met anywhere else. It was the memo on his desk, from the school board, demanding that teachers come up with a plan to raise the academic achievement levels in Hillsboro Elementary.

"No matter what we do, it's never enough," he thought. "Maybe the problem is that we don't know what we ought to do, so we try and do everything. It sure seems like the rest of the community wants us to deal with problems they won't handle. But it's all a matter of trade-offs. We can't do everything well—there isn't the time or money. How will we chose?"

He rose, gathered the student papers to be read that weekend, put on his coat, and went to the door. Looking back into the classroom he thought of the students who sat in each desk—white, black, and Hispanic, male and female, affluent and poor. Each one was an individual, each one dependent on Steve in a different way, and each one a challenge. He would be back on Monday to try and meet that challenge again. Right now he just wanted to go home and take a nap.

INTRODUCTION

■ Steve is facing questions not unlike those faced by all teachers. Over time, the mission of the school and teachers has continually expanded. When our society resolves questions of who should be educated, it is teachers who carry out the task. If it is decided that certain social problems are the domain of the school, teachers are the ones to enact the proposed solutions. If other social institutions or even families do not meet the specific needs of youth, teachers are often expected to fill the void. Additionally, what we commonly see as "adult" problems, such as unemployment, often have an impact on children in ways that influence their work in school.

This means that the social context of schooling, the nature of the culture in which the school is located, often impacts on the job of the teacher. In this chapter we want to explore the current social context of education and the demands that context generates for teachers. How do these demands affect the joys and rewards of teaching? More specifically, what is the role of schooling today and what does that imply for teaching? To do this we will examine the ongoing debate over what social tasks the schools have been expected to perform and what schools should do in our democratic society.

THE NEW CONCERN FOR PUBLIC EDUCATION

☐ **The Continuing Debate**

Since schools are our single largest public institution it is only logical that a great deal of public debate swirls around them. At one time or another politicians, ministers, merchants, generals, social reformers, and parents have fought to mold the school as each sees fit. For that reason, the recent debate about American public schooling should not surprise teachers. Nor should teachers ignore the current debates. In all likelihood these debates will alter the role of today's teacher as similar debates have in times past.

Who "Wrecked" the Schools?

Over 20 years ago, Mary Ann Raywid saw educational criticism in this way:

> Not only is American education under fire; the practice of criticizing our schools is well on its way to becoming a national pastime. For some it is already a favorite sport. For others, it has become a full-time career.[1]

Raywid reacted to a continuing pattern in which schools were seen as the reason for a variety of social ills. It is important to discuss that pattern in order to understand current educational controversy.

THE SPUTNIK ERA   On October 4, 1957, the Soviet Union launched the first artificial earth satellite. Called *Sputnik* (for "fellow traveler"), this technological achievement sent shock waves through American society. Sputnik was conclusive proof that our Cold War adversary had outstripped our scientific capabilities. In particular, schools were blamed for our lack of scientific achievement owing to their so-called anti-intellectual tenor. As Vice-Admiral Hyman Rickover, father of the nuclear navy, put it: "We are in our present predicament because education in America has deteriorated in quality for lack of standards."[2]

The solution to this public or social problem of international military superiority was to overhaul public schooling. In addition to Rickover's influential book, *Education and Freedom,* the Council for Basic Education, founded by Arthur Bestor, issued a call for a return to basic education. The Council's publication discussed subjects essential to a good education, including 4 years of English, French, German, and history, 3 years of math, and 2 years of science.[3]

These calls led to President Dwight Eisenhower's promotion of a larger federal role in public education. Congress was convinced to fund National Science Foundation (NSF) appropriations to train science and mathematics teachers in summer institutes, develop new science and mathematics curricula, and, through graduate fellowships, convince students to pursue science as a career. Additionally, the National Defense Education Act (NDEA) was passed in 1958 with the express aim of insuring "trained manpower of sufficient quality and quantity to meet the national defense needs of the United States."[4] This program was to provide funds to enhance curriculum and the recruitment of teachers in the areas of science, mathematics, English, and foreign languages.

THE HUMANISTIC CRITIQUE OF THE 1960s AND EARLY 1970s
Beginning in 1964 a new critique of public schools was heard. In direct opposition to critics of the 1950s, the claim was made that schools were too rigid, formal, and overly concerned with the basics. John Holt, in *How Children Fail,* argued that schools caused failure, proved by the fact that students were afraid, bored, and confused by schools that impeded students' natural desires to learn.[5] Holt's work was followed by a wide range of the so-called radical school critics. This included Jonathan Kozol's startling revelations of the dehumanizing nature of many urban school systems,[6] Charles Silberman's survey of the flatness of much school life,[7] and even the call by some for the abolishment of schools.[8]

FOCUS 3.1   Death at an Early Age

by Jonathan Kozol

Stephen is 8 years old. A picture of him standing in front of the bulletin board on Arab bedouins shows a little light-brown person staring with unusual concentration at a chosen spot upon the floor. Stephen is tiny, desperate, unwell. Sometimes he talks to himself. He moves his mouth as if he were talking. At other times he laughs out loud in class for no apparent reason. He is also an indescribably mild and unmalicious child. He cannot do any of his school work very well. His math and reading are poor. In Third Grade he was in a class that had substitute teachers much of the year. Most of the year before that, he had a row of substitute teachers too. He is in the Fourth Grade now but his work is barely at the level of the Second. Nobody has complained about the things that have happened to Stephen because he does not have any mother or father. Stephen is a ward of the State of Massachusetts and, as such, he has been placed in the home of some very poor people who do not want him now that he is not a baby any more. The money that they are given for him to pay his expenses every week does not cover the other kind of expense—the more important kind which is the immense emotional burden that is continually at stake. Stephen often comes into school badly beaten. If I ask him about it, he is apt to deny it because he does not want us to know first-hand what a miserable time he has. Like many children, and many adults too, Stephen is far more concerned with hiding his abased condition from the view of the world than he is with escaping that condition. He lied to me first when I asked him how his eye got so battered. He said it happened from being hit by accident when somebody opened up the door. Later, because it was so bruised and because I questioned him, he admitted that it was his foster mother who had flung him out onto the porch. His eye had struck the banister and it had closed and purpled. The children in the class were frightened to see him. I thought that they also felt some real compassion, but perhaps it was just shock.

Although Stephen did poorly in his school work, there was one thing he could do well. He was a fine artist. He made delightful drawings. The thing about them that was good, however, was also the thing that got him into trouble. For they were not neat and orderly and organized but entirely random and casual, messy, somewhat unpredictable, seldom according to the instructions he had been given, and—in short—real drawings. For these drawings, Stephen received considerable embarrassment at the hands of the Art Teacher. This person was a lady no longer very young who had some rather fixed values and opinions about children and about teaching. Above all, her manner was marked by unusual confidence. She seldom would merely walk into our class but seemed always to sweep into it. Even for myself, her advent, at least in the beginning of the year, used to cause a wave of anxiety. For she came into our class generally in a mood of self-assurance and of almost punitive restlessness which never made one confident but which generally made me wonder what I had done wrong.

The Art Teacher's most common technique for art instruction was to pass out mimeographed designs or suggested color plan. An alternate approach was to stick up on the wall or on the blackboard some of the drawings on a particular subject that had been done in the previous years by predominantly white classes. These drawings, neat and orderly and very uniform, would be the models for our children. The art lesson, in effect, would be to copy what had been done before, and the neatest and most accurate reproductions of the original drawings would be the ones that would win the highest approval from the teacher. . . .

If Stephen began to fiddle around during a lesson, the Art Teacher generally would not notice him at first. When she did, both he and I and the children around him would prepare for trouble. For she would go at his desk with something truly like a vengeance and would shriek at him in a way that carried terror. "Give me that! Your paints are all muddy! You've made it a mess. Look at what he's done! He's mixed up the colors! I don't know why we waste good paper on this child!" Then: "Garbage! Junk! He gives me garbage and junk! And garbage is one thing I will not have." Now I thought that that garbage and junk was very nearly the only real artwork in the class. I do not know very much about painting, but I know enough to know that the Art Teacher did not know much about it either and that, furthermore, she did not know or care anything at all about the way in which you can destroy a human being. Stephen, in many ways already dying, died a second and third and fourth and final death before her anger.

From Jonathan Kozol, *Death at an Early Age* (New York: Houghton Mifflin, 1967), pp. 1–4.

A great deal of the radical critics' claims rang true. Research pointed out how minority and female students were given a more limited education than were white male students. Additionally, much schooling continued to be rather dull and unimaginative, focusing on drill, repetition, and recitation with little room for creativity or originality. Perhaps what gave these critics' claims the most strength was the growing general distrust in the late 1960s and early 1970s of our public institutions. It was a period of disillusionment. President Lyndon Johnson decided not to stand for reelection after the quagmire of the Vietnam War; assassin's bullets ended the lives of Martin Luther King and Robert Kennedy; President Richard Nixon and Vice-President Spiro Agnew resigned from office under a cloud of suspected unethical, if not illegal, behavior. It was in this atmosphere of institutional distrust that the humanist critique was heard and occasionally acted on.

The humanistic critique, however, seemed to have only a limited effect on public schooling. The most notable success on a national level was the amending of the Elementary and Secondary Education Act, first passed in 1965 to provide funds for the educational needs of poor students. For example, amendments in 1966 (PL 89-750) provided funds for the education of low-income American Indian and migrant worker families. In 1967, amendments (PL 90-247) were added to help school dropouts and begin bilingual education. Title IX of the Educational Amendments of 1972 was designed to eliminate and prevent discrimination against women in public education. But the actual practice of classroom teachers barely changed. As Ken Sirotnik's recent survey suggests, little has changed in American classrooms as teachers still rely on workbook pages from texts, recitation, and drill.[9]

THE 1980s: A DECADE OF REPORTS   In the early and mid-1980s public attention once again focused on schools. Following an established pattern, this renewed debate about schooling occurred at a time of general social uncertainty. International incidents have reminded us of the limits of our power, economic productivity has declined in comparison to other countries, and unemployment, inflation, and high interest rates eat into our standard of living. Again, society turns to the schools as both the cause of and solution to our national ills.

This context helps us best understand the recent surge of reports on the state of public education. Since 1982, dozens of reports have chronicled the shortcomings of public education and prescribed reforms. Most of these reports are concerned with a social problem that is traceable, the critics claim, to the schools. We turn to a review of these reports now.

RESEARCH NOTES 3.1   Required Reading: Major Reports on Public Education Issued in the 1980s

The topic of public education has generated a wide range of recent reports and books. Below you will find a bibliography of the most important recent reports, some of which you may want to read.

Bennett, William. *First Steps: A Report on Elementary Schools in America.* Washington, D.C.: U.S. Government Printing Office, 1985.

Boyer, Ernest. *High School: A Report on Secondary Education in America.* Princeton, N.J.: Carnegie Foundation for the Advancement of Teaching, 1983.

Business–Higher Education Forum. Task Force of the Business–Higher Education Forum. *America's Competitive Challenge: The Need for a National Response.* Washington, D.C.: Business–Higher Education Forum, 1983.

Committee of Correspondence on the Future of Public Education. *Education for a Democratic Future: Equity and Excellence.* St. Louis: Committee of Correspondence, 1985.

Cusick, Philip. *The American High School and the Egalitarian Ideal.* New York: Longman, 1983.

Education Commission of the States. Task Force on Education for Economic Growth. *Action for Excellence: A Comprehensive Plan to Improve Our Nation's Schools.* Denver: Education Commission of the States, 1983.

Goodlad, John I. *A Place Called School: Prospects for the Future.* New York: McGraw-Hill, 1984.

Lightfoot, Sara Lawrence. *The Good High School: Portraits of Culture and Character.* New York: Basic Books, 1983.

The National Commission on Excellence in Education. *A Nation at Risk: The Imperative for Educational Reform.* Washington, D.C.: U.S. Dept. of Education, 1983.

The National Science Board Commission on Precollege Education in Mathematics, Science, and Technology. *Educating Americans for the 21st Century.* 2 vols. Washington, D.C.: National Science Foundation, 1983.

Powell, Arthur G., Farrar, Eleanor, and Cohen, David K. *The Shopping Mall High School.* Boston: Houghton Mifflin, 1985.

Ravitch, Diane. *The Troubled Crusade: American Education, 1945–1980.* New York: Basic Books, 1983.

Raywid, Mary Ann, Tesconi, Charles A., and Warren, Donald R. *Pride and Promise: Schools of Excellence for All the People.* Westbury, N.Y.: American Educational Studies Association, 1984.

Sizer, Theodore R. *Horace's Compromise: The Dilemma of the American High School.* Boston: Houghton Mifflin, 1984.

The Twentieth Century Fund Task Force on Federal Elementary and Secondary Education Policy. *Making the Grade.* New York: Twentieth Century Fund, 1983.

A NATION AT RISK   The report that started it all, refocusing public attention on schools and school reform, was *A Nation at Risk*.[10] This report was issued by the National Commission on Excellence in Education formed by Terrel Bell, Secretary of Education during President Ronald Reagan's first term. Secretary Bell was concerned with the widespread public perception that the quality of public schools was deteriorating. The Commission was to assess the quality of teaching and learning in American schools; compare American schools with those of other advanced nations; study the relationship between high schools and college; see how recent social and educational changes have affected student achievement; and suggest a course for excellence in education.

Claims by the Commission on Excellence fueled the growing debate over the schools. The Commission noted that "business and military leaders complain that they are required to spend millions of dollars on costly remedial education and training programs in such basic skills as reading, writing, spelling and computation."[11] School failure was the assumed cause of diminished industrial output, a general international devaluing of American manufactured goods, a weakened national defense, and a fraying of the fabric of American culture. Thus, similar to other periods of educational upheaval, schools were to blame for complex cultural problems.

The solutions the Commission recommends for the poor state of schooling sound strangely reminiscent of the proposals offered by the Council for Basic Education in the 1950s. With regard to content, a program of five basic subjects (English, mathematics, science, social studies, and computer science) are recommended for all students with additional work in foreign languages for most students. Increased standards were recommended in grading, testing, and textbooks. Further recommendations included more homework, more strictly enforced discipline, and lengthening of the school day and year. Career ladders for teachers, including merit pay plans, were encouraged to attract a more able teaching corps from talented college students. Finally local, state, and federal officials were challenged to take a more active role in encouraging and promoting academic excellence.

Many educators have pointed out the shortcomings of the Commission on Excellence report. For example, Charles Tesconi demonstrated how the statistics used on student achievement are often misleading or inaccurate.[12] Others argue that the report focuses much too narrowly on schools as the cause *and* cure of broad social problems.

Regardless, *A Nation at Risk* signaled that we are in another period of general public consternation with the schools, leading to proposals for reform of this vast public institution. We should see the public concern with schools as the continuation of a trend, a trend that we have traced through the nineteen fifties, sixties, seventies, and now into the eighties. Yet what is different about this concern today is that there is not one unified, major position on the "failure" of the schools. Rather, many voices have been added to the chorus, voices that we survey here.

EDUCATION FOR WORK AND DEFENSE   On the heels of *A Nation at Risk* came a series of reports whose primary concern was the preparation of youth for jobs and the maintenance of our national defense. These included the Education Commission of the States' (ECS) *Action for Excellence,* the National Science Board's (NSB) *Educating Americans for the 21 Century,* and the Twentieth Century Fund's *Making the Grade.*[13] All these reports share a common consensus that declining American industrial productivity and international stature are both due to the failure of the public schools to provide students with an adequate education.

During the 1950s the concern was for America's scientific skills; the concern today seems to be for technological skills. Worried that American productivity is falling and that our international balance of trade is worsening, these commissions turn to the schools for a solution. The problem they see is Americans not being adequately trained to meet the demands of an increasingly technological workplace—particularly in science and mathematics. This claimed educational failure is especially dangerous since "education is perhaps the most important key to economic growth."[14] The rhetoric behind this point seems to echo that of the 1950s, as in the NSB report:

> Already the quality of our manufactured products, the viability of our trade, our leadership in research and development, and our standards of living are strongly challenged. Our children could be stragglers in a world of technology. We must not let this happen; America must not become an industrial dinosaur.[15]

A similar argument is made relevant to our national defense. It is claimed that our national strength and military might depend on the education of America's children. Without the proper schooling the armed forces will be unable to secure an adequate pool of manpower to defend our shores.

The recommendations these reports make in the face of this "crisis" can be summarized in one word—"more." All call for increased emphasis in traditional academic courses as well as the more recent fields of technology and computer literacy. Additionally, it is recommended that more time is to be spent in the classroom, more homework assigned, and more money allotted to materials and teaching in mathematics and science. Part of the plan is to link schools closely to businesses in order to further aid the schooling-to-work transition. Finally, teachers need upgrading through the vigorous recruiting of more capable students, more rigorous training in their subject disciplines, and the provision of career ladders for teachers.

An erroneous assumption runs through all three reports. It is what David Cohen has called the "Toyota problem." Cohen contends that recent calls for schools to prepare better workers is merely the most recent expression of the belief that schools can be the chief means of "making America more productive, more efficient, more competitive." Cohen continues:

> This is an idea that becomes increasingly problematic the deeper one digs into the relationship between education and productivity, yet few seem inclined to question the notion that schools are responsible for the many failures of General Motors, or Ford, or Chrysler. It is odd, since schools never were praised for causing earlier successes in that industry.[16]

Even more unfortunate about the assumption of these reports is that they focus nearly all debate on a very limited component of schools. This means subjects like science, math, and basic English take precedence over the arts and humanities. Or, as Eleanor Duckworth has put it:

> None of the reports gives due attention to the qualities we might wish to develop in young people for their lives outside the marketplace and university. . . . They give the schools no role in enabling people to see themselves as "fit" to contribute to public discourse, in developing people's sense of responsibility for one another, in helping people to understand the need to struggle individually and collectively for a more just world.[17]

SCHOOLING AND EQUALITY   Based for the most part on extensive research in schools, another set of reports challenges the assumption that schools should prepare students for jobs. These argue that social equality, usually defined as equality of opportunity, should be the central purpose of schools. Included among such reports are Ernest Boyer's *High School: A Report on Secondary Education in America,* John Goodlad's *A Place Called School,* and Theodore Sizer's *Horace's Compromise.*[18]

While these reports agree that something is wrong with our schools, the problem is what schools are, rather than are not, doing.

This is a twofold argument: First, the schools try to do so much that there is no single, agreed-on mission that can unite and thus motivate parents, teachers, and students. Second, the major agenda that is agreed on—the preparation of students for jobs—is wrongheaded in that it both creates the conditions for unequal school opportunities and is also not achievable.

Let's examine the first of these points: that schools lack a general purpose and thus attempt to do too much. What Boyer, Goodlad, and the others remind us of is that the role of the school has been expanded into areas traditionally left to other institutions. The point these authors make is that by expanding the school's role into social and vocational areas little time is left for academic tasks. Schools, they argue, "are unable to find common purposes or establish educational priorities that are widely shared. . . . The institution is adrift."[19]

FOR REFLECTION 3.1   "What Should Schools Do?"

According to Ernest Boyer, in response to the question of what Americans want from their schools the answer is simple—we want it all. This is an argument also made by John Goodlad when he describes parental and public demands that schools meet academic, vocational, and social goals. The human side of all this is presented by Theodore Sizer when he describes this fictitious morning announcement:

At 9:57, the public address system goes on, with the announcements of the day. After a few words from the principal ("Here's today's cheers and jeers . . ." with a cheer for the winning basketball team and a jeer for the spectators who made a ruckus at the gymnasium), the task is taken over by officers of ASB (Associated Student Bodies). There is an appeal for "bat bunnies." Carnations are for sale by the Girl's League. Miss Indian American is coming. Students are auctioning off their services (background catcalls are heard) to earn money for the prom. Nominees are needed for the ballot for school bachelor and school bachelorette. The announcements end with a "thought for the day. When you throw a little mud, you lose a little ground."*

Are schools indeed losing ground because we try and throw mud at too many problems? With several classmates compile a list of the tasks that schools attempt to carry out. Why do schools do these things? Should they try to carry out these disparate tasks? If schools decided not to do any of these tasks who would do them? How would they be undertaken?

---

*From Theodore Sizer, *Horace's Compromise* (Boston: Houghton Mifflin, 1984), p. 73.

As to the second point, the claim is that when schools attempt to focus on preparing for jobs they often segregate, and thus discriminate. This happens through both the practice of "ability grouping" at the elementary level and the "tracking" of the secondary curriculum into vocational, general, and college preparatory programs. All these authors point out that these practices have no research justification and, indeed, do much more harm than good to our students. Behind this argument is the claim that grouping, tracking, or any similar arrangement is not only pedagogically unsound but is inherently unequal as well.

This returns us to the issue of equality. These reports focus on linking together the issues of excellence in education with equal educational opportunities. To do this, they suggest one major reform: a common core of learning experiences for all students. While the proposal varies somewhat in each report, the essence is that every student would engage in a core curricular experience, which leans heavily on the humanities, sciences, and social studies. Additionally, students would pursue in depth, either individually or as a group, particular areas of interest. Finally, several of these reports call for a unit of community service required of all students in order to increase their sense of civic responsibility. The curriculum would thus be one of a broad, general or "liberal" studies nature, with little or no vocational training. Perhaps this proposal could be summarized in the following way: Schools should not teach children how to do *something*—they should prepare them to do *anything*.

FOCUS 3.2 "Critical Thoughts on Education"

by Ernest L. Boyer
President of the Carnegie Foundation
for the Advancement of Teaching

During the academic year 1983–84, excellence was at the forefront of everyone's agenda. Actually, this great wave of renewed interest in the public schools may reveal less about their present state than about our underlying feeling about education in America. Fervor has always characterized the way we speak about our schools; in fact, it can be said, without a hint of irreverence, that education is the secular religion of our nation. While we may be quarrelsome about the public schools, very deep in our traditions is the conviction that whatever progress we hope to make as a nation will be carried through our dedication to education.

In my opinion, this faith has not been misplaced. One cannot read history without observing that much of our progress has been the result of an enlightened belief in universal public education. I do not whitewash the failures, nor do I suggest that we have totally fulfilled our dream, but it is clear that through our educational institutions waves of new immigrants and new generations of children have found their way to greater opportunity in this country.

We honor this great tradition, but what of the actual state of our schools in 1984? If I were to describe the present American educational system, I would try to avoid panic-inducing metaphors, such as "the rising tide of mediocrity." I would want to acknowledge that some of our schools are not only outstanding but, in my view, the best in the world. Still, there are problems which we must face if we are to deal successfully with the challenges thrown at us in recent months by various commissioned studies and reports.

The first problem is a lack of clear goals. The simple truth is that it's impossible to achieve excellence in education if our schools are caught in the crossfire of competing goals, acquiring purposes like barnacles on a weathered ship. I am convinced that institutional health will occur when we are able to focus our efforts and resources on several goals and then give the schools the backing to pursue those purposes with conviction.

Second, schools must stress the central importance of language. We hear constantly of the need for more emphasis on math and science to get our automobile and technology industries rolling again. The computer has become the new security blanket for school improvement. I think frankly that computer literacy and more demanding math and science requirements are important, but the emphasis on these areas may be a diversion. The central issue for all learning is the mastery of language. It is that skill which makes us truly human and makes all students potentially successful.

The third criterion for excellence in education is a curriculum with coherence. Here the debate quickly becomes heated. Is there a core of knowledge appropriate for all students? If so, who determines it? The question of content in education is profoundly important, and we cannot skirt the issue of piling on more courses in more subjects. I must say that I am deeply troubled by the call for one more Carnegie unit of history, one more of math, one more of English, and, in a burst of ingenuity, one-half unit of computer literacy—whatever that means. I'm troubled by those who assume that more of a subject will automatically lead to better education. Quantity means little unless we constantly question the quality and significance of what we teach. How do courses relate to the world in which we live? Will students gain wisdom as well as knowledge? There are no easy answers, but the questioning is essential.

The fourth proposal for reform deals with the centrality of teaching. The largest chapter in *High School,* our Carnegie report, focuses on renewing the profession of teaching. It includes at least seven major proposals, ranging all the way from rewarding existing teachers to changing various aspects of teacher preparation.

Dan Lortie wrote on one occasion that teaching in America is both honored and disdained; it is praised as dedicated service and lampooned as easy work. Lortie says teaching, from its inception in America, has occupied a special but shadowed place. He then concludes by saying that real regard shown for those who teach has never matched professed regard. And yet, I suspect that most people, were they to reflect for a moment, could recall one or perhaps a half-dozen teachers who had influenced them deeply.

Teachers are the first group of people, after parents, who, in a disciplined and sustained way, shape the values and priorities of children. Why we seem so ambivalent about honoring the power and significance of that influence bewilders me. But, if there is anything in the current debate that encourages me, it is the fact that the centrality of teaching has once again become part of the nation.

The much-talked-about subject of merit pay for teachers (while an interesting and, in the long term, appropriate issue to pursue) is in my judgment out of place if presented first. More urgent priorities are the problems of base pay and of adequate working conditions, which, if we are to believe the results of our survey, are even more important to teachers than the salaries they receive. Time after time, we heard the teachers talk about the aggravations of bureaucracy, the lack of recognition from students, the pressure to add more classes and even hall duty to their jobs. Teachers were concerned about such embarrassingly simple things as having no desk of their own and having to meet in faculty rooms converted from closets. In most school districts, not a dime was being provided for teacher travel to attend professional meetings. This all adds up to a disgraceful, demeaning set of circumstances which causes good teachers either to suffer in silence or, more frequently, to leave. I believe, therefore, that we must find ways to reaffirm the centrality of teaching, and some of that effort must begin in the simple recognition of a job well done.

I conclude with the observation that, in the past, the nation's public schools have risen to every challenge, and I am convinced they can do it yet again. In 1647, we responded to a mandate of the Massachusetts Bay Colony that all children should be taught to read and write. At the nation's birth, we responded to Thomas Jefferson's vision of civic education. At the turn of the century, we responded to the waves of immigrants who wanted a new and better life. At the time of Sputnik, we responded to the threat of diminished world leadership, and in the decade of the sixties we responded to the challenge of equal opportunity for all. But, if we are to meet the challenge of the future, I think more than rhetoric is needed. The nation must deepen its commitment to the belief that a human mind is a terrible thing to waste. We must renew our commitment to public education. To me this means establishing a clarity of goals in education, restoring language to a central place in the classroom, developing coherent curriculum, and reaffirming the centrality of teaching.

James Agee said on one occasion that with every child who is born, no matter under what circumstance, the potentiality of the human race is born again. I believe this is the vision of our public schools and this must also be the vision of the nation.

From Ernest L. Boyer, "Critical Thoughts on Education," *National Forum* (Winter 1985), pp. 33–34.

The work of Boyer et al. reminds us that schools do not operate in a vacuum, but rather function in a social context. Many of the problems schools deal with are beyond their control; many of the demands they try to meet are not of their own making. Each proposal for school reform that we have examined suggested that schools meet a broad social concern—the defense of our shores, the preparation of good workers, a more humane environment, or more equality of opportunity.

As a prospective teacher, it is vital that you understand that schools are indeed often used in order to resolve issues that the culture at large cannot manage. The role of the teacher has often been altered to accomplish a wide variety of social goals. Perhaps then, it would be useful to turn to a consideration of the current context of schooling in order to better understand the social roles schools, and the teachers within them, are expected to play.

THE MULTIPLE ROLES OF PUBLIC SCHOOLING

■ Recall that Boyer, Goodlad, and others have argued that we want schools to "do it all." This means a variety of things. To some, it means that we expect schools to accomplish large social goals. To others, it means that the schools are expected to solve the personal problems of students. To yet others, this means schools should have exclusive domain over the area of academics.

Indeed, schools have been called on to perform all the tasks mentioned above. Each of these is related to the perceived needs of American society at large. Educators can only understand the most recent pressures put upon schools when these demands are viewed within the context of our society at large. This is indeed the criticism made of the "back-to-basics" and "education for work and defense" movements and reports—they focus exclusively on only one task of the schools and often seem to forget the social context of schooling. It is this context that the "schooling and equality" reports consider and to which we now turn.

☐ **Solving the Problems of Democracy**

American schools have always been seen as fundamental to democracy. A sentiment first expressed by Thomas Jefferson, public schooling's main task was to insure a general level of intelligence enabling citizens to govern themselves. The particular task given to the schools has often been to overcome social barriers to the equal distribution of knowledge and thus the power to govern.

The schools have not always been up to this task. Indeed, internal school practices such as tracking in the high school and middle school grades and grouping in elementary schools often seem designed to perpetuate social inequality. However, when Americans have decided to act on our promise of equal rights for all the task has been given to the schools to oppose discrimination and segregation. When the schools fail or have limited success at these tasks, perhaps it is due to lack of public commitment rather than school people's efforts.

The Rights of Minorities
In 1953 and 1954, the Supreme Court of the United States ruled that schools segregated by race were unconstitutional. The Supreme Court, in *Brown* v. *The Board of Education of Topeka, Kansas,* ruled that

Our students come from a variety of backgrounds.

segregated schools for blacks were inherently inferior and unequal. It is important to acknowledge that the Court did not concern itself with issues of whether or not separate schools were "equal." Rather, in its opinion the court argued that "the policy of separating the races is usually interpreted as denoting the inferiority of the Negro group."[20] If democracy was to have any meaning such artificial vestiges of status or privilege had no place. Thus, given their perpetuation of social inequality based on race there could be no justification of separate schools.

While the Court's decision had the effect of striking down discrimination in all public facilities, the school bore its broadest consequences. Schools were to be a tool for desegregating society. Rather than attack racism through adults, children were to be the bearers of the egalitarian dream. It may seem hard to believe that today, over three decades after the Supreme Court ordered that schools be desegregated "with all deliberate speed," we still debate integrating schools. After years of magnet schools, busing, and consolidation many school districts still find it difficult to desegregate. Additionally, recent data from the Census Bureau points out that the incidence of poverty among blacks continues to be about three times that of whites—a situation unchanged for over 30 years.[21] Schools appear to be having a problem desegregating American society.

Bilingual Education

Similarly, schools were to integrate language minorities into American society through the provision of bilingual education. Practiced in a variety of ways, the intent of these programs is to help students obtain proficiency in English while gaining academic skills in their native tongue. The idea was that without these skills language minorities cannot compete equally for economic gain and political power. Unfortunately, the success of these programs is now widely contested and they appear to be losing much of their funding base.

Is it fair in either case to say that schools have failed? We can understand this claim if it means that the direct practices of schools discriminate against minorities. But the argument that schools are to carry the entire blame for continued racial segregation in American society cannot be accepted. Again, this is an issue of context, often forgotten while discussing schools. The question should not be *have* schools desegregated society, but *can* they. Is it possible for schools, dealing almost exclusively with children, to solve the problems created by adults? Perhaps schools can be part of the solution by working to insure equal treatment for all within. However, schools cannot be held responsible for racist images on television; segregation in the workplace, neighborhoods, or churches; or political practices designed to pit whites against blacks.

The 51% Minority—Women

Just as minorities found themselves out of the economic and political mainstream, so did America's major minority, women. As we know, historically women have had to fight for the political rights granted *pro forma* to men. The right to vote, to hold public office, even to work have been granted only after prolonged political struggle. Even the granting of constitutionally protected civil rights for women (previously granted to minorities in the Fourteenth Amendment to the Constitution) through the Equal Rights Amendment (ERA) proved so controversial it failed to obtain ratification.

The most recent attempt to expand the rights of women has focused on the schools. The Educational Amendments of 1972, passed by the 92nd Congress, included a Title IX, part of which read as follows:

> No person in the United States shall, on the basis of sex, be excluded from participation in, be denied the benefits of, or be subject to discrimination under any program receiving Federal financial assistance.[22]

This meant that schools could not discriminate against women by excluding them from any school program. The most obvious consequence of this has been the expansion of athletic opportunities for women in schools. But it has also influenced the whole range of curricular and extracurricular activities of the school.

Again, however, if the intent was to have schools resolve for society the problem of sex discrimination, Title IX has been, at best, a limited success. This is not to say that it has not changed the internal workings of the schools—it has, and schools are a more successful place for many women because of it. In society at large though, women are still paid less than men for similar jobs, are less likely to hold elective office, and in a recent poll women report that they feel recent job discrimination has increased rather than decreased.[23] Again, the issue here is not should the schools treat students more equally—our answer to this is an emphatic yes. At issue is whether or not the school alone can bear the burden of solving democracy's problems.

Expanding the Mainstream

The most recent attempt by schools to expand economic and political equality is in the treatment of the handicapped. For many years relegated to school boiler rooms, hallways, and even separate buildings, handicapped schoolchildren were seldom seen in the mainstream of school life. A lawsuit brought by the Pennsylvania Chapter of the National Association for Retarded Children (PARC) against the Commonwealth of Pennsylvania in 1972 began the attempt to change this relationship. PARC claimed that retarded children were being unlawfully discriminated against by their segregation into separate educational facilities. The outcome of the suit was that the courts found for an extension of the Equal Protection Clause of the Fourteenth Amendment, which mandated that handicapped students be brought into the regular school setting where possible.

The judicial ruling was to be given the force of legislation with the passage of the Education For All Handicapped Children Act of 1975, more commonly known as Public Law (PL) 94-142. The main intent of PL 94-142 was to "assure that all handicapped children have available to them . . . a free and appropriate public education."[24] While the term "mainstreaming" is not found in the legislation (the actual phrase used was "least restrictive environment"), the administrative regulations later released by the Department of Health, Education, and Welfare assumed mainstreaming would play a major part. In operation were two assumptions, first, that if handicapped children were more involved in "regular" schooling they would individually have more opportunity in the society at large; second, that through exposure to handicapped children, nonhandicapped students would accept and display fewer discriminatory actions toward the handicapped.

It is too early to judge the success of PL 94-142. The news is encouraging: handicapped students are succeeding in schools in ways previously not thought possible, and students and teachers in schools seem more accepting of special students than ever before. But can classrooms alone change the views of an entire society toward the handicapped? As in other cases, the answer is yes and no: Yes, in schools, we can do a better job of treating individual student differences. No, schools alone cannot change society's discriminatory treatment toward handicapped citizens.

In each of these cases we see how social forces influence the schools. Democracy requires nondiscriminatory treatment of individuals. When society fails in this respect, rather than tackle the problem head-on it is handed to the schools. Society reasons: if children grow up in an integrated, egalitarian setting they will, some day, remake the larger society; children become the bearers of the democratic dream. Later we will examine in what ways schools attempt, succeed, and fail to make their internal practices consistent with this dream. But here we are left with the nagging question of how much schools can do. For what should schools be held responsible? Indeed, more and more of the struggles for fair and equitable treatment of minorities, women, and the handicapped go on outside the school walls. Barriers based on race and national origin are challenged in a variety of settings, women work for "comparable-worth" pay legislation, and the handicapped fight for increasing access to both public and private facilities. But the school, as our largest social institution next to the military, continues to be seen as the main force for resolving the problems of discrimination in our democracy. We will return later in the chapter to this issue of whether or not the school can do this and at what cost.

☐ **Solving the Personal Problems of Students**

Schools have not only been asked to solve what we might call the macro-problems of our society but the micro-problems as well. These are the problems that do indeed spring from broad social trends but that are often considered to be the personal problem of a student. Examining these problems again forces us to reflect on what the school can and cannot do.

Getting a Job
Several of the reports cited in the last section were concerned primarily with the issue of employment. Given the decline in national productivity, schools were seen as the place to restore our productive might. But why the schools? Why not a public policy devoted to reindustrialization, public investment in emerging technology, or even a national economic plan? The point of raising this question is not to answer it, but rather to show that the school is only one choice for solving the problems of unemployment and productivity.

That schools should be considered the most useful for resolving employment problems is not a new phenomenon. Schools have often been used as tools for solving unemployment. This is because problems of unemployment are not generally seen as problems of the economy at large. Rather, it is claimed (often incorrectly) that people do not work because they either do not have the skills necessary to obtain a job or the desire to go get one. The problem is purely personal. So schools, where most future workers spend a minimum of 10 years, logically are the perfect place to resolve such issues.

This focus has resulted in schooling's heavy vocational emphasis, not only in the wide range of activities and classes commonly referred to as vocational, but also in the entire organization of the school. Virtually the entire academic program is devoted to vocational tracks (general, academic, and vocational). Course work is often devoted to the jobs to which students are presumed destined. We are struck with how easily this becomes the sole purpose of schooling.

The Hazards of Growing Up
The American public is preoccupied with its youth. Television screens are populated with characters struggling to grow up. The press carries

daily reports of the latest fads in music or dress, the newest vice in terms of drugs or alcohol, and the latest form of adolescent rebellion.

Three "youth problems" have captured the public's attention over the past decade or so: drug and alcohol abuse, sex, and child abuse. Drug and alcohol abuse among children, often referred to as substance abuse, has been a constant source of worry to parents since the 1950s. The relatively free access to these materials for youths spawned report after report of widespread "experimentation." With the introduction of "the pill" a whole universe of sexual taboos were exploded. Pregnancy was no longer a consequence of sexual relations. This made sex even more available to adolescents with no desire to be parents. Child abuse, most recently "out of the closet" as reporting of incidents has increased, is frequently a topic of television docudramas and flashy investigative reporting. It is not difficult to get the impression that every American child is abused or will be, experiments with drugs, and, given the subsequent diminished moral state, rolls in and out of bed with a variety of sexual partners without guilt or responsibility.

The accuracy of these perceptions is discussed in Chapter 5, Students. We recount these impressions here because they are focal points for school reformers. In fact, we can see the direct consequences of such concern displayed in curricular reforms. Virtually every junior high, middle, and high school child will go through programs in sex education and substance abuse. More and more elementary schools are engaged in assault prevention programs. All these programs are designed to provide students with the ability to make appropriate moral choices, which they will do when provided with "the facts."

This claim leaves two questions unanswered. First, why should schools do these things? We want to stress that this question is not intended as an objection to the value of these school programs. Instead, we are asking that you reflect on whether or not schools are the best places to deal with these issues. You might ask: Do school programs absolve the rest of society from any responsibility? Seemingly, the answer has recently been that schools should go it alone relevant to combating drugs, alcohol, sex, and abuse.

But, secondly, can schools solve the personal problems of students? Television, magazines, and music all bombard children with messages that seem to encourage substance abuse. Sex is used to sell cars, television programs, and even music in some rock videos. Our society is a violent one, a fact children learn early as they buy army toys and guns, see violent cartoons, and watch as adults resolve both international and domestic confrontations with force. Why are schools expected to solve all the problems of growing up when grown-ups themselves cannot deal with them?

☐ Social or Academic Skills?

Much of the foregoing discussion raises implicitly the debate over whether schools should focus primarily on social or academic skills. This debate is not about excluding one function in favor of the other. Few argue that schools should be solely academic and no one argues that schools should supply only social skills. But what is the mix to be and what, if anything, should not be done by the school?

The Case for Social Skills

The teaching of social skills refers to the concept of socialization. This is the process of bringing an individual, usually the child, into the social group by teaching him or her the moral, ethical, and social standards shared by the group. Additionally, attempts are made to prepare the child to eventually take a productive place in the society as a worker and community member. By socialization we mean all those skills and attitudes discussed above when we talked about schools solving social problems.

Two arguments are usually made in defense of schools carrying out the task of socialization. The first is that schools are where children are. Every young person in this country must attend some form of schooling—and the vast majority go to public schools. Any national agenda item is easily focused on schools if we want to get to children.

Building on this logical argument, a second, practical argument is made for socialization skills. It goes like this: "If the schools don't do it, who will?" In one sense this argument is historically incorrect. Much of what schools now do in terms of socialization was carried on in the larger community outside the schools. Particularly with regard to personal development problems, these functions were often taken from, not given to, the school.

With regard to racism and discrimination, however, it is just as clear that no other social institution was willing to handle the problem. This, schools were forced into trying to fill a social void—a void bigger than they could ever hope to fill. When they often failed to fill it they were blamed for the very ills they set out to cure. This void continues to exist and present schools with irresolvable problems.

The Case for Academic Skills

Counter to those who argue that schools should focus on social skills are those who say that schools should concern themselves primarily with academics. Their argument is that socialization is best left to the rest of the community. Schools, they insist, should focus on academics, a claim made most recently by proponents of the back-to-basics movement.

The contention here is that schools are the only public institution charged with the inculcation of academic skills in children. This has been their historical purpose and mission. By providing, or attempting to provide, all future citizens with basic academic skills all individuals will have an equal opportunity for success. Additionally, when teachers trained in subject matter, as well as pedagogy, take time away from teaching academic skills they are in unfriendly waters for which they are not prepared.

On the negative side of the equation, those concerned primarily with academic skills feel that socialization is not properly the domain of the schools. Those who favor socialization argue that no one else will do these things; those opposed to it argue that functions left to the society will be claimed by the community. Besides, it is argued, when schools try to engage in socialization skills they invariably make a mess of it. It leads to a watering down of the curriculum with such courses as "Bachelor Living" or "Comparative Shopping." Students take these courses, which have limited usefulness, instead of courses in math, science, English, and the rest that apply to all aspects of human life. There is a trade-off being made here for socialization over academics that is, in the eyes of some, indefensible.

Can We Have It All?

Given an institution with unlimited funds and time we might be able to argue that schools should perform all the functions listed above. But clearly this is not the case with schools. They function on a limited budget, the national average per pupil expenditure being only slightly over $2,300 per year. They operate on a limited time frame, with average attendance requirements being 180 days for 5½ hours a day. Thus, they have to make choices: choices between academics and socialization, personal and national problems, basic subjects and vocational needs. These are choices that teachers will always face, regardless of resources, because sooner or later every student leaves school, limiting the time teachers have with them.

THE CONTEXTUAL CHALLENGE TO EDUCATORS

■ What should be clear by now is that many of the problems faced by schools come from problems in the society at large. Unemployment, international uncertainty, and personal problems all find their way to the schoolhouse door. At the same time as schools are asked to solve these problems, faith in all social institutions, including schools, continues to decline. Schools are seen as an instrument, albeit imperfect, for resolving social problems. Put another way, they are guided by what we commonly call instrumental reason.

□ **Schooling and Instrumental Reason**

As we pointed out above, in many ways schools are to be instruments of social reform. They are either to carry out specific national policy (like the elimination of racism or reducing unemployment) or to serve as a mediator of the problems of the young. The assumption is indeed that schools can do it all.

This instrumental reason has affected all agencies dealing with children. As Grubb and Lazerson point out, this is because children themselves "are not valued for the individuals they are, but as instruments in achieving other goals—economic growth, the reduction of welfare costs, stable and fluid labor markets, a high level of profits, social peace."[25] With regard to schooling, this tendency to view the child as a means to an end is captured by Sara Lawrence Lightfoot:

> Part of the focus away from the child as a whole person . . . reflects the broad social and economic functions of schools in our society. Schools are considered transitory, preparatory environments where the child's *future* status becomes the overriding concern of his adult sponsors.[26]

Thus, schools are seen as the best place available to solve adult problems—not immediately, but some time in the future.

And yet, what happens when they fail? What happens when the social problems are not resolved or when children seem unable to solve their personal problems? What happens when schools, exerting their limited influence through meager resources, do not deliver the goods?

Additive Reform and the Prescribed Curriculum
Perhaps the failure of the instrumental justification of schooling is nowhere clearer than in the recent reports on schooling that simply call for "more." If workers are not productive, give them more schooling; if our defenses need shoring up, the solution is more schooling; if substance abuse or teenage pregnancy rises, the answer is more schooling. But while schooling always seems to be the answer we are never clear about the questions. Why these trends occur, what causes them, how they are creatures of forces perhaps outside of the school's control, are never considered. It is simply assumed that schools can deal with them.

The curriculum does then indeed come to look like a cafeteria. There is something for everyone, maybe not much in the way of supply, but certainly a lot of variety. Demand after demand is placed on the school, and meanwhile nothing is removed from its mandate. As Mortimer Adler has put it, when the "school is made the repository of every social concern, education itself is bound to be crowded out—and the social problems will remain. More is less."[27]

Furthermore, the more the school is asked to take on, the more the task of the teacher is prescribed. One mandate after another, the increased specification of learning objectives, and greater reliance on standardized exams, all continue to limit the range of teacher autonomy in the classroom. The "art" of teaching is gradually lost to a new "technology" where exact measures replace intuition, repetition replaces creativity, and routine replaces serendipity.

Additive reform seems not to solve any of the problems we face. But given our instrumental mentality with regard to schools we seem destined to continue repeating our mistakes. Adding without taking away makes the school a "jack of all trades, master of none." Schools, by promising to be all things to all people also raise expectations they cannot meet.

THE LOSS OF FAITH   As we pointed out in Chapter 1, public support for public education continues to decline. Some point to test scores, others to the failure of industry as reasons for the declining faith. We would offer another explanation of such a decline: schools by promising all things to all people have become a convenient target for criticism when any of the promised tasks are not performed. Ernest Boyer summarized this phenomenon: "Today's school is called upon to provide services and transmit the values we used to expect from the community and the home and the church. And if they fail anywhere along the line, they are condemned."[28]

What should schools do? An instrumental approach to schools would suggest that whatever happens to be the most prevalent problem at the time should be the task of the school. But this seems to be the process of deciding by not deciding. It does not provide a way to choose between the many demands put on schools. Schooling seems to be adrift, a ship without a compass. Until such purpose is established there seems little hope of schools' adequately meeting any of the demands put on them.

EDUCATORS AND THE SEARCH FOR PURPOSE

■ Given the contextual pressures upon schooling there seems to be no way to avoid seeing schools as instruments of social reform. Yet on the other hand, schools seem to have a mixed record as an agent of social change. We would propose a twofold approach to the problems of purpose and additive reform: first, that educators willingly take on one social purpose that is well within their control—that of making schools the most humane, bias-free, supportive environments within which children can grow. Second, that educators lead the search for a genuinely educative purpose for schools.

☐ **Creating a User-Friendly Environment**

By the time students complete 12 years of schooling they have spent nearly 10% of their lives within the school. We would argue that those should be some of the best hours of every child's life. Pursuing educational excellence while simultaneously recognizing that children come to schools with a variety of personal needs requires that we pay close attention to the school environment. We borrow this idea from *Pride and Promise,* where the following argument is made:

> We need to make schools into what computer lingo would dub "user friendly" institutions. All who enter it should experience the school as a concerned, responsive, supportive environment. Our interest in education's outcomes often leaves us indifferent to what school means and feels like to the young people and adults who work within it. Yet, as several recent studies have suggested, this is probably the single most important feature of a school for those who inhabit it daily. . . . Thus, instead of trying to make schools places of stern discipline and adult-regulated order as some suggest, ways should be sought to make them more relaxed and, yes, places of enjoyment, challenge, excitement.[29]

FOCUS 3.3   Creating A User-Friendly School

In their book *Pride and Promise* Raywid, Tesconi, and Warren describe a user-friendly school this way*:
The three attributes named—efficacy, collegiality, and user friendliness—are certainly not exhaustive of the qualities which school organization should reflect. But they are perhaps the currently most overlooked requisites of durable, successful school improvement. They satisfy some basic human desires for community, belonging and interdependence, engagement in creating and sustaining a commonly valued enterprise, and assurance that one's efforts count and one's interests and concerns matter.
If the above considerations were taken seriously in the design of school structure and operations, here are some of the many features that would appear:

- Schools would be small in size or large ones would be divided into small, independently functioning units to permit considerable personalization.
- Schools and schools-within-schools would be engaged in considerably more decision-making than individual units now undertake.
- Site management, budgetary development and budgetary control would be taken seriously at the local school level.
- Schools and schools-within-schools would be encouraged to cultivate their own distinctive climates, to innovate, and to differ from others in the particular way they pursue curricular goals.
- Both staff and student time would be invested in deliberate, conscious effort to maintain the ethos or moral order of the school.
- Parents would be welcome in schools as respected clients, as allies, and as irreplaceable sources of help in the effort to educate their children.
- Principals would encourage and make time for a great deal of staff communication and interaction both within and outside the school day.
- Teams of teachers would together work out solutions to the perennial challenges of teaching—content and its arrangements, instructional activities, classroom order.
- Teachers would have opportunity to select their school of assignment, in the interests of dovetailing the educational orientation of individual and institution.
- School staff would exert collective responsibility for the selection and retention of teachers.
- Schools would work more like institutions trying to respond to and serve a clientele than like organizations set on adapting the clients to the institution.
- Schools would differ as to how much power students exert in school decision-making—because educators differ over that, and because student needs and capacities differ.
- In all schools, students would recognize that their interests, concerns, and welfare were an important consideration in determining the way things are.

---

*From Mary Ann Raywid, Charles A. Tesconi, and Donald R. Warren, *Pride and Promise: Schools of Excellence for All the People* (Westbury, N.Y.: American Educational Studies Association, 1984), pp. 18–19

By creating user-friendly schools educators could perform a distinct and valuable social service: that is, giving every child the ability to see himself or herself as a valuable and useful human being. Research tells us that the deepest scars of discrimination are borne by one's self-concept. Further, social scientists provide us with evidence suggesting the stronger one's self-concept the most likely one is to achieve academically. The user-friendly school, valuing each child as an individual and as a member of the group, is perhaps the most schools can do in the way of an academic and social role.

So what would the teacher do in the user-friendly school? We attempt to answer this question throughout the remainder of this book. First, teachers would value children as children. This valuing would be shown by working to understand children's backgrounds, needs, and experiences and by incorporating all these in daily lesson plans. Second, teachers would work to make schools a place of free and open communication where every child felt valued. Finally, teachers would vary their methods and instructional strategies to meet and complement the diverse ways in which students learn.

It is important to note that this text is indeed just an introduction to these topics. We fully expect that good students, those who will go on to become educators, will use this material as a springboard to future investigations into what it means to be a teacher. But before entering this discussion, one last word remains to be said about the purpose of the schools.

CHAPTER SUMMARY

■ We started this chapter raising the issue of the purpose of the school. Steve, the fictitious teacher in our opening scenario, was struggling with the all-too-real classroom consequences of our current confusion over purpose. We then investigated many of the reports about schooling and the context of schooling as often dictating purpose. Now what can we say about the purpose of schooling?

The establishment of a central, guiding purpose for schooling, which will give meaning to teachers' actions, is more than mere speculation. It may be, as John Goodlad suggests, an act of survival:

> [I]t is no longer reasonable to assume that schools can or should do all or perhaps even most of the educating. It may be necessary to recognize that the school will continue to be a viable, appreciated institution only if we define its mission more precisely, including only those things educational which the rest of the society cannot do well.[30]

The attempt to establish a purpose for schools is beyond the scope of this, or any book. It is a project that must involve the whole of the educational community, including teachers, parents, students, and other community members. Together, by surveying both the general needs of all students and the particular needs of each community that the school alone can meet, purpose can be achieved.

FOR DISCUSSION

1. Much of what was discussed in this chapter had to do with school reform. If you could institute three reforms in public schooling what would they be? Why would you choose those three? What would you expect the results of such reform to be?

2. What do you believe to be the most important tasks of public schooling? How should these tasks be accomplished?

3. What current tasks undertaken by public schools do you believe should be eliminated? Why? Who else in the community should assume these tasks and why?

4. Given your answers to questions number 2 and 3 what does that imply for your preparation as a teacher? What particular skills do you need to develop, what knowledge base is crucial? How will you achieve this level of preparation?

5. Think back to teachers you had in the grade level you want to teach. At what tasks were they the most successful, social or academic? How do you believe this influenced your decision to enter teaching?

IN THE SCHOOL/IN THE CLASSROOM

1. Obtain a curriculum guide from the school in which you are doing field work. With several other students review the guide and answer the following questions:
   a. What are the primary goals for the curriculum (either grade level or subject matter)?
   b. How are these goals to be accomplished?
   c. How would this curriculum have to be altered to meet the demands of the National Commission on Excellence in Education? Compare that to any of the other reform reports mentioned in this chapter.

2. Return to exercise no. 2 in this same section in Chapter 2 that asked you to shadow a teacher for a day. Review this account of the teacher's time with respect to the following questions:
   a. How much time is spent on academic skill development? (List activities and time.)
   b. How much time is spent on social problems of students? (List activities and time.)
   c. What trade-offs could this teacher make?
   d. Show your list to the teacher and discuss his or her reaction to it.

SUGGESTED READINGS

In addition to the reports listed in the text you might also want to read the following:

Adler, Mortimer. *Paideia: Problems and Possibilities*. New York: Macmillan Publishing Company, 1983. This is Adler and the Paideia group's attempt to answer some of the many questions raised by *The Paideia Proposal*. It covers a variety of issues ranging from curriculum and financing to problem students. It also presents three examples of *The Paideia Proposal* in action.

Gross, Beatrice, and Ronald Gross, eds. *The Great School Debate: Which Way for American Education?* New York: Simon and Schuster, 1985. This book claims to be "the first authoritative source book on the controversy over the quality of our schools"—and it is! An excellent collection of essays on the recent debates over educational excellence. With 64 entries every important voice is heard.

Holt, John. *How Children Fail*. New York: Pitman Publishing, 1964. One of the first voices in the humanist critique of schooling in the 1960s. Holt argues that school failure is more the product of school practices rather than student inability. This book has just been updated and reissued.

Karp, Walter. "Why Johnny Can't Think: The Politics of Bad Schooling." *Harpers* (June 1985): 69–73. A review of eight of the recent reports on schooling. The focus is on the political rhetoric of *A Nation at Risk* versus the in-depth analysis of other reports.

Koerner, James D., ed. *The Case for Basic Education: A Program of Aims for Public Schools*. Boston: Atlantic Monthly Press, 1959. This was the most important document of the "back-to-basics" movement in the 1950s. Still a standard, it takes a variety of subject matters, argues why each is basic, and proposes a curricular plan for schools.

Kohl, Herbert. *Basic Skills*. New York: Little, Brown, 1982. A member of the humanist critics of schooling, Kohl has previously published *36 Children* and *The Open Classroom*. Here he reexamines the notion of "basic education" with an eye toward those skills children need to become democratic citizens.

Kozol, Jonathan. *Death at an Early Age.* New York: Houghton Mifflin, 1967. This book rocked the country with its systematic exposure of the racist and abusive treatment of black children in Boston schools. Kozol was a teacher who recounts his attempts to make life better for children and his ultimate firing.

Kozol, Jonathan. *The Night Is Dark and I Am Far From Home.* New York: Houghton Mifflin, 1975. In this follow-up to *Death at an Early Age,* Kozol examines the whole of the school system. It is an impassioned plea for a more careful consideration of teaching and learning with the child at its center.

CHAPTER REFERENCES

1. Mary Ann Raywid, *The Ax-Grinders* (New York: Macmillan, 1962), p. 11.
2. H. G. Rickover, *Education and Freedom* (New York: E.P. Dutton, 1959), p. 223.
3. James D. Koerner, ed., *The Case for Basic Education* (New York: E.P Dutton, 1959), p. ix.
4. U.S. Statutes at Large, Vol. 72, part 1, 85th Congress, 1958, p. 1582.
5. John Holt, *How Children Fail* (New York: Dell, 1964).
6. Jonathan Kozol, *Death at an Early Age* (Boston: Houghton Mifflin, 1967).
7. Charles Silberman, *Crisis in the Classroom* (New York: Random House, 1971).
8. Ivan Illich, *Deschooling Society* (New York: Harper and Row, 1971); Everett Reimer, *School is Dead: Alternatives in Education* (Garden City, N.J.: Doubleday and Co., 1971.
9. Ken Sirotnik, "What You See Is What You Get: Consistency, Persistency, and Mediocrity in Classrooms," *Harvard Educational Review 53* (February 1983), pp. 16–31.
10. National Commission on Excellence in Education, *A Nation at Risk: The Imperative for Educational Reform* (Washington, D.C.: U.S. Department of Education, 1983).
11. Ibid., p. 9.
12. Charles A. Tesconi, Jr., "Additive Reform and the Retreat from Purpose," *Educational Studies 15* (Spring 1984), pp. 1–10.
13. See citations for these reports in Research Notes 3.1 in the text.
14. Education Commission of the States, Task Force on Education for Economic Growth, *Action for Excellence: A Comprehensive Plan to Improve Our Nation's Schools* (Denver: Education Commission of the States, 1983), p. 18.
15. National Science Board Commission on Precollege Education in Mathematics, Science, and Technology, *Educating Americans for the 21st Century* (National Science Foundation: Washington, D.C., 1983), p. v.

16. David K. Cohen, " . . . The Condition of Teachers' Work . . ." *Harvard Educational Review 54* (February 1984): p. 12.
17. Eleanor Duckworth, " . . . What Teachers Know: The Best Knowledge Base . . ." *Harvard Educational Review 54* (February 1984), p. 17.
18. See citations for these reports in Research Notes 3.1 in the text.
19. Ernest Boyer, *High School* (Princeton, N.J.: Carnegie Foundation for the Advancement of Teaching, 1983), p. 63.
20. Brown vs. Board of Education of Topeka, Kansas, 347 U.S. 495 (1954).
21. See *Statistical Abstracts of the U.S.: 1983–1984* (Washington, D.C.: U.S. Bureau of the Census) for this and other data on income distribution.
22. *U.S. Statutes at Large,* Vol. 89, 92nd Congress, 1972, p. 373.
23. *Washington Post Weekly,* February 25, 1985, p. 38.
24. *U.S. Statutes at Large,* Vol. 91, 94th Congress, 1975, p. 775.
25. W. Norton Grubb and Marvin Lazerson, *Broken Promises: How Americans Fail Their Children* (New York: Basic Books, 1982), p. 53.
26. Sara Lawrence Lightfoot, *Worlds Apart: Relationships Between Families and Schools* (New York: Basic Books, 1978), p. 84.
27. Mortimer Adler, *The Paideia Proposal* (New York: MacMillan, 1982), p. 45.
28. Ernest Boyer, *High School,* p. 57.
29. Mary Ann Raywid, Charles A. Tesconi, and Donald R. Warren, *Pride and Promise: Schools of Excellence for All the People* (Westbury, N.Y.: American Educational Studies Association, 1984), p. 17.
30. John I. Goodlad, *A Place Called School: Prospects for the Future* (New York: McGraw-Hill, 1983), p. 59.

4

Learning About Teaching

■ Every Wednesday morning Jenny was eager to discuss the topic of her weekly education seminar with her classroom teacher, Mrs. Phillips. Most discussions were amiable and Jenny found herself better informed because her teacher could add a personal interpretation. This was one of the ways Jenny learned about real classroom teaching during her field experience. Besides, Mrs. Phillips didn't mind the time the discussions took. In fact, she found that Jenny's questions often encouraged her to think more deeply about teaching.

"Jenny, you look troubled today. Does this have anything to do with your seminar?"

"How can you tell?"

"Well, Jenny, after 12 years of reading students' faces you get pretty good at it I guess. What's troubling you?" asked Mrs. Phillips.

"I thought I had teaching all figured out and that I knew what really happened in schools, but now I wonder. Last night our instructor had us examine some reports on education that were written several years ago so we could discuss what's still wrong with schools. The reports were usually negative and so were the comments of my classmates. It seemed that nobody had anything good to say about schools and teachers. One report particularly bothered me. It spoke of mediocre education, acts of war, civil violence, and similar problems—as if schools were to blame for all of our country's troubles and made us vulnerable to attack. Many of the reports made the pupils sound so dumb, and they really seemed to come down hard on teachers. Now I wonder if I want to teach!"

"Jenny, I think I know how you feel. After all, in the things those reports describe they are talking about teachers—people like me, you know. Maybe we have some of the same feelings, and maybe teaching is not as bad as some make it seem."

"I guess it's especially the part about teachers that bothers me most," Jenny offered. "I've been watching you for a few weeks now and the other teachers, too. I don't see how people can believe that *all* teachers are unintelligent, can't write, don't know their subjects, can't maintain order in classrooms, don't care about students, and other things like that. Mrs. Phillips, you've been around for a while and kids really seem to like you; they seem cooperative and look as if they are eager to learn. Do you think teachers are as poor or mediocre as some of those reports say?"

Mrs. Phillips paused for a long while and then replied, "No and yes. No, not all teachers are mediocre. You've seen that for yourself. I know many marvelous teachers. In fact, our building alone has several distinguished teachers. But, I can't honestly say that teachers in general *are* or *are not* mediocre. It seems that some teachers don't even like to teach; they act like they are stuck in a rut and appear as if they don't care. Their attitudes can rub off on others—teachers and students—and bring the morale of a whole school down with them. That is what happened to me a while ago. I felt depressed and hopeless. That's why I decided to transfer to another school—here—and now I see some things differently and it's mostly because of the talented teachers that I work with. I respect them and can exchange ideas with them. I guess that's what you call collegiality, but whatever it is, it helps when I feel stale or just don't know what to do."

"Then why don't they just quit if they don't like teaching?" offered Jenny with disgust.

"Easy now, Jenny. There may be several reasons for the way some teachers feel: low salary, a teachers' strike, parents, students, principals, family problems, health problems—you name it. Teachers are human too, don't forget. And I guess sometimes publicity like those reports you spoke about doesn't always help either. But, the fact that *you* started to ask questions about teaching, though, is one way those reports can help. What do you think would happen to education if new teachers, like you, didn't ask tough questions to gather the facts so they could decide about teaching for themselves?"

BECOMING A TEACHER

☐   **Is a Teacher Born or Prepared?**

Mrs. Phillips welcomed Jenny's questions and she seemed to suggest that all persons who are thinking about teaching would benefit from asking pointed questions. In fact, Mrs. Phillips suggested that the teaching profession would benefit overall if those who enter it continue to ask tough questions. This seems to suggest that teachers can be prepared, that people who do not naturally possess the skills needed for teaching can actually learn to teach by refining skills they already have and by adding new skills. These assumptions support the position that teachers can learn to teach because they are specially prepared, not because they were born to be teachers.

Are teachers just naturally born with the capability for teaching? Probably some are and we suspect that quite a few people are excellent teachers, perhaps not because of their preparation, but in spite of it. Yet this affirmation of heredity does not mean that just anyone who feels called to teach can, in fact, teach properly.

A widely held belief is that all that teaching requires is common sense. The common sense view of what it takes to teach seems to be validated by the achievements of some who teach quite well without any formal education whatsoever in the methods of teaching. In fact, many teachers are able to do just that.[1]

Philip Jackson maintains that people can teach quite well just by using the common sense theory *if* three assumptions are true: (1) that

Is a teacher born or prepared?

the teacher actually *has* a class of students—the presumption of a public; (2) that the students haven't already learned what the teacher wishes to teach—the presumption of ignorance; and (3) that the teacher has a background and character similar to the students—the presumption of identity.[2]

Teachers could find themselves in situations where these assumptions are true and be quite successful at teaching. But what if they do not? Does this make them unsuccessful teachers? Can we assume that the common sense theory is actually true? On this point Jackson says:

> Teachers who *think* their students are with them when they are not, who assume ignorance when there is none, who envision their students as being carbon copies of themselves, when in fact they are quite different, are obviously courting failure; the irony is that so long as they cling to their erroneous assumptions they may never find out they have failed.[3]

Even if some teachers fail at what they do and never find out about it, the most common senseful of them will be faced with situations sooner or later in which they have to make choices and take actions without having any guidance, nor be able to benefit from a particular domain of knowledge. Yet no teacher has to labor under this type of deficit. Knowledge about teaching can be acquired through special preparation for teaching, through deep reflective thought, and through discussions with or advice offered from teacher colleagues.

□   **Your Personal Responsibility**

Perhaps teachers can continue their routines, with little harm done, even when their students aren't "with them" and when some students have already learned what is being taught. Time may be wasted and students may be frustrated if they lag behind the pace of the teacher. Those who are already beyond what is being taught simply have to bide their time and are usually creative at finding other things to occupy their minds. Here common sense can be applied. Alert teachers will notice that some students are falling behind or that some students are ahead and take common sense steps to synchronize their teaching with their students.

When teachers and students are very much alike, much of what the teacher needs to know and do may be supplied by common sense. Yet it seems that the most potential for classroom conflict and damage to any form of education can occur if the teacher and students are not much alike. What if the teacher and students are from different "worlds"? To this Jackson replies:

> When teachers are working with students *who are very much like themselves,* there is relatively little to learn about teaching, at least insofar as technique is concerned, that is not supplied by either common sense or knowledge of the material taught. But when teachers and students are *not* very much alike in important ways—that is, when the presumption of shared identity is *in*valid—there may be quite a lot to learn about how to proceed. The knowledge called for under those circumstances is genuinely knowledge about teaching *per se.* It is not a part of what most people would call common sense, nor is it deducible from knowledge of the material to be taught. Instead, it has to do with such things as the developmental characteristics of students and how to adapt instructional procedures in light of those characteristics, how to handle social situations involving the potential for conflict, how to proceed in the face of disagreement over the purposes and goals of instruction, and so forth.[4]

The assumption that teachers and students automatically share a common identity is becoming less valid, not to mention less probable. Most teachers are white and middle class, and probably will be for a long time. Meanwhile, lower and middle class nonwhites are among the fastest growing portion of the student population. The probability for a common shared identity between teachers and students, overall, seems quite slim. Therefore, it should be clear that teachers who do not, or who will not, share a common identity with their students can benefit from teacher preparation, especially where they have opportunities to (1) think about the issues surrounding education, (2) learn new skills and gain experiences from their education that will help them conceptualize their role as teachers, and (3) use these skills to arrange materials and select teaching approaches that help span the distance between teacher and student identities.

The fact that your courses in education *can* be useful does not make them so. The final analysis—your teaching and judging the quality of your *own* education—will determine the usefulness of your teacher preparation. So you must be the judge. But consider that your role as judge carries certain responsibilities. What are your responsibilities to the *quality* of your own education?

The process of becoming a teacher is not easy, nor is it simple. You will see as you progress through your preparation that there are often different possible solutions to the many problems teachers face. Becoming a teacher requires that you learn to make many decisions and accept

FOCUS 4.1 Well Below His Ability

by James A. Mecklenburger
Director of the Institute for the Transfer of Technology to Education,
National School Boards Association, Alexandria, Va.

Dear Mr. and Mrs. Brandt,

Would you please make an appointment one day next week after school to meet with me again about Charles, Jr.

Just as when we met last fall, Charles remains a very pleasant child but he still performs well below his ability. In writing he shows no imagination. He would never open a book unless I force him. Arithmetic is obviously a bore to him, and his attention to neatness in his writing and his work is non-existent.

I believe Charles lacks motivation. But his daydreaming not only hurts him, it also sets a bad example for the other children in his class.

I know that Charlie's poor performance troubles you as well as me. Perhaps together we can find a key.

Yours truly,
Sandi Crystal, Teacher
Grade 4

Dear Grandma Brandt,

Sure I've been thinking about growing up. I'd like to be like the newsman on TV who knows a million words and puts them on my screen and says Hi to David in Tokyo and Marlene in France and draws lines on maps where the rain is coming and shows people about golds and stocks and basketball and cars and soups and koolaid. Marlene would say Hi Chuck back to me in Dallas and I would watch her say the President met today with the one in France at a summit in a palace and they looked worried and went to dinner and had a toast. Or like my dad who taps words on a screen at his work and zips them to a man in a bank in some place like Kentucky who sees what my dad says and puts OK Charlie on my dad's screen, Good Job, you did nice work today. Or like Aunt Patti who draws circles and boxes and lines and squiggles and puts them all in colors on her screen and changes them squeezes and stretches and twists them and until they look just like a picture of a building somebody can build and then she puts the picture on paper and tapes it on her big wall with lots of other buildings and houses and shapes she thought up.

But I'm just in school where there's only pencils and papers and books and Miss Crystal talks to us about words and numbers and firemen and stuff and told my Mom I daydream a lot.

Love,
Charlie

From *Phi Delta Kappan*, April 1986, pp. 576–577.

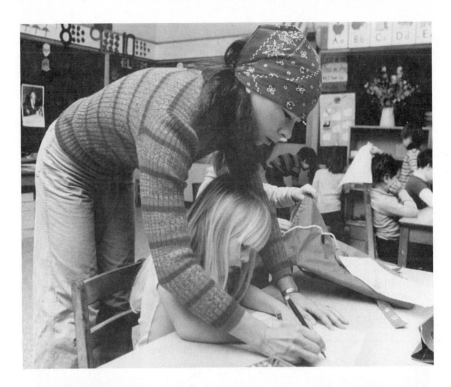

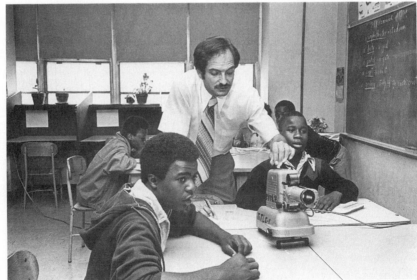

More than common sense is needed when teachers and students differ in important ways.

responsibility. In brief, you bear a large portion of the responsibility for your own education and preparation in becoming a teacher. Not all this responsibility rests on your instructor's shoulders. You can begin this process of becoming a teacher by learning about teaching.

Perhaps the first step in learning about teaching is to take what you already know—your present common sense—and expand it; specialize your common knowledge of teaching so it becomes more useful. Use your good sense and knowledge to explore the responsibilities of teachers. What do you need to know to become a good teacher? Are you ready to accept the tasks of teachers?

☐ Accepting the Tasks

If you know how schools are organized, and you know about the social context of schools, and if you understand the nature of pupils, you will probably be better equipped to endure the induction period of teaching. This enlightening will also enable you to continue your growth as a teacher and to participate in improving your profession. Knowing about the tasks of teachers—that is, knowing what you are expected to be able to do—can help you prepare for teaching so you do not fall victim to false assumptions.

Relentless paperwork: one of the tasks of teaching.

First-year teachers often report "reality shock." This shock occurs while making the transition from the secure, controlled teacher preparation program to real classroom teaching where conditions may be considerably different from those previously experienced and studied. Reality shock often represents ". . . the collapse of the missionary ideal formed during teacher training by the harsh and rude reality of everyday classroom life."[5] Why is this missionary ideal shaken? Mostly because beginning teachers find many problems to solve that at first they assume to be less important than they really are. Problems associated with the task of teaching usually have to do with classroom discipline, motivating students, recognizing and coping with student differences, evaluating students' work, dealing with parents, organizing the classroom, and not having sufficient or adequate teaching materials and supplies. Supervisory duties and noninstructional chores are piled on top of these tasks of teaching and tend to add to the reality shock.

Even veteran teachers express their frustrations with the cumulative tasks of teaching. In time, the teachers who *master the tasks* become respected and known for their commitment to education and outstanding teaching, while those who are *mastered by the tasks* become frustrated even further and often try to cope by entrenching themselves in comfortable, invariable teaching routines. This type of entrenchment is a self-protective function. What type of teacher do you wish to become? Do you have a choice?

The choice you have seems related to your ability to perform three primary but critical functions in the classroom. You must learn to (1) facilitate learning, (2) manage the classroom, and (3) make decisions.[6] For now we will explore these tasks briefly as one way of

"What homework? These are hall passes, insurance forms, attendance reports, competency updates, and my grocery list."

Phi Delta Kappan, May 1985, p. 638.

thinking about and learning about teaching. Each topic is presented in more detail in later chapters.

Facilitating Learning

"Facilitate" means to make easier or to help along. How can you learn to facilitate learning? First you must know your pupils. Chapter 5 will help you to learn about students in more detail, but for now let's think of knowing your pupils in terms of being able to identify levels of achievement, finding out about any learning problems your pupils have, and recognizing their interests—all these factors help to reduce the liabilities associated with differences in teacher-student identities.

Teachers must work with pupils individually and in groups. In each case teachers must use different teaching techniques, teaching materials, and different forms of technology that are best suited to different pupil learning styles. Careful consideration must also be given to planning learning experiences and in using well-constructed questions if you will succeed in encouraging independent thought and in helping students learn to solve worthwhile problems. And, of course you must also learn when it is appropriate and what is the best way to present information directly to students. All these teaching tasks suggest the importance of proper classroom management.

Managing the Classroom

The term "facilitate learning" connotes the multiple responsibilities teachers have. Teachers must develop effective ways to organize the classroom atmosphere so that it stimulates learning and helps to foster proper discipline. Successful classroom management requires ongoing evaluation to determine if teaching goals are accomplished. Decisions about classroom organization must be made and accompanied by proper changes. Other factors that are ancillary to the classroom must also be managed. For example, teachers must manage their communications with parents, the community, special service personnel, and community agencies. Nearer the classroom, and usually on the teacher's own time, pupil records must be examined, regularly updated, and constantly maintained. Also, the assistance of volunteers, invited guests, classroom aides, and paraprofessionals must be correlated with instruction.

Making Professional Decisions

The few tasks already mentioned give us only a small sample of the responsibilities that teachers have, and describe a few occasions when teachers must make professional decisions. The most obvious decisions teachers must make concern what to teach, what materials to use, and how to teach in a way that best fits teaching goals, lesson objectives, and students. Other decisions are less obvious, like those that have to do with reorganizing lesson plans—usually on short notice—because of school assemblies, special events, field trips taken by other teachers, class pictures, or fire and tornado drills, and so on.

Responsible decisions must also be made about which materials to use for proper student assessments and in providing appropriate student services through other personnel such as school nurses, school psychologists, social service agency workers, school librarians or media specialists, and career or guidance counselors.

MAKING DECISIONS

■ Decisions can also reach beyond the classroom and are necessary because conditions external to the school can affect the role and functions of teachers. Teachers must determine how best to deal with political, economic, and social pressures, as well as professional factors that may affect classroom functions. Teachers must also decide how to work with educational and noneducational professional organizations, the school community, and the larger public if they are to do all that others expect of them. For now, we ask you to consider making decisions relevant to four factors: (1) your personal expectations, (2) what specialized knowledge you will need, (3) what professional knowledge you will need, and (4) what type of a career in teaching you expect.

☐ Personal Expectations

What you expect from a career in teaching affects your decisions about the other factors. Consider your personal reasons for choosing to teach. Are you actually interested in teaching, or are you considering it because someone else thinks that is what you ought to do?

Also consider carefully how you will impact on students. What will your decision to teach mean to them? What kinds of personal and professional relationships do you think you will have with pupils, teaching colleagues, school administrators, and parents? How motivated are you to complete the tasks of teaching as demanded by the average 47-hour teacher work week? Are you willing to devote extra time and energy to a profession of human service? What kind of teacher do you think you can become? How do you think pupils will respond to you? Will they respect you?

What age and type of pupil do you think you prefer? Do you prefer a generalist teaching assignment typical of elementary schools? Do you favor a position as a subject specialist usually found in secondary

FOR REFLECTION 4.1

How do you answer the following questions and how do you think your future students should answer the same questions?
1. Do you like to learn new things? Why? What are some examples of efforts you have made to learn new things?
2. Are you a curious person? Why? How do you know?
3. Should you keep up with technical and social developments and with current events? Why? If yes, what are some examples when you have done this?
4. Do you enjoy solving problems and creating new ideas or things from the ideas you learn? Why? How do you use what you have learned?

schools? Do you have those extra qualities needed for teaching special education for exceptional children? What type of school do you prefer: suburban, rural, small city, urban, high school, elementary school, middle or junior high school? What do you ultimately expect from a career in teaching?

☐ Specialized Knowledge

Students benefit from a teacher's broad and general education that is usually acquired through liberal arts studies. This knowledge may include languages, literature, philosophy, psychology, history, and so on. Most colleges require some liberal arts studies as a way of expanding the general knowledge of college students and broadening their intellectual scope. This type of study also provides samples of specialized fields and helps to make the selection of teaching specialties easier.

For teachers, a broad education can be a valuable tool. While teaching, you will find it easier to elaborate on students' ideas, cite practical examples, and penetrate the artificial barriers of subjects that separate learning. Such knowledge can have a positive influence on pupil attitudes toward learning.

General knowledge provides an important context for the special, in-depth knowledge of teachers. But your own pupils may not share an interest in the same subjects. Therefore they will need someone to help them acquire essential subject-related skills and develop broad ideas as one form of their own general education. What subjects do you prefer? Why? How do you think pupils regard these same subjects? Would you enjoy teaching pupils these subjects? At what age or ability level would you prefer to teach these subjects? How can you relate your preferred subjects to the other subjects taught in school?

☐ **Professional Knowledge**

Desire, enthusiasm, and knowledge are important attributes of teachers. Yet without an ability to identify and interpret what pupils need and which teaching conditions are best for meeting these needs, you may have difficulty applying the successful methods for teaching that you will learn. Interpretation (or diagnosis as some prefer to call it) of classroom environmental cues requires artistic as well as systematic means for figuring out what will work when teaching pupils. Careful teacher observation and impartiality are required for effective teaching analysis. An additional requirement is a ready repertoire of teaching approaches including traditional and progressive methods of teaching, classroom management, and communication skills. What observation and teaching skills do you have? What teaching methods do you recognize and how have you seen teachers use them? What skills do you think are suited to the subject, type of school, and age of pupils you prefer? Why? How do you think you can best teach students? How do you think you should be educated to help teach others?

REFLECTING ON TEACHING

■ Your decision to teach, or not to teach, will be based on answering several questions. Whether you decide to become a teacher or pursue

FOR REFLECTION 4.2

When becoming a teacher you need to ask yourself some demanding questions and search out the answers that represent a valid portrayal of who you are. How do you answer these questions?

1. How interested are you in becoming a teacher?
2. What personal qualities do you have that may make you suited for teaching?
3. What kind of teaching assignment do you think you prefer? Why?
4. Do you like to learn? How do you learn? What are the best ways to learn something new? Should students feel the same way about learning as you do? Why?
5. What special skills and interests do you have that may be helpful to a career in teaching? How can you use these special skills or interests to teach?
6. If you decide to devote your time and talents to a teaching career, what do you expect in return?

Effective teachers successfully adapt their teaching.

some other career, you can count on being faced with many questions or problems and with having to make countless decisions.

If you do decide to become a teacher, you will be faced with the need to make several decisions about the kind of teacher you will become. You must make decisions about personal goals, professional goals, educational priorities, what you will teach, what learning materials you will use, how you will manage the classroom, what type of school you prefer, and so on.

Some teachers are comfortable with these decisions being made more through default than by active personal choice. The teacher education program offers a type of social immersion into teaching and helps to acquaint its neophyte teachers with the dominant ideas of education, at least as its faculty sees them. Possibly teachers-to-be face few decisions during their preparation that require real choices. In fact, any choices could be prefabricated during the process of becoming a teacher because little or no real responsibility for making decisions is required. These decisions may have already been made by your teachers through the class experiences provided and assignments required. The end result can be that decisions are made rather mechanically or they are made by others through impulse, tradition, or authority.[7] This is similar to what seems to happen to teachers as they acquire many years of experience. Over time some teachers mechanically do what they have been doing all along, or accept the views of an authority with few questions. Little attention is given to the reasons for doing what teachers do. Alan Tom comments on this point:

> Personal inquiry into the potency and effectiveness of our ideas which stem from these dominant conceptions tends to be abandoned as teachers gain experience. Without attention to the linkages between our conception of teaching and our daily practice, our professional lives become ritualized, that is, our teaching activities become grounded in a rigid adherence to current practice or tradition.[8]

Becoming a teacher by being a passive recipient of information can reinforce what has been authoritatively passed along. Reflecting about teaching, exploring alternatives available to teachers, and making active decisions about teaching help to assure planned, quality teaching and personal satisfaction with your own professional growth. These things are possible when you learn about teaching in a reflective way.

☐ What It Means to Reflect

Reflection is a process that you can use to conduct your personal inquiry into learning about and becoming a teacher. The idea of reflection is not new. John Dewey, educator and philosopher, made an important distinction between routine and dynamic teaching during the early 1900s. To Dewey, routine teaching was unreflective and was guided by impulse, tradition, and authority in which goals, problems, and solutions were narrowly defined and approached in prescribed ways. No problems were apparent as long as the daily teacher routines continued without disruption. This method of teaching, when left to dominate, obstructed teachers' views in recognizing and trying all viable, prospective solutions to educational problems. Carl Grant helps to give Dewey's thoughts a contemporary context:

> Teachers who are unreflective about their work uncritically accept this everyday reality in schools and concentrate their efforts on finding the most effective and efficient means to achieve ends and to solve problems that have been largely defined for them by others. These teachers lose sight of the fact that their everyday reality is only one of many possible alternatives. They tend to forget the purposes and ends toward which they are working.[9]

Grant seems to make a case for teachers thinking about their mission and looking closely at what they do. We encourage you to think deeply about what it means to teach and to establish this technique as a habit and as a method for avoiding unreflective, routine, or even misapplied practices of teaching. Dewey saw the action of reflection as an "active, persistent, and careful consideration of any belief or practice in light of the ground that supports it and the further consequences to which it leads."[10]

Reflecting on teaching provides us with a method for identifying and solving problems. Teachers who reflect actively think about their actions, their relationships with students, and why they do what they do. Reflective teachers are in touch and make plans for improving their teaching.

☐ Prerequisites for Reflection

Teachers who successfully learn to reflect have three essential attitudes that are prerequisites. Reflective teachers are: (1) open-minded, (2) responsible, and (3) wholehearted.

Open-mindedness
Teachers who are open-minded look for all sides to a problem and consider all available information before making a teaching decision. How will you decide what content and teaching procedures to use in your classroom? How will you decide how to handle discipline problems, when to remind, when to reprimand, or when to punish? Will you take a dominant role in discipline or empower students to discipline themselves? Will you accept, without question, teaching procedures suggested by a teacher's textbook guide? Will you teach as all other teachers in the school teach? Will you continually think about your teaching, monitor its effects, and change when desired results are not received?

Sense of Responsibility
Are you willing to accept responsibility for your teaching decisions? Sometimes students do not do what you expect. Even the best plans run amok from time to time. Reflective teachers are aware of this possibility, strive for excellence, and do not resort to what is always the easiest approach when a lesson's objectives require a new approach or extra effort. Your teaching actions must have definite purposes and you must accept responsibility for successes and possible failures.

Wholeheartedness
The extent to which you practice open-mindedness and accept responsibility for your decisions provides an indication of your wholehearted

Teachers must reflect on the impact of their teaching.

commitment to teaching. Reflective teachers exercise active control over their preparation for teaching. Reflective teachers are dedicated to teaching all pupils and to fulfilling the requirements of their profession. It is easy to like polite, cooperative, attractive, and intelligent children; it is less easy to dislike unruly children. Reflective teachers are always open-minded and responsible to their profession; they are not reflective only when it is convenient.

☐ **How to Reflect**

Being a reflective teacher means continued growth. Think about the more than 12 years you have spent as a student in classrooms. How has your participation helped to socialize you into teaching even before you decided to consider becoming a teacher? The thousands of hours you spent in classes with several teachers and other students helped to provide you with particular conceptions about teaching, what students should do, how students learn, why we have schools, and so on. Your present conceptions are good places to start your reflection about teaching. Your reflection should consist of an analysis of your present beliefs. Any beliefs that cannot be supported might be replaced by other ideas. Supported ideas can be enhanced or even supplemented by adding contrasting points of view. Using this technique helps you learn about teaching and helps sustain your personal development as a teacher.

Your Personal Development
The following steps are suggested while you are examining your beliefs and assumptions about teaching. These steps are useful to your present study of teaching and can help provide a framework for making future decisions about teaching, or in confronting choices throughout life.

1. *Identify* and express your current *beliefs* about the many issues raised during your introduction to teaching; examine your *assumptions* that underlie these beliefs.
2. *Compare your beliefs* with the beliefs of classmates and practicing teachers. Try to understand the beliefs of others and maintain an open mind toward alternative viewpoints.
3. Try to *identify the origins of your beliefs*. What aspects of your background influence the way you think about teaching? What psychological theories or educational philosophies undergird your beliefs?
4. *Consider the possible consequences* of holding certain beliefs. How might your beliefs influence what children learn? If your beliefs spill over the boundaries of the classroom, how might the social, political, religious, or economic order of the school community be affected?
5. *What do you need* in order to teach successfully and be consistent with your beliefs? What knowledge, skills, attitudes, and values will you need in order to teach as you believe? Many of these needs can be filled through formal preparation for teaching. But, what about your needs that are not included in courses and practical teaching experiences? How will you provide for them? What must you do to complete your personal development for teaching? How will you keep your preparation up to date?

Another important part of your preparation for teaching will come at some point during your education program. Time spent observing and working in classrooms with teachers and pupils can help meet some of your specific needs. The knowledge, skills, attitudes, and values you need to become a successful teacher can be identified and acquired in a setting of real teaching experiences if your participation is reflectively guided.

Reflecting About Teaching

When you enter a teacher's classroom you find yourself in an environment of organized time, space, and operating procedures. The teacher in charge has already made the environmental decisions and may not take the time to explain the reasons behind the selected classroom organization and teaching action. Often decisions have been made partly on the basis of routine choices. As a visiting prospective teacher it is easy to take what is seen for granted. How do you think the classroom, as you see it, came to be? How would you organize a classroom of your own?

The most basic problem suggested by the questions above is in understanding the thinking and decision-making processes that underlie the teacher's classroom. Even experienced teachers may often take the many important factors for granted. If you want to understand what goes on in classrooms you will need to raise questions about what you see. Questions about these occurrences are best directed to a variety of real teachers in real classrooms.

The need for questions about real classrooms suggests the need for an active and personal responsibility for your teacher preparation. These real classroom experiences are commonly called "field experiences."

Field experiences consist of observing, assisting teachers, and doing practice teaching in classrooms under the supervision of an experienced teacher or college supervisor. These experiences have become an important part of many teacher preparation programs. There is a general belief among many teacher educators that "the more prospective teachers can participate in guided interaction with students, the more successful they are likely to be when they themselves are in classrooms directing that process."[11]

Significant learning about teaching occurs if you have opportunities for real teaching experiences. You realize the need for making rather specific teaching decisions as you confront the realities of actual classroom problems. Your need to seek answers to questions, and questioning the methods of practice places you in a position to reflect as you identify alternatives, make decisions, and take action. Field experiences may provide abundant opportunities: (1) to recall what you have learned or studied in campus classes, and (2) apply what you learn about the profession. This is a concrete form of practical learning acquired from meeting the actual classroom challenges of teaching.

MEETING CHALLENGES

□ **Society's Challenge**

Our study of the current context of teaching in Chapter 3 should suggest that the public's confidence in schools has been shaken. Historically our society has learned to expect schools to perform and produce observable results in brief spans of time. This led to faith in schools. More recently, however, higher and higher expectations have been held for our schools, requiring teachers to accomplish more and more.

Schools have been given the responsibility for solving problems that are more social than educational in nature. For example, schools have been legally required to help stamp out discrimination through integration and busing, as well as to remedy the social ills of poverty, unwed adolescent parents, drug abuse, malnutrition, pollution, and management of our natural resources—only to cite a few problems delegated to our schools.

Perhaps schools and teachers are held accountable for too many diverse problems beyond the scope of the structure of schools and the abilities of teachers. Teachers hear so much criticism about their classroom performances and preparation for teaching that they may begin to believe what is said is true. Consequently, teachers may behave in ways that our society expects of them. Recent years have shown small but tangible gains in SAT and ACT score averages. An apparent academic turnaround seems to have started within 2 years of the critical reports that Jenny referred to earlier in this chapter. When told of their positive gains and noteworthy accomplishments, teachers felt renewed pride and a better sense of accomplishment. Still, some critics claim that a teacher is a teacher is a teacher. It was, after all, the increased standards placed on teachers that caused the academic gains, wasn't it? After all, teachers do not make that much of a difference, do they?

CHAPTER SUMMARY

■ Do teachers make a difference? Several years ago, while trying to identify what makes an effective teacher, researchers reported what they found after analyzing good teaching. What they had to say was not very encouraging. It seems that after 75 years of research, not much was reliably known about effective teaching. Some influential writers actually declared that teachers were not very important in contributing to student achievement. But, each of us can usually identify some teachers who have had a profound positive influence on our lives. What makes the difference? How then do people learn to teach?

Successful teachers take a large part of the responsibility for their own learning and preparation for becoming a teacher. They become informed about teaching responsibilities: stimulating learning, effectively managing all that happens in classrooms, and making the countless decisions required of teachers. Successful teachers actively reflect on their actions and the consequences of their decisions. Some teachers may do these things intuitively, but there is more to teaching than what appears to be common sense.

Common sense has long suggested that a single teacher can make an important difference in the life of a student, but that same teacher is not so influential for all students. Students with different backgrounds, abilities, preferred styles of learning, personality types, and cultural influences seem to need teachers with differing characteristics. Students need teachers who understand them, teachers who share an identity with them. In fact, at least one researcher has documented that effective teachers in the schools of low socioeconomic communities differ in their teaching behaviors from those effective teachers who teach in schools of high socioeconomic communities.[12] The research tends to support the claim that effective teachers are those teachers who are successful at adapting their teaching to student needs and capabilities.

Effective teachers do not entrench themselves in one teaching approach; rather they have a repertoire of teaching skills and approaches that can be used according to the situational demands and needs of students. This makes up the largest challenge of teaching students—knowing them, being able to communicate with them effectively, and being able to relate to them properly. These challenges are the topics explored in the next section of this book.

FOR DISCUSSION

1. What is your position on the argument that teachers are born? Provide evidence from your own experiences as a student to support your position.

2. Jenny believes that teachers should leave the classroom if they no longer enjoy teaching. What is your recommendation for dealing with the anxiety that teachers may feel from being trapped by their circumstances?

3. "Good teachers make an impact; they make a real difference," it is claimed. What kind of difference have teachers made in your life?

4. The failures of schools seem to make the news more than their successes. Attention drawn to failures appears damaging to school and teacher credibility. How can teachers turn negative press into an advantage?

5. What recommendations would you make to the best and worst teachers you have had?

IN THE SCHOOL/IN THE CLASSROOM

1. Observe several classrooms, paying particular notice to classroom organization, how the teachers teach, and how they communicate with the students. Do the teachers and students share an identity? Support your response with examples.

2. To what extent do you find evidence that these teachers make the assumptions described in this chapter? Are any assumptions correct? What additional assumptions do you notice? How do these assumptions influence teaching and learning?

3. Interview several teachers and ask them about their preparation for teaching. Ask them to describe what they had to do to become a teacher. Ask them to comment on how well prepared they were for beginning a career in teaching. Speculate about the extent that each accepted responsibility for learning about teaching as described in this chapter. From the interviews and your observations, to what extent do you believe the teachers "reflected" in conjunction with their preparation for teaching? To what extent do these teachers appear to reflect now that they are teaching?

SUGGESTED READINGS

Grant, Carl A. *Preparing for Reflective Teaching*. Boston: Allyn & Bacon, 1984. Grant's book provides a thoughtful introduction to reflection and reinforces the techniques suggested by including a wide variety of brief articles and timely pieces guaranteed to tease the brain. Chapters consist of relevant collections of material by other authors, and chapters cover the topics of the teacher, schools and society, curriculum and materials, instruction and classroom management, and kids.

Jackson, Philip W. *The Practice of Teaching*. New York: Teachers College Press, 1986. This book is an edited collection of essays originally written and delivered by Jackson throughout his distinguished career. Several of his chapters are useful in helping you think about and learn about teaching. We recommend careful reading of the chapters "On Knowing How To Teach," and "The Uncertainties of Teaching."

Kohl, Herbert. *Growing Minds—On Becoming A Teacher*. New York: Harper & Row, 1984. This book is a thoughtful collection of Kohl's experiences in becoming a teacher. Part I, "Beginning To Teach," provides an inspiring account of how Kohl learned to teach and how he learned to adjust to the rigidity and apathy of the education system. His views can open the minds and stimulate the imaginations of experienced and novice teachers alike.

CHAPTER REFERENCES

1. Philip W. Jackson, *The Practice of Teaching* (New York: Teachers College Press, 1986).
2. Ibid., p. 24.
3. Ibid., p. 25.
4. Ibid., p. 26.
5. S. Veenman, "Perceived Problems of Beginning Teachers," *Review of Educational Research* 54, no. 2 (1984): 143–178.
6. National Educational Association, *Excellence in Our Schools: Teacher Education* (Washington, D.C.: National Education Association, 1982).
7. Carl A. Grant, *Preparing For Reflective Teaching* (Boston: Allyn & Bacon, 1984).
8. Alan R. Tom, *Teaching as a Moral Craft* (New York: Longman, 1984), p. 2.
9. Grant, *Preparing for Reflective Teaching*, p. 4.
10. Ibid., p. 4
11. P. G. Elliot, *Field Experiences in Preservice Teacher Education* (Washington, D.C.: ERIC Clearinghouse on Teacher Education, 1978), p. 2.
12. Jere E. Brophy, "Reflections on Research in Elementary Schools," *Journal of Teacher Education* 27, no. 1 (1976): 31–34.

II

Working with Students

In the first section of this text we introduced you to the breadth of the field of education. You should now have some understanding of the demands made on the schools and the teachers who work within them. For the remainder of this book we want to focus on specific aspects of the various tasks that face teachers and schools.

Section II examines the clientele the schools are designed to serve—students. We begin, in Chapter 5, by looking at students themselves. Who are the individuals who face us, expectantly, every day? What needs, problems, hopes, and dreams do they bring with them to the classroom? We believe that it is important to know who students are before we claim that we can teach them.

Teaching students involves communicating, and this is the focus of Chapters 6 and 7. While the need for good classroom communication may seem obvious, the fact is often overlooked that communication skills are learned. Thus, in Chapter 6, we examine the communication skills that can help teachers reach their students and the various communication pitfalls that can limit or even stop learning in the classroom. Additionally, we explore human relations skills, particularly how to overcome the often hidden biases in the classroom. These are biases based on race, class, socioeconomic status, or handicapping conditions that limit student achievement.

Chapter 7 addresses a concern that many teacher education students have—classroom management. In our discussion of this, we focus on the broader and more positive notion of classroom atmosphere. We see your classroom atmosphere not as something you add on to your lesson plan or methodology, but as something that sets the stage for all your teaching.

After reading this section you should have a better understanding of what teaching is all about. It is a complex process in which teachers and students try to communicate as clearly as possible in order to obtain a desired learning outcome. How these communication tools can be specifically used within your teaching will be explored in Section III.

5

Students

Previous chapters of this book have begun with an imagined scenario. In this chapter we begin by allowing students to speak for themselves. What follows are two conversations, the first about teachers and the second about administrators, compiled by Diane Slyfield of the Glenbard East *Echo* (Glenbard East High School, Lombard, Illinois). Listen to students talk about schooling.

SCENARIO: REACTION TO TEACHERS

■ *Melanie:* I think the worst part can be the teachers. I can get a bad grade and learn a lot. I think of a science teacher in the seventh grade. I didn't do as well as I could, but I learned so much from him and he was one of my favorite teachers. It was the same with geometry as a freshman. I got the worst grade in geometry that I got all through high school, but I still appreciated that teacher the most because of the respect he had for me. But there are so many teachers throughout high school who are like, "If you don't get the A or the B that I know you can, you are worth nothing!" You respond, "Oh I must be worthless because I got a C plus in your class. I'm sorry."

Kelly: I think the worst thing about school is when it gets boring. A lot of that often has to do with the teacher or the course. Health is one of the most boring classes I've ever had. I was doing the same thing in biology and in chemistry and in medical science. When it's boring, you have no ambition. And when the teacher is boring, it's just as bad.

Melanie: I should reverse what I said before. One of the best things I've found is the teachers. The teachers can also make the best part of school.

Diane: They can be the worst.

Melanie: Both ways.

Diane: A teacher can totally destroy your ambition in a class.

Melanie: You can't let it, though. If that happens, that's your responsibility.

Jeff: That's not a teacher's job—to destroy.

Diane: I only met one teacher in all of my years of going to school that I could not stand. She could not stand me either, and she told me in front of the class. Not only did I not like the class, I did not try simply because she didn't care. I think one teacher can ruin one class for you, but they can't ruin your whole education.

Kelly: Until I got to high school, I didn't know you were allowed to not like a teacher. I was such a puppy in class. I didn't know a teacher could be a bad person. I always respected the teachers and thought they were the best. I started to learn that maybe every teacher wasn't a wonderful person.

Jeff: When I was a freshman, I was naive. I came in expecting to learn something and thinking that teachers were gods. What they said was law. Now that I've experienced a lot more teachers, I've realized many are BS artists, not gods. I use them for all they're worth. I use what little knowledge some of them have. It's not a very nice way to put it, but you could be good friends with a teacher and yet use them, too.

Melanie: I think it's important that teachers in a math class or history or whatever do not say, "Now these are the dates. Memorize them." You get all of the trig or whatever, all these rules down, and then that's all there is to it. But I like it when the teacher gets you into it so it's more than memorization; it's experience. And through the experience, you pick up the rules and dates. I don't like it when the teacher is standing in front of you and says, "All right, we're going to study Chapter 3. Chapter 3 is this and this and this"—she just goes on and on.

Then the hour's up, and you're told the assignment and how to do it. And it's like there's no thinking on your own. A class is really interesting when I can add my opinions to it. I like it to be open—not just preaching. I like to express my own opinions and form my own thoughts—and to discuss them so the teacher can discuss back what's wrong or right with them.

☐ Reaction to Administrators

Steve: What really irritates me is the red tape. There seem to be so many petty bureaucrats running around the high school that drive me crazy.

Jeff: Administrators.

Steve: Yeah, that and all the dumb rules and regulations and people's attitudes towards these rules and regulations just get on my nerves.

Kelly: They expect you to act and be like adults, but they treat you like kids. For example, not being able to talk or use materials other than library materials in the library. Not being able to sit and talk with friends even if you can keep it down. Not being able to go to the washroom without a pass.

Manish: Privileges of using the gym or other facilities without a supervisor. They kick you out otherwise.

Kelly: That's mostly for safety reasons. But I know some examples when we were not able to be in school without a supervisor. We had work to do for a play, and the teachers had a meeting. They wouldn't let us work because we didn't have someone standing over our shoulders.

Steve: Idiot things like this big confrontation about smoking across from the school irritate me. I don't smoke, but it's just a ridiculous thing. It's just so stupid. It makes absolutely no sense whatsoever. Just the general attitude.

Okay—admittedly the kids on that street are causing a problem for people who live there. That's not cool. But the administration should say, "Well, we've got a problem here. Let's deal with it." The way to deal with it was not to suspend anyone smoking there or in the general area, not to call the Lombard police and make them cruise every day and night to make sure it didn't happen. They don't have to go through all that bullshit.[1]

INTRODUCTION

These are some of the voices of students—the main reason schools exist. They are the primary consumers of the school's product. They are the reason we hire people called teachers. And if surveys are correct, they are the main reason teachers choose to go into teaching.

Given these factors it is surprising that teachers often know very little about their students. While much attention is devoted to the psychological makeup of students, little is paid to their social situation. That is, who are students, what is their world like, what do they hope and dream for, what do they fear, how do they see school and teachers, where do they think they are going? Questions like these guide this chapter.

There are three main reasons for considering, in depth, the social nature of the students that teachers face. The first is given to us by students themselves. When talking about their favorite teacher, or the teacher from whom they have learned the most, students frequently say it is a teacher who "cares" about them as a person. Often this means the teacher "understands" or can "communicate" with students.

While not actually a friend, the good teacher, the educator, knows where his or her students are coming from and knows how to relate to them. He or she takes the time to know students as human beings, not numbers in a grade book.

If we compare the role of the teacher to that of a doctor we see the second reason teachers need to know their students. Imagine your physician prescribing medication for an illness if he or she had never examined you. You would be outraged. How could the doctor treat you if you had not been examined? Teachers play the same role. There is a treatment to be administered: teaching in a variety of fields. Yet how can the teacher be sure the treatment (or teaching) rendered will be effective if he or she is not fully aware of the needs of the student (patient)?

Finally, we believe good teaching begins where students *are,* and not where we want them to be. Here, we echo John Dewey's belief that unless we can connect subject matter with students' experiences they will not retain what is taught. If teachers expect to be effective they have to reach out to the social experience of students and connect their material with that experience.

For these three reasons we will be exploring the makeup, culture, and experience of today's youth. We look first at the school performance of children. Then we will focus on the culture of youth, the pressures they face living in the modern world. How these forces combine in the perceptions children have about today's world and schooling will then be explored. Finally, the challenges children pose for teachers will be set forth. In all this we will be trying to understand if and how today's youth are changing and what that means for teaching and learning.

STUDENT ACADEMIC PERFORMANCE

■   How well do children perform in school? This question has recently become perhaps the most discussed aspect of American education. Most frequently publicized has been a reported decline in standardized test scores. But press reports with dramatic headlines tell only half the story. When headlines like *U.S. News and World Report*'s "Are We Becoming a Nation of Illiterates?" (May 17, 1982) catch our attention, we are often misled into simplistic answers. With little or no evidence, the public comes to the conclusion that schools are failing, that students are illiterate, that teachers cannot teach. The lack of good information about student academic performance both confuses and trivializes the debates on education.

It is important for educators to know what is behind the test score debate. Most news magazines, television networks, and newspapers do a poor job of covering education. Experienced reporters with a background in education are few and far between, and educational issues that do make the headlines—violence, drugs, falling test scores—are often reported in their most superficial and sensational way. To combat this manufactured impression of schools' and students' performances, teachers must be informed about the meanings behind the numbers.

This is not to say that schools should cover up their failures. Rather, they should understand them so that they can correct their faults. This is the second reason for looking closely at school performance. Getting behind the numbers helps us more clearly identify the problem so that we may work more directly at solving it.

☐ Falling Test Scores

Perhaps one of the most misunderstood educational issues of our time is the phenomenon of falling standardized test scores. In fact, people occasionally pay more attention to these than to the high school football scores. More seriously, the concern over a perceived drop in a variety of measures of academic success has led to grave concern over the quality of our schools. This is because they are taken to be the best indication of what children learn, which is, we assume, the main reason for them to be in school. What has actually happened to test scores and what reasons might be behind any change in them?

The clearest way to put it is that scores on the SAT declined throughout the 1970s and have shown a slight upward trend in the 1980s. These scores seem to be reflected in a variety of other tests as well.[2] Given this, what do we know?

What we know from these scores is in fact very confusing. Take the SAT, for example. It is supposed to be a measure of *aptitude,* not *achievement.* If this is the case it tells us very little about what children learn (achieve) in school. But let's assume for a moment it does tell us something about student achievement; in fact, tests like The National Assessment of Educational Progress (NAEP) do claim to measure student achievement. Why the decrease in scores?

Put simply, we really do not know. After years of study, a variety of competing claims are still made concerning test score declines. These include the claims explored in Chapter 1 that schools and teachers are not doing their job. Other explanations have focused on who is taking the tests. Since the SAT is not required, it is taken by only a sample of students who intend to go to college. Perhaps more and more less able students were taking the tests, or maybe the increase in broken homes, childhood poverty, divorce, television watching, and so on is to blame. The unfortunate truth is that we really do not know.

☐ Dropping Out or Staying In?

There are two ways to examine the issue of dropping out of school. The first is survey reports on how many dropouts there are and who is or is not staying in school. The second is to look at figures that tell us what percentage of the American population finishes what levels of schooling.

As to survey reports, recent estimates place the dropout rate (that is, students not finishing high school) at 16%. This figure varies by race and sex. For white males the dropout rate is 17.9% compared with 18.9% for black males. White female dropouts figure at 13.2%, while 19.7% of black females are dropouts.[3]

Figures on high school completion for the entire population are a bit more encouraging. In 1960 only 24.6% of the population had completed high school. The median school years completed stood at 10.6. By 1982, however, nearly 38% of the population had finished high school and the median years of schooling was up to 12.6. Of course, disparities remained between races and sexes. Of white males, 34.5% finished high school as did 42.7% of white females. Black males finished high school at the rate of 32.1% and 32.8% of black females did the same. For those of Spanish origin the figures were dismal, with 25.9% of males and 28.3% of females finishing high school.[4]

How do these figures help us understand student achievement? If we take attendance at school to mean anything, the figures are encouraging and discouraging at the same time. First, there is still a very serious dropout problem, especially among selected racial groups. However, as reflected in the *adult* population (statistics here are for individuals 25 years and over), more and more people are finishing high school. Much of this is due to attempts by public schools to include more and more diverse groups. As we pointed out earlier, public schooling has gradually expanded to include minorities previously left out.

So we are faced with a paradox. On one hand, test scores drop. On the other hand, more children are getting more schooling. There is no easy way to resolve this muddle. But perhaps one last source of information could shed some light on the quality of students.

☐ Teacher Perceptions

We have looked at the statistics on student performance from the angle of both test scores and dropout rates. These numbers tell us part of the story of student performance in school. We get even a broader picture by listening to what teachers say about their students.

Experienced teachers seem generally to agree that today's students are more difficult to reach than their predecessors. From kindergarten through the university, teachers say their students are "different" than they used to be. What do they mean by this? In Focus 5.1 you will find a report on how teachers in one district perceive this change. Indeed, their perceptions seem to be echoed in reports nationwide.

FOCUS 5.1   Changes in Children and Youth over Two Decades: The Perceptions of Teachers

To learn if and how children and adolescents have changed over the past 10 to 20 years, we turned to "real experts"—elementary and secondary school teachers. Veteran teachers (is there any other kind now?) are in a position to observe and interact directly with hundreds, thousands, of young people in a controlled setting over a great many years. Their experiences represent a rich source of data and insight regarding child and adolescent development. Yet too often we deprive ourselves of their insights, relying instead on the findings of social scientists, whose contact with this age group tends to be sporadic and limited to survey and interview data rather than continuous observation.

Our experts were 300 teachers and administrators in a suburban school district in Minnesota. . . . [They] responded to the following question: "What are the major changes you have observed in students over the years you've been working with them?"

Nearly every respondent reported noteworthy differences between today's students and those they had encountered as "rookies." On two issues there was substantial agreement between elementary and secondary teachers. Both groups reported that students today are 1) more assertive and outspoken, and 2) more oriented toward instant gratification.

Under more assertive, teachers described students as being more expressive, more sure of themselves, more willing to challenge authority, more likely to openly express dislike of school, more at ease with adults, and less fearful of adult authorities. . . .

This new assertiveness was sometimes viewed as a positive, constructive change; in other cases it was reported with a tinge of resentment and disapproval. But clearly, quiet, docile, "seen but not heard" students have been replaced by more open, expressive, impatient, challenging, questioning, aggressive, and assertive youngsters.

The second area of agreement between the two groups was that young people have a strong need to be entertained and expect instant gratification for both their personal and educational desires. Children and adolescents were perceived as having shorter attention spans, being insatiable in their need for attention, being harder to please, having higher expectations, being less willing to put forth effort to learn, and being motivated more by external than by internal rewards. . . . ,

The passivity and dependence described by elementary teachers becomes ingrained by adolescence and, according to high school teachers, tends to harden into a generalized pattern of self-centeredness and lack of social concern. . . .

On one major issue, whether students "know more" now than in the past, there was a significant difference between the observations of elementary and secondary teachers. Elementary teachers emphatically asserted that they do, and secondary teachers believed they do not. According to elementary respondents, children are more aware, knowledgeable, sophisticated, and worldly; they come to school knowing more than they did in the past, both in terms of readiness to learn and in breadth of knowledge. Again, the teachers are ambivalent about the change. Some suggested that it showed up mainly as "pseudo-sophistication and street smarts," while others saw it as enhancing interest and readiness for reading and removing the fear of dealing with formerly taboo issues such as incest and alcoholism.

In contrast, not a single secondary school teacher perceived that students possess more knowledge than in the past. Instead they saw adolescents as less intellectually curious, less interested in learning, less inquisitive about the world around them, and less willing to put effort into education. In general, they observed that school is not as central to the lives of teenagers as it once was and that the job, not school, is the first priority for many of them.

It may be that there is no real contradiction between the perspectives of the elementary and secondary teachers. Perhaps the reason that junior and senior high students show less inherent interest in their education is precisely because they have been exposed earlier to more information. By the time they reach secondary school, they may indeed be, as James Coleman observed, "information rich but action poor." The students may feel that they have already studied the content of much of the secondary curriculum, while in actuality they have had only a superficial encounter with it. In their discussion of student "pseudo-sophistication," teachers focused on a frustrating dilemma in public education: Students feel satiated with information and knowledge and find school increasingly repetitious and monotonous—merely an empty ritual to pass the time until they are old enough to fill adult roles.

As a final note, we must report that teachers hardly mentioned the current "high profile" topics such as increased drug use, violence, and pregnancy, or the much-debated "decline" in basic skills. Perhaps these are not serious problems in this community. Perhaps also they are mere symptoms of the more fundamental problems that the teachers focused on in their discussions.

From *Phi Delta Kappan,* June 1980, pp. 702–703.

In these reports, again we are faced with paradoxes concerning American youth. On one hand, they seem to be more assertive. They speak out, challenge, and attempt to take control of many situations. On the other hand, they want to be entertained. They can remain passive and unmotivated, waiting for something, anything to happen. Some teachers say kids know more (primarily, elementary school) and others say they know less (secondary school). An interesting trend seems to emerge from all this.

Students seem to be more worldly yet at the same time bored with their world. Demands are made for their rights, but they often seem ignorant of their responsibilities. Not only is the student body more diversified, it is becoming more disconnected. While not the case for a majority of students, it seems a significant minority are not very excited by their future.

Perhaps this is one way to understand the various indicators we have looked at with regard to student performance. It may not be a failure of the educational system with which we are faced. Instead,

Is the lure of the video arcade stronger than that of the classroom?

there may be a larger, social crisis that is taking its toll on our children and showing up in schools.

YOUTH CULTURE

■ What is it like to "grow up American" today? What special problems do children face and how do these problems affect school achievement? In what follows we look at a variety of problems and pressures that children face today. These include the changing family structure, social pressures, the media, and social problems. We conclude by suggesting that modern society may be witnessing the disappearance of childhood.

A note of caution is appropriate. No one should gain the impression from reading this that every child is threatened by some type of personal crisis. Most children come to school well adjusted, happy, and glad to be there. At the same time, every child is at risk from forces much larger than himself or herself. Only by understanding the pressures children face can educators reduce that risk and increase school success.

□ **The Family**

The American family is perhaps the major building block of American society. Because of this, a great deal of attention is paid to its condition. The perceived ideal family is one with a father, mother, and

The Washington Post National Weekly Edition, January 21, 1985.

children. However, today the family is changing and here we present the nature of these changes and how they have affected school achievement and behavior.

Family Structure

Most children are still raised in conventional, two-parent homes. Family size has dropped as we have become a more urban society, but usually children can expect to have one or two siblings around the house. Most marriages survive, not ending in divorce or separation. Yet for a significant number of children this is not the case.

DIVORCE At one time in American society divorce was almost socially unacceptable behavior. Perhaps this was unfortunate, for many unsuccessful marriages continued much to the detriment of all involved. Regardless, much of that has changed as the stigma of divorce has been greatly reduced, accounting, perhaps in part, for rising divorce rates.

Currently, more than one million couples a year end their marriage with divorce. Put another way, the average duration of an American marriage is less than 9.5 years.[5] Of course, divorce significantly alters the family setting, often with children caught in the middle. Battles over custody and visitation, financial arrangements, and disagreements over how children are to be raised all take their toll on the children involved.

This is *not*, we repeat, *not* to say that every child of divorce has the problems discussed below. Many such children grow and develop quite normally with few, if any, problems. Yet we do know that children whose parents separate suffer from higher rates of delinquency, depression, aggressiveness toward parents, acting out sexually, and school behavior problems. Furthermore, these children are more likely to experience school failure, a problem more likely the younger the child is at the time of the divorce.[6]

Thus, schools are faced with a growing problem. As divorce rates increase so do the number of children attending school at risk from the problems of divorce. The problem of divorce has become so intense in some schools that specific programs have been devised to meet these children's needs.[7] These programs focus on rebuilding the students' self-esteem and helping them cope with the increasing strains at home.

SINGLE MOTHERS A similar alteration in the family unit has been the increase in children born to unmarried women. The numbers are startling. Nearly one child in five (20%) are born today to unwed mothers. This compares with 11% of children born in similar conditions in 1970. Unfortunately, this number is not color-blind. While 12% of white births take place out of wedlock, the number is 51% of black births.

These children face many of the same problems experienced by children of divorce. Additionally, as we shall see below, many of these mothers are students in school when they get pregnant. The school is often unequipped to deal with such students, since we are frequently unsure whether to even allow pregnant young women to attend school.

Poverty is another problem that children of single-parent homes face. One-third of all female householders subsist at or below the poverty level. These individuals account for more than half (56%) of the children in single-parent households. That is, nearly 7 million children of single-parent families are living below the poverty level. Of course, poverty strikes two-parent families as well. However, no group is so impacted by poverty as those children living in a single-parent home headed by a female.[8]

As with so many statistics these numbers should not be taken to apply to every situation. Many single mothers, and fathers as well, do quite well in providing for their offspring. Furthermore, while many of these numbers seem to pinpoint women as particular failures that is not our intent at all. The problem of poverty among single mothers is as much a social as personal problem. Living in a society that discriminates against women in terms of hiring, promotion, and pay, we should not be surprised at all that single mothers have a hard time supporting their children. We should also be concerned with why the fathers of these children seem to see no need for personal responsibility for their children's well-being.

ABUSE, RUNAWAYS   Unfortunately, one last aspect of the changing American family needs to be addressed—child abuse. There are no clear figures on child abuse because much of it goes unreported. However, there seems to be agreement that there may be as many as half a million cases of child abuse yearly. This includes physical abuse, neglect, and mental or psychological cruelty.

There are few clear-cut facts about why child abuse occurs. It is not limited to one socioeconomic class or geographical area. What is apparent is that parents who were abused as children are more likely to abuse their children. Additionally, social stress, such as the loss of employment or income, can increase the possibility that abuse may occur.

In response to abuse and other family problems many children simply run away. Government estimates place the number of runaways at over 1 million per year. The vast majority of these children return after only a couple of days. But over 45,000 stay away for extended periods of time, sometimes never going home.[9] These figures, as with those on abuse, single mothers, and divorce, seem to rise yearly.

THE CHANGING FAMILY Clearly, the American family is under stress. Some suggest that this indicates a period of evolution, with new family forms appearing. Others suggest that we have neglected the family, that we have not supported it sufficiently in order for this institution to survive. Regardless, it is clear that what is happening challenges educators in many new ways.

More and more children come to school with family problems. Fewer and fewer have the support system at home necessary to insure that homework assignments are completed, meals are eaten, and the necessary amount of sleep obtained.

An example of this is the phenomenon of "latchkey children." These are children who return to empty homes at the end of the school day. Nearly half of the 13 million schoolchildren age 13 and below come home to an empty house because one or both parents are still at work.[10] Quite often this is a situation beyond the parents' control since it is an economic necessity that they work. But what does this mean for educators? How will it affect their work?

For one thing, it means teaching will get harder. Students will bring more problems to school and teachers will get less help from home. For another, schooling will become more important. The schoolhouse is perhaps the last public institution left that is primarily concerned with children. There is nowhere else for many children to go for help. Examples of the expansion of schooling to serve the social needs of students include free lunch programs, breakfast programs, lessons on preventing sexual abuse, and special classes for children coping with divorce. Finally, the teacher will have to be more responsive to the needs of his and her pupils. We cannot assume the faces that greet us each morning will be smiling, and we will need to be ready for the various traumas they bring to the classroom.

RESEARCH NOTES 5.1 Where Our Children Live

With both biological parents: 63%
With mother only: 20%
With non-relatives, foster parents or institutions: 1%
With father only: 2%
With other relatives: 2%
With two adoptive parents: 2%
With one biological parent and one step-parent: 10%

Source: U.S. Senate Select Committee on Children, Youth and Families

☐ **Peer Pressures**

One of the most difficult things about growing up is dealing with one's peers. The pressure to conform, to be like everyone else, is so strong it can even lead to self-destructive behavior. Who has not had to respond to the taunt, "Come on, everyone else is doing it!"

In this section we look at the push to conform. By this we do not mean the pressures to conform in matters of dress, hairstyles, choice of music, and the like. Rather, our focus is peer pressure to engage in self-destructive actions, such as drug and alcohol abuse and teenage sex. This provides us with another insight into the culture of childhood.

Alcohol and Drugs
Parents and teachers have always voiced concern about young people's use of alcohol and drugs. And substance abuse by young people continues to be a major social concern. What exactly are the numbers behind the debate?

ALCOHOL Alcohol use by American youth is far more widespread than drug abuse. While over 50% of our students use or have tried drugs, over 90% of children age 18 and under have used alcohol. Not only is use of alcohol more widespread, it begins at a much earlier age.

In recent studies, over 10% of the respondents reported their first use of alcohol to be in the sixth grade or before. Seventh and eighth graders saw over 22% of their classmates using alcohol for the first time. Add that to the number of first-time users in sixth grade or before and we see that by the end of junior high school one-third of the students have tried alcohol.

Alcohol use continues to escalate throughout the high school years. By 9th grade, 56% of students reported having used alcohol; 10th grade, 74%; 11th grade, 86%; and 12th grade, 92%. Only 7.4% of students reported *not* having used alcohol at all during their public schooling.

Unfortunately, alcohol use among students is increasing. While this is not so much the case with older students, the real increase is among younger students. Children in the sixth grade and below try alcohol at a younger age and use it more frequently than students before them.[11]

DRUGS Interestingly enough, drug use among children is actually decreasing. From a high in the mid 1970s, drug use has fallen off through the 1980s. There are no accurate figures on drug use—it is illegal and thus difficult to measure. But virtually every survey demonstrates that use of all forms of drugs, excepting cocaine, continues to fall.

That's the good news. The bad news is that by the time students graduate from high school over 50% of them reported they have used marijuana and over 16% have used cocaine. Additionally, 5% of high school seniors reported they are heavy marijuana users (20 times or more per month). Even more disturbing is the trend toward younger and younger drug users. Today, teachers in the upper elementary grades report that students in the fifth and sixth grades have experimented with drugs. Students report further that drug abuse is the biggest problem facing them today. In a poll of 13- to 18-year-olds, 42% cited drug abuse as the major problem in their young lives.[12]

RESEARCH NOTES 5.2   Drug Use Declines in High Schools

American high school seniors are becoming less likely to use drugs including marijuana, stimulants, sedatives and tranquilizers, according to a recently released survey conducted by the University of Michigan. However, cocaine use has not declined, the most recent survey found.

Here is the trend for high school seniors who have used marijuana/hashish and cocaine:

PERCENT WHO HAVE EVER USED:

MARIJUANA/HASHISH	COCAINE
Class of '75 - 47.3%	Class of '75 - 9.0%
Class of '76 - 52.8%	Class of '76 - 9.7%
Class of '77 - 56.4%	Class of '77 - 10.8%
Class of '78 - 59.2%	Class of '78 - 12.9%
Class of '79 - 60.4%	Class of '79 - 15.4%
Class of '80 - 60.3%	Class of '80 - 15.7%
Class of '81 - 59.5%	Class of '81 - 16.5%
Class of '82 - 58.7%	Class of '82 - 16.0%
Class of '83 - 57.0%	Class of '83 - 16.2%
Class of '84 - 54.9%	Class of '84 - 16.1%

From *The Washington Post National Weekly Edition,* March 11, 1985, p. 38. Note: surveys were sponsored primarily by the National Institute on Drug Abuse. About 17,000 high school students were interviewed annually in about 140 public and private U.S. high schools.

Sex

The prevalence of sex among America's youth was recently summed up by a *New York Times* headline: "U.S. Leads Industrialized Nations in Teenage Births and Abortions."[13] The *Times* story was reporting on an international study of teenage pregnancy carried out by the Alan Guttmacher Institute. The study demonstrated that "by the time they reach 20, nearly 1 in 10 American women will have been pregnant at least once."[14] More importantly, only in the United States have the rates of teenage pregnancies been steadily *increasing* for the past several years.

These numbers mean that there are nearly 1 million teenage pregnancies per year in the United States, with over half of them ending in abortion. The future for these children and their parents (usually just the mother) is not very bright. Simply put, most teenage mothers and their children will end up in poverty.

The consequences of teenage pregnancy are dire for both parents and child. The mothers are forced to give up their schooling and devote all their energies to child rearing and wage earning. Fathers, when they do take the responsibility, have to leave school for work at minimum-wage jobs. If the risks are so high, why take the chance? The Guttmacher study explored this issue and found that many of the commonly suspected causes were incorrect. American teenagers don't start having sex earlier than other nations, abortions are not easier to obtain, and welfare stipends for children are minimal and far below those in other industrialized nations. The study did suggest that the lack of access to birth control and appropriate sex-education for American teenagers were the biggest problems.[15]

But of course this begs a larger question: If there is so much to lose, why try it at all? Of course, the same could be said for drug and alcohol use. In what follows we attempt to point to several sources of such self-destructive behavior. These include the media, the social problems children face, and the institution of childhood itself.

□ The Media

Item: A group of former sports stars are gathered to tell stories and share memories. The location, a bar. The beverage, a beer whose merits are the central part of the conversation.

Item: The qualities of a new car are being discussed by an announcer. But as much attention is paid in the accompanying pictures to the well-dressed, shapely young woman posing with the vehicle.

Item: A muscular young man pauses after climbing a dangerous mountain peak. To relax he reaches into his shirt pocket and pulls out a pack of cigarettes.

These are the images children encounter daily in our media age. Print, audio, and visual media suggest to them what it means to be grown up, to be successful. Children, exposed to a limited version of adulthood, presume that these behaviors constitute all there is to being grown up. Unable to access other adult roles, such as work or community service, children imitate the more publicized and primarily recreational roles.

It is impossible to underestimate the impact of media on childhood and children. They are bombarded daily with sights and sounds directed either at them or adults. Usually there is no attempt to distinguish between the audiences, since most images use pictures and sound rather than words. The adult skill of reading is not necessary to get the message.

What can be said about the nature of the images presented? How do they lead children to perceive their world? And what does this mean for educators?

The Media Image

A popular song in the mid 1980s by the rock singer Madonna uses the refrain, "We are living in a material world." Indeed, the images created by the mass media would lead us to believe that material things are to be valued above all else in our culture. In print, audio, and visual media, a great deal of emphasis is placed on the immediate, the material, pleasures of life.

If you have completed the exercise in For Reflection 5.1 you begin to grasp how broadly these images of the good life run. Advertisements in magazines push products meant to enhance our attractiveness to the opposite sex—from clothes, to makeup, to automobiles. Television shows often promote a life-style that revolves around drinking, sex,

The "plug-in drug."

and violence. Our cultural heroes are sports stars, rock stars, and movie stars.

FOR REFLECTION 5.1   "Living in a Material World"

With several classmates, collect a variety of magazines that young people read. Additionally, take turns watching the top-rated television shows. Now imagine that you had no other knowledge of American culture but these samples. Answer the following questions:

What does this culture value?

Who are its heroes?

What do most people do?

What do you need to know to be successful?

Compare your group's answers to others in your class. Can you come up with any overriding themes? What do these imply for the task of the teacher?

The problem in all this is that it often suggests to students that what happens in school is not very important. If the road to fame is to be found outside the classroom why pay attention to the teacher? Why be concerned with the life of the mind when what really counts are the material goods one possesses?

Teachers also have to compete with the stimulus of television. Television is perhaps the most pervasive element of our culture. By the time a child graduates from high school he or she will have spent as many hours in front of the television as in a classroom. Before even arriving in school some children spend over 2,000 hours in front of the tube. What is the effect of all this television?

Perhaps the most telling critique of television and children has been offered by Marie Winn. In her book, *The Plug-In Drug,* she claims that it is not what children watch, but the very act of watching that is dangerous for children. As she puts it:

> There is, indeed, no other experience in a child's life that permits quite so much intake while demanding so little outflow.[16]

Her argument is that while children need activity to stimulate intellectual, social, and emotional growth, television encourages passivity. Such passivity reduces the intellectual curiosity and natural inquisitiveness of children as they spend hours passively waiting to be entertained.

Teachers often find themselves ill-equipped to deal with such a visual medium. The colors, sounds, and rapid pace are beyond the

*"Sure it's sloppy! You ever try
to do homework and watch TV
at the same time?"*

Phi Delta Kappan, November 1978,
p. 12.

range of the classroom. Furthermore, such exciting, immediate stimuli are probably not well suited to many of the intellectual demands of school. Learning takes time, careful thought, and sometimes is a painfully slow process. Learning also needs the active mental engagement of the learner, rather than the passivity of the viewer.

Television may make it harder to reach children. As we saw earlier in this chapter, teachers complain that their students are too passive. They find it difficult to engage them in the classroom. One side of this may be the psychology of television watching—the passivity, the waiting to be entertained, that characterizes the tube. On the other hand, teachers say that students come to them knowing more. This may be the effect of the content of television.

For example, television news programs, often a part of family viewing, depict graphic violence that would gain many movies an "R" rating; cartoons are filled with violent acts that have no lasting effects on the show's characters; evening shows depict adults as using alcohol to relax and sex as a vehicle for either friendship or personal advancement. Television makes it difficult to keep anything from children. By the time a child reaches sixth grade he or she has seen it all.

No wonder teachers see today's students as knowing more—there is literally nothing kept from them. However, today's children may not know what they think they know. Their ability to separate fact from fiction is limited because they have little prior experience to use for judging others' actions. Ignorance about the realities of daily life may lead them to believe that the flickering images on the television screen are all there is to adult life.

In these ways the media, especially television, help to mold many of the peer pressures that students face. Seeing no barrier to adulthood, they pressure one another to grow up fast. Children are thus hurried by peers, social pressures, and the media to grow up too fast, too soon.

THE HURRIED CHILD

■ Recently, an entire body of literature has focused on the social phenomenon of "the hurried child." Works by Elkind, Postman, and Winn all point out the pressures on children to grow up too fast, too soon.[17] This concept is the best way to understand the combined effects of the social forces we have been discussing.

☐ The Social Construction of Childhood

Childhood as we know it is a relatively recent social construct. In fact, as Postman points out, up until the 15th and 16th centuries, children were merely viewed as miniature adults. There was no distinction made between adults and children in terms of dress, social manners, and living quarters. Most importantly, there were no social secrets kept from children. Children were exposed to adult problems and activities virtually from birth. This lack of separation from adults and no withholding of secrets was due to a number of factors, including short life span, poverty that made separate living quarters impossible, and the need for all family members to work. But the most important factor was the existence of primarily an oral culture.

Before the invention of the printing press, most knowledge was transmitted in either an oral or visual manner. Thus, the only precondition for entering into adulthood, accessing all that the culture had to offer, was the ability to speak and comprehend the language. With the printing press, developed in the middle of the 15th century, a new barrier to becoming an adult rose—one had to be able to read. This new definition of adulthood gave rise to a new definition of childhood.

Gradually, childhood became a period of protected status. Children were not presumed to be capable of living an adult life from the time they were able to speak. Rather, adulthood was something children were gradually brought into through the transmission of adult skills. This made it possible to keep secrets from children, social and personal secrets, since they were not immediately able to access the world of print.

This is not to say that childhood burst forth fully developed from the printing press. It only gradually spread to the middle and lower social classes. Early in this century we still witnessed children hard at work in factories alongside adults for 10 to 12 hours a day. It took child labor laws to bar these children from the ravages of industrial labor. Behind this legislation was a well-developed principle—that childhood was to be a protected period. Childhood is a time in which the immature mind gradually opens up to the world of adult secrets, dreams, hopes, and responsibilities. The question we now pursue is whether this distinction between children and adults is now disappearing.

☐ **The Disappearance of Childhood**

The last 20 years have seen a dramatic increase in children displaying adult behaviors. Among children, violent crime, drug and alcohol abuse, pregnancy, tobacco use, and suicide rates have all increased since the early 1960s. The figures are deeply troubling: the National Institute on Alcohol Abuse and Alcoholism estimates that 1.3 million children between the ages of 12 and 17 have serious drinking problems; in the 1960s, 10% of teenagers were sexually active as compared with 60% today; there are 5,000 teenage suicides a year, out of 500,000 attempts.[18]

We touched on a variety of these trends above in suggesting that all our children are at risk today. But how can we understand these trends in order to do something about them? The best way to see it may be as the erosion of childhood.

On one hand, it is a product of hurrying children to grow up. Parents, seeing this as an ever more competitive world, hurry their children to progress in school in the competition for jobs. Other parents, under financial or marital stress, expect their children to take over the adult tasks of running a home or raising siblings. Schools hurry children to succeed in adult endeavors on the sports field as younger and younger children are organized into teams meant to replicate professional sports. New pressures to measure all student academic performance hurry children to learn as much as possible for the standardized examinations.

There is a commercial side to this hurrying as well. Children are once again, as in the Middle Ages, encouraged to dress like adults. Fashions seem to vary only in size from age group to age group. Music with explicit lyrics dealing with sex and violence is the daily fare of radio stations aimed at children from ages 7 to 17. Our youth are more and more seen as a consuming public to be exploited.

Additionally, it seems no longer important to keep secrets from children. The clearest example of this is the influence of television.

RESEARCH NOTES 5.3   Young Worries

Worry	5th	9th
School performance	54%	60
My looks	42	57
How well other kids like me	45	47
Parent might die	50	41
How my friends treat me	42	45
Hunger and poverty	52	31
Violence in U.S.	43	30
Might lose best friend	40	29
Drugs and drinking	40	32
Might not get good job	31	30
Physical development	31	17
Nuclear destruction	29	21
Parents might divorce	30	13
That I may die soon	26	13
Sexual abuse	23	14
Friends will get me in trouble	25	13
Drinking by a parent	21	11
Getting beat up at school	18	9
Physical abuse by parent	17	9
That I might kill myself	16	9

5TH - - - - - - -
9TH _____

From *Young Adolescents and Their Parents,* a study conducted by the Search Institute, of Minneapolis. Eight thousand students were asked which of the following worried them "very much" or "quite a bit." The chart contrasts the responses of fifth graders and ninth graders.

Above we pointed out Postman's argument that television eliminates the possibility of concealing things from the young. Graphic violence, sex, and human tragedy and suffering is easily accessible in every home at every hour of the day. In this way, childhood ceases to become a gradual period of protected maturation. Instead, in a throwback to when there was no childhood, as soon as a child can understand the language and visual images of the television screen he or she may enter the adult world.

One graphic example of this is the range of adult social problems of which children are now aware. As we see in Research Notes 5.3, childhood worries go well beyond just school performance and peer acceptance. We may be happy that young people are concerned about these problems. Yet if they are so tied up in their worries about problems that are now beyond their control, what will that do to their own personal development?

It is important to note we are not suggesting that young people should turn inward, concerning themselves only with their own lives. But the issue is how to make sure children are personally stable before facing the types of difficult issues we face as adults. Simply put, do we want childhood to disappear?

Much of this disappearance of childhood is taken for granted and seldom do we stop to ponder if this is a move for the good. The issue is whether or not children are both psychologically and socially ready to grow up as fast as we seem to want them to. Perhaps by hurrying them as we do we deny them the opportunity to be all that they can be. As children jump into adult life and activities they often do so in ways that are self-destructive. We saw above how the choices children make today are so serious that they may alter their lives forever.

FOCUS 5.2   All Grown Up and No Place to Go

by David Elkind

Sigmund Freud was once asked to describe the characteristics of maturity, and he replied: lieben and arbeiten ("loving and working"). The mature adult is one who can love and allow himself or herself to be loved and can work productively, meaningfully, and with satisfaction. Yet most adolescents, and certainly all children are really not able to work or to love in the mature way that Freud had in mind. Children love their parents in a far different way from how they will love a real or potential mate. And many, probably most, young people will not find their life work until they are well into young adulthood.

When children are expected to dress, act, and think as adults, they are being asked to playact, because all of the trappings of adulthood do not in any way make them adults in the true sense of lieben and arbeiten. It is ironic that the very parents who won't allow their children to believe in Santa Claus or the Easter Bunny (because they are fantasy and therefore dishonest) allow their children to dress and behave as adults without any sense of the tremendous dishonesty involved in allowing children to present themselves in this grown-up way.

It is certainly true that the trend toward obscuring the divisions between children and adults is part of a broad egalitarian movement in this country that seeks to overcome the barriers separating the sexes, ethnic and racial groups, and the handicapped. We see these trends in unisex clothing and hairstyles, in the call for equal pay for equal work, in the demands for affirmative action, and in the appeals and legislation that provide the handicapped with equal opportunities for education and meaningful jobs.

From this perspective, the contemporary pressure for children to grow up fast is only one symptom of a much larger social phenomenon in this country—a movement toward true equality, toward the ideal expressed in our Declaration of Independence. While one can only applaud this movement with respect to sexes, ethnic and racial groups, and the handicapped, its unthinking extension to children is unfortunate.

Children need time to grow, to learn, and to develop. To treat them differently from adults is not to discriminate against them but rather to recognize their special estate. Similarly, when we provide bilingual programs for Hispanic children, we are not discriminating against them but responding to the special needs they have, which, if not attended to, would prevent them from attaining a successful education and true equality. In the same way, building ramps for handicapped students is a means to their attaining equal opportunity. Recognizing special needs is not discriminatory; on the contrary, it is the only way that true equality can be attained.

All children have, vis-a-vis adults, special needs—intellectual, social, and emotional. Children do not learn, think, or feel in the same way as adults. To ignore these differences, to treat children as adults, is really not democratic or egalitarian. If we ignore the special needs of children, we are behaving just as if we denied Hispanic or Indian children bilingual programs, or denied the handicapped their ramps and guideposts. In truth, the recognition of a group's special needs and accommodation to those needs are the only true ways to insure equality and true equal opportunity.

From David Elkind, *The Hurried Child: Growing Up Too Fast Too Soon* (Reading, Mass.: Addison-Wesley, 1981), pp. 20–22.

As educators we need to think carefully about the role we play in this process. Given the problems children now face, what should the school provide? Should we take part in the hurrying process in order to equip students to deal with the pressures they face? Or is there an alternative that challenges the assumptions of the disappearance of childhood in which we could engage?

THE CHALLENGE FOR THE TEACHER

■ Clearly, it is a very difficult world for children of all ages. The pressures they face to grow up and become adults cause them to engage in a variety of dangerous behaviors. Much of this lands at the schoolhouse door. The social problems children face come with them to school, not only in the more overt behaviors, but in the covert, internalized problems children have. Preoccupied with family distress, a parent's loss of work, pregnancy, dating, drugs, and world problems, our students often seem physically present yet intellectually and emotionally absent from the classroom.

It is possible to just ignore these problems, to go on teaching as if we all come from a safe and sane world or to act as if childhood is not under attack when we face a classroom failure. Certainly this is a recipe for classroom failure, in which content is covered yet not learned.

We suggest that teachers need to be aware of the pressures of childhood and deal with them directly. A positive self-concept is necessary for school success. Clearly, many of the pressures on children work against such a positive understanding of self. How can schools and classrooms become places that deal with a more positive notion of childhood and its possibilities?

□ The Hope

The Children

The argument could easily be made that in this chapter too many negative things have been said about children. Intentionally, this has been the case. Problems that children face cannot be underestimated and must be presented in the most direct terms possible. But this does not mean that every child succumbs to such pressures.

Look around your community and note all the positive things in which children are engaged. Find how many places they volunteer their time and their energies for the good of the community or neighborhood. The list of activities and groups and clubs is probably endless. Additionally, charity drives can always count on children for vast amounts of support.

In schools, we find children involved in a wide variety of positive projects. Music groups of all types and levels offer frequent concerts. Drama groups put on plays and skits for both the student body and the community. Newspapers and yearbooks are published, often on students' own time. These are only a sampling of the activities that can be found in elementary, middle or junior high, and high schools.

Students are the community's most valuable resource.

The best hope for childhood begins with children themselves. Their desires to make sense of their world and perhaps to make it better is manifested in many of the projects just mentioned. The teacher's task is to draw on that resource base and recognize childhood for all its possibilities as well as problems.

Their Parents

Often forgotten in our discussions of childhood are parents. They are too frequently cast as the villains, and it is easy to forget how difficult parenting can be. Virtually all parents hope that their children will succeed—which may mean different things to different parents.

FOR REFLECTION 5.2　The Best Our Kids Can Be

While much is said about the problems and troubles for childhood, little is reported about the good children do in our communities. Of course, not to be overlooked is the fact that we should value children in our communities just for who they are, children. As such, they often give common purpose and meaning to our communities.

Additionally, we often find children active in a variety of very positive ways. Take some time to survey your community with respect to the following questions:

1. In what specific ways do children add to the health and well-being of our communities?
2. What projects have groups of children undertaken to make this a better place to live?
3. What clubs and groups are made up primarily of children in this community and how do they add to its strength?
4. What could we as adults do to make the positive activities of children more possible?
5. Interview adults in the community to find out which they would prefer, a neighborhood with or without children, and why.

Unfortunately, parents have become a target of much of the campaign to hurry children. Today parents are led to believe that they can give children a head start by working on academic skills with babies still in the crib. Psychologists are reporting an increase in the number of stressed children ages 3, 4, and 5 that they are seeing.[19] Frequently, they report that this is due to parental attempts to accelerate learning prior to entering school. Exclusive preschools spring up daily promising parents an academic program that will get their children started on the road to an Ivy League college or university.

Concerned with their children's future in a world of seemingly diminishing opportunities parents often, for all the best reasons, hurry their children with unfortunate side effects. What is not to be missed here is the genuine concerns of parents for their children. Given the problems children face, the task for the teacher is to turn that concern into positive support and action for teaching and learning.

Communities

At their best, our communities and neighborhoods offer the perfect haven for childhood. When they are tightly knit, but not exclusive, they offer children the chance to explore the world without risk.

For example, civic associations can provide protected space for play and recreation. Youth clubs offer children places to deal with their problems, finding solutions in something other than drugs or alcohol. Special interest groups encourage children to try to develop new talents and interests without the pressure of failure.

The school should and can be a vital part of the community. John Dewey suggested that schools replicate communities where all individuals are valued for their contribution to the collective whole. Projects like the Foxfire program in Georgia draw from community resources to build a curriculum that helps students appreciate their culture and roots.[20] In Atlanta, students are required to complete over 75 hours of community service work before graduating.

Each of these programs and recommendations have, at their center, one aim: to integrate the best of school and community so that students will have a protected place to mature. They seek both to recover childhood and also to reaffirm all the best things about our children today. This is also the task of the classroom teacher.

CHAPTER SUMMARY

■ What can teachers do in the face of this onslaught faced by children? In this chapter we have considered the many problems children must face and the pressure on them to grow up fast. Certainly many of these are social problems for which the school cannot be held responsible. Yet it seems unjustified to suggest that teachers ignore these problems. The problems children face do affect academic performance, reducing for many children their ability to learn. They also damage self-concept, again hindering learning. Finally, if we are concerned with the learner as well as learning we simply cannot ignore what does seem to be the disappearance of childhood.

Teachers can do something positive to help children grow and mature in socially, psychologically, and academically sound ways. It requires that they confront the problems faced by children with all the human resources (children, parents, communities) at their disposal. And the task requires constructing a space where children are valued for what they are, that is, children, rather than for what they might be.

Simply put, schools and classrooms need to become places where childhood is possible. Children need a place where they are not rushed to grow up, but encouraged to grow at their own pace; where they are encouraged to experiment, think, and discover without fear of failure. Perhaps the best way to put this is to say that schools need to become islands of decency in a fundamentally indecent world.

What would decent classrooms look like? They would be communities in the best sense where everyone was valued both for what he or she is as well as for his or her addition to the shared community; places where the self-worth of all individuals is fostered. They would be closely connected with parents and the larger community in order to seek the task of schooling as part of the larger social task of fostering humane, self-directed individuals. How to build such classrooms is the focus of much of the rest of this text.

FOR DISCUSSION

1. We often look to standardized test scores to see how children are doing in schools. Are there other indicators of school success that should be examined? If so, what are they and how would we use them to determine school success or failure?

2. What pressures do you feel students might be under today that were not present as you were growing up? How might that make growing up more difficult?

3. Television is often seen as an enemy of childhood. Why would someone see that as being the case? Do you agree or disagree with that claim? Why?

4. How might some of the problems faced by students today affect the job teachers do? Be specific, give examples.

5. Should teachers and the school deal directly with the social problems students face? Or, rather, are there ways of indirectly dealing with them that are more within the scope of the school?

IN THE SCHOOL/IN THE CLASSROOM

1. Throughout this chapter we have mentioned a variety of problems that children face. Using this material, compile your own list of potential childhood problems. Survey students at a variety of grade levels to see how much these problems affect their lives. Compare your results with those in the text and with those of other students. Focus on the following questions:

    a. What seem to be the most important problems faced by students today?

    b. Do these problems change by grade level? If so, why?

    c. How could these problems affect student performance in school?

    d. What challenges do these problems present for teachers?

2. Find some of the more experienced teachers in your building. Ask them if they have noticed a change in students over the years. Probe their answers, seeing if you can answer the following questions:

    a. What, if any, changes have occurred in the student body? (This might include demographic changes as well as social or psychological changes).

    b. When did these changes begin?

    c. To what would you attribute these changes?

    d. What do these changes mean for the teacher's job?

SUGGESTED READINGS

Children's Defense Fund, The. *A Children's Defense Budget*. Washington, D.C.: The Children's Defense Fund, yearly. This is one of the most comprehensive surveys of the status of youth at risk available. Published yearly by the Children's Defense Fund, an action group concerned with child welfare, it is full of information on public spending on children. It does an excellent job of comparing money spent on children as compared to defense, and so on.

Elkind, David. *All Grown Up and No Place To Go*. Reading, Mass.: Addison-Wesley, 1984. A sequel to his *The Hurried Child,* here Elkind looks at the problems of adolescence. His argument is that by forcing teenagers to become adults too fast we force them into many of the problems they face. He suggests alternatives to hurrying, focusing on creating safe spaces for kids to grow up within.

Elkind, David. *The Hurried Child: Growing Up Too Fast Too Soon*. Reading, Mass.: Addison-Wesley, 1981. The first of Elkind's important studies on the pressures facing today's children. Concerned mostly with preteens, Elkind focuses on the forces that hurry children in growing up. In particular, he looks at families, schools, and the media. Important reading for those concerned with helping children grow and mature positively.

Grubb, W. Norton, and Marvin Lazerson. *Broken Promises: How Americans Fail Their Children*. New York: Basic Books, 1983. An investigation of the history of public policy toward children. The focus is on whether or not public policy has actually had children at its center, or as an afterthought. A wide ranging historical study with implications for current policy and practice inside schools.

Postman, Neil. *The Disappearance of Childhood.* New York: Dell, 1983. Postman's impassioned study of the historical rise and fall of childhood. He traces how childhood as a social construct came into being and how it is rapidly disappearing. It is a critique of mass media and the ways in which television forces children to grow up before they are ready by exposing them to adult secrets.

Winn, Marie. *Children Without Childhood.* New York: Pantheon Books, 1981. Winn is also concerned with the historical evolution of childhood. She works to point out the sociological roots of current social treatment of children and how this treatment denies children the space they need to grow. Her argument focuses on the psychological development of both children and parents.

Winn, Marie. *The Plug-In Drug: Television, Children, and the Family.* Rev. ed. New York: Penguin Books, 1985. This classic study of the effects of television on children was first published in 1977. It now includes material on video games, computers, and television in the school. The key issue is how the passive act of watching television affects the developing child's relationship to the real world.

CHAPTER REFERENCES

1. Glenbard East *Echo, Teenagers Themselves* (New York: Adama Books, 1984), pp. 69–71.
2. Lynn Olson, "9-Point Jump in S.A.T. Scores Is Highest in 22 Years," *Education Week,* October 2, 1985, pp. 5, 16.
3. Velema Plisko and Joyce Stern, eds., *The Condition of Education: 1985 Edition, A Statistical Report* (Washington, D.C.: National Center for Educational Statistics, 1985). These figures are for 18- and 19-year-olds.
4. From *Statistical Abstracts of the United States: 1985–86* (Washington, D.C.: U.S. Bureau of the Census, 1987).
5. Jeanette Lauer and Robert Lauer, "Marriages Made to Last," *Psychology Today* 19, (June 1985): 22–26.
6. Arnold L. Stolbery and James M. Anker, "Cognitive and Behavioral Changes in Children Resulting from Parental Divorce and Consequent Environmental Changes," *The Journal of Divorce* 7, no. 2 (Winter 1983): 23–41.
7. Charles Leerhsen, "Reading, Writing, and Divorce," *Newsweek,* May 13, 1984, p. 74.
8. C. Emily Feistritzer, *Cheating Our Children* (Washington, D.C.: National Center for Education Information, 1985).
9. James Mann, "An Endless Parade of Runaway Kids," *U.S. News and World Report,* January 17, 1983, pp. 64–65.

10. Deborah Burnett Strother, "Latchkey Children: The Fastest Growing Special Interest Group in the U.S.," *Phi Delta Kappan,* December 1984, pp. 290–293.

11. Lloyd Johnston, *Use of Licit and Illicit Drugs by America's High School Students, 1975–1984* (Ann Arbor, Mich.: The University of Michigan Institute for Social Research, 1984).

12. Kenneth E. John, "Teenagers Say Drug Abuse Is the Biggest Problem Facing Them," *The Washington Post Weekly Edition,* January 14, 1985, p. 39.

13. Nadine Brozan, "U.S. Leads Industrialized Nations in Teenage Births and Abortions," *New York Times,* March 13, 1985, pp. 1, 22.

14. Jerry Adler, "A Teen-Pregnancy Epidemic," *Newsweek,* March 25, 1985, p. 90.

15. Ibid.

16. Marie Winn, *The Plug-In Drug* (New York: Penguin Books, 1985), p. 4.

17. David Elkind, *The Hurried Child: Growing Up Too Fast Too Soon* (Reading, Mass.: Addison-Wesley, 1981) and *All Grown Up and No Place To Go* (Reading, Mass.: Addison-Wesley, 1984); Neil Postman, *The Disappearance of Childhood* (New York: Basic Books, 1983); Marie Winn, *Children Without Childhood* (New York: Pantheon Books, 1981).

18. Elkind, *All Grown Up and No Place To Go,* Chapter 1.

19. Elkind, *The Hurried Child,* Chapter 1.

20. See Eliot Wigginton, *Sometimes A Shining Moment: The Foxfire Experience* (New York: Doubleday, 1985).

6

Communicating with Students

■ Marcia and Pam were sharing a cup of coffee in the teachers' lounge before school.

"You had Loretta last year in first grade, did you have any problems with her?" Pam asked Marcia.

"Well . . . no, not really. Oh, she required a bit more attention than some of the other children, but she wanted to cooperate." Actually, Marcia thought to herself, she was one of my best students.

Pam went on, "Well, I can't get a thing out of her this year. She doesn't do her work, doesn't pay attention, doesn't seem to have any intention of being involved in my class."

"Really," Marcia said, "well, she must have changed a lot in one year." But I know better than that, her thoughts to herself continued. It has more to do with Pam than with Loretta.

That night Marcia shared with her husband, a high school teacher, the situation at school with Loretta and her teacher, Pam. "Loretta is a wonderful little girl. She was one of my bright spots last year. But this year, well, I'm just hoping that there isn't too much damage done to Loretta."

"You might explain this a bit more," John, her husband, replied.

"Well, it's simple, really. Pam does little in her classroom to make it a place where children want to be. It's only her first year, so I can understand it when her methods or plans fail. But the problems come when she doesn't admit those failures and try to adjust. She tries to force kids to learn."

"And this really doesn't work with Loretta?" asked John.

"Especially not Loretta," continued Marcia. "Kids like Loretta, all kids, need to have communicated to them that they matter in the classroom. You can't force them to work, you have to encourage them to work. But when there is nothing about the classroom that *invites* students to learn they have little incentive to be involved."

"That's funny, I've been thinking about the same problem at the high school," John interrupted. "While some teachers rarely have problems with students, others seem to have them all the time. And that isn't to say that some teachers are easy and so kids like them. No, I think some teachers communicate clearly to kids that they like them and like being there. Others, well the kids see them as just drawing a paycheck."

"And to hear your students talk, you're one of the communicating kind," added Marcia. "That's why you're always asked to be involved in their activities—and why they work so hard for you."

"Well, thanks, some days it doesn't seem that way though," John laughed. "But that doesn't solve Loretta and Pam's problem."

"I know, I know," Marcia shook her head. "I just don't know what to do. I mean, I can't confront Pam about her teaching—and I won't take anyone's side against Loretta. If only Pam would open up the lines of communication in her class."

INTRODUCTION

■ Opening up the lines of classroom communication is what this chapter is about. We believe that classroom communication is one of the most important yet difficult and often overlooked aspects of teaching. As one educational researcher has put it:

> Teaching and communication are inseparable. Teachers' success with students is to a large extent related to their competence and effectiveness as communicators. Many variables and factors can affect whether or not someone learns in the classroom, but there is little argument that a teacher's communicative effectiveness is among the most important. In fact, learning cannot occur without communication.[1]

Here we explore the ways in which teachers can effectively communicate with their students. This will not include the technical aspects of public speaking, although all teachers should be able to speak with clarity and precision. Rather, we will focus on the messages teachers send to their students. This refers to what they communicate in terms of student worth, values, and beliefs through not only what they say, but *how* they say it. This is where communication in the classroom gets complicated.

To examine classroom communication we will divide this chapter into two parts. The first will look at barriers to effective communication. The second part will look at tools teachers have at their disposal to promote effective classroom communication. In both cases we will look at the actions of the individual teacher as well as those of the school system. By doing this we hope to introduce you to the tools available to communicate most effectively with those for whom the school exists—the students.

BARRIERS TO EFFECTIVE CLASSROOM COMMUNICATION

■ Walk into any classroom and observe carefully—you will be amazed at the amount and diversity of communication taking place. One moment the teacher addresses the entire class; later, students ask questions about an assignment. There are small group discussions, animated and often boisterous. Or the room may be very quiet as the teacher walks from student to student asking questions, giving advice.

Of course, that is only half the picture: the verbal half. Additionally, nonverbal messages are being sent from student to teacher, teacher to student, and back again. A glance from the teacher toward an unruly group brings quiet. A smile to the same group encourages them to keep at a project they are having success with. A pat on the back, or a hug, brings renewed effort from a student working hard at a problem that confused her. Rapt attention by students as they lean forward to catch every word tells the teacher that the book she is reading is one they enjoy.

In each classroom such communication between students and teacher goes on every day. In fact, Phillip Jackson in one of the first major studies of classroom communication recorded over 1,000 daily interactions between elementary school teachers and their pupils.[2] The importance of these interactions and their effects on students cannot be overlooked. They each communicate to students what is important and what is not, what is acceptable and what is not, and often which students are valued and which are not.

Unfortunately, some of these messages are unintended. And most frequently, these unintended messages communicate negative expectations to students. This was Pam's problem with Loretta; Pam was telling her through both words and actions that she was not an important and valued member of the class. In response, Loretta refused to participate.

We can change the negative messages we send students—the barriers to communication we erect—only by being aware of them. In this section we discuss those barriers so that we might then move on to tools for more effective classroom communication.

☐ **Teachers' Verbal and Nonverbal Messages to Students**

The most obvious way in which teachers erect barriers to effective communication with students is through their verbal and nonverbal behavior in the classroom. As we noted above, teachers engage in almost a limitless number of exchanges with their students every day. Through these we let our students know what we think and feel about their work, their behavior, and their personalities. Often the messages students receive are not those that encourage them to achieve in the classroom.

It's More Than Talk
WHAT GETS SAID   Pay close attention to what a teacher says to students the next time you get the chance. How often are students praised or encouraged? How often does the teacher literally tell students that he or she is excited about being their teacher and enjoys being with them? Unfortunately, in many classrooms such statements are not frequently heard.

In fact, research demonstrates that teachers may spend only about 2% of their time praising or encouraging students. On the other hand, nearly 5% of class time can be spent on criticizing students.[3] It shouldn't surprise us that students do not respond well in classrooms where criticism is more prevalent than praise.

Besides an overuse of criticism, several other verbal barriers to communication exist. The use of sarcasm is seldom effective in communicating with students, because it is most often misunderstood and taken personally. Humiliating students in front of their peers always hinders future communication and students will try to save face in some way rather than address what you see as the problem. Also merely raising one's voice, making threats, or demanding attention has little positive effect on classroom communication.

The best way to think about verbal behaviors that are barriers to classroom communication is to reflect on your own experience. Does criticism motivate you more than praise? Do you prefer sarcasm over honest criticism? Do you enjoy other people humiliating you in front of your friends and peers? Most likely the answer to all three questions is no, that is not how you want to be treated. And it is probably not the way to treat your future students.

WHO GETS TO TALK   In addition to looking at what gets said, it is important to look at who gets to talk in the classroom. If classrooms are to be places with positive learning climates, that requires teachers and students to be able to freely communicate with one another. Unfortunately, available research seems to indicate that the communication climate in most classrooms is very limited.

John Goodlad's *A Place Called School,* based on observations in nearly 1,000 elementary and secondary classrooms, came to the conclusion that the emotional tone of the American classroom is "flat."[4] While 70% of classroom time is given over to verbal instruction, student talk takes up less than 20% of that time. More notably, barely 5% of the instructional time is spent on direct questioning, with less than 1% of that time spent on open-ended questions. Less than 5% of class time is spent responding to students, while students spend 10% (secondary level) to 15% (elementary level) of classroom time responding to teachers. Finally, less than 3% of classroom time is given over to positive, or even negative, statements of affect. "In other words, the affect present over 95 percent of the time can best be described as neutral."[5]

The picture that emerges is of quiet classrooms, with teachers lecturing, and students occasionally called on to answer questions. Certainly, teacher lecture is called for occasionally. But if students are to enjoy schooling, to expand both their creative and intellectual powers, and to have experience in communicating with others, a broader use of verbal options in the classroom is required.

FOCUS 6.1   Just Two Words

by Robert Lucking

I have an obsession. While I like to think that in most situations I am capable of maintaining my composure, undulating in life's ebb and flow, I walk into an elementary classroom and nearly always lose control. I listen to the dialogue between teacher and children, and I soon become a green-skinned monster tearing at my hair and flesh in anguish. So what triggers this fevered fury although I normally conduct myself in a reasonable fashion? Two words do it for me; just two words cause me to feel pain for those youngsters and resent the linguistic climate in which they are held captive. Those two words are "tell me."

Over and over I hear teachers asking children questions, hundreds of them, and the vast majority of those questions begin with "tell me." Those queries are presented as follows: "Who can tell me the noun in this sentence?" "Can you tell me if this is a long vowel or short vowel?" "Tell me which syllable is accented." I want to be transmigrated immediately to one of those young bodies and shout to the teacher. "No, I will not tell you. I will tell my classmates, I will tell myself, but I will not tell you. I am not here for your benefit; I am here for my education." I want to plead with that teacher to let me learn, make me learn, for my own pleasure and self-fulfillment, not for the sake of the teacher. Every time I hear those two venal words I have visions of a hoop being held up for me to jump through to satisfy some distorted sense of pleasure, the same sense of pleasure derived from seeing one's dog clear the hoop.

Unfortunately, those two words are only too typical of the many indicators of the locus of authority in the classroom, and they are a part of a larger scheme in which teachers establish dominance in the discourse sustained in that classroom. Researchers have validated quite clearly teachers' proclivity for monopolizing the dialogue in their instruction. The teacher sets forth the questions; however, the majority of these queries call for student responses which are brief and simple. The pace is fast and predictable, and such an environment cannot be seen as nurturing children's expressive abilities or inclinations.

The structures that are placed on the flow of language in a classroom are also evident in question-answer routines which take place. Students are asked to engage in a "discussion" of a topic; however, they are quick to realize that their role is an insignificant one. And if that realization should be slow in forming, teachers tend to be direct in communicating just who will be engaged in talk and under what circumstances. The teacher has the right to speak at any time, to determine the topic, to select the speaker, and to ascertain the quality of that speech. Children are asked for isolated facts that provide the teacher with an opportunity to explain a concept or react to an idea. Students are called upon to bark out answers to a barrage of questions, and once again the image comes to mind of a dog performing tricks to please a master.

Perhaps even more revealing is the manner in which teachers respond to students' answers. Research shows that teachers tend to wait less than a full second before responding to what a child has said. Such a brief time span clearly indicates less than a thoughtful response to the ideas of children. Additionally, that teacher response is usually judgmental, intended ostensibly to provide positive reinforcement for correct answers. While it may be an old joke, the story of the boy who is asked a question by his teacher bears repeating here. It seems that Johnny was asked by his teacher, "Who can tell me what four plus three are?"

Johnny replied, "Seven."

"Good!" said the teacher with emphasis and enthusiasm.

"Good?" Johnny smirked, "Hell, that's perfect!"

Perhaps the majority of children's answers are perfect, and perhaps the greatest tribute a teacher can pay to a child's ideas is respect and a considered pondering of those remarks.

Classroom dialogue is often very unnatural and contrived. I wonder how many teachers have imagined being invited to someone's house for dinner and being asked by the host "Who can tell me about the political situation in Central America?" and then being told "Good" as praise for their opinion. All children develop their understanding of functions of language in a human context where real consequences hinge on the exchange of words, they learn competence by putting language to work expressing feelings, formulating ideas, and gathering information. If teachers are to capitalize on the intrinsic excitement of language at work in the classroom, they will have to surrender some of their authority in the manner in which they involve children in talk and in the manner in which they respond to talk. Only through the creation of a more natural, spontaneous environment might we find children who are skilled at giving verbal shape to ideas rather than barking to satisfy those two words.

From Robert Lucking, "Just Two Words," *Language Arts* 62 (February 1985): 173–174.

It's How You Say It

Patrick Miller, in a review of research on nonverbal communication for the National Education Association, has pointed out five reasons why humans rely on nonverbal communication. These include:

1. Words have limitations in displaying affect or emotion.
2. Nonverbal signals are powerful.
3. Nonverbal messages are more likely to be genuine.
4. Feelings too disturbing to state are often more easily displayed nonverbally.
5. Complex messages often need more than one channel for effective communication.[6]

Since we rely so heavily on nonverbal messages in general, it makes sense that teachers should be aware of their use in the classroom. In this section we examine teacher nonverbal behaviors that discourage classroom communication.

We all remember the classrooms in which we felt it was clear that our input was not wanted. We sat quietly, even cautiously, hoping not to offend the teacher's "excellent" classroom control. Yet the consequence of this control is to squelch students, to limit their input, and to make them feel that the classroom is an uninviting, if not fearful, place. As students are convinced they have little to add to the classroom, they avoid attempting to contribute. They often adopt a strategy of simply getting through a class, surviving it in order to do other things.

What are some of the nonverbal behaviors that discourage communication? The first, according to Charles Galloway, is simply inattention. Often we find our minds wandering when listening to someone. While we hope they do not notice, our features often give us away as we avoid eye contact, or our gestures and posture communicate impatience, preoccupation, or concern with other thoughts.[7] What do we tell students when we exhibit this type of behavior? No doubt it

Communicating with students depends upon listening to what they say.

rapidly becomes clear to students, as it would to anyone, that what they have to say is not very important. The message is that they are just not worth listening to. It doesn't take much of this sort of treatment to convince a student to stop trying to contribute in class.

The unresponding teacher can generate the same reaction. If a teacher fails to respond to students' questions, ignores students' nonverbal signals such as raised hands or questioning looks, or withdraws physically from the classroom, students soon stop trying to reach the teacher. The teacher who sits behind the desk or stands out in the hall while class goes on is telling students not to bother him or her.

Perhaps the most powerful nonverbal tools for cutting off communication are signs of disapproval. Simple frowns, scowls, or threatening glances inhibit communication. Another such weapon is the pointed finger. Pointing at someone when addressing them indicates superiority (how often do teachers point at principals, or principals at superintendents?). It can be a way of demeaning students, or showing them their place. Similarly, the teacher who guards the door with arms crossed tells students who is in charge and who are to take orders. All these signals work to put students in the position of feeling that their efforts are not valued by their teacher.

These examples are just a sampling of the nonverbal behaviors that can limit teacher-student communication. You can probably think of others you have seen displayed in classrooms. What is important to remember about all of them is that actions do speak louder than words. Galloway elaborates: "When the nonverbal cues are not congruent with the verbal, they (students) accept the nonverbal as the more valid."[8]

□ **Communicating Expectations and Stereotypes**

Imagine that within the first few days of your education class you notice that the instructor pays more attention to some students than others. These students soon find seats in the front of the class, they are called on more often, they take part in discussions more frequently, and the teacher praises them frequently. The rest of you seem almost ignored. When it comes time for group work the students who sit in the front all seem to be grouped together while the rest of you are put in separate groups. Soon, you begin to realize the instructor has differing expectations for the students in the class, perhaps based on academic major, past academic record, race, gender, or even appearance. Think for a minute about how you would react in each case. If you were placed in the group for which the instructor had high expectations do you think you would respond with greater effort? Or if you were put in a group for which the instructor held low expectations would you respond with decreased effort or even resentment?

This may all sound farfetched to you, yet in the elementary through high school levels we find this treatment of students frequently. The way we organize the classrooms and schools communicates to students what we expect of them—and students react to these expectations. Only when we become aware of this form of communication can we constructively alter it.

Pygmalion in the Classroom
You may have heard of or seen the classic George Bernard Shaw play *Pygmalion,* which was later turned into the movie *My Fair Lady.* In it, Eliza Dolittle, a flower girl from the streets of London, was taken under the wing of a well-to-do university researcher. His plan was to change her into a "refined" lady whom no one would recognize as being

from "lowly" origins. Not only was the experiment successful, but the two are wed at the end of the play.

The effect of the professor's expectations on Ms. Dolittle has come to be known as the "Pygmalion effect"; because the professor believed Eliza could change her behavior, she did. Of course, this was due to the careful work by the professor because of his expectations. Additionally, Eliza reacted to the attention paid her in a positive way and began to believe in herself and her own potential.

First explored in schooling by Robert Rosenthal and Lenore Jacobson, this effect is also known as the self-fulfilling prophecy.[9] In schooling there are actually two forms of prophecy. On one hand, there is the self-fulfilling prophecy, and on the other hand, the sustaining prophecy. Good and Brophy discuss them as follows:

> A self-fulfilling prophecy occurs when an erroneous belief leads to behavior that makes [an] original false belief become true. Self-fulfilling prophecies are the most dramatic form of teacher expectation effects because they involve *changes* in student behavior. . . . The term sustaining expectations refers to situations in which teachers fail to see student potential and hence do not respond in a way to encourage some students to fulfill their potential. In summary, self-fulfilling expectations bring about a change in student performance, whereas sustaining expectations prevent change.[10]

As mentioned above, Rosenthal and Jacobson's work first created interest in these effects in the classroom. While their work has since been much debated, it is of value to us in understanding the power of teacher expectations. Their experiment involved administering a test to several classes in grades one through six. They told teachers that the test had identified "bloomers" in their classes, students who would do well academically that year. Even though the test told them no such thing, at the end of the year those students labeled as bloomers had indeed bloomed. More importantly, those students who were not labeled as bloomers but who did bloom were viewed negatively by teachers.[11]

The researchers hypothesized that teacher expectations about these children had caused the teachers to act differently toward them. The children, in turn, responded to this increased attention and progressed academically as expected. The process became a cycle as this academic success brought on more positive attention, yielding more success, and so on.

Mentioned above was the fact that there has been some controversy over these findings. In particular, students may reject the expectations communicated to them if they are too out of line with reality, or teachers may not be good at communicating their expectations to students.[12] However, it does seem clear that the expectations of teachers when communicated to students can and do have an effect on their achievement and success. How we communicate negative expectations through classroom structure is discussed in what follows.

COMMUNICATING NEGATIVE EXPECTATIONS THROUGH TEACHER BEHAVIOR   Teachers communicate negative expectations to students by modifying their behaviors toward high- and low-achieving students. A list of these behaviors is included in Research Notes 6.1.

If you look closely at this list you will see an unfortunate pattern: students who need the most help get the least. Additionally, Goodlad points out that programs designed for lower achieving students are more often a hindrance than a help to these students. The reason is that these courses do not demand as much from students as they can deliver.[13]

Students are, in fact, aware of these feelings. According to Weinstein and Middlestadt students believe that:

1. High-achieving students are given more special privileges.
2. High-achieving students are given more opportunities to define and choose their academic projects.
3. High-achieving students have more freedom to work in the way preferred.
4. Low-achieving students are not as often expected to complete their work.
5. Low-achieving students are monitored and supervised more closely by their teacher.[14]

Recall earlier when you were asked to reflect on how you would respond to such treatment. Through our behavior it becomes clear to students what we expect of them and they often respond accordingly. As we have seen, this is often a function of past or perceived records of achievement.

GROUPING AND TRACKING   Just as individual teachers and individual classrooms communicate expectations, statements of personal worth, and values to students, so does the entire school environment. The way we organize the school day, the curriculum, the activities in which students are allowed or encouraged to engage in, all convey messages to students. Often, this form of communication is referred to as the "hidden curriculum."

RESEARCH NOTES 6.1   How Teachers Alter Their Behavior Toward High- and Low-Achieving Students: A Review of the Research

1. Waiting less time for lows to answer.
2. Giving lows answers or calling on someone else rather than trying to improve their responses by giving clues or repeating or rephrasing questions.
3. Inappropriate reinforcement: rewarding inappropriate behavior or incorrect answers by lows.
4. Criticizing lows more often for failure.
5. Praising lows less frequently than highs for success.
6. Failing to give feedback to the public responses of lows.
7. Generally paying less attention to lows or interacting with them less frequently.
8. Calling on lows less often to respond to questions.
9. Seating lows farther away from the teacher.
10. Demanding less from lows.
11. Interacting with lows more privately than publicly, and monitoring and structuring their activities more closely.
12. Differential administration or grading of tests or assignments, in which highs but not lows are given the benefit of the doubt in borderline cases.
13. Less friendly interaction with lows, including less smiling and fewer nonverbal indicators of support.
14. Briefer and less informative feedback to the questions of lows.
15. Less eye contact and other nonverbal communication of attention and responsiveness in interaction with lows.
16. Less use of effective but time-consuming instructional methods with lows when time is limited.

From Thomas L. Good and Jere E. Brophy, *Looking in Classrooms,* 3rd ed. (New York: Harper and Row, 1984), 104–105.

One of the central components of the hidden curriculum is the way we organize students for instruction. In elementary classrooms students are often grouped by academic level for instruction in areas such as reading, language arts, and math. Students in the middle and high schools are tracked either by curriculum (vocational, general, business, or college prep) or by level of difficulty of each class. These practices can communicate some of the most negative messages students receive about what is expected of them in school.

As Oakes has pointed out in her study of tracking, such practices were designed to meet the differing needs of students. However, rather than meet such needs the consequences of tracking are more likely to have an adverse effect on student achievement.

TABLE 6.1 Tracking Assumptions and Reality

Assumption 1:	*Reality 1:*
Students learn better in homogeneous groups. Bright students are likely to be held back if they are placed in mixed groups and the deficiencies of slow students are more easily remediated if they are placed in classes together.	Research evidence clearly indicates that no group of students has been found to benefit consistently from being in a homogeneous group. Many studies have found the learning of average and slow students to be negatively affected by homogeneous placement.
Assumption 2:	*Reality 2:*
Students, especially the slower ones, feel more positively about themselves when they are in homogeneous groups. Classroom competition with bright students is discouraging to slower ones and may lead to lowered self-esteem, disruptive behavior, and alienation from school.	Students placed in average or lower classes do *not* develop positive attitudes, rather than tracking fosters *lower* self-esteem. Lower tracked students are seen and treated as dumb by teachers and students. Students in lower-track classes have lower career and educational aspirations. Lower track students participate less in extra-curriculars, are alienated from school, and have higher drop-out rates.

From Jeannie Oakes, *Keeping Track: How Schools Structure Inequality* (New Haven, Conn.: Yale University Press, 1985), p. 6–8.

Why is this the case? The first reason is that the instruction in lower tracks, rather than helping slower students with difficult material, is merely watered down in both content and expectations. Oakes and Goodlad have both pointed out that in lower track classrooms students are exposed to less content, have fewer academic interactions with teachers and fellow students, are exposed to a predominance of rote-memory and drill activities, and experience a more punitive discipline climate.[15] Good and Brophy make this point clear:

> Content presentation to low-achieving students often result[s] in content fragmentation, simplification, repetition, low quantities of theory, and limited expense to powerful or integrating concepts. [Low-grouped students] spent much of their time on repetitive drill activities that were inadequately related to relevant integrating concepts, so that students were unlikely to receive the intended benefit from their activities even if they did them correctly.[16]

The second reason tracking and grouping fail to meet student needs is due to the messages such practices communicate to students about their self-worth. Labeling of students often occurs quite early in their educational careers and tends to stay with them throughout school.[17] The differential treatment these students receive conveys to them the expectation that they are either "smart" or "dumb." For smart students the effect is positive; for the rest, it is devastating. Put simply, "students in high-track classes [have] significantly more positive attitudes about themselves . . . than do students in low-track classes."[18]

Communicating Stereotypes
Another barrier to effective classroom communication is the stereotypical behavior often displayed to students on the basis of their gender, race, socioeconomic status, or handicapping condition. In all grades, students who are seen as somehow different are often treated in ways that communicate negative expectations. Through the books they read and the treatment they receive many students come to see themselves as having little value in school.

STEREOTYPING IN TEXTBOOKS For years the textbooks students used at all grade levels and in all subjects presented racist images of minority groups in the United States. Frequently, this was a function of omission. Blacks and other minorities were just not included as authors in anthologies, as important figures in science, history, or mathematics, or as characters in the stories children read. Sadker and Sadker, writing on children's literature, suggest that such omissions may have been a "saving grace." The images presented were so often racist and demeaning that children were better off not seeing any at all. "For decades," they write,

> black characters were presented as shuffling, lazy, shiftless, singing sub-humans. Without mind, purpose, or aspiration, blacks danced across the pages of children's books fostering prejudice and ignorance in the minds of countless young readers.[19]

To compound the problem, other ethnic groups have received similar treatment in the books children read. Native Americans have often been portrayed as "the savage Indian, engaged in howling dances, covered by ferocious combination of paint and feathers, scalping helpless white women and children." Jewish Americans have been stereotyped as having overprotective parents, a domineering mother, and a closed family. Hispanic Americans have too often been portrayed as rural, uninterested in education, and poor. And of course we are all familiar with the portrayal of Orientals as untrustworthy, close-knit, even clannish families, and adhering to ancient custom and tradition.[20]

One would expect that these stereotypical portrayals of ethnic groups would be dismissed in texts, but this has not been the case. As mentioned above, the contributions of ethnic Americans are often overlooked completely in textbooks. When they do appear it is usually in a stereotypical role. Blacks are slaves, Native Americans appear on horseback, and Hispanics eke out a living in the desert.

The National Coalition of Advocates for Children has recently issued a report that points out how these practices continue in schools:

> Surprisingly, few school systems have made significant investments in revising curriculum to reflect the variety of cultures in the nation and in the world. Witnesses told us of Native American children sitting through lessons about "taming the frontier" and of Columbus "discovering America"; of world history texts which devote no more than a few paragraphs to Africa; of Asian history courses that treat "all Japanese, Chinese, and Filipino people, whose histories are all different and all need to be told" as if they were one; of schools in the Southwest which teach the history of their region with little more than a cursory look at its rich pre-Anglo culture. Such accounts reminded us again and again of how devastating it can be for students to attend schools which disconfirm rather than confirm their histories, experiences, and dreams.[21]

A report by the U.S. Commission on Civil Rights echoes the findings of the Coalition. In a review of the literature on characters in textbooks it was found that texts are culturally biased not only in what they present, but in what they do not present. In particular, the culture, history, and achievement of many ethnic groups represented in our schools are omitted in most textbooks.[22]

TEXTBOOKS AND WOMEN   Concern over the portrayal of ethnic minorities in school texts has expanded into concern over stereotypical portrayal of women as well. As with minorities, one of the biggest sins is that of omission. Put simply, women just do not figure greatly in American history as portrayed to students. Frazier and Sadker comment:

> If a student were to tell what American life was (and is) like, based on a reading of academic books, (s)he would have to conclude that it had very few women. . . . In the decisions and deliberations of who should be celebrated in the history text, *women are selected out*.[23] [Emphasis in original.]

The same pattern of exclusion shows up in readers for elementary school children. The Women on Words and Images project uncovered the following ratios in readers.[24]

Boy-centered to girl-centered stories	5:2
Adult male to adult female main character	3:1
Male to female biographies	6:1

Male to female animal stories	2:1
Male to female folk or fantasy stories	4:1

As with minorities, women fare little better when they are actually depicted in books. Researchers have found that women are stereotyped both by sex role and by attributes. As to the latter, women are seldom displayed having the supposedly male traits of bravery, curiosity, autonomy, creativity, and ingenuity. Rather, female characters more often were passive, incompetent, fearful, and domestically oriented.[25] In history texts women are often "drawn as creatures concerned with trivia, helpless and ineffectual when it comes to serious matters. One text spends more time talking about the lengths of women's skirts than about their struggles to achieve civil and political rights."[26]

Stereotypical role models are also prevalent in textbooks. In an area seemingly value-free such as mathematics, blatant stereotypes of women are portrayed. In story problems girls are more often baking, cleaning, shopping, sewing, and cooking while boys camp, hike, earn money, build things, and go places.[27] The same problem shows up in readers and other textbooks.

The important point is that these stereotypes affect boys as well as girls. They limit the role choices either sex might make through limiting the available role models. We communicate with students both what they are and what they might become through such material. Similar expectations are communicated through our actions as well.

STEREOTYPES IN TREATMENT   In Research Notes 6.2, the differential treatment students receive based on external conditions is cataloged. As we can see, schools communicate negative expectations to students of various social groups in a variety of ways.

The point in surveying these forms of discriminatory treatment is not to say that teachers or schools intend to mistreat students. Rather, our hope is just the opposite. We believe that teachers want to effectively communicate with students. They want to share their knowledge, insights, and experiences with students. But they can only do that when effective channels of communication are open. Understanding the barriers to communication in the classroom helps us as teachers understand what we should not do. We now turn to what we can do in order to promote effective communication.

RESEARCH NOTES 6.2   Discrimination and Negative Expectations

Class Discrimination
- The average child from a family whose income is in the top quarter of the income range gets four years more schooling than the average child whose family is in the bottom quarter.
- Many school districts allocate substantially fewer dollars to schools in poor and minority neighborhoods. The disparities among schools within a district are often just as great as the gap between low-income urban and rural districts and affluent suburban districts within the same state.
- Studies of classroom interactions reveal significant differences in teacher expectations and behavior towards students based on the social class of the students.
- Of the more than 40 million public school students, between 20 and 25 percent were eligible for Title I programs in 1980–81. Only about half of those eligible actually received services.

Racial Discrimination
- 62.9 percent of Black students attend predominantly minority schools.
- Only 8.5 percent of all teachers are minorities.
- Black children tend to drop below grade level expectations in elementary school and fall further behind as they get older.
- At the high school level, Blacks are suspended three times as often as Whites; while minority students are about 25 percent of the school population, they constitute about 40 percent of all suspended and expelled students.
- The national drop-out rate for Blacks in high school is nearly twice that of Whites.
- Black students are more than three times as likely to be in a class for the educable mentally retarded as White students, but only half as likely to be in a class for the gifted and talented.

Cultural Discrimination
- Only about one-third of the estimated 2.7 million limited English proficient students aged five to 14 receive any form of special programming responsive to their linguistic needs.
- In 1980, only 10 percent of Hispanic children with limited English proficiency were in bilingual programs.
- Studies conducted in urban high schools have revealed dropout rates as high as 85 percent for Native Americans, and between 70 to 80 percent for Puerto Rican students.
- Many textbooks remain culturally biased, both in their presentation of material and in their omission of material on the culture, history, or achievement of many of the national and cultural groups represented in our schools.

- Nearly 25 percent of all public school teachers in the United States had students with limited English proficiency in their classes in 1980–81; but only 3.2 percent of those teachers said they had the academic preparation or language skills to instruct their LEP students.

Sex Discrimination

- Males and females achieve equally in most major subject areas at age nine; by age 13, females begin a decline and by 17 end up behind males in math, reading, science and social studies.
- Vocational educational programs remain overwhelmingly segregated by sex, with females clustered in those programs that prepare them for the lowest paying jobs. Females comprise 92 percent of those studying to be secretaries, or cosmetologists, but only five percent of those in electrical technology.
- Women are less likely than men to complete four years of college; they are much less likely to continue through higher levels of education and obtain doctorates or professional degrees.
- At all educational levels, women have higher unemployment rates than men.
- Women college graduates on the average earn less than men with an eighth grade education. The average woman worker earns about 69 percent of what a man does, even when both work full-time; minority women earn less than any other group of worker.
- Pregnancy is the major known cause of dropping out among school-age females. Three-fifths of women at or below the poverty level were high school drop-outs.

Special Students

- Some children with special needs remain unserved. According to the Office of Civil Rights Elementary and Secondary School Surveys of 1980 and 1982, between 5.6 and 8.4 percent of students needing services were not receiving them.
- Large numbers of poor and minority students are misclassified, excluded from the mainstream, and stigmatized by placement in classes for the mildly mentally retarded. In 1980–81, 3.35 percent of Black students and 1.06 percent of White students were assigned to such classes.
- Special education programs and services sometimes fail to realize the goals of PL 94-142. For example, classes for the educable mentally retarded are often characterized by extremely low expectations and poor achievement outcomes.
- Because of problems in service availability, many students are not served in the least restrictive settings.

From National Coalition of Advocates for Children, *Barriers to Excellence: Our Children at Risk* (Boston: National Coalition of Advocates for Children, 1985), pp. 5, 10, 16, 21, 22, 26.

CHANNELS OF EFFECTIVE COMMUNICATION

■ In what ways can teachers open up effective channels of communication? Certainly teachers can work to avoid those behaviors that act as barriers to communication. But beyond that what can be done by teachers to improve classroom communication? In this section we consider tools for effective classroom communication. These include classroom communication skills, human relations skills, ways to develop high expectations, and methods of overcoming stereotypes.

Before going through this section, take a moment to complete the exercise in For Reflection 6.1 on classroom communication. Perhaps you will see that there are positive ways of communicating in the classroom that can be learned, practiced, and perfected. Use this list to help build your own repertoire of classroom communication skills.

☐ **Classroom Communication Skills**

As we pointed out in the previous section, teachers communicate both verbally and nonverbally with students. In what follows, we consider three areas of communication skills that you can use for effective classroom communication. These include the use of praise, organizing your speech, and questioning for higher levels of thought.

FOR REFLECTION 6.1   Good Teaching, Good Communicating

Communication skills are vital to the good teacher. Think back to the best teacher you have had. Now we would like you to consider one specific characteristic of that teacher (or teachers): his or her communication skills. Below you will find two lists; on each list write the communication skills displayed by the teacher(s) you chose.

Verbal Communication	*Nonverbal Communication*
1.	1.
2.	2.
3.	3.
4.	4.
5.	5.
6.	6.
7.	7.
8.	8.
9.	9.
10.	10.

Praise in the Classroom

Perhaps one of the most valuable tools of effective classroom communication is the use of praise. Unfortunately, as we pointed out earlier, teachers seldom praise students. And, as we have seen, teachers often use praise in differential ways for differing groups of students. Another problem with the teacher's use of praise is that it is often repetitive, with no real emotion. For example, praise often amounts to only the perfunctory "good" that follows a student's answer. What follows are guidelines for the positive use of praise in the classroom.

VERBAL PRAISE   For praise to be effective, teachers should follow several rules. Praise should be genuine—it should be used only when deserved, never in a satirical manner, and it should be given with enthusiasm. Praise should be prompt—it should follow immediately or as soon as possible after the positive action by the student. (This includes promptly returning all written work.) Praise should be specific—focus on those particular things you are pleased with. Finally, praise should be personal—rather than the standard "good," teachers should vary their praise to reflect the actions of students.

NONVERBAL PRAISE   Verbal praise must be accompanied by nonverbal praise if students are to perceive the praise as genuine. Teachers' nonverbal behaviors let students know what teachers think about them. Nothing could be less genuine than praise delivered by a teacher who is not really paying attention to a student.

Demonstrating enthusiastic support is a nonverbal way of telling students that you value their contributions to the classroom. Smiles and nods, a pat on the back or a hug, leaning forward and really concentrating on what the student is saying through sustained eye contact, all demonstrate to the student that you value his or her contribution. Backing up verbal praise with such nonverbal signals doubles the power of praise in the classroom.

Organizing Your Speech

Nothing is more distracting to students than an unorganized classroom. As teachers, we communicate a lack of interest in our students and our subject matter if we are unorganized in our presentations. Part of the solution to this is careful classroom planning, discussed later in Chapter 11. Another solution is to carefully choose our verbal messages in classrooms.

Arno Bellack and his colleagues suggest that teachers make four general types of classroom verbal moves: structuring, soliciting, responding, and reacting.[28] Carefully organizing these in the classroom improves the flow of class activities. Structuring moves are used to

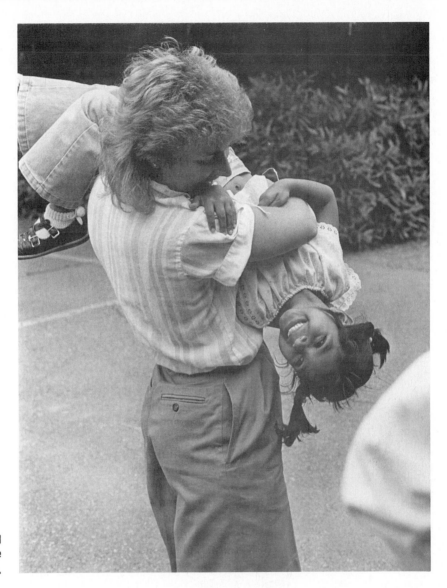

Sometimes a hug makes all the difference.

begin a class—directing student attention, organizing a plan of in-quiry, or presenting information. Soliciting moves request students to involve themselves in the classroom—through assignments or ques-tions. Responding moves come about as a result of student requests—answers to questions, guidance, additional information. Reacting moves are used to clarify something that has gone on previously in class—such as the use of praise or elaborating on a student's answer.

On first glance, all these moves may seem fairly obvious. However, they are all valuable to effective classroom communication. Imagine a classroom, for example, where the teacher uttered no structuring moves. The chaos would be devastating for students. With no clear statement of the day's agenda, or teacher expectations, students would be set adrift. Thus, classrooms without clear structuring moves are often classrooms with discipline problems. This is not to suggest that the teacher needs to be domineering or control-minded. Rather, the shared expectations of teachers and students need to be clear for a mutually satisfying classroom environment.

Questioning for Higher Levels of Thought
Later we will discuss in detail the soliciting moves known as questioning. Questions are one of the most effective tools a teacher has for engaging students in classroom dialogue. But what is often overlooked is that the quality of the teacher's questions affects the quality of students' responses. That is, as teachers we get from students what we ask for.

Consider the following questions:

Who fought in the American Revolutionary War?
Why was the Revolution fought?
When is a revolution, such as the American Revolution, justified?

"I can't explain what I just read, because I wasn't listening."

Phi Delta Kappan, December 1984.

Each of these questions calls forth a different level of thought on the part of students. As teachers we need to carefully consider what we ask of students. If we want students to think in our classes, and not merely memorize, we need to communicate our expectations to them through our questions. We return to this topic in Chapter 12.

☐ Human Relations Skills

Human relations skills are specific patterns of behavior that help us understand others better. In the classroom, teachers use these skills so they may communicate more effectively with students. George and Glazer-Waldman put it this way:

> As teachers, we need to develop those skills that will enable us to understand the behavior of another person from that person's internal frame of reference so that we can work toward modifying the person's perceptions of self and/or situation in such a way as to bring about the desired change. The skills for doing this are basically human relations skills.[29]

In this section we outline a variety of human relation skills for the classroom.

WARMTH AND POSITIVE REGARD Showing warmth and positive regard means showing an interest in the feelings of others. Teachers do this in order to show students that they are valuable members of the classroom, that they are important.

Ways in which teachers can show warmth and positive regard include the verbal actions of asking leading questions and using sounds that display interest. Nonverbal behaviors that show warmth and positive regard include turning toward the speaker, stopping an activity to listen, moving closer to a speaker or leaning forward, exhibiting facial expressions that show interest, and maintaining eye contact.

There are a variety of benefits to be derived in the classroom from using warmth and positive regard. George and Glazer-Waldman list four:

1. They make it easier to listen and remember.
2. They enhance the self-respect of students.
3. They facilitate self-exploration.
4. They model appropriate behavior.[30]

The focus here is to let students know that we care about them as persons through our actions. When students know they are valued, they gain a positive self-concept in the classroom. However, this is only the case when we express genuine warmth, not a hurried or perfunctory expression of interest. In fact, when we honestly do not have time for a student concern, the best thing to do is suggest another time to meet and talk. Nothing is more demeaning to a person than to believe that we are being manipulated by shallow expressions of warmth.

Comprehensif

EMPATHIC UNDERSTANDING   As a complement to warmth and positive regard, empathic understanding tells students that teachers care about them as people. When we take the time to understand students' feelings from their point of view, we let them know that they have the right to those feelings. Through empathic understanding we can build a classroom climate of patience, understanding, and personal safety. How does empathic understanding work?

We begin by clarifying, in a nonjudgmental way, the feelings of the student. It is important not to deny a student's feelings but to accept them when he or she is excited, happy, angry, frustrated, or upset. Then, teacher and student explore where those feelings come from. We cannot deal with our feelings unless we know why we have them. Finally, we can collaboratively set out a course of action for dealing with those feelings.

The teacher who uses empathic understanding not only helps build student self-esteem but also models effective adult behavior. Such understanding shows students the worth of caring about others and believing that they are important. Again, this is not to be an artificial activity but should be a genuine response to students' feelings.

SINCÉRITÉ   *AUTO - RÉVÉLATION?*

GENUINENESS AND SELF-DISCLOSURE Genuineness and self-disclosure involve the "communication of one's opinions, thoughts, and values to another person(s)."[31] We might assume that we always do this. But, in fact, teachers often act as if they are somehow not human between the hours of 8 A.M. and 4 P.M. We put up a defense in order to keep our distance from students. This is not to say that some distance is not important. However, research indicates that the effective teacher is more likely to be self-disclosing as opposed to self-concealing.[32]

Self-disclosure consists of two steps. First, it involves being honest with ourselves about our experiences and our feelings about them. Second, it means allowing students to see us as we really are. An example is to share with students an experience from our past in order to help them see how you identify with their experiences. Or letting students know when you are really pleased (or angry) with their behaviors. Self-disclosure lets students know that we are real.

S'EXPOSER

Since genuineness and self-disclosure are such powerful tools in the classroom, several notes of caution are necessary. First, overextended self-disclosure ("war stories") are not useful in the classroom and make students think we are more interested in ourselves than in them. Second, messages of self-disclosure should be appropriate to the level of trust already established in the room. Emotional outbursts and deep analyses of our feelings accomplish little. Finally, we always need to keep in mind the purpose of self-disclosure. It is not to soothe the fears of lonely teachers who need someone to talk to. Rather, it is to open up broadly the communication lines in the classroom.

CONFRONTING   Often overlooked in discussions of human relations skills is the skill of confronting. We can go overboard with human relations, accepting all student feelings and behaviors in a supportive manner. However, teachers need to *positively* confront both their own and students' behaviors that are unfair or disrespectful. Positive confronting should be seen as an invitation to improve behavior. Students should be helped to examine their actions with an eye toward more effective behavior. The result of such effective confronting is likely to be increased mutual respect and understanding leading to sounder classroom relationships.

Tamminen and Smaley suggest that positive confronting is seen as a progression, while negative confronting is a dead end. Below are the aspects of each:

Negative Confronting:

1. *Acquiescing:* Ignoring or in some other way allowing the self-defeating behavior to continue.
2. *Scolding:* This is an attempt to force or manipulate change and usually fails because it puts students on the defensive.

Positive Confronting:

1. *Identifying ineffective behavior:* A clear description of the behavior or behavior pattern that hurts the student or others.
2. *Realizing negative consequences:* This has an element of empathy as the teacher points out the unfortunate consequences of continuing the action.
3. *Committing to change:* Challenging the student to be responsible for taking a new pattern of action more likely to be successful.[33]

We will return to helping students build more positive behaviors in Chapter 7, Classroom Atmosphere. But here it is important to note that, as with the other human relations skills, confronting may be abused. The way to avoid such abuse is for the teacher to stop and consider his or her motives. If confrontation is merely a way to punish or carry out revenge on a student it will most likely not be positive. If it is, on the other hand, a genuine way to encourage students toward more positive behavior, it will most likely be a success.

□   **Positive Expectations**

We discussed in the first part of the chapter the way in which the organization of our classrooms often leads to negative student expectations and thus achievement. Through both teacher actions and instructional strategies such as tracking and grouping, some students have communicated to them that they are not valued members of the class. This often leads to student disaffection and behavior problems. One way of overcoming this problem is communicating high expectations for all our students; another is structuring our classrooms to be cooperative as opposed to competitive.

Positive Teacher Expectations

Merely expecting students to do better will not alter student achievement. However, if high expectations are communicated through the actions of the teacher, students will often strive to meet those expectations. Further, student self-concept can be enhanced when teachers show students that they expect them to achieve.

COMMUNICATING POSITIVE EXPECTATIONS   It is important to plan instruction and school settings that communicate positive teacher expectations. As we have seen, these expectations can directly affect student self-perceptions. As Beane and Lipka have put it:

> The problem with not paying attention to self-perceptions through careful planning is that the consequences may be largely unpredictable. In other words, school programs and features that are *not* planned so as to enhance self-perception may have one of three consequences. First, they may actually be enhancing; second, they may have no real effects; or third, they may hinder development of self-perceptions or even act in a debilitating way. Since self-perceptions are so important in human development and since most schools include enhancement of self-worth among their goals, the first outcome is too risky and the second and third are simply not acceptable.[34]

So how are teachers to communicate positive expectations to students that enhance their self-concept? Good and Brophy, in their

Sometimes laughter is the best communication tool.

work on teacher expectations, suggest a variety of strategies for building and displaying positive and high expectations. They can be summarized as:

1. Teachers should enjoy their work, and let students know they like being with them.
2. Teachers should remember that their main job is to teach, not to mother or entertain. Students should see the classroom as a place to learn, and the teacher should support them in that endeavor. EFFORT, TENTATIVE
3. Teachers should focus on all aspects of instruction—task presentation, diagnosis, remediation, and enrichment. Merely demonstrating and handing out worksheets ignores the needs of students who then see themselves as poor learners.
4. Teachers need to constantly assess students' understandings of classroom material. Discussing material with students

individually helps to focus teachers' attention on student needs, keeping all students involved in the classroom.

5. Teachers should let all students know they are expected to meet class objectives.
6. Teachers should create a learning environment where students enjoy learning.
7. Teachers should deal with individual students, not members of stereotyped groups.
8. Teachers should assume students have good intentions and want to learn.[35]

If a teacher displays these characteristics, it is more likely that all students will be engaged in classroom goals and see themselves as valuable members of the group. Displaying such characteristics requires designing learning activities that draw on all students' strengths, that engage students in helping other students, and that provide many ways for students to receive recognition for their efforts.

COOPERATIVE CLASSROOMS   Another way to communicate higher expectations to students is through cooperative classroom organization. The two ways we often structure classrooms and schools both focus solely on individual achievement. In one model, students compete against one another for grades, since all grading is done on a curve. In the other model, some fixed standard (say, the number of problems correctly worked) is set by the teacher, and students work individually to approach that goal. In both models, individual differences are the most important factor in determining who gets rewarded. Thus students who know more to begin with or are faster are likely to have a definite advantage.

In opposition to this model, teachers concerned with the self-esteem and high achievement of all students can use a cooperative learning model. Such a model includes group investigation of an issue, team-learning and peer tutoring, and student teams being responsible for classroom instruction. Each of these models can be adapted to any classroom or subject. For more details on cooperative learning strategies see *Circles of Learning* by David Johnson et al. in the Suggested Readings at the end of the chapter.

All cooperative models have two basic characteristics. First, students work in mixed ability groups with each student contributing from his or her own area of strength. Second, students are evaluated as a group in addition to individual assessments. For example, there may be a group project that is produced for a group grade. Or the group may work to get the highest possible group average on an exam or quiz.

Certainly, teaching to such heterogeneous groups can be more difficult than teaching homogeneous groups. The teacher has to teach to a wide range of student abilities. Additionally, fostering cooperation in a group is a difficult process that does not just happen overnight. Again, you are encouraged to research and study cooperative activities carefully before trying them.

To Foster
Stimuler
Encourager
Favoriser

However, such activities have three advantages over individualistic approaches:

> (1) A built in incentive for students to interact with one another as learning resources; (2) a means of accommodating learner differences in the learning process; and (3) a way of greatly minimizing or eliminating the effects of initial differences in students' skill levels or learning rates in the assigning of rewards for learning.[36]

More importantly, the research on cooperative learning strategies demonstrates that such practices increase academic achievement for all groups of students. Further, they enhance intergroup and interpersonal relationships and individual student's self-concept.[37] In other words, cooperative classroom practices can work to communicate messages of self-worth and self-esteem to our students.

☐ Overcoming Stereotypes

More than anything or anyone else, the classroom teacher plays the central role in overcoming stereotypes in the classroom. It is what the teacher communicates to all students in terms of their worth that ultimately makes the difference. Lightfoot found that the positive messages teachers communicated to students distinguished good schools from average or poor ones:

> I will remember the general attitudes of respect and good will towards all students in these good schools. In every case, adults interacted with adolescents in ways that underscored their strength and power. Occasionally I heard faculty voice words of discouragement, frustration, and even outrage to one another about difficulties they were having with students. But even the backstage conversations in the faculty rooms were not abusive to them. Teachers did not use students as targets of their own rage or projections of their own weaknesses. . . . Good schools are places where students are seen as people worthy of respect.[38]

Using multicultural and nonsexist teaching practices communicates that respect to all students.

Multicultural Education

Multicultural education begins with the premise that we live in a culturally pluralistic society and each of us chooses our own ethnic or cultural affiliations. In addition, these affiliations are not to encourage exclusiveness but rather to give us all the basis from which to interact fully with other ethnic or cultural groups.[39] Thus, multicultural education is designed both to legitimate each student's cultural choices as well as to enhance acceptance of a wide variety of cultural differences.

For teachers this means taking three steps in examining our classroom behaviors: First, introspection—examining carefully our beliefs toward student differences, identifying biases and stereotypes, and working to alter them. Second, exploration—examining our students' cultures to find within them the cultural diversity and richness every child brings to school. And third, readiness—designing and implementing learning activities that are unbiased, diverse, and open to personal cultural interpretation.

These steps will result in a learning environment that embraces all the children in the classroom, builds their self-confidence, and expands their horizons. We now turn to putting these three steps into practice in a multicultural program.

MULTICULTURAL PRACTICES   Often when we think of multicultural education we think only in terms of racial groups. However, cultural contexts include those of ethnicity as well as socioeconomic status. Keep in mind the variety of ways in which multiculturalism can work when you read the following examples.

Language. Central to all that is done in schools is language. Just as there is a variety of cultural groups in the United States, there is a variety of dialects of English spoken. Perhaps the best known of these is black nonstandard English. However, there are a variety of dialectal styles related to place and socioeconomic status as well. For example, a combination of these two factors has led to the creation of a rich and lively dialect throughout the Appalachian Mountain region.

The point to be made here is that these speech patterns are indeed dialects, not deficits. They follow established rules and patterns and facilitate a perfectly adequate system of intracultural communication. The problem that arises is that the dialect is not suitable for intercultural communication. Thus, there is a need for a standard English language. The goal of the multicultural educator is not to condemn students for their dialects, but to instruct them in the appropriate time and location for the use of standard English as opposed to their dialect.

An example of this was witnessed by one of the authors. Visiting a colleague's house, he was introduced to the children who were adopted and were black (the colleague was white). During dinner a phone call was received for one of the teenagers. Amazingly, the young man shifted from the standard English of the dinner table to a dialectal conversation with a friend. Returning to the table he rejoined the more formal conversation. He used the correct dialect for the correct context.

In each classroom there are times when a particular speech pattern is acceptable. It is perhaps one of the most important lessons a student from a minority culture can learn if he or she is to successfully enter the majority culture. The chances of such learning taking place is greatly enhanced when it is not at the expense of the home dialect.

Use of Cultures. A multiculturally sensitive teacher take the time to inventory the cultural backgrounds of his or her students and uses this diversity in the classroom. Taking time for personal interviews with students, exploring their neighborhoods and communities, taking interest inventories, all yield information about students' backgrounds and histories. Provided with this information, teachers can more readily identify the needs and strengths of each child and develop a more personal approach to education.

On one hand, this means giving students more direct experiences with the differences and similarities among cultures. This could involve students in sharing their traditions, stories, and cultural practices when appropriate (say, in units on food, language, history, oral or written expression). Additionally, it might mean reaching out into the community for members of various cultural traditions and using their knowledge as a classroom resource. All of this works to broaden students' cultural perceptions and acceptance.

On the other hand, direct experience can deepen appreciation for one's own culture. For example, the Foxfire folk life project in Georgia encourages Appalachian youths to deepen their appreciation of their heritage through chronicling the lives of community elders.[40] Similar projects go on throughout the country. Students in these programs not only learn history or English, but a respect for who they are as well.

Classroom Interaction. Beyond special projects there are the daily classroom interaction patterns that can enhance multiculturalism. The teacher can further foster multicultural understanding in the classroom by involving students in cooperative endeavors with racially or culturally different students. In a study by Slavin, teachers had students work together cooperatively in English classes. The result was that students were able to overcome biases and stereotypes and develop interracial friendships that were maintained beyond the classroom.[41] As Garcia has put it:

Heterogeneous classes present the opportunity to build positive
interethnic and interracial relationships among students. Activities should be planned that allow the students to work together
over a sustained period of time.[42]

Nonsexist Education

Simply put, nonsexist education is education that proceeds from an
assumption of nonstereotypical roles for males as well as females. That
is, students are not treated as if, because of their sex, they come to
school with a prescribed set of characteristics or that they will leave
school to take prescribed roles in the world of work. Additionally,
nonsexist education sees every child as an individual with unlimited
potential deserving of unlimited opportunity.

Note that much of what has been said, and will be said below,
could also pertain to multicultural education. This is by design. In both
cases we are suggesting that teachers become more sensitive to the
needs of those who have often found themselves outside of the
American mainstream. This means, first, working to find ways to
include the excluded. Additionally, it is important to work to break
down biased and stereotypical views held by members of the majority
culture. Obviously, the strategies for dealing with this in both cases
will be similar. Just as obviously, it is important to deal with each of
these separately, because all exclusionary practices must be confronted
and changed on a variety of fronts.

NONSEXIST CLASSROOM PRACTICES   As with multicultural education, nonsexist classroom practices proceed in a wide variety of areas.
In ways similar to multicultural education, there is a focus on teacher
attitudes and classroom materials. Somewhat dissimilar is the attention paid not to bringing the child's culture to the classroom but to
exposing children to nonstereotypical cultural alternatives.

Teacher Attitudes. Given the school's commitment to equal opportunity, it is important for teachers to examine their own attitudes
toward students. Our behaviors usually reflect our attitudes; thus
sexist attitudes may often turn into sexist behavior. As a prospective
teacher, you need to examine the potentially stereotypical view you
hold of boys and girls. Listen for self-fulfilling prophecies such as "boys
will be boys" or "she acts like such a nice young lady." Only when we
change our own biases can we begin to make nonsexist education a
reality in the classroom.

Teacher Actions. Nonsexist teachers do not act toward their
students in ways that are predetermined by a student's sex. To
examine our actions, Foxley suggests a series of questions for teachers
to ask themselves in order to insure we treat females and males
equitably:

Do I have different expectations for male and female students?

Do I interact with male and female students differently, including frequency and type of interaction?

Do I evaluate the work of male and female students differently?

Do I encourage sex-role stereotypic behavior among my students in any way?[43]

The key here is to develop an increased sensitivity to the ways in which we interact with all students.

Student Actions. As Frazier and Sadker put it, when it comes to student actions in the classroom, "we cannot tolerate incidents in which children demean other children."[44] Students should not be allowed to make fun of other students based on sex, race, or ethnic characteristics. Further, describing another student in a way that demeans not only that student but others as well should not be allowed. Claims that "crying is just for girls" or "he runs like a girl" need to be challenged by the teacher. Students should see that not only are taunts like these incorrect, but that they also hurt all of us including the offender.

Classroom Materials. The first step in dealing with classroom materials, as with multicultural education, is to review the materials for stereotypical images of boys and girls, and men and women. Certainly, such materials should be avoided if at all possible. However, a good teacher could take the opportunity when using biased material to help the students explore the biases, why they occur, and what to do about them. Additionally, students need to be shown materials that offer alternatives to stereotypical roles, in which men and women are displayed in a variety of activities and occupations.

Students can benefit as well from direct experiences with nontraditional role models. Women who are firefighters, doctors, lawyers, and such can be invited to the classroom or visited on the job. Similarly, students should see men in nontraditional roles.

Finally, issues of sex roles can be introduced into the teaching on a wide range of subjects. In history, for example, we can point out the often omitted references to great women who were instrumental in the building of our nation. Why not study Sojourner Truth, Susan B. Anthony, and Rachel Carson as opposed to Martha Washington or Betsy Ross? English studies as well offer many noted female authors and plenty of stereotypical fictional characters.

Classroom Activities. In the classroom Frazier and Sadker see nonsexist education as insuring that

[students are] given every opportunity to see themselves as individuals relating to other individuals, rather than as boys or girls relating to members of the same or opposite sex. Not that sex differences do not exist, it is just that they must be put into the proper perspective as one of the small contributions to a person's individuality.[45]

There are a variety of ways to provide such opportunities. The most obvious is to avoid ever dividing the classroom into boys and girls when such divisions are not fundamental to the activity. The organizing of classroom competitions, tasks, games, or any other activity by sex promotes an unnecessary distinction between groups. This is a simple but important first step.

Second, it is helpful to find ways to reward cooperation as opposed to aggressive, competitive, or docile behavior in the classroom. Students often bring with them cultural messages that boys are to compete whereas girls are to sit by passively and observe. This serves neither group. Classroom activities that involve all students in cooperative goals draw on each child's strengths and support each one's weaknesses.

Finally, it is important to avoid labeling any task or activity as just for girls or just for boys. It would be detrimental, for example, in any elementary classroom to place all the activity-oriented toys in one area and the playhouse and dolls in another. Or in a secondary classroom you would not put boys in charge of research reports, while girls only type or present them. These practices encourage the separation of boys and girls and further limit their visions of who and what they might become.

CHAPTER SUMMARY

■ By now it should be clear to you both how important and multifaceted classroom communication really is. The way we speak to and hear our students, how we organize our classrooms, how we structure the school, all communicate with students. On a daily basis we send them messages that establish the climate of our classrooms. We hope you have picked up ideas on how to create a climate that is open, accepting, and exciting for your students.

Behind all this is the notion that we communicate much more than subject matter to our students. Most importantly, we communicate to our students messages of self-worth or self-esteem. How they come to see themselves often depends on how we treat them. There are many factors aside from schools that impact on a student's self-esteem. However, that does not relieve us as teachers from being concerned with those factors inside the school that we control. As Eliot Wigginton of the Foxfire program puts it, "school may be the only place where steadying, stabilizing and sane forward-looking forces have a chance to rule."

If students are to live democratically—a central goal of public schooling—we must communicate to them that they are capable of such a life. We need to create classroom climates where students gain a sense of autonomy, relatedness to others, and self-confidence. How we communicate with them, through our words, actions, and school organization, has a great deal to do with developing those attributes. For these reasons, teachers should be acutely aware of how they communicate with students and of the human relations skills involved in creating a positive classroom atmosphere.

FOR DISCUSSION

1. What forms of teacher verbal and nonverbal behaviors would foster in students a positive self-concept? Why? What forms of teacher verbal and nonverbal behaviors would foster in students a negative self-concept? Why?

2. Teachers often group students within their classroom for the purpose of instruction. On what basis is such grouping carried out? Why do you think teachers do this? What seems to be the effect of such grouping?

3. What would a lesson plan look like that fostered student cooperation as opposed to competition? Design such a plan for a classroom in your subject area or grade level.

4. How do teachers produce role-model expectations in the classroom? Give specific examples of particular role models and ways that teachers might reinforce or attempt to alter them. Use examples from your own schooling.

5. Gather together a representative sampling of classroom textbooks or materials for your grade level or subject area. Evaluate them for examples of biased or unbiased treatment of minorities, the handicapped, women, and ethnic groups. How would you deal with the examples of biased treatment in your classroom?

IN THE SCHOOL/IN THE CLASSROOM

1. Discuss with your cooperating teacher the students in your class. Be alert for any indications of a self-fulfilling or a sustaining prophecy held by the teacher for his or her students. Now, next time you observe in that classroom, watch to see if the teacher acts on that prophecy. In particular:
   a. How are different students treated by the teacher?
   b. Does that treatment seem to reflect the expectation for that student held by the teacher?
   c. How might the teacher alter his or her expectation or treatment of the student?

2. Make a chart of where each student sits in your cooperating student's classroom. Find out how each student is doing in that particular class. While observing, watch to see which students are:
   a. Called on more often
   b. Given more or less praise
   c. Given more or less help
   d. Given more positive nonverbal signals from the teacher
   In analyzing your material see if the teacher's behavior follows any pattern with respect to high- and low-achieving students.

3. Interview students from various tracks or ability groups. Discuss with them:
   a. How they like school
   b. Future plans
   c. How they think other students see them
   d. How they think teachers see them
   e. How they feel about their own school performance
   f. What extracurricular activities they are involved in
   g. How long they will stay in school
   Review your findings with an eye toward any differences among students in various tracks or ability groups.

4. Interview women and members of minority groups in the school where you are working. Explore with the students their aspirations for the future, how they see schooling, and how they feel about themselves. Examine the findings of your interviews with other students and see if you can identify patterns that might be the result of stereotyping and bias. What programs would you suggest to help change these negative images or continue to reinforce the positive ones?

SUGGESTED READINGS

Colangelo, Nicholas, Dick Dustin, and Cecelia H. Foxley, eds. *Multicultural Nonsexist Education*. Dubuque, Iowa: Kendall/Hunt, 1985. This is a collection of essays dealing with a wide variety of human relations issues. It includes sections on human relations skills, multicultural education, nonsexist education, and a section on special problems. The book has a variety of practical approaches as well as theoretical selections.

Galloway, Charles. *Silent Language in the Classroom*. Bloomington, Ind.: Phi Delta Kappa Foundation, 1976. Galloway is the recognized expert in the area of nonverbal communication. This short booklet reviews much of the research and suggests practical skills and strategies for teachers to employ in improving classroom communication.

Johnson, David, and Roger Johnson. *Circles of Learning: Cooperation in the Classroom*. Alexandria, Va.: Association for Supervision and Curriculum Development, 1984. An excellent handbook of practical strategies for cooperative learning. Deals with the technical aspects of setting up groups, use of materials, and types of learning activities. Includes first-person accounts of successful cooperative classrooms.

Johnson, David, and Roger Johnson. *Learning Together and Learning Alone: Cooperation, Competition, and Individualization*. Englewood Cliffs, N.J.: Prentice-Hall, 1975. This is an excellent collection of methods for developing cooperation in the classroom. The choices offered fit a variety of grade levels and subject matters. Important readings for those who want to alter the prevailing patterns of grouping in public schools.

Oakes, Jeannie. *Keeping Track: How Schools Structure Inequality*. New Haven, Conn.: Yale University Press, 1985. Perhaps the single best work available today on tracking in public schools. Oakes not only reviews previous literature, but uses her recent research from John Goodlad's A Study of Schooling project to demonstrate the effects of tracking. She questions tracking practices not only from an effectiveness viewpoint, but also from the angle of what these practices do to student self-esteem and their constitutionality.

CHAPTER REFERENCES

1. William J. Seiler, L. David Schuelke, and Barbara Lieb-Brilhart, *Communication for the Contemporary Classroom* (New York: Holt, Rinehart, and Winston, 1984), p. 3.
2. Phillip Jackson, *Life in Classrooms* (New York: Holt, Rinehart, and Winston, 1968), p. 11.
3. Ned Flanders, *Analyzing Teaching Behavior* (Reading, Mass.: Addison-Wesley, 1970), p. 24

4. John Goodlad, *A Place Called School: Prospects for the Future* (New York: McGraw-Hill, 1984), pp. 108–114.

5. Kenneth A. Sirotnik, "What You See Is What You Get—Consistency, Persistency, and Mediocrity in Classrooms," *Harvard Educational Review* 53 (February 1983): 21.

6. Patrick W. Miller, *Nonverbal Communication* (Washington, D.C.: National Education Association, 1981), pp. 4–5.

7. Charles Galloway, *Silent Language in the Classroom* (Bloomington, Ind.: Phi Delta Kappa Educational Foundation, 1976), p. 25.

8. Ibid., p. 21.

9. Robert Rosenthal and Lenore Jacobson, *Pygmalion in the Classroom: Teacher Expectations and Pupils' Intellectual Development* (New York: Holt, Rinehart, and Winston, 1968).

10. Thomas L. Good and Jere E. Brophy, *Looking in Classrooms,* 3rd ed. (New York: Harper & Row, 1984), p. 93.

11. Rosenthal and Jacobson, *Pygmalion in the Classroom,* pp. 99–148.

12. Rhona Weinstein, "Student Perceptions of Schooling," *Elementary School Journal* 83:4 (March, 1983): 287–312.

13. John Goodlad, *A Place Called School* (New York: McGraw-Hill, 1984).

14. Rhona Weinstein and Susan Middlestadt, "Student Perceptions of Teacher Interactions with Male High and Low Achievers," *Journal of Educational Psychology* 71:4 (August 1979) 421–431.

15. Jeannie Oakes, *Keeping Track: How Schools Structure Inequality* (New Haven, Conn.: Yale University Press, 1985), see especially Chapters 4, 5, and 6; John Goodlad, *A Place Called School* (New York: McGraw-Hill, 1984), pp. 144–166.

16. Good and Brophy, *Looking in Classrooms,* p. 107.

17. Oakes, *Keeping Track,* Chapter 7.

18. Ibid., p. 143.

19. Myra Sadker and David Sadker, *Now Upon a Time: A Contemporary View of Children's Literature* (New York: Harper and Row, 1977), p. 129.

20. Ibid.

21. National Coalition of Advocates for Children, *Barriers to Excellence: Our Children At Risk* (Boston: National Coalition of Advocates for Children, 1985), p. 17.

22. Jeana Wirtenberg, Robin Minez, and RoseAnn Alspektor, *Characters in Textbooks: A Review of the Literature* (Washington, D.C.: U.S. Commission on Civil Rights, 1980).

23. Nancy Frazier and Myra Sadker, *Sexism in School and Society* (New York: Harper & Row, 1973), p. 115.

24. Women on Words and Images, *Dick and Jane as Victims: Sex Stereotypes in Children's Readers* (Princeton, N.J.: Women on Words and Images, 1975).

25. Ibid.

26. Frazier and Sadker, *Sexism in School and Society,* p. 116.

27. Anne Grant West, ed., *Report on Sex Bias in the Public School* (New York: National Organization for Women, 1971).

28. Arno Bellack, Herbert Kliebard, Ronald Hyman, and Frank Smith, *The Language of the Classroom* (New York: Teachers College Press, 1966).

29. Richy L. George and Hilda Glazer-Waldman, "Human Relations Skills in Teaching," in *Multicultural Nonsexist Education,* 2nd ed., ed. Nicholas Colangelo, Dick Dustin, and Cecelia H. Foxley (Dubuque, Iowa: Kendall/ Hunt, 1985), p. 29.

30. Ibid., pp. 30–31.

31. Dick Dustin and Jay Curran, "Genuineness and Self-Disclosure in the Classroom," in *Multicultural Nonsexist Education,* 2nd ed., Colangelo et al., eds. (Kendall/Hunt, 1985), p. 49.

32. Arthur Combs, *The Professional Education of Teachers* (Boston: Allyn & Bacon, 1965).

33. Armas W. Tamminen and Marlowe H. Smaley, "Confronting: A Human Relations Skill," in *Multicultural Nonsexist Education,* 2nd ed., Colangelo et al., eds. (Dubuque, Iowa: Kendall/Hunt, 1985).

34. James A. Beane and Richard P. Lipka, *Self-Concept, Self-Esteem, and the Curriculum* (Boston: Allyn & Bacon, 1984), pp. 29–30.

35. Good and Brophy, *Looking in Classrooms,* pp. 112–120.

36. Oakes, *Keeping Track,* p. 20.

37. D. W. Johnson, David W. Johnson, Geoffrey Maruyama, Roger Johnson, Deborah Nelson, and Linda Skon, "Effects of Cooperative, Competition, and Individualistic Goal Structures on Achievement: A Meta-Analysis," *Psychological Bulletin* 89:1 (January 1981): 47–67; Robert Slavin, Shlomo Sharan, Spencer Kagan, Rachel Hertz Lazarowitz, Clark Webb, and Richard Schmuck (eds.), *Learning to Cooperate: Cooperating to Learn* (New York: Plenum Press, 1985).

38. Sara Lawrence Lightfoot, *The Good High School: Portraits of Character and Culture* (New York: Basic Books, 1983), p. 350.

39. Horace M. Kallen, *Cultural Pluralism and the American Ideal* (Philadelphia: University of Pennsylvania Press, 1956).

40. See Eliot Wigginton, *Sometimes A Shining Moment: The Foxfire Experience* (New York: Doubleday, 1985) for an account of this program.

41. Robert E. Slavin, "Effects of Biracial Learning Teams on Cross-Racial Friendships," *Journal of Educational Psychology* 41 (1979): 381–387.

42. Ricardo L. Garcia, "Countering Classroom Discrimination," *Theory Into Practice* 30 (Spring 1984): 108.

43. Cecelia H. Foxley, "Eliminating Sexism: What Can Teachers Do?" in *Multicultural Nonsexist Education,* 2nd ed., Colangelo et al., eds. (Dubuque, Iowa: Kendall/Hunt, 1985), p. 386.

44. Frazier and Sadker, *Sexism in School and Society,* p. 188.

45. Ibid., p. 183.

7

Classroom Atmosphere

■ (The following incident was reported to us by one of our field-experience students.)

It was another routine day in the high school music appreciation class. Students, somewhat bored, were working away on dittos assigned after the usual 20-minute lecture. Not much excitement, nor any disturbances—just listless students putting in time.

With about half an hour left in the period, Beth approached Mr. Jackson's desk. After she had stood there a minute or two, he finally looked up as she made what seemed a simple request.

"Mr. Jackson, could I take Friday's test early? My family is going out of town and I . . ."

"Go wash off that eye makeup," came the abrupt reply, cutting Beth off in midsentence.

"Huh?"

"I said go wash off that makeup," this time a little louder.

By now, Terry, an education student observing in the class, had focused on the discussion. In fact, so had all the students in the class because the discussion was getting too loud to ignore.

"Young lady, you know what the rules are on makeup, now go wash that off or I will wash it off for you!"

Terry had to admit to himself that Beth did have, well, a distinctive way of adorning her eyes. But then again, this confrontation did not seem like the best way to resolve the issue.

"Listen, I only hit my momma one time in my life, and it was over my makeup. So keep it up if you want the same," Beth clenched her fists, seeming genuine about her threat.

"Well! No student speaks that way to me! We'll see what the principal has to say about this! Come with me . . . NOW!"

"Damn straight."

And with that Beth and Mr. Jackson disappeared out the door accompanied by a loud chorus of "oohs" and "aahs" from their rather appreciative audience.

Terry, so caught up in watching the drama that had just unfolded, suddenly realized he was now alone with the students. The incident had them excited, and he was sure their noise level would annoy other teachers. His only hope, he felt, was to engage the students in a useful discussion of what had occurred.

"Well," he cleared his throat and gulped down his nervousness, "that was interesting."

"She was right, he can't do that."

"Ah, he's just afraid of girls."

"Bet she could have floored him."

"He's so boring, at least that was interesting."

Student comments came in a flood, and Terry could see it was going nowhere. Besides, he did not want to engage in a gripe session about the teacher with whom he was working.

"Ah, let's look at it a different way. Seems like you have a lot of complaints about school in general and, ah, about the ways you are treated. Maybe that would help us understand all this—how do you feel about the way you are treated at school?" Terry felt he had recaptured the focus of the class.

"They treat us like children, always telling us what to do. They make up stupid rules, like on makeup, for no reason."

"Yeah. Nobody ever asks us what we want, or talks to us about the rules. There are so many rules it's hard to know which one you might be breaking!"

"It's like this, they don't care what we learn as long as we behave. It's just that simple."

For the next 20 minutes Terry found out more about schooling than he ever imagined possible. Certainly some of the students' claims were not well thought out. But he also had to admit that many of them were very true. It did seem that a great deal of emphasis was put on school rules—and he had never seen a student directly consulted on the important issues. Students had very little control over the classroom, where they were expected to be passive and obedient day after day.

Most of all, one question continued to trouble Terry, long after the day had ended. "If students are treated like children who have no voice in the way their lives are run, when do they get a chance to grow up?"

INTRODUCTION

■ Terry witnessed and dealt head-on with an issue that deeply concerns many education students, and teachers—classroom atmosphere. Most of the time this is referred to as discipline or management, but we believe these terms send the wrong message. Discipline often implies some sort of punishment, and management reduces teaching to that of overseeing an assembly-line process. What we will suggest in this chapter is that the atmosphere a teacher and school generates is crucial to students' enjoying learning and developing self-discipline. Such an environment reduces what are often called behavior problems and enables students and teachers to have more enjoyable exchanges in the classroom.

Additionally, we hope you will come to see these practices not as something added on to your teaching. Too often so-called behavior management techniques are taught separate from issues of communication, human relations, methodology, and philosophy. This assumes that such concerns are separate parts of classroom life. What we will be suggesting is that the flow of the classroom is deeply related to student behavior and the two cannot be considered separately.

In what follows we will look at several aspects of classroom atmosphere. First, we need to explore how serious a problem student misbehavior really is. Although the public is concerned with discipline, what is the reality behind the impression of students' lack of discipline? Second, we will look at some "add-on" approaches to classroom management to see what possibilities and problems each one holds. Finally, we will look at how to bring together a variety of teaching skills to make our classrooms and schools places that foster self-discipline. That is, to use a phrase from the work on self-discipline by Carducci and Carducci, how to create the "caring classroom."[1]

DISCIPLINE IN SCHOOLS—IMAGE VS. REALITY

■   According to Gary Bauer, deputy undersecretary in President Ronald Reagan's Department of Education, "student misbehavior is one of the most serious problems facing our schools today."[2] Ronald Reagan himself claimed that "in schools throughout America, learning has been crowded out by alcohol, drugs and crime."[3] The picture one can take from these statements is that of a "blackboard jungle," schools where violent chaos is the norm.

On the other hand, many of us recall our schools as very safe places, with a minimum of disruption. The school in our neighborhood today, or that we visit for practice teaching, does not seem to be a place of confrontation or drug-dealing.

So which perception is correct? Perhaps both are in some ways. Each individual school has its own personality, a personality heavily dependent on location. But what about public schooling as a whole—

Is this how discipline in schools should be managed?

what are schools like throughout the country with regard to discipline? In this section we attempt to lay the groundwork for talking about classroom environment by looking both at perceptions of school discipline as well as the reality of daily school life.

☐ **Perceptions of Discipline in the Schools**

Many public pronouncements about schools foster a view of schools as violent, often dangerous places. A story of one assault or attack, a drug deal, or similar disturbance usually can find its way to the front page of the local paper. A story such as this is often repeated and shared until the assumption is made that such incidents are the daily fare of public school life. It is probably fair to say that such stories greatly exaggerate the truth. Yet it is important to understand these perceptions so that one may begin to see how important classroom atmosphere is.

Public Perceptions
One cannot underestimate the public's concern with discipline in the schools. As we can see in Research Notes 7.1 the public continues to rate "lack of discipline" as one of the biggest problems faced by public

schools. In the 18 years that the Gallup Poll of public attitudes toward the school has been taken, lack of discipline has topped the list of problems faced 16 times! In 1986, drug use, another discipline-related item, finished first in the Gallup Poll.

RESEARCH NOTES 7.1 Perceptions of Discipline Problems in the Schools

Perceptions of the Public[a]

When asked to name the biggest problems facing schools today, parents answered as follows:

	National Totals	Public School Parents	Non-Public-School Parents
Use of Drugs	28%	27%	22%
Lack of Discipline	24%	23%	26%
Lack of Proper Financial Support	11%	15%	14%
Poor Curriculum/Poor Standards	8%	10%	11%
Difficulty in Getting Good Teachers	6%	6%	5%
(22 other categories at under 5%)			

Perceptions of Teachers[b]

When asked about the seriousness of each of the following problems with schools, teachers responded as follows:

Teachers of Grades 7–12
Base: 820

	Very Serious	Some-what Serious	Not Very Serious	Not at All Serious	Not Ap-plicable	Not Sure
The number of students who lack basic skills	% 30	50	16	4	—	*
The amount of drinking by students	% 27	39	20	13	1	2
The number of students using drugs	% 14	44	29	11	1	1
The number of teenage pregnancies	% 19	30	29	20	2	1

(Continued)

		Very Serious	Some-what Serious	Not Very Serious	Not at All Serious	Not Ap-plicable	Not Sure
The number of dropouts	%	13	27	34	22	3	1
The number of teenage sui-cides	%	4	13	33	45	3	1
Teachers of Grades K–6							
Base: 1,124							
Overcrowded classes	%	18	31	29	21	*	—
Inadequate pro-grams for gifted and talented	%	17	28	27	25	2	*
Inadequate pro-grams for reme-dial students	%	8	29	35	27	*	*
Inadequate pro-grams for bilin-gual education	%	13	16	23	26	22	1
Inadequate pro-grams for the handicapped	%	8	19	30	33	9	*
Absenteeism	%	6	22	41	30	*	*

*Less than 0.5%

When asked of teachers who were considering leaving teaching what were the main things that prompted their concern the following answers were given:

Inadequate, Low Salary	62%
Working Conditions	41%
Student-Related	31%
(Note: 21% related to lack of student discipline)	
Administration related	25%
Lack of Respect	25%
Emotional Aspects	22%
Parent and Community-Related	21%
Miscellaneous	7%

(Figures add to more than 100% because teachers were free to offer more than one answer to the open-ended question.)

[a] From Alec M. Gallup, "The 18th Annual Gallup Poll of the Public's Attitudes Toward the Public Schools," *Phi Delta Kappan* 68, no. 1 (September 1986): 43–59.
[b] From *The Metropolitan Life Survey of The American Teacher 1985* (New York: Metropolitan Life Insurance, n.d.), pp. 14, 30–31.

It is never clear how the public gathers its impressions of public schooling. Students themselves are one source of information. The stories that are shared over the dinner table are perhaps the most important "newsletter" any school sends home. (We know of several teachers who finish their day with a review of the day's events so that children have a ready answer for the "what happened in school today" question.) Additionally, the stories reported in the media are often taken to reflect what goes on in schools.

Recently, the rhetoric about school discipline has increased in both volume and intensity. We would suggest the reason for this is the increased pressures children find themselves under coupled with the school's unique social role. Nowhere else in our culture do we find children gathered for the purpose of being inducted into the culture. Schools, as age-segregated institutions, are the focus of most of the social, recreational, intellectual, and economic activities of citizens between the ages of 5 and 18. Thus, if children in general have a problem with drugs or alcohol it becomes a school problem. If the pressures of poverty, family discord, or peers take their toll on children the effects are always present first in the school. For example, we often hear reference to a drug problem at the local school as if the school itself offers illegal drugs in the cafeteria line. In reality, the problems children have with drugs are brought to the school because that is where children spend their time.

Teacher Perceptions

Up to this point we have talked about the perceptions outsiders have of school discipline problems. Perhaps a more realistic perception is that of teachers, those who are in the schools daily. As we can see in Research Notes 7.1, teachers, while concerned about student discipline, do not see that as the major problem in schools. In fact, depending on grade level, they are much more concerned about student ability levels, overcrowded classrooms, and inadequate programming. When teachers do see student discipline as a problem it is usually in the area of drug and alcohol abuse and these are problems that seem to touch every segment of our culture.

The reasons teachers give for leaving teaching is another indicator of different perceptions. For example, the main reason, overwhelmingly, is low pay. However, low teacher pay was mentioned as an important problem only 3% of the time in the Gallup survey of the general public! What is even more startling is that while teachers rank working conditions as the second leading reason for leaving teaching, this response was not even offered by the public in their list of problems.

How are we to interpret this difference of perception? One explanation is that teachers tend to think of their *classrooms* while the public thinks of *schools*. For example, in a National Education Association (NEA) survey of teachers, 66% indicated relative satisfaction with the student behavior in their classes.[4] It is possible that when parents and the public think of their own child's school the discipline problem might not look so large. In fact, when parents think of their own schools they generally rate them more positively than schools in general. Thus, media reports of violence, lack of discipline, drug use, poor academic achievement, and so on are often taken to represent schools in general while we feel very differently about our school in particular.

Additionally, the problems of children make news. It is easier to point to discipline problems and say *"They* ought to be tougher with those kids" than it is to point to teacher salaries and say *"We* need to raise taxes to better reward our teachers." In order to sort out these conflicting perceptions it is important to try to find the reality behind the opinions. Only when we do that can we begin to think about building an effective classroom atmosphere with the students we teach.

Discipline Realities

Definition is one of the problems in talking about discipline in the schools. For example, we know that drug and alcohol use have both increased and involved younger and younger children. But is this a school problem or a social problem brought to the schools? Indeed, there are many violent acts that occur on school grounds. But according to one study of such acts most of those were committed by intruders, not students (in the case of rape, 100% of teacher rapes were committed by such intruders).[5] Further, violent crime reports are never clearly defined; teacher assault often ranges from throwing a piece of candy at a teacher to physical beatings.[6]

Of course, who does the reporting creates a problem too. Building administrators, wanting to present the best image possible, might tend to hold back evidence of school problems. Law enforcement officials or school guards might exaggerate school problems in order to make their services seem more necessary. Again, perhaps the best source about the actual nature of school discipline problems comes from teachers themselves.

In the NEA survey 28% of the responding teachers indicated they had personal property stolen or destroyed by a student. Further, 4% of those teachers surveyed reported being physically attacked by a teacher. Nearly one-half of those attacked reported no physical damage or emotional trauma as a result of the attack.[7] What emerges here is a picture of schools in general as being one of the safest places to be in our society.

However, we do not want to minimize the problems. Students and teachers are subjected to far too much violent behavior in schools. But as we have indicated, many of these are problems brought *to* schools, not, as is often implied, *caused* by schools. The task for the school is to create a safe haven for learning and growth in an often violent society. It is unfair to blame the school for violence that is commonplace in too many homes and on television screens. Yet it is the teacher's task to find ways to counteract these forces that interfere with learning.

The nature of behavior in the classroom is the issue that often gets left out of much of the discussion on student violent misbehavior. It is not so often misbehavior as lack of student involvement that concerns teachers. As we saw earlier, student apathy ranks high as a frustration for teachers.

Nothing speaks directly to this problem more clearly than a letter received by one of the authors from a former teacher education student. In it, the young woman we'll call Beth described her frustrations in a very successful year of teaching:

> I have to honestly admit to you that my college education . . . did not prepare me for what I encountered this year. And I'm not sure any fault can be directed towards the University. I don't think any book or professor can make you believe that teaching will be difficult. I thought I could handle anything and anybody. I was unprepared for the attitude and gall of the students I taught. They have such an apathetic way of life, I was dumbfounded. How do you make someone care about school and learning? Teach me that.

Perhaps the most important reality teachers face when it comes to discipline is being active as opposed to being reactive. Students bring with them from their culture and lives a variety of problems often classified as discipline problems and teachers have to deal with them. But perhaps the task is best seen as setting an environment and atmosphere where students are engaged and encouraged to develop self-discipline.

Earlier we discussed the major recent reports on public education. It is important to remind ourselves that in the most in-depth studies of schooling the major problem found was *not* discipline in the sense of violent misbehavior. Rather, the issue was one of detachment, of *lack of student involvement* in emotionally flat classrooms. That was the issue Beth was raising in the letter she sent. How do we build an atmosphere in our schools and classrooms that engage and encourage students as opposed to controlling them?

"It's moments like this—when they're all so very, very quiet—that I get a strange, uneasy feeling."
Phi Delta Kappan, February 1981.

CLASSROOM MANAGEMENT

■ Unfortunately, as we mentioned in the introduction to this chapter, when we think about classroom atmosphere we often refer to "management" techniques or "discipline." Usually, the argument presented in such discipline models is that "any teacher can become effective at classroom management."[8] Then a series of prescribed practices are set forth for managing behavior wholly separate from classroom instruction. It is as if the teacher is operating in two distinct worlds at once in the classroom, one instructional, the other managerial.

This is not to deny that an organized classroom, relatively free from major disruptions, is not important. Indeed, it is only in climates where children feel safe that they can learn. More importantly, the problem with many classroom management or discipline approaches is that they are both reactive and absolutist: reactive in the sense that they assume a behavior problem exists, the focus of which is the individual student, that must be solved; absolutist in that the suggestions given for solving the problem are usually cookbookish in form and are to be followed in a step-by-step manner. As Daniel Duke and Adrienne Meckel point out in their survey of classroom management techniques:

We regard with concern the tendency of school officials, consultants, and teacher educators to learn and utilize a single "best" approach to teaching. Nowhere has this tendency been more pronounced than in the area of classroom management, where dozens of approaches currently are purveyed to educators as panaceas.[9]

However, even with these shortcomings, two important points may be taken from the work in the area of classroom management. The first is that teachers who feel they are in control of their classroom are more likely to feel positive about their work. The second point is that for teaching and learning to occur there must exist an environment that makes possible sustained inquiry and undisturbed study. In what follows we will examine the assumptions behind much of the classroom management literature and examples of methods in this tradition.

☐ Behavior Modification

A great deal of the classroom management literature comes from the application of behavior modification theory, or behaviorism. Perhaps in a psychology course you have already been exposed to the psychological underpinnings of behaviorism. The theory is that most behavior is guided by an individual's desire to achieve rewards as opposed to punishment for his or her actions. Thus, actions that lead to rewards are more likely to be repeated while those that result in punishment are likely to be extinguished.

More specifically, behavior modification techniques operate from three basic assumptions. The first assumption is that behavior is influenced by the consequences that follow the behavior. Thus, behavior followed closely by a reward will occur more frequently, while behavior followed closely by a punishing consequence will occur less often. Further, a behavior may be completely extinguished when it is no longer reinforced.

The second assumption is that programs for behavior change must focus on specific and observable behavior. For example, in a classroom it would be inappropriate behavior modification technique to focus on changing a student's attitude about a subject matter. Rather, the focus would be on altering a particular student behavior, say, arriving late to class, that conveys to the teacher a negative attitude.

The last assumption is that any behavior change strategy requires careful, systematic, and thoughtful data collection. A behaviorist system that relies on either rewards or punishment must be directly linked to the behavior that we desire to change. Unless we are carefully informed about actual behavior it is possible that we may reward or punish the student inappropriately.

Assertive Discipline

One of the most popular recent attempts to apply behavior modification techniques to the classroom is Lee Canter's Assertive Discipline model. Canter developed this model in working with children with severe or profound behavior disorders. The model was then adapted for classroom practice in the regular school setting.[10]

The Assertive Discipline model is based on one key premise—the teacher should be in charge of the classroom. The goal of this model is to foster in teachers the feeling that they are indeed in charge. Canter suggests that there are three types of teachers: (1) nonassertive teachers who allow themselves to be pushed around by students; (2) hostile teachers who harm students through arbitrary or negative controls; and (3) assertive teachers who believe in their abilities and their right to teach without disturbance. As Canter puts it:

> An assertive teacher will actively respond to a child's inappropriate behavior by clearly communicating to the child her disapproval of the behavior, followed by what she wants the child to do.[11]

The Assertive Discipline model consists of the teacher's initially establishing and conveying to the class a set of specific guidelines for student behavior and the consequences of violating the guidelines. The first time a student violates a guideline his or her name is put on the board and he or she is told what the misbehavior is. The second infraction leads to a check placed after the student's name, which requires the student to stay 15 minutes after school. A second check means staying 30 minutes after school, with the third check resulting in a call to the student's home. The ultimate penalty is a severe clause that involves an administrative conference to mete out punishment. A severe clause may also be invoked immediately for serious misconduct.

On the reward side, the teacher develops a model for keeping track of those times the entire class is on task. This should involve something obvious like dropping a marble into a jar. When the jar, or similar object, is filled the class is rewarded through a special activity.

ADVANTAGES   Canter and his associates claim that over 300,000 teachers have been trained in Assertive Discipline techniques. Certainly one reason for the popularity of this approach is the ease with which it can be applied. It requires little training and can be used as a model for an entire school.

Additionally, the Assertive Discipline model is based on setting clear expectations for students. Canter argues that children need and want limits, and appreciate having limits set for them. In such cases, children know how to behave with little uncertainty.

Finally, the biggest advantage to the model is giving a teacher a sense of being in control. Many teachers feel harassed and unable to control their classrooms. Assertive Discipline techniques help teachers set the bounds of reasonable classroom behavior. Once those bounds are exceeded, especially if the student reaches the severe clause, the disruptive student is removed from the classroom so that the teacher may return to teaching.

DISADVANTAGES In recent years there seems to be a move away from the Assertive Discipline model.[12] One reason is that some of the students it was primarily designed to control—the most disruptive—are not controlled by it. This is only a system to control classroom behavior and much misbehavior occurs outside the classroom. Further, many of the negative consequences (such as a call home) are not threatening enough to control some student behaviors.

That leads us to the second problem with the Assertive Discipline system—the locus of control. Assertive Discipline is based primarily on external controls, either punishment or rewards. As Duke and Meckel put it:

> Within class, the approach may reduce rule-breaking but not without negative by-products. Assertive Discipline provides no opportunites for students to learn or practice conflict-resolution skills. Rather than learning to be responsible, students remain dependent on the teacher to intervene and handle behavior problems.[13]

Indeed, there is no research available on Assertive Discipline that demonstrates its effectiveness in promoting self-discipline.[14]

Finally, the Assertive Discipline system ignores one possible reason for student misbehavior—the teacher. It places total blame on the student for classroom disruption while teacher behaviors go unexamined. Jones and Jones voice a similar concern:

> Too frequently [Assertive Discipline] creates a "sit down, shut up, or get out" philosophy in classrooms where teaching methods are failing to meet students' basic personal and academic needs. Too often teachers use the Assertive Discipline procedures rather than examining their own teacher methods to consider how to prevent disruptive behavior.[15]

☐ **Advantages and Disadvantages to
    Behavior Modification Strategies**

As we have seen, there are some advantages to a classroom management strategy based on behavior modification. They are (1) simplicity,
(2) clear expectations, and (3) focus on teacher controls. However, as
we will argue below, we believe the disadvantages clearly outweigh
the advantages.

Perhaps the central advantage to such systems is found in their
application to individual problem students. When a student occasionally seems unable to behave in a manner that is conducive to the whole
class' welfare, learning a behavioristic approach might best assist that
particular child. Jones and Jones find that "most teachers indicate that
these techniques are extremely helpful in assisting students with
serious or persistent discipline problems to positively alter their
behavior."[16]

An example of an individual approach would be "contracting."
Here the teacher and student decide together what behavior they want

Students and the principal cooperatively solving school problems.

to change and what the consequences will be if such a change does or does not occur. A specific example of an expected behavior change is clearly spelled out (say, the number of successive times a student would arrive to class on time). At the end of a specified time the reward for the behavior change would be administered. Gradually, the teacher would extend the time between rewards until the behavior change continued without need for reinforcement.

However, too much has been made of behavior modification techniques as classroomwide management schemes. In order to solve the problems of a few students entire classes have been exposed to methods that assume students will not be responsible for their actions. Thus, students face a system of external controls, controls that seem to serve little purpose except to manage children.

Two problems then loom large in schools and classrooms using behavior modification techniques. First, students are given little opportunity to learn the self-control we often assume they should gain in school. Second, when management becomes detached from questions of teaching and learning we ignore evidence that our methods or content may be failing. Student behavior may be a way of communicating to teachers that there is something more generally wrong with the classroom or school. In fact, by concentrating solely on the discipline side of classroom management we may be losing excellent opportunities to teach self-discipline as in Robert Rubinstein's example in Focus 7.1. We now turn to classroom management plans that have at their heart a desire to teach teacher self-discipline through a positive learning atmosphere.

CLASSROOM ATMOSPHERE

■   What alternatives are there to behaviorist approaches to classroom management? What we want to explore here are approaches to the classroom that focus on its overall atmosphere. The notion that guides us is that classrooms and schools must be areas that invite student self-discipline as opposed to places that attempt to impose teacher controls. Self-discipline is the target of such approaches.

What do we mean by self-discipline? Duke and Jones summarize self-discipline as

> the capacity and desire to (a) behave properly without direct supervision, (b) try and correct one's own behavior when it is improper, and (c) assist others in behaving properly.[17]

The difference between this and behavioristic approaches is the focus on self or internal control as opposed to external control.

FOCUS 7.1   "Do We Discipline Students Too Much?"

By Robert E. Rubinstein

Again and again, the national studies of education mention discipline. Students need stricter discipline, and teachers must exert more control in classrooms. Over and over, the same horror stories of student misbehavior are recounted.

So we educators make rules. No eating in the hallways. Right-handed traffic only between classes. Students who are late to class will be locked out, whatever their excuse. Then we lie in wait to pounce on transgressors.

But perhaps, instead of making strictness our goal, we should focus on developing true discipline in students; perhaps we should stress individual self-control and personal responsibility. For the past 15 years, we have tried such an approach at Roosevelt Middle School in Eugene, Oregon. We expect our students to be responsible and to behave well. And, in general, they do.

But we have not left students completely to their own devices. We have established a support system of teacher/advisors to guide students when they have problems. Each teacher at Roosevelt acts as an advisor for approximately 20 sixth-, seventh-, and eighth-graders in what we call a "house." There are currently 38 such houses at Roosevelt.

We also distinguish between minor and major problems. For such minor problems as tardiness, unexcused absences, minor disruptive behavior, or talking in class, a teacher either sends a note to the involved student's advisor or sends the student to the advisor to discuss the problem. If necessary, the advisor and the student meet with the teacher to discuss the matter. At such a meeting, the student has the opportunity to present his or her view of the situation to both the teacher and the advisor, as well as to find out why the teacher reacted in a particular way.

Such communication is central to helping students learn self-control. At Roosevelt, a teacher does not simply demand obedience and then expect a student to change his or her attitude immediately. Minor problems are worked out through mutual understanding.

Of course, there are occasional major problems—committed by a very small percentage of the total student population. For example, a student may get into a fight, be insubordinate or verbally abusive, or harass others. Dealing with such situations is an administrative matter. Usually the student's advisor is called on to act as an advocate for the student—not to defend the student's behavior, but to help the student explain his or her actions. In this way, the lines of communication remain open, and the situation doesn't blow up into a futile confrontation that pits the school against the student. Minor offenses that are repeated often and cannot be taken care of with a note from the advisor to the involved student's parents also become administrative matters.

Using this system frees administrators to deal with the 5% to 10% of the student body who cause most of the serious problems in the school.

Focusing attention on those problem students allows the school to do without a great many rigid rules.

The absence of all those rules has made possible a number of benefits for both students and staff members. For example, teachers do not have lunchroom duty at Roosevelt. Even in an overcrowded school with 800 middle-schoolers, problems in the lunchroom are rare. The counselor and an administrator are usually in the lunchroom. Most of the time they walk around, stopping to chat with students, and the atmosphere is relaxed. Sometimes teachers voluntarily eat in the lunchroom just to talk with their students.

We also allow students to eat lunch in the halls. At times this creates a problem with litter, but seldom does it lead to any other problems. And usually a morning announcement by the principal mentioning the litter and requesting help from the students is enough.

Teachers do not have hall duty at Roosevelt—not even during the students' 10-minutes break in the morning. Nor do students have to walk on only one side of the hall. They mill around, talk, and joke. Teachers and administrators move freely about the halls, talking with each other and the students, carrying out whatever business they have, but certainly not prowling around looking for students walking the wrong way. Between classes, at lunch time, and during the morning break, there is no sense of having to supervise or spy on the students.

The organization of Roosevelt has also helped us arrange several unusual activities. For example, we had a successful "Beautification Day," when members of houses went out and picked up litter; cleaned walls and lockers; planted trees, flowers, and bushes; and painted basketball courts and foursquare lines on the playground. An art class designed and directed the decoration of the hallways with colorful murals.

I suspect that a school administration with a long tradition of rigid rules and strict enforced obedience would have a difficult time at Roosevelt. However, such a change, managed in a positive way, can reduce stress in the classroom and allow teachers to pay more attention to teaching than enforcing rules. Such a change can also bring about greater personal growth on the part of students and a warmer, more personal, and more productive relationship among students, teachers, and administrators, and parents.

Teaching students self-discipline is a lot like training horses. Keeping the reins taut only makes horses (and students) aware of them and encourages rebellion. Relaxing and showing a measure of confidence, tightening the reins only when necessary, allows students to learn to respond appropriately to particular situations and to discipline themselves.

From Robert E. Rubinstein, "Do We Discipline Students Too Much?" *Phi Delta Kappan,* April 1986, pp. 614–615.

The importance of such an internal locus of control is twofold. On one hand, the evidence is clear that such self-discipline has a positive effect on student learning. Joseph Rogus, summarizing the research on locus of control and achievement, points to three basic findings:

> (a) Persons who believe they can control their destinies are likely to use previously learned skills in acquiring new ones; (b) internality is positively related to such desired outcomes as classroom participation, scores on academic achievement tests, and ability to delay gratification; and (c) students with an internal locus of control demonstrate greater flexibility and attentiveness as well as better performance and higher rates of knowledge than students with an external locus.[18]

On the other hand, such self-discipline is fundamental to a democratic society. We live in a culture that, at its best, demands that each individual contributes and cooperates for the social welfare. Arthur Combs explores this broader function of self-discipline:

> If our democratic society is to function effectively it requires self-disciplined, caring citizens who are willing to pull their own weight and contribute to their own and the community's welfare.[19]

What this implies is that to live democratically requires being treated democratically. To learn the self-discipline necessary for such a life means living in a culture that directly promotes and engages us in democratic processes.

One of the best known advocates of the teaching of self-discipline is William Glasser. In his books, lectures, and work he has promoted teaching methods that encourage self-discipline for democratic living. In one of his most widely read books, *Schools Without Failure*, Glasser directly links school life with social life:

> Children should have a voice in determining both the curriculum and the rules of the school. Democracy is best learned by living it! Children who attend school in which they are asked to take some responsibility for the curriculum and rules discover democracy; they also discover that in a democratic school, as in a democratic country, many problems have no clear cut solutions. Rather, they learn they have a *responsibility for finding the best alternatives to a series of difficult problems, problems that they themselves help to pose. The process of stating the problem, finding reasonable alternatives, and implementing what seems to be the best alternative in education.*[20]

What is being promoted here is looking at comprehensive classroom atmosphere as opposed to simply classroom management. By seeing the classroom as a whole, linking together instructional, communication, and human relations strategies, the idea is to promote self-discipline through actual experience. If we want children to achieve in school and mature into participating, democratic citizens they need to have direct experience with self-governance. In what follows we examine models of comprehensive classroom management and atmosphere and elucidate their specific principles.

☐ Comprehensive Classroom Management and Atmosphere

Looking at classroom management in a comprehensive way means seeing it as a form of instruction as opposed to a form of discipline or control. As the exercise in For Reflection 7.1 points out, the focus is to create a learning environment that engages students in tasks that enhance their own self-perception and thus self-control. Two models of such strategies are presented in what follows, but you should remember that there are many other models available that could meet this criterion. Of course, as with the behavior modification examples, we cannot present any model in its entirety and you are encouraged to consult the author's work itself for a broader discussion.

FOR REFLECTION 7.1   Positive Self-Perception and Self-Discipline

Arthur Combs suggests that self-discipline is a function of a person's self-perception. One's feelings, attitudes, beliefs, and aspirations make up this self-perception and act together in the following ways:

   a. Self-disciplined persons see themselves in positive ways;
   b. Success experiences contribute to positive views of self and self-discipline;
   c. A feeling of belonging or oneness with others is requisite for self-discipline.[a]

Using these criteria, discuss the following questions:

   1. How do the behavior modification techniques of classroom management take Combs's ideas into consideration?
   2. In what ways do teachers today use these principles in their classrooms?
   3. How do the two examples of comprehensive classroom management and atmosphere, the Logical Consequences model and the Social Literacy model, use these principles?

[a] From Arthur W. Combs, "Achieving Self-Discipline: Some Basic Principles," *Theory Into Practice* 24 (Autumn 1985): 260–263.

Logical Consequences

The Logical Consequences model was developed by Rudolf Dreikers and associates.[21] Their concern was that most discipline systems saw student resistance to the curriculum or the teacher's influence as something to overcome by external pressure. "Unless teachers learn to stimulate and to influence children from within instead of applying pressure from without, they are in no position to overcome the resistance they encounter in the classroom."[22]

Dreikers feels that such internal motivation can come from two sources. First, teachers need to see all student behavior as goal directed. Misbehavior in the classroom comes from trying to meet attention seeking, power seeking, revenge seeking, or inadequacy-displaying goals. The first step in helping students take self-control is helping them understand the goals they have and alter them as necessary.

The process of alteration comes about by setting logical consequences through group cooperation. Dreikers believes that through democratic classroom processes ways can be found to meet or redirect the needs of all children:

> The child's potential for learning is greatly enhanced when the child is viewed with mutual respect and when he is given a sense of equality and of equal responsibility along with an acknowledged role in decision making. In such a democratic atmosphere, children can learn skills far more advanced than those they are now learning.[23]

The Logical Consequences process involves classroom discussions where rules for the classroom are set and the consequences of not adhering to these rules are discussed, understood, and mutually agreed on. Such consequences must be directly related to the violated rule, consistently applied, and involve choices. For example, if a student fails to observe a rule on taking turns he or she may lose a turn (the consequence would not be homework or some other unrelated punishment). On future occasions the student will continue to be given a choice between adhering to the rule or suffering the consistently applied consequence.

Classroom discussions of rules and consequences are central to Dreikers' model. It is here that students learn to collaboratively set rules and thus gain ownership over them. Students are more likely to hold to rules of their own making. Dreikers continues:

> Group discussion in the classroom is a necessary procedure in a democratic setting. It is a means by which children can integrate

A classroom meeting in progress.

themselves into the class as a unit with status, responsibility, and active, voluntary participation.

Using group discussion not only helps children to develop better interpersonal relationships but also enhances learning through accumulated information. Effective communication of ideas leads to problem solving. Children learn through discussions to explore controversial matters and to deal with people of difficult backgrounds.[24]

Such group discussions should start at the beginning of the year and should occur whenever a classroom problem or issue arises. The guidelines for such discussions are simple:

1. Help each other; do not hurt one another.
2. Establish how to take turns and listen to one another.
3. Establish trust and mutual respect.
4. Cooperate with each other.[25]

The teacher's role is to guide the discussions until such guidance is no longer needed. However, the teacher must be careful not to impose his or her own ideas, preach, or lecture.

A classroom run on Dreikers' Logical Consequences model would engage students in planning and implementing classroom rules and curricula, value creative thinking over exact answers, work for cooperation as opposed to competition, and operate from the assumption that children are trustworthy and will respond to a positive, collaborative, and accepting classroom climate. According to Dreikers, teachers can do little else:

> [A] question arises whether students should be given the right to decide whether or not they will learn and what they will learn. This is no longer a question, because children have already taken this decision upon themselves, and the teacher is in no position to force a reluctant student to learn.[26]

Social Literacy

Alfred Alschuler and his colleagues began working with discipline problems in newly desegregated school systems in the 1970s. After observing in classrooms they came away with the conclusion that the "central battle was for students' attention."[27] Unfortunately, teachers were losing the battle. Even when students were silent they were passively resisting the teacher and the instructional style by simply not paying attention and not causing trouble—they just tuned out.

What this situation was leading to was an endless cycle of win-lose games between teacher and students. In these games either the students were able to win and the teacher lose through disruption, or the teacher would win and students lose through the direct use of force or authority. What was needed was a way to find mutually agreeable methods for meeting the needs of both the students and the teacher through "cooperative, win-win learning games."[28]

Fundamental to such a process is the development of student self-discipline. As Alschuler sees it: "Self-Discipline involves the personal control of one's own attention. . . . As a quality of consciousness, a powerful tool for action, and a characteristic of cooperative life in organizations, discipline is both a means for learning and a goal for life."[29]

What Alschuler and his colleagues did was to apply the principles of the Brazilian educator Paulo Freire to the problem of engaging students in taking more control of their education. The concern was that students, having no control over the schooling process, saw little need to cooperate in it. Rather, the "lack of participation by students in determining the rules governing even the most trivial aspects of their lives in school is a nationwide phenomenon and one cause of nationwide violence in the school."[30] It was Alschuler's goal to alter this fundamental dynamic in order to increase cooperation and learning in the classroom.

Utilizing the work of Freire, Alschuler helped teachers set up Social Literacy groups in the classroom. The process was to engage the entire class in a three-phase approach. First, the class and teacher name and analyze the formal classroom rules. This involves examining each rule to find those that promote the quality of life in the classroom and those that seem to exist for no reason but to control the students. Second, the informal rules of the classroom undergo the same process. These are the rules that everyone knows of but that are not explicitly listed. The most burdensome of these rules, those that limit communication in the classroom as discussed in Chapter 6, are exposed and eliminated. Finally, classroom rules are collaboratively redrawn so that they are democratic, positive, simple, and clear.

Social Literacy work is also applied to particular problems that occur in the classroom or school. In problem solving, four steps are followed: First, the problematic incident is clearly defined. Second, an attempt is made to see if this is part of a pattern as opposed to a particular incident. Third, alternative solutions are brainstormed for the problem. Finally, a democratic plan is developed to implement the first steps of a solution to the problem.

Two additional notes are important to fully understand Alschuler's Social Literacy approach. First, the model operates on the assumption that the rules and roles of the institution are largely responsible for behavior or discipline problems. That is, in school the way students are treated (and teachers as well) creates problems that need not exist. Thus, the focus in both setting up classroom rules and in solving problems is on changing the system to better meet the needs of the individuals rather than changing the individuals to meet the needs of the system.

Second, Alschuler puts a great deal of emphasis on democratic processes to solve problems. This means that teachers must share authority with students in arriving at solutions. While Alschuler realizes that this might be problematic for some educators, he, as does Dreikers, sees little choice:

> A major block to the creation of democratic classrooms is teachers' fear of losing their authority, and that with democracy will come a loss of control, less learning, and unreasonable demands endorsed by a majority. Typically, these fears are unwarranted. Authority is power to authorize. Teachers do have the legal authority to order students to work and to evaluate that work. In practice, however, students often resist, evade, or ignore autocratic authority, reducing learning time in classes by over 50 percent. Students must give their consent, by cooperation, for learning to occur. In this sense, students always authorize or do not authorize in the classroom the legal authority given to teachers.[31]

☐ Advantages and Disadvantages to Comprehensive Classroom Management and Atmosphere

From the two models presented above we can draw several commonalities that exist in all programs that focus on comprehensive classroom management and atmosphere.

1. They see management as a part of instruction, not something added to the classroom.
2. They focus on *preventing* problems through the active engagement of students in setting rules and curriculum.
3. They require that the teacher share his or her authority in the classroom.
4. When problems do arise, the solution to these problems is looked for in the nature of the institution, not in the nature of individuals.
5. They rely on open and free dialogue between students and teacher in order to organize classroom life and solve classroom problems.

Disadvantages
Although we favor comprehensive models over behavioristic models, that is not to suggest they are without drawbacks. The primary problem is time. If these models are to be pursued seriously they require the use of significant amounts of class time to discuss and resolve problems. They also require spending a fair amount of time at the beginning of the year teaching students how to fruitfully involve themselves in discussion and in decision making.

Furthermore, if students are not well prepared to take the exercises seriously, if they see it as just a way to avoid school work, little of worth will be accomplished. The teacher must work at impressing on students the value of their contributions and the importance of the class interaction.

Finally, teachers may find these more comprehensive approaches threatening. Already beset upon by mandates from administrators, state and local school boards, and district curriculum committees, teachers may see this as another erosion of their authority. An insecure teacher, or a teacher who is confident that he or she knows what should happen in the classroom at all times, is unlikely to venture into sharing authority with students.

Advantages
There are three distinct advantages to the comprehensive models discussed. First, there is clear evidence that they improve student

achievement. Alschuler, reporting on his use of Social Literacy in the Springfield, Massachusetts schools, found that "students in the experimental classes (using Social Literacy methods) reported significantly more democratic participation in decision making and more orderly classes, and they learned significantly more as measured by the objective portions of their final exams."[32] This leads us to the other two advantages, student self-discipline and democratic learning.

With regard to self-discipline it seems clear that the more involved students are in rule making the more likely they are to follow those rules. As Wayson points out, before individuals will accept the norms of any social group they need to feel a sense of "belonging to, contributing to, and benefitting from" the group. In schools, he says:

> Good discipline is closely associated with schools that elicit high levels of belonging and participation from all members including students. Belonging and participation enhance the ownership and commitment each person feels, and impels responsible behavior.[33]

Educators can enhance student self-perception and thus increase student self-discipline by actively engaging students in their own education.

Finally, if the goal of schooling is to prepare students for democratic citizenship the most likely way to do that is through democratic and comprehensive approaches instead of autocratic and behavioristic forms of control. When the student leaves the school there will not be a teacher standing over him or her, commanding attention and directing behavior. Rather, our students as future citizens will be required to make their own social, economic, and political decisions; direct their own behavior; and motivate themselves to contribute to the general welfare. It is incumbent on the school to use those methods that best inculcate future self-discipline and democratic action.

BARRIERS TO DEVELOPING SELF-DISCIPLINE

■ Before concluding this chapter we want to point out several discipline practices that hinder the development of student self-discipline. These practices are not easily included in the above sections because while they are certainly not embraced by advocates of comprehensive strategies, there is not agreement among advocates of behaviorist strategies of their worth either. In what follows we consider corporal punishment, suspension, and arbitrary rules.

☐ **Corporal Punishment**

American education has for too long embraced the concept of beating
obedience into the child. Corporal punishment, spanking, has been an
accepted practice in the majority of American classrooms. However,
extensive research evidence indicates that such use of force does little
to encourage student compliance with school rules or regulations. In
fact, rather than promote good behavior, corporal punishment is more
likely to drive students away from the norms of the school. Furthermore, there is more than a little inconsistency built into physically
punishing children for offenses such as violent behavior on the
playground or in the classroom.[34]

   More specifically, research documents the following about corporal punishment:

- Corporal punishment often has a negative effect on student
  achievement.
- Corporal punishment often generates new disruptive behaviors.
- Corporal punishment produces strong negative emotional side
  effects.
- Corporal punishment often is followed by aggressive behavior.
- Corporal punishment leads some students to avoid further
  interaction with the teacher.
- Corporal punishment provides a model of aggressive behavior.[35]

Of course, corporal punishment is also another form of external as
opposed to internal control.

☐ **Suspension**

Suspension is the removal of the student from the school setting for the
violation of a school rule. There may indeed be occasions when a child's
behavior is so dangerous that removal from the school and the securing
of professional help is necessary. But students are also suspended for
such rule violations as gum chewing, talking out in class, or inappropriate apparel. When so used it is not a mutually agreed-on consequence but a punishment meted out by adults to children. This use of
suspension inhibits the development of self-discipline.

   Gay Su Pinnell, in reviewing the research on suspension, found
that school policies on suspension often work in ways to discourage
self-discipline. In particular, she points out that suspension policies:

- Teach that power is absolute and arbitrary.
- Removes the student from the place where he or she is to be taught.
- May put the student irreparably behind in school work.
- Is often disproportionately applied to minority groups.
- Teaches students a sense of helplessness and builds anger if applied without proper due process.
- Sometimes functions as a reward since one of the major offenses resulting in suspension is truancy.[36]

In all these ways the control of student behavior is located outside of the student as opposed to being a process of developing and internalizing controls.

☐ Arbitrary Rules

Arbitrary rules are perhaps one of the most frustrating elements of classroom management, for both teachers and students. These are rules that have little relationship to the teaching and learning process and often cause the most conflict between teachers and students. The best example of such rules is the apparent fetish that teachers and administrators have with quiet in the lunchroom. The lunchroom is the single site of free social exchange granted most students in the entire school day. It should be expected that they would talk, even shout, to one another as they share common interests, games, and plans. Yet for some reason school people want children to sit quietly and eat as if they were studying another lesson. Perhaps the absurdity of this becomes clearer if you reflect on the level of noise at the last dinner or cocktail party you attended.

Such arbitrary rules can only convey to students the total lack of control they have over their lives in school. There are no reasons for them, and yet they are punished for not obeying them. The best way to overcome this obstacle is to engage in Alschuler's Social Literacy process to root them out and change them.

CHAPTER SUMMARY

- This chapter introduced you to ways of looking at classroom management and atmosphere that go beyond a mere discipline plan. The management and atmosphere of the classroom is closely related to the communication strategies, human relations skills, and instructional practices of the teacher. Those management systems based on behavioristic approaches, while they may work in the short run, avoid the hard questions that must be asked about the reasons for student misbehavior. These reasons may often be found in the practices of the teacher and the school and perhaps require a reexamination of our beliefs as educators.

As an alternative to behavioristic approaches we have explored models that look comprehensively at classroom management and atmosphere. We suggest that many classroom problems can be prevented by altering the approach to classroom organization and rule-setting. Students learn about decision making and gain a sense of self-discipline through self-respect when they are included in the process of making educational choices. This is not to deny that these efforts are time-consuming and often threatening to the teacher. But we believe that the clearly established benefits of comprehensive strategies are worth the effort.

Behind all these suggestions is the intent that the classroom be a caring place. We take this position not only for humanistic reasons but for pedagogical reasons as well. The evidence seems clear that students achieve more both academically and socially in classrooms that engage them in taking responsibility for their own education and behavior. It is the caring classroom and school, not the punitive one, in which such responsibility is taken.

The task before teachers is to implement comprehensive methods of communicating and teaching that make the caring classroom possible. Such action will be difficult, and will not always meet with immediate success. But these methods do offer a way of preventing problems before they occur. Comprehensive strategies bring together the teachers' best intentions with the resources of students to create an environment that is rewarding for both parties.

FOR DISCUSSION

1. Compare and contrast behavioristic and comprehensive management strategies with regard to the following areas:
   a. Difficulty of use
   b. Short-term versus long-term effects
   c. The role of the teacher in the classroom
   d. The role of the students in the classroom

2. What are some of the potential problems linked with having students make decisions about classroom rules or curriculum? How might a teacher overcome these?

3. In Chapter 6, Communicating with Students, we discussed a variety of useful strategies for engaging students in the classroom. Do you think behavioristic management techniques are consistent with these strategies? Comprehensive management techniques? Why or why not?

4. What possible areas in the classroom or school could students have more control over? Would this differ in relation to student age? What other factors should be considered?

IN THE SCHOOL/IN THE CLASSROOM

1. Observe your cooperating teacher closely with regard to classroom management. Focus on the following areas:
   a. Does the teacher seem to have a consistent approach to classroom management?
   b. Is the orientation behavioristic or comprehensive?
   c. How are rules set? How are consequences set?
   d. What would you say is this teacher's greatest discipline problem? How would you attempt to resolve it?

   (Explore the same questions for the school as a whole.)

2. Form a social literacy group in your university education class. Work through the social literacy exercise below with regard to the school classrooms in which you are placed.
   a. List the formal class rules. Analyze them for their value in actually promoting learning or merely maintaining order.
   b. List the informal class rules. Analyze them for their value as above. Identify the most toxic of these informal rules and identify strategies to change them.
   c. Develop a plan for instituting new class rules in a democratic fashion.

   (Undertake the same process for the school as a whole.)

SUGGESTED READINGS

Alschuler, Alfred. *School Discipline: A Socially Literate Solution*. New York: McGraw-Hill, 1980. Alschuler and associates set out the theory behind and the actual practice of social literacy groups. The work draws from the theory of Paulo Freire. A direct and clear manual for those interested in pursuing socially literate solutions to classroom problems.

"Developing Self-Discipline." Theme issue of *Theory Into Practice* 24, no. 4 (Autumn 1985). This special issue of *Theory Into Practice* contains a series of articles on self-discipline. Included are reviews of research, discussions of the theory behind developing self-discipline, and loads of practical suggestions. An excellent resource with a broad base in research.

Dreikers, Rudolf, Bernice Bronia Grundwald, and Floy C. Pepper. *Maintaining Sanity in the Classroom*. 2nd ed. New York: Harper and Row, 1982. This volume explores the theory and practice of Logical Consequences management strategies. It begins with a discussion of the nature of children's needs as found in Adlerian psychology. Readers are then provided with a wealth of practical suggestions drawn from classroom experiences.

Duke, Daniel L., and Adrienne Meckel. *Teacher's Guide to Classroom Management*. New York: Random House, 1984. This work provides an excellent summary of the major management models discussed today. Each model is briefly summarized and then applied to particular situations. A useful reference book but limited in its depth.

Glasser, William. *Schools Without Failure*. New York: Harper and Row, 1969. This is a classic in the management literature. Glasser explores the application of Reality Therapy (also developed by Glasser) to classrooms. He draws from his own experiences in teaching to argue for classrooms that invite self-discipline as opposed to those that demand discipline through the threat of failure.

Jones, Vernon F., and Louise S. Jones. *Comprehensive Classroom Management: Creating Positive Learning Environments*. 2nd ed. Boston: Allyn & Bacon, 1986. More complete than the Duke and Meckel work, Jones and Jones explore approaches to classroom management from both the behavioristic and comprehensive perspectives. They are clearly in favor of comprehensive approaches, but are fair to behaviorism. Both the theory and application of each perspective is explored.

CHAPTER REFERENCES

1. Dewey J. Carducci and Judith B. Carducci, *The Caring Classroom* (Palo Alto, Calif.: Bull Publishing Co., 1984).

2. Gary L. Bauer, "Restoring Order to the Public Schools," *Phi Delta Kappan,* March 1985, p. 488.

3. Bernard Weinaul, "Reagan Asks Curb on School Crime," *New York Times,* March 1, 1985, p. 3.

4. National Education Association, *Nationwide Teacher Opinion Poll, 1983* (Washington, D.C.: National Education Association, 1983), p. 9.

5. Jackson Toby, "Violence in School," in *Crime and Justice: An Annual Review of Research, Vol. 4,* ed. Michael Tomry and Norval Morris (Chicago: University of Chicago Press, 1983).

6. Irwin A. Hyman and John D'Alessandro, "Good, Old-Fashioned Discipline: The Politics of Punativeness," *Phi Delta Kappan,* September 1984, pp. 39–45.

7. National Education Association, *Nationwide Teacher Opinion Poll,* p. 10.

8. Joan C. Carson and Peter Carson, *Any Teacher Can! Practical Strategies for Effective Classroom Management* (Springfield, Ill.: Charles C. Thomas, 1984), p. 11.

9. Daniel L. Duke and Adrienne M. Meckel, *Teacher's Guide to Classroom Management* (New York: Random House, 1984), p. vii.

10. Lee Canter (with Marlene Canter), *Assertive Discipline* (Los Angeles: Canter and Associates, 1979).

11. Ibid., p. 30.

12. Vernon F. Jones and Louise S. Jones, *Comprehensive Classroom Management: Creating Positive Learning Environments,* 2nd ed. (Boston: Allyn & Bacon, 1986), p. 345.

13. Duke and Meckel, *Teacher's Guide to Classroom Management,* p. 13.

14. Jones and Jones, *Comprehensive Classroom Management,* pp. 345–346.

15. Ibid., p. 345.

16. Ibid., p. 341.

17. Daniel L. Duke and Vernon F. Jones, "What Can Schools Do to Foster Student Responsibility?" *Theory Into Practice* 24 (Autumn 1985): 277.

18. Joseph F. Rogus, "Promoting Self-Discipline: A Comprehensive Approach," *Theory Into Practice* 24 (Autumn 1985): 271.

19. Arthur W. Combs, "Achieving Self-Discipline: Some Basic Principles," *Theory Into Practice* 24 (Autumn 1985): 260.

20. William Glasser, *Schools Without Failure* (New York: Harper and Row, 1969), pp. 37–38.

21. Rudolf Dreikers, Bernice Bronia Grundwald, and Floy C. Pepper, *Maintaining Sanity in the Classroom,* 2nd ed. (New York: Harper and Row, 1982).

22. Ibid., p. x.

23. Ibid., p. 6.

24. Ibid., pp. 143, 144.

25. Ibid., p. 145.

26. Ibid., p. 70.

27. Alfred S. Alschuler, *School Discipline: A Socially Literate Solution* (New York: McGraw-Hill, 1980), p. 26.

28. Ibid., p. 32.

29. Ibid., p. 27.

30. Ibid., p. 49.

31. Ibid., p. 150.

32. Ibid., p. 44.

33. William W. Wayson, "Opening Windows to Teaching: Empowering Educators to Teach Self-Discipline," *Theory Into Practice* 24 (Autumn 1985): 232.

34. Irvin A. Hyman and James H. Wise, eds., *Corporal Punishment in American Education* (Philadelphia, Pa.: Temple University Press, 1979).

35. John Lamberth, "The Effects of Punishment on Academic Achievement: A Review of Recent Research," in *Corporal Punishment,* ed. Hyman and Wise, pp. 384–393; Anthony F. Bongiovanni, "An Analysis of Research on Punishment and Its Relation to the Use of Corporal Punishment in the Schools," in *Corporal Punishment,* eds. Hyman and Wise, pp. 351–372.

36. Gay S. Pinnell, "The 'Catch-22' of School Discipline Policy Making," *Theory Into Practice* 24 (Autumn 1985): 289.

III

The School and the Teacher

So far you have explored teaching from the viewpoint of the individual teacher or student. Now it is time to turn to the larger arena within which your work as a teacher will go on—the school itself. Teachers undertake many more tasks than are usually visible to the average student. That is, they are part of an institution, the school, which requires them to play multiple roles. It is this multiplicity of roles that is explored in Chapter 8. We asked two former school principals, Crystal Gips and Paul Bredeson, to help us introduce you to the organization of contemporary schools and to how school organization impacts on the individual teacher. You should find this to be an excellent introduction to the school and your possibilities as a teacher within it.

But how did schools come to look as they do? No institution just springs out of the ground, fully developed, without some attention and direction. The nature of American schools today is heavily influenced by the history of school development, which we take up in Chapters 9 and 10.

Often chapters and texts on the history of public education in the

United States read like any other history text—a recounting of the events and individuals that influenced the institution in question. We have decided to take a different approach and emphasize the expectations that have been held for schools and how these expectations have influenced the school's organization. Each of the two chapters deals with a specific historical period and expectations, or often philosophies, that guided the development of schools.

Through an understanding of these expectations you should be able to locate the evolving role of the teacher in the classroom. Being clear about this process should enable you, the future teacher, to begin to understand what you will be asked to do as a teacher and what options you have in your choice of roles.

8

School Organization and the Role of the Teacher

■ After two lengthy rehearsals and the helpful coaching of class advisors, the assistant principal, the guidance counselor, the band teacher, and of course, the high school principal, the graduation ceremonies were beginning. The long-awaited strains of "Pomp and Circumstance" poured out of the open gymnasium doors. Wondering whether or not all their relatives were able to make it, Tim Mitchell and Janet Darcy waited anxiously to begin the march to the area where the senior class would sit. The two students who were about to become graduates had negotiated with Mr. Mason, the assistant principal, to walk and sit together through the ceremony. They had argued that since they had spent most of their high school years together, it was only right that they graduate together, and Mr. Mason had given in. They thought of graduation as one more part of the world they knew and understood.

Grandparents, aunts, uncles, neighbors, and friends were all squeezed into the chairs that covered the gym floor, and many more filled the bleachers. Flashbulbs were going off all across the room, and people here and there rose out of their seats in an attempt to see their favorite graduates as the procession began.

"Hey, this is a bigger deal than I thought," Tim whispered to Janet. "I wonder if I can pick out my parents while we walk."

"Knowing you, you'll trip. I'd better find them for you," Janet, always quick with her words, quipped back in a whisper. Within a couple of steps, she raised her arm and pointed across Tim and off to his right. "Look, there they are, next to Coach Miller." Then suddenly remembering the many reminders of the seriousness of the occasion from the marine-sargent-like principal, she whispered, "Whoops! Arm down," and held her arm rigidly to her side.

The line of graduates was moving slowly, and Tim and Janet

turned their attention to the area where the class would sit. The large bunches of flowers up front looked funereal, but the purple and gold colors of Columbia High School brought back memories of pep rallies, cheerleaders, and proms over the last 4 years. Behind the flowers sat several people who had not been a part of the rehearsals. "The stage looks pretty crowded already," Tim commented. "Who are those people anyway?"

"Well, obviously, the principal is up there. And next to him is Ms. Morris, the class advisor," Janet stretched up onto her toes as she walked to get a better view. "But what is Doc Anderson doing sitting next to her? I know he comes to all the football and basketball games in case a player gets injured, but they don't expect one of us to fall off the stage, do they?"

"Maybe graduates faint from excitement," Tim said sarcastically. "And look! Art Malleck, from the Town Market, is up there too. You don't suppose he's furnishing all the refreshments for the reception afterward, do you?"

"It's possible. He's a great guy, Tim. For a man without any kids, he sure comes to a lot of school activities."

Janet and Tim reached the beginning of the row in which they were to sit. They stopped whispering, filed in, and turned to face the crowd while the rest of their classmates found their places. "This place sure is full," Janet observed as she looked around. "Look, there are people at the end of our class line who aren't a part of our class either," she said, leaning over toward Tim. The pair watched as George Kearney and another man they didn't know filed in behind the last two seniors and then went across the seating area and sat with Doc Anderson and the grocer. Mr. Kearney carried an official-looking leather folder in his right hand.

Tim looked at Janet. "George Kearney? They're prepared for plumbing problems, too?"

"I don't think so," Janet laughed. "But who's that other guy with him? I don't think I've ever seen him."

Their conversation ended as Pastor Schulz stood and asked the entire group to rise and join him in prayer. Tim and Janet stood with their classmates. As they sat down again, Tim whispered, "Whew! That was long. I hope all those people on the stage aren't going to be making a speech of some kind."

"I hope not," Janet agreed. "But why would they be up there?" Tim shrugged his reply.

As the principal went up to the podium and adjusted the microphone to fit his six-foot-three stature, Janet continued to look around. "There are lots of people from town here today that I didn't expect to see. You know, people who don't have kids in school and whom I don't think of as having any connection with anyone who's graduating." She shook her head. "This isn't exactly like I expected it."

"Shh, Ms. Morris is looking at you." Tim nudged her.

INTRODUCTION

Scenes similar to this one are played out in schools across the country every May and June. Though the colors of the ribbons adorning the flowers and the characters filling the seats on and off the stage vary from school to school, the cast of people on any one stage bear striking similarities to those assembled at any other school. Schools, like most organizations, sponsor a variety of formal occasions for students, staff, and community members. When formal events such as high school graduation occur, the important people usually end up on stage. But who are these people on the stage? Why are they there? What makes them important with respect to school activities? What do they have to do with schools? And finally, what do you as a prospective teacher need to know about them?

These unknown individuals are important people in the educational community. They are, in part, actors in the ceremony, but they also represent crucial dimensions of the educational enterprise beyond the classroom. They are part of the organizational structure that helps carry out local public education in some 15,500 school districts in the United States.

Even without knowing your particular school district or any of the individuals who sat on the stage during your high school graduation, we could provide a composite picture of those people, and be fairly accurate in our assessment. We could identify these people as members of the Board of Education—a legislative body of sorts for your school district. A study of school boards reveals, for example,

> the typical board member, if there is such a person, is a white male between the ages of 40 and 51 who's married and has children in the public schools. A college graduate, he holds a professional or managerial position, earns a family income of from $30,000– $40,000. He was elected to his school board between four and seven years ago and at the time had no previous experience.[1]

In the same way we can describe a typical superintendent. The "average superintendent" is a married white male, age 48, who at age 23 entered education in a rural or small-town district. He typically took his first administrative or supervisory position, usually a principalship, just before the age of 30. He decided to become a superinten-

Many non-teaching personnel add to the organization of schools.

dent by the time he reached 32, and achieved that goal within 2 years. He's been a superintendent for approximately 7.6 years and believes he was hired because of personal characterictics and qualifications.[2]

The people on the stage then have a great deal to do with what happens to you as a teacher. They will be the ones to hire you, supervise you, pay you, question you about your work, and support you in your efforts both in and out of the classroom. Now where do these people fit in the school organization? And where will you fit with respect to them? How will they affect the roles you play as a teacher and how you play out those roles?

This chapter takes a look at the combination of people, roles, and expectations called school. It presents many persons other than teachers who play significant roles in the school and describes a variety of ways in which teachers interact with them in these people's official capacities. Finally, it presents the complexities of teachers' roles and the expectations placed on them by a multifaceted organization. By the time you finish this chapter, you should be quite skilled in explaining the structure of school organization and anticipating what impact the structure will have on you as a teacher.

We will help you through this process by first examining the elements that are common to many thousands of schools. We will illustrate this in a frame of reference you may be able to apply to other school organizations you know. Then we will look at the individual's impact on the organization and on other individuals within it. This should help us to consider the interaction of people, structure, and expectations.

Then the chapter moves to a discussion of organizational expectations for teachers' roles. In this section we will look at the many roles teachers fill, the rules that grow out of the school organization, and what the rules will mean to you as a teacher. Here you will have an opportunity to consider how expectations for teachers and students affect the ways in which teachers behave and whether you want to spend your professional life within those expectations.

SIMILARITIES IN SCHOOLS ACROSS THE NATION

■ What are the common elements of schools across the nation? Although there are many thousands of school buildings and more than 15,000 school districts, they are similar in many ways. The commonalities we think most significant fall into four general categories. They include (1) matters of organizational structure—basically, who has the power and the responsibility to act within the organization; (2) funding and governance, which includes the relationship of the local school district to the public and to other governmental bodies; (3) academic programs; and (4) male dominance in the roles of professional administration and elected school board membership.

□ **Organizational Structure**

School organizations are quite often described as bureaucracies.[3] That is, there are many people at the bottom of the organization (teachers), a few in the middle (principals), and only one superintendent at the top. An individual at the bottom of the pyramid or organization has much less power than an individual at the top. We generally find this to be true in our schools especially if we look at the powers given to persons by their job descriptions. There are of course exceptions that arise primarily out of the force of an individual's personality; we will explore this factor more fully later in the chapter.

Bureaucracies are also characterized by the fact that people are assigned to those tasks for which they have the technical expertise. That is, people in different roles do different jobs (see Figure 8.1). Surely you have heard the stories of the old one-room schoolhouse in which the teacher chopped the firewood, swept the floors, and reported the status of the school to the community—all of this in addition to teaching children in several grades. Now that we have larger schools, we differentiate jobs more specifically, and then we employ people to do just what those positions require. In contrast to the example of the one-room schoolhouse, we now have a business manager who contracts for oil delivery to the school buildings, custodians who do the cleaning, and perhaps even a public relations specialist to disseminate the news of the school system.

It may seem rather puzzling to you that more than 15,000 organizations have emerged in nearly the same format. Perhaps you might even conclude that this is the right format or perhaps the only format that will work. We would urge you to question these conclusions and, as you become more knowledgeable about the workings of schools, to continue to explore variations of the structure, especially for the purpose of accomplishing certain outcomes. We will introduce you to some of the issues in this area later in the chapter.

FIGURE 8.1 Organizational chart of a typical school district. An organizational chart illustrates the relationships between positions within the organization and demonstrates spans of control.

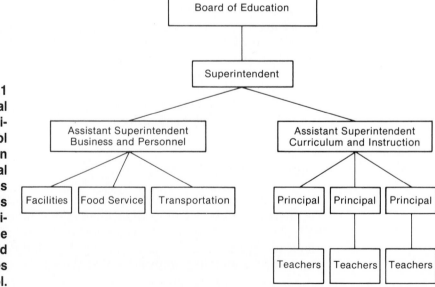

☐ Funding and Governance

Another important source of similarity among our schools is governmental responsibility for education, which is assumed on three levels. First, education is the responsibility of the states in this country. That means that in all states there is a primary relationship between the nature of the state's economic health, the prevailing social and political issues, the concerns of current politicians, and what happens in the schools. Second, the federal government, especially in the last 50 years, has assumed considerable responsibility for education, especially through the establishment of specific educational programs (special education, for example), and through the determination of significant legal issues (for example, decisions on desegregation of schools affect all schools). Finally, and most important, many decisions regarding schools are left to the local community, which still bears much of the financial responsibility for education. Clearly there are conflicts among desires and expectations at the three levels, with the power to determine specific issues being granted in some cases to one governmental level, and sometimes to another.

For example, the question of the level at which teacher competency will be determined and ultimately who will be able to decide whether a teacher may be hired for a particular role is currently under debate in many circles. In the 1600s and 1700s, a group of town fathers

"As you know, Miss Henson, the school board has had to stretch its resources rather thin. Could I have some of your lunch?"
Phi Delta Kappan, November 1983.

hired a teacher. When superintendents became common in the 1800s, they took on this task with the approval of the school board. Then teacher certification was approved first by the teacher training institutes, and then by state departments of education. Today many states have legislated examinations by which teachers will be certified, thus removing the power from the colleges and universities. In addition there is talk of a standardized certification examination for teachers nationwide. Thus we see how educational issues are often questions of the locus of power in educational decision-making. That is, matters of local importance may be determined by standards that are set for the state or the nation and are not the most appropriate for the individual school district.

A picture of the sources of governance for schools includes several persons. In the last section we mentioned the professionals within the school system itself. The hierarchy we described is a part of a much larger one. Each individual school district in this country is headed by a school board or committee. The superintendent of the school district serves as the board's executive secretary. Since the board members are themselves for the most part elected, the professional staff of the schools are thus responsible to political boards of directors composed of laypersons. This organizational factor often gives rise to some interesting conflicts, as you can imagine.

The district board of education exists under the immediate influence of three important governmental bodies at the state level. They are the state legislature, the state board of education, and the state department of education. The legislature makes decisions that establish significant policy guidelines—for example, how monies at the state level will be distributed to individual districts—and passes laws that govern everyday operations and influence local political activity. For example, one state legislature recently declared that on a daily basis the school must contact the parent of every child absent from school.[4] Think about the impact of this decision on the workload and its cost in those schools where that had not been a practice. The legislature in the same state recently passed a law that for the first time allows a local board of education to forbid its employees from using corporal punishment on students.[5] This action has led to intense debate among board members and voters.

Teachers feel the impact of these distant decisions in both direct and indirect ways. Teachers who are suddenly forbidden to use a means of punishment to which they had become accustomed must find new ways of managing student behavior. When a school must redirect its resources to meeting a legislative mandate—for example, calling the home of each absent student—teachers feel the effects of it as well. Either secretarial assistance on which they depended is no longer

"Wilson sometimes has a little difficulty handling parent conferences."
Phi Delta Kappan, May 1984.

available, or perhaps money once spent on a classroom aide is now spent on an office aide to make the telephone calls. These and many other potential changes affect teachers' use of time in the teaching process.

Forty-nine states (Wisconsin excepted) govern their schools with a state board of education. From 5 to 24 elected or appointed persons serve on each of these boards. Each state also has a chief executive officer for education called a state superintendent or commissioner. Under them serve vast bureaucracies, or state departments of education, of nearly 20,000 persons who help to direct and shape the local educational systems from their state-level offices.[6] They affect teachers through their decisions and directions on the inclusion or exclusion of certain curricular topics, the format of lesson plans, emphasis on specific goals, and in countless other ways.

At a national level, the Secretary of Education, a member of the President's Cabinet, heads the U.S. Department of Education. Its responsibility centers on the administration of all projects that are funded or mandated by Congress. Through this role, it also affects policy and operation at the local level. At the national level, Supreme Court decisions also have a significant impact on school operations and teacher behavior. For example, affirmative action policies determine to some extent who may be hired in a local district, and student disciplinary procedures are significantly affected by some Supreme Court decisions.

The issues of control, as you can see, are complex ones, for the actions of many governmental bodies are interwoven. In just the last 40 years, the number of school districts has decreased from 100,000 to 15,500. This has made coordination with the state and federal levels much more possible. The increasing ease of communication and travel has supported this increased coordination. But at the same time, the consolidation of so many small districts into larger ones has given some of these districts so much power that they have power bases quite capable of standing against state-level power. Yet those small districts that have given up their independent status are viewed by many as having lost the valuable ability to respond to the needs and desires of their immediate constituents.

☐ Academic Programs

Schools across the country have remarkable similarities in academic programs. Does it seem surprising to you that nearly all elementary school children study mathematics nearly every day? Or that nearly every high school offers algebra to ninth graders? Or that nearly every high school requires at least 1 year of American history of its students? Why is it that nearly everyone in this country knows who we are speaking of when we mention Dick and Jane? While our discussion in the previous section may have given you some ideas regarding possible answers to these questions—for example, the roles of the various state departments of education—what is most important now is that you understand the impact of these curricular similarities on you as a teacher. What we are suggesting is that despite the excellence of the training you receive to fill the role of teacher, many decisions concerning what you will teach and when you will teach it either already have been made or will be made by someone other than yourself.

These decisions come from many sources. Some states have standardized examinations in various subject areas; certainly teachers' interest in their students' good performance on these tests affects what they teach, when they teach it, and how thoroughly. Instruction on controversial subjects—sex education or genetics, for example—is often a matter of the values of board of education members. Whether or not you share certain works of literature with your students may have already been determined by the district administration's response to a small pressure-group among the citizens of the district. And finally, the role you take as an informal counselor to your students may indeed be affected by the local and state level conceptualization of the teacher's role.

☐ Male Dominance in Leadership Roles

Our earlier descriptions of school board members and superintendents display another commonality in the schools worthy of our consider-

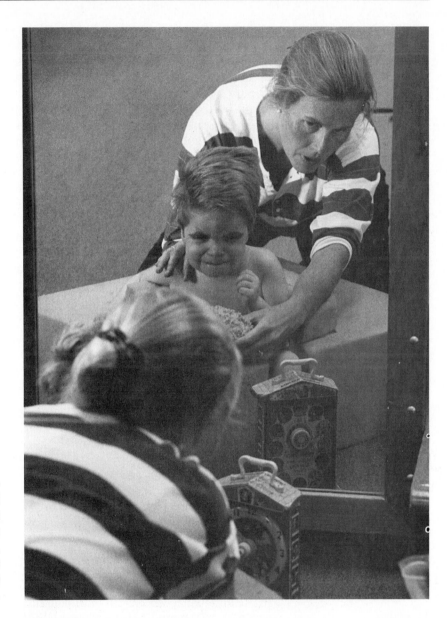

Government policy and special programs help students with special needs, yet remove some control from the local school.

ation: that is, the disproportionate number of men in leadership positions in the schools. Approximately two-thirds of all teachers are women. Yet less than 15% of administrators[7] and 30% of school board members[8] in the United States are women. We might safely guess that because membership on a school board is political it is more often open to men, like other political positions in this country. We also know that in selecting employees, or even people with whom we will work, we are more likely to select those who most closely resemble ourselves.[9] Thus it is likely that male school boards will hire male superintendents.

We can raise questions about the impact of primarily male leadership on our schools from a number of perspectives. One might ask if their representation of their employees is accurate. Are the values that govern the educational program well-balanced in their representation of both male and female viewpoints? Does the small likelihood that female teachers will rise to positions of leadership affect their view of their careers? Does the fact that the male dominance is nationwide and that the questions are therefore pertinent across the country affect the process of education as a whole in the country?

We have pointed to broad-ranging, deep, sometimes amazing, and perhaps permanent similarities in our schools. Perhaps you have been thinking as you read that you could name some differences among schools. We don't deny these differences at all. In fact we see them as well, and believe that they are the products, first of all, of local differences, and second, of powerful local individuals.

SOURCES OF DIFFERENCES IN SCHOOLS

■   The situation is not quite as simple as one might imagine from the information just noted. Our schools do not look like so many cookies pressed out with the same cutter and put in the oven to bake. When we recall how many organizations we are talking about, we must consider the effect of certain local differences pressed into the same basic pattern. Perhaps we could think of giving a cookie to each local community and allowing the residents to reshape it and decorate it before baking it. In the United States there are approximately 59,000 elementary school buildings, 27,000 secondary schools, and an additional 1,700 buildings that house grades K to 12.[10] These large numbers suggest the complexity of modifying the philosophical and concrete similarities we have mentioned with local preferences.

Financial dependence on the local community has made schools very responsive to community interests over the years. The story of the schools in a particular community may reflect changing interests and power groups in that community. If you were to dig deep into the history of the schools in your town, you would probably uncover events, changes, and conditions that were the product of specific local conditions or of the preferences of certain powerful local individuals at a given time.

Female school leaders are rare in a male-dominated profession.

Think of our cookies again. They may be made of the same flour, sugar, and spices. But they have been reshaped by many forces—pinched, joined together with others next to them, frosted with many colors, and so on. What this analogy shows is that while the organizational structure does determine the nature of our schools to some degree, there are other factors that can have just as much impact. If you choose to become a teacher, you will be choosing to have some impact. Whatever you do as a teacher, however you choose to play your role, will contribute to the total of that entity called school. That is why we are urging you at this early time to think deeply about yourself as a teacher. In this chapter we are urging you especially to think about yourself in the context of the school organization and about the impact you want to have.

☐ Two Schools and Their Communities

In our discussions of the organization, structure, and activity of schools, we have suggested something of the roles of the persons on the stage in the scenario at the beginning of the chapter. We have tried to provide the organizational focus for understanding the work life of a teacher in virtually any school setting. Let's take a look at brief descriptions of two high schools and the towns in which they are situated. Two high schools, School A and School B, with like enrollments and facilities may be qualitatively very different enterprises. Either one or both of them may sound familiar to you, yet you may feel very differently about them.

The course list for School A, with 1,200 students, includes nine different foreign languages as well as advanced classes in biology, chemistry, and physics, along with other specialized science classes. One home economics teacher and two industrial arts teachers serve small lab classes that enroll a total of 125 students. Eighty-five percent of the graduates go on to 4-year institutions of higher education. Athletics play a small role in the life of the school. The teams usually finish a little above the bottom of their league.

Nine hundred miles away in another part of the country, a city of comparable size houses its 1,200 high school students in a building that on the outside looks much like the one we just visited. A glance at the high school course list indicates that a student may select from French or Spanish if he wishes to study a foreign language. Enrollments are small, however. There are three sections of chemistry taught this year and two of physics, with no advanced class in either. Approximately one-half of the seniors and nearly one-third of the juniors enroll in home economics. What captures a visitor's attention on entering School B are the huge trophy cases just inside the front door. They are filled with athletic trophies—not just for league championships but for state victories as well. Framed pictures of outstanding athletes run along the walls on either side. The principal remarks that the best tackle he has ever known is not represented yet since he just graduated in the spring. He finishes apologetically by saying that no college would accept the boy. But that boy is like many others who leave this high school; about 85% never attempt college.

What accounts for these differences when schools appear to be structured for conformity? Think of something you all know about on a college campus. University dorm rooms illustrate the impact of the personal dimension on what appears to be a rigid structural conformity. Perhaps you have never thought of schools being as rigidly structured as dorm rooms, but the analogy seems appropriate. With little variety in location, space, color, and furniture, each dorm room presents itself as banal and uninteresting to the new resident. However, what results from the impact of individual personalities on these spaces can be remarkably creative, wonderfully inspiring, and distinctively accommodating. We can see the same basic similarities and then the same range of differences in School A and School B. Let's take a look at what might be behind these differences. We can attribute differences noted in the decorating of the rooms to the effect of individual personalities, imagination, creativity, skills, values, and, to be sure, money. These same factors significantly affect schools, their purposes, their formal and informal structures, and their major activities. Thus, it is impossible to discuss school organization and function without recognizing the importance of the personal dimension.

The people related to School A and School B differ. School A's community is home for several hundred men and women with faculty or administrative roles in one or more major universities or medical facilities in neighboring communities. Large numbers of residents are lawyers, doctors, or professionals in a growing high-tech industry. The metropolitan area is filled with cultural activities to suit varied tastes. Employment rates seldom fall as low as 95%. Families in the local community travel widely and introduce their children to a wide range of experiences. The local papers show no houses for sale for less than $160,000. The principal of the high school educated himself at a small liberal arts college and has completed most of his doctoral work at a respected private university. Eighty-five percent of the teachers have master's degrees; two teachers have doctoral degrees.

Now let's consider School B and the influences on it—they are quite different from School A. The community of School B sags under its broken industry and high rate of unemployment, currently 25%. Professionals who lose their jobs leave town for work elsewhere. House prices are low, but no one is buying. The city, which was once a center for coal mining, river trade, and agriculture, has few cultural activities to offer its residents. Most of the residents have lived there all their lives and few have traveled far from home. School B's principal is viewed as an outsider—from about 90 miles away in the same state. He attended the state college in his hometown and then earned a master's degree there as well, after teaching and coaching for a few years. Most of the teachers completed undergraduate programs in one of two colleges within commuting distance. Few have a second degree.

These sketches indicate that we must consider the structural commonalities and the human differences together if we are to develop a true picture of life as a teacher. In thinking about the two high schools we visited one might consider several questions. Do students graduating from these two high schools necessarily get radically different educations? How is it that some graduates we know from School B seem better prepared for college than others from School A? Could we as individual teachers work effectively in either school? Would our work in one school be different from our teaching in the other? If these differences are significant, can we intentionally decrease the differences?

By now, you should guess that the position of the authors of this book is that individual teachers—so long as they recognize their power—have an enormous opportunity to modify the educational outcomes within a given school organization.

The problem of understanding the relationship between organizational structure and persons within the organization is a very complex one because it is many-faceted. In attempting to sort the pieces of the puzzle we must at least recognize a number of assumptions that govern public education: that the major purpose of schools is to "socialize" children and to teach them the appropriate values and norms for maintaining social order[11]; that schools are to serve students with the foremost question always, "Is it good for the students?"[12]; that services in schools are provided to clients who have no choice in the matter—not the most conducive situation for learning.[13] If we accept these assumptions and agree that schools are required to maintain the status quo with clients who have no choice about being served and that the service is often provided by persons whose chief concerns are not for the children, then we seem to have a rather difficult situation before us. In fact, it contradicts our notions of good education. With the addition of these concepts to your ideas of the role of the teacher, you may be once again finding yourself at a point of introspection. You may be thinking, "If it is really like this, how do I make a difference?" That is a legitimate question, and an answer we want you to continue to seek personally as you read on in this chapter.

FOR REFLECTION 8.1   Impacts of Personal Experiences on Organizational Structure

People display many personal characteristics that we can see played out through their roles in the schools. Suppose that several members of the school board have had to scrimp and save all their lives just to get by. Or suppose that the principal's best days of his life were during the week in which he played on the team that won the state basketball championship. What effects would you expect these memories, traits, and experiences to have on the organization of the school? Suppose the president of the school board is the steward of the local unit of the United Mine Workers? How might that situation affect decisions made in the school organization?

What other examples of the effect of personal experience on school environment and organization can you suggest?

What traits and experiences may affect your behavior and attitudes as a teacher?

We believe that one of the assumptions about schools we just mentioned is inaccurate. It is true that schools contribute to our heritage and culture by maintaining the past. But we think we have another responsibility: to help our students decide what is worth keeping, and then to create new contributions of equal or greater value. This depends on our asking, "Is this good for the students?" first, and then changing the conditions if necessary so that we can answer affirmatively. We must find ways to serve students rather than sacrificing them to the service of other groups in and around the school organization. This comes about through the interaction of the individual and the organizational structure. We believe that this interaction makes a school what it is.

☐ **Metaphorical Representations of Schools**

Think about your future role in school in terms of how you envision the organization, its operation, administration, purposes, and activities. If you were to compare a school to something else, what would help you to understand the school? Complete the following sentence: A school is like a _____.

A sampling of suggestions from a group of educators includes gardens, patchwork quilts, bubble gum machines, sand on the beach, laundries, and sewage treatment plants. The point of this exercise is

FOR REFLECTION 8.2   Integration of Organizational Structure and Individual Impact

> Try to imagine how all the pieces of the educational puzzle fit together in a school system. Think about their relationships to one another. A useful activity for understanding the structure of an organization and the people in it is to create a mental picture that expresses not only who these people are but how they relate to one another. Think of objects or entities, animate or inanimate, that might illustrate a school. Now actually draw that image. Try to illustrate in a pictorial fashion what your particular school district looks like. Share your drawings with your classmates.
>
> 1. What common themes, ideas, and structures appear in the drawings you and your classmates have made? List the elements.
> 2. Why do you think these elements tend to recur in the drawings?
> 3. What do these common features mean in terms of how schools have developed as organizations?
> 4. What do they suggest about your role in school as a teacher?

not to promote or defend the legitimacy of any of these analogies. Rather it is to help you consider the impact on the school, the students, and yourself. What if you think and behave as if schools are shopping malls? What if you think they are similar to museums? To rush hour traffic jams? What do various metaphors tell us about the people in schools, their values, their priorities, and most important, how individuals put the values and priorities into practice?

We believe that the metaphors people hold determine how they act out their teaching roles. Even more significant, we believe that the metaphors actually determine what students learn about both subject content and human interaction.

THE COMPLEX ROLES OF THE TEACHER

■ How did you know what was expected of you as an elementary school student? As a high school student? Today as a college student? There are many possible answers to these questions. Perhaps one answer is that you were given a set of rules to govern your behavior. You may recall rules posted on the wall in your classrooms, written in student handbooks, or in school folders on which the rules were printed, or even rules you wrote 500 times after you violated them. Some schools have hundreds of rules specifying either acceptable or unacceptable student behavior, and others have just a few.

Think about the school rules with which you are familiar. Before you read on, try to answer each of the following questions:

1. Why do rules exist?
2. Who decides what the rules will be?
3. What are the benefits of these rules?
4. What difficulties might these rules cause?
5. Why are the same rules desired by some and hated by others?

Your answers to these questions may be varied and complex. It is important to recognize that rules serve as the visible aspect of the structure of an organization; they give it shape and form by controlling its operation. Rules exist in every organization. They differ in content, origin, and number or degree from organization to organization, and most especially they differ among various kinds of organizations. That is, we are more likely to find similarities among the rules of all the high schools in a 100-mile radius than we are between the high school and the Rotary Club in a particular city.

Most probably you think of school rules as those that are developed to control student behavior. If this is a major function of school rules, and we agree that it is, then we believe that these same rules must also control the behavior of persons who interact with students. Certainly when we consider the impact of laws that are designed to govern student behavior, then we find persons connected with the schools to be affected by these same laws. For example, most states have statutes that determine the age at which a student may choose to leave school without graduating—in most cases it is 16 years old. Not only does this law affect students, but it becomes the basis for the school attendance policy that must be enforced by administrators; it is in part the reason why teachers must take attendance; it is the basis for the position of attendance officer or truant officer; it stands behind the work of guidance counselors; and it results in parental presence in court in the cases of some reluctant students. We could demonstrate many ways in which the roles of teachers are affected by student rules. As a prospective teacher, you must think about the ways school rules and state and federal laws will affect you. For example, attendance laws affect the efforts you will be expected to make to encourage reluctant students to come to school regularly. Due-process requirements limit the freedom of school authorities in the administration of certain punishments and sanctions. In the case of these regulations and many others, the purpose is to guarantee students an opportunity for an education; in so doing, they also place restraints on the nature of the delivery of the education and on its content as well.

☐ Role Definition

We have suggested that there are two forces within an organization that interact to determine the nature of the role of any individual within the organization. The structure of the organization with its rules is one major factor. The specific persons within each of the roles make up a second significant factor.

New teachers often find themselves struggling for definition of their roles as teachers for just this reason: there is no one definition applicable to all places and all times. In fact, the variation may be enormous. For example, we generally accept the principal's role as evaluator and shaper of teachers' roles, at least in theory. But even this is not simple. When the ladder of power and authority gives the principal the role of determining the adequacy of your performance, it at the same time constrains you. You may not be allowed to make some of the choices you would like to make. As a teacher you will not have complete freedom to teach as you wish or even as you think best. Other people in other roles in the schools—principals, supervisors, the superintendent, board members, even the plumber on the stage at graduation—will have some part in determining how and what you will teach.

Another aspect of this complex issue of role definition arises when teachers feel they are asked to do things that do not obviously fall within the teaching role. They frequently ask: "Why should I straighten up the room? Why should I monitor the hallways and restrooms? Why should I supervise the cafeteria? Why should I collect money for pictures? None of these jobs sounds like teaching to me."

Answers to these questions may be as varied as the questions themselves. For example, keeping the classroom neat and clean may serve as a model for students to learn habits of neatness and cleanliness, which may in turn make the teacher's job more pleasant. On the other hand, teachers argue that cleaning up the room takes away from their teaching time and effectiveness. Here we see that one's view of the purpose of school is crucial.

You may be wondering, Shall I expect anything and everything to be part of my role as a teacher? The answer is not simple. On some days it will be yes, perhaps because that is what is necessary for 200 or 400 or 1,600 children and adults to function compatibly in a relatively small space.

By now you may be thinking that life as a teacher sounds like a situation completely out of your control. True, there is a certain degree of ambiguity. But something else is present as well—the opportunity for you to make a difference, to make some decisions of your own. Now we want you to think about how you will interact with the organiza-

"Cafeteria duty!"
Phi Delta Kappan, June 1985.

tion—actually the rules—as a teacher. This involves both how you will live within the structure and also make a difference.

☐ Teachers and Roles

The issues of education are complicated by questions of the organization, management, and direction of large numbers of persons who are expected to share a common set of goals and get along in a relatively small space. This understanding brings us to a recognition of the need to articulate the various roles of the teacher. There must be some agreement about what people will do and how they will do it if we are to assure the members of the group both productivity (learning) and safety.

Teacher roles can be looked at in five broad categories—academic, social, managerial, legal, and organizational. We can easily agree that each of these roles is crucial, and even that teachers probably engage in playing out each of these roles on a daily basis. At the same time, we may find that the carrying out of one role interferes with the carrying out of another. That is what makes the life of a teacher both complicated and challenging.

The academic role of the teacher is generally the most commonly accepted one. There is little disagreement that the teacher is responsible for transmitting knowledge and skills that enhance the students' ability to learn. In the same category but somewhat more controversial is the expectation that teachers will transmit culture and values, and that they will teach their students to think. Here one often encounters a situation in which content and methodology are decided by someone other than the teacher. For example, the teacher's decision to transmit a segment of American culture by using the novel, *The Grapes of Wrath* in English class may be met with objections from citizens who are in turn supported by the Board of Education. We regularly face conflict over the teaching of (or the failure to teach) certain values, and even the teaching of thinking becomes problematic when it results in students' questioning ideas and procedures held dear by their elders.

Another role of the teacher involves responsibility for the socialization of young people. Even new teachers are generally aware that we hold two concepts to be fundamental to our society—a sense of group cohesion that forms the basis for our version of democracy, and a sense of individuality that is essential to our capitalistic society. Teachers are also aware of the potential for contradiction within these concepts and for the varying interpretations our citizens put on them. Nevertheless, it is the responsibility of the teacher to inculcate in his or her students a sense of belonging to a group and the skills required to live responsibly within a group, at the same time that he or she teaches students to do their individual best, to compete, and to excel. In many cases, the parent–counselor–scout leader role requires some very delicate integration with other roles.

Effective management of instruction is dependent on the teacher's taking on a managerial role. The teacher must keep records of such things as attendance, test scores, use of books, condition of instructional materials, students' behaviors, and contacts with parents. The role of manager also involves the making of arrangements for field trips, class plays, use of parent volunteers, and trips to and from the cafeteria or the bathroom. While it may seem sad, it is true that many teachers' careers rise or fall on their ability to move their students around the school building rather than on what they teach in the specified curriculum. Many teachers contend that the performance of this role detracts from the performance of their instructional role.

Teachers also have legal responsibilities within their role as teacher. Although teachers are not at the top of the power structure in a school, they are certainly not absolved of responsibility for rules. Perhaps their most obvious role with respect to rules is that of enforcer; they help students to live within the rules of the school, and they redirect those who find themselves running at cross-purposes with the school's rules.

Teachers are also makers of rules. In some cases they do so by actually constructing specific rules and presenting them to their students. In other cases the rules are the product of an agreement reached by teacher and students. And other rules arise in more subtle ways, frequently out of a set of generally held understandings.

The last of the five role responsibilities facing a teacher is that of being a member of the school organization. This role involves such activities as participation on committees, and doing one's share in curriculum development, as examples. But in actual practice, there is another aspect to organization membership that we often tend to ignore. That is the idea that all people in organizations, no matter who they are, are governed by rules. The rules are not always written on paper but they do make up the expectations for persons in specific roles. The difficulty for an inexperienced teacher lies in uncovering these expectations before he or she runs amok of something everyone else takes for granted.

Prospective teachers must give some thought to the effects of either accepting or violating the school's rules. Blind followers are hardly the kind of people who are effective stimuli for students or creators of interest in learning. Rather we look for you to consider all sides of a rule. For example, you don't like being at school by 7:35 A.M.

"I'm giving you a 'Marginal' on your attitude toward construc-
tive criticism."
Phi Delta Kappan, January 1985.

because you would rather sleep later than that, you must drop your
child at nursery school after 7:30, the traffic is unpredictable, or you
don't need the time before school to get organized because you complete
everything before leaving in the afternoon. From another perspective,
however, your failure to arrive on time may affect others. The area you
supervise on the students' arrival in the morning is uncovered; your
homeroom is unsupervised; students cannot find you for extra help
before classes actually begin; an administrator or secretary will spend
time rescheduling to cover your absence; parents trying to contact you
by telephone will not reach you. Even though it is possible that the rest
of the world could adapt to your irregularities, they must give time,
energy, and tolerance to do so. Multiply that effort by the number of
teachers in the school, and even the most self-centered person can
imagine the problems that some rules are designed to prevent.

CHAPTER SUMMARY

■ In this chapter we have pointed to many sources of expectations for
schools and teachers. Most of these sources are outside the schools and
involve people who may be far less knowledgeable about education
than you will be as a teacher. We have noted the influence of federal
and state legislators who of course respond to their constituents;

federal and state departments of education and their vast bureaucracies; textbook manufacturers and testing agencies; and the local board
of education members and their constituents. While teachers are most
directly responsible for achieving the expectations, the expectations
themselves have many sources.

You may argue that as many concepts of the role of teacher exist
as do teachers. From one perspective, we agree that such diversity is
crucial to good education. From another viewpoint, we see a need for
some agreement on what life as a teacher really is. Perhaps a parallel
example can illustrate the point. Imagine a grade K to 6 elementary
school of three classrooms at each grade level with no curricular
guidelines. Even if each teacher maintained his or her own set of
educational experiences over the years and there were no staff changes,
a child spending 7 years in that school could potentially have any one
of 2,187 different 7-year educational packages. Since schools cannot
handle such unconstrained diversity, they establish curricular plans.
For similar reasons, the sources of expectations that we have explored
have contributed to a definition of school as an organizational structure, and have defined a teacher role that will assure some chance of
achieving these expectations.

Just as we pointed to the variety of roles each teacher must play
in order to assume the entire "teacher" role, we also contend that it is
the integration of these roles—conflictual as they may seem at some
moments—that is the essence of being a teacher. We have argued
throughout this chapter that it is how you integrate the many roles of
a teacher that makes a difference to your students and to your own
level of satisfaction with your being a teacher. It is how you bring
balance to the multifaceted expectations from all the constituent
groups and individuals that affect schools, students, and teachers that
determines what kind of education your students will gain from you.

We have also shown you in this chapter that the definitions and
the structures we create continue to influence themselves. That is,
some of the expectations grow out of the structure of the organization,
and the roles created by the structure are filled by people who have
values, skills, and experiences. Remember those people who were on
the stage at graduation. They share something with you—they too
went to school. They may not have graduated, but they had the
experience of school, which forms the basis for some of the expectations
they exert through their legal power. The parents of your future
students had school experiences too, and their expectations for their
children's education grow out of their own expectations. Even you, as
a prospective teacher, will never leave behind your elementary or
secondary school experiences, nor will you escape the impact of the
class for which you are reading this book.

The next two chapters present the story of education in this country from the earliest Puritan community schools to those we know today. You will see clearly how decisions about schooling were made on the basis of the earlier experiences of the decision makers—often not persons with the level of professional expertise of a teacher. The history of the ungraded class movement is a good example. Learning theory supports the practice of mixing students of various ages—perhaps 7-, 8- and 9-year-olds—together in one classroom and teaching them what they are ready to learn in the manner they would best learn it. But at the time that teachers and others attempted to implement this practice, virtually all school board members, voters, principals, and parents recalled their own third-grade years and remembered that they had experienced third grade in a classroom with other third-grade students only. Emotional ties triumphed over well-supported theory, and decisions were made on the basis of personal needs of the expectation-setters rather than the needs of students. In fact, what we see here is the hidden set of expectations contributing to the structure of the organization and thus to its operation.

We know that as a teacher you will encounter many situations similar to the one just described. You will work with persons (perhaps your superior) who will make decisions that are consistent with what they have always done and are not necessarily the best decisions in the current situation. But we want you to remember what you have experienced in this chapter: reading, thinking, and discussing have carried you beyond an unknowing acceptance of such decisions.

As you move along the path to a classroom of your own, we want you to think about the issues we have raised. We believe that you can be successful as a teacher, and that you will be happy only if you have considered what your role will be in a school and how that role will interfere with other persons in the organization. Only you will know for sure if that role in both its definition and its ambiguity will be well-suited to you. As a teacher you will be educated in content areas and teaching skills. And yet you will be subject to the expectations—often contradictory ones—of many other people. It will be your difficult but nonetheless important task to select the best from these expectations for your students in whose interest you must always work.

FOR DISCUSSION

1. How is the structure of a school organization affected by the source of its money? What do you predict would happen if the resources were to become more predominantly local? Came more predominantly from the state? From the federal government?

2. How do you think the role of the teacher has been affected by the decrease in the number of school districts? Do you think you would rather work in a small district or a large one? In a small school or a large one? Why?

3. Think about the school handbook you knew when you were in high school. Who do you suppose wrote all the rules? What role do you think the teachers had in their formulation? What role would you like to have when you become a teacher?

4. Think back either to your high school or to an organization of which you are presently a part. Try to determine what rules or practices are a function of an individual's personal needs. Can you recall any personal needs that may have caused conflict within the organization?

5. Which organizational needs result in particular rules in a school? Name the needs you can identify and then write the rules that must follow.

IN THE SCHOOL/IN THE CLASSROOM

In an effort to determine what elements are essentially the same in schools across the country and which ones seem to vary from place to place, plan a visit to two or three schools containing the same grade levels. With the permission of the principal, interview several teachers and perhaps some students as well. Be sure to arrange for a bit of time with the principal, too. Based on your observations of similarities and differences and on some ideas you might have gotten through your reading and class discussion, check out your hunches. Try to get at the reasons for the similarities and differences. Consider such factors as curriculum, grading systems, building structure and appearance, extra-curricular and social activities, use of the school by other groups, student handbooks, and any other ideas you may have.

After visiting the schools and talking to people, try to classify factors as those that seem to be present in every school and those that show some variation from school to school. Wherever you can, add explanations for the factors' placement in one of the two categories.

SUGGESTED READINGS

Blumberg, Arthur and William Greenfield. *The Effective Principal: Perspectives on School Leadership*. Boston: Allyn & Bacon, 1980. This book presents case studies of eight practicing principals. It provides insight into how they view their jobs and how that thinking shapes the school.

Goodlad, John. *A Place Called School: Prospects for the Future*. New York: McGraw-Hill, 1984. A detailed collection of actual practices in schools that gives the prospective teacher a basis for determining what practices he or she wishes to engage in and which ones should be avoided or adjusted for.

Lightfoot, Sara Lawrence. *The Good High School: Portraits of Character and Culture*. New York: Basic Books, 1983. Lightfoot presents a positive view of what can happen (and does happen) in some of our schools in which leadership facilitates teaching and learning, and teachers make the kinds of choices we are suggesting in this chapter.

Lortie, Dan. *School Teacher: A Sociological Study*. Chicago: University of Chicago Press, 1975. This book presents the clearest picture we know of the nature of teachers and teaching. Reading it now will afford the prospective teacher a view of the cohort of professionals he or she is about to join.

Sizer, Ted. *Horace's Compromise*. Boston: Houghton Mifflin, 1984. Sizer and his research team studied numerous American high schools, described what they saw happening there, and then drew up some recommendations for structural changes that they believe could result in a dramatically different kind of education for students.

CHAPTER REFERENCES

1. "Heads Up: Professionally and Financially You're Better Off Than Ever Before," *The American School Board Journal* 172 (1985): 29.

2. Luvern L. Cunningham and Joseph Hentges, eds., *The American Superintendency, 1982: A Full Report* (Arlington, Va.: American Association of School Administrators, 1983), pp. 31–54.

3. Max Weber, *The Theory of Social and Economic Organization,* trans., A.M. Henderson and Talcott Parsons; ed. Talcott Parsons (Glencoe, Ill.: Free Press, 1947), pp. 328–329.

4. *Baldwin's Ohio Revised Code* (Columbus: Banks-Baldwin Publishing Co., 1986), p. 55.

5. Ibid., p. 129.

6. Council of Chief State School Officers, *Educational Governance in the States* (Washington, D.C.: U.S. Department of Education, 1983).

7. Roald F. Campbell, Luvern L. Cunningham, Raphael O. Nystrand, and Michael Usdan, *The Organization and Control of American Schools,* 5th ed. (Columbus, Ohio: Charles E. Merrill Publishing Co., 1985), p. 179.

8. Norma Mertz and Frederick Venditti, "Advancing Women in Administration: Study of an Intervention Strategy," *Journal of Educational Equity and Leadership* 5 (1985): 31.

9. Leonard L. Valverde, *Successive Socialization: Its Influences on School Administration Candidates and Its Implication to the Exclusion of Minorities From Administration,* Project 3-0813 (Washington, D.C.: National Institute of Education, 1974), pp. 1–5.

10. Stephen J. Knezevich, *Administration of Public Education: A Sourcebook for the Leadership and Management of Educational Institutions,* 4th ed. (New York: Harper and Row, 1984), p. 173.

11. Wayne K. Hoy and Cecil G. Miskel, *Educational Administration: Theory, Research, and Practice* (New York: Random House, 1982), p. 32.

12. Ibid., p. 34.

13. Ibid., p. 48.

9

Contexts for Teaching: Perspectives Before the Twentieth Century

A SCENARIO: A MATTER OF VALUE

■ For most beginning teachers the first day on the first job is filled with both anxiety and anticipation. The days that follow are characterized by "settling in": getting to know the students, the routines, and the "system" in general. Facing the first class in the first year is accompanied by a conviction to overcome self-doubt, to make the most of one's skills, and above all to survive. The students and parents are unknown; the administration seems friendly, but in command. Of most concern is not saying the "wrong thing," the phrase that might arouse suspicion. But for the moment, all is well, and the task is to keep it that way.

The gradual accommodation of student, teacher, and parent takes place. The emphasis on basic skills and information gives direction to the elementary class. Slowly, however, there develops a need for something more. Students ask questions that take the teacher outside the familiar territory of texts, workbooks, and unit plans. The teacher is uneasy, but with growing confidence spends more time engaging the class in dialogue. "Neutrality" is the key word, or so the new teacher remembers having been told in some college class. The students' questions seem innocent enough: "Is life more important than anything else?", "Is war okay?", "Is the President always right?"

The teacher has fielded most of the questions without incident. There are a number of uncompromising opinions voiced by students. These are usually accompanied by the justification that, "My father said. . . ." The dreaded day comes eventually with the call by the parent requesting a conference. The call is a simple, "I'd like to see you." But when asked for more specifics, the mystery continues in the sentence, "I'd like to talk to you about something."

The appointment is made, and parent and teacher meet for the first time. The teacher is affable, the parent demure. When asked if there is any problem with his daughter's work, the parent says, "No, no problem, but I think you're saying some things that are incorrect. There is something you said in class about a week ago that was way out of line from our point of view."

The use of the word "our" turned out to be more than symbolic, for the parent had had discussions about the matter with his neighbors. The source of the problem turned out to be a remark by the teacher to the effect that war was seldom justified because of the high value that we place on life. Though this seemed a rational, objective statement at the time, it became highly provocative when put in the context of the community's attitude that "there are some things worth fighting for." The reaction of those to whom the parent had talked had ranged from "maybe we should set her straight" to comments about the pinkish color of the teacher's illegitimate origins.

The parent-teacher conference that ensued was less than satisfying for the teacher although it was without verbal hostilities. This was due primarily to such deflecting statements by the teacher as "I can respect that," "It does seem something else could have been said," and "It didn't seem controversial at the time, but I see what you mean." At the same time, however, the teacher could not help but feel that she had "lost," that what was really an honest statement of conviction was sacrificed. That was a lot of humility for one day. Even going over in her mind the hundred things that could have been said to change the outcome didn't help. When all was said and done it still seemed that no one had the right to put her in that position: "It wasn't fair."

INTRODUCTION

■ Such confrontations—many of them far more severe—number in the hundreds of thousands each week. They are, of course, personally significant. But they also reflect the larger issues of the differing purposes of schooling and the different constituencies that attempt to control schools. Historically you will see that the moral mission of elementary schools has been equally important as their academic mission. The gradual emergence of teaching as a profession has also tended to widen the gap between teacher and community. After all, if the teacher is to be a professional, then surely he or she ought to have some say about what goes on in the classroom.

But what does it mean to have more say? Does it mean making decisions about content, values, and instructional techniques? For the most part, it has meant the last of these three. This is one of the dilemmas that elementary (and secondary) teachers have faced. In deciding to "open up" the classroom, the teacher in the scenario undoubtedly made a technical decision about how to conduct her class. Yet at the same time the decision placed a priority on a free exchange of ideas. What appeared to be only a decision about instructional technique actually involved assumptions about the values to be communicated in the classroom. Substance (content), as the teacher found out, could not be separated from technique.

What teachers do depends, in part, on what other teachers have done in the past. It also depends on what the current public expects them to do. Looked at in this way, being a teacher is a result of both tradition and expectations. In this chapter we will look at how teachers were expected to behave in the past and how these behaviors relate to more general philosophic issues that have recurred in education.

The history of American teaching is a history of responses to the continuities as well as the changes in the priorities of American culture. Changes in the structure of family life, for example, brought changes in the demands made on teachers. Increasingly the teacher became a parent away from home and took on additional responsibilities associated with child rearing. Changes in the education of teachers then followed closely on the heels of these demands.

It is important to distinguish between what teachers actually did and what people expected them to do. The latter is not too difficult to describe; the former is quite difficult to investigate historically. For example, people visualized the teacher as an important person in making America more democratic, more moral, and stronger in the face of external threats to its security. Yet the teacher's career and his or her classroom behavior were dominated by many routine and mundane tasks necessary to keep the classroom running from day to day. These two dimensions of a teacher's life were not necessarily incompatible, but they were very different. Moreover, they were not easily linked together in how teachers were perceived and what they actually did. The same difficulty is present for contemporary teachers.

COLONIAL PRECEDENTS

■ New England Puritans of the early 17th century and their cultural heirs during the next 100 years asked all parents to discipline their children spiritually and intellectually. They asked the same of their teachers. Throughout 17th century colonial America, elementary schooling was an extension of family values considered important by the clergymen of the New World. Family, church, and community set educational standards and priorities. In general, however, there were very few differences in the purposes and methods of education in early colonial America from those of the mother country, England.

If we are to believe the accounts of diaries and the sermons delivered in colonial New England, important teaching took place in nonschool settings. Teaching basic skills, proper behavior, and morality were responsibilities of the family. Proper socialization was clearly a family obligation. Lessons in rhetoric and logic could be learned by listening to a persuasive sermon. Learning was a far more important activity than teaching. Only in a generic sense, not a professional sense, was teaching a priority in Puritan life.

Teaching within the family and church was a matter of bringing children, servants, and apprentices to a recognition of their sinful nature, their responsibility to obey God, community, and parents, and their duty to learn the lessons of the Scriptures. Benjamin Wadsworth's essay on the "Well-Ordered Family" (1712) gives the rationale for keeping a close watch over children:

> Children should not be left to themselves, to a loose end, to do as they please, but should be *under Tutors and Governours,* not being fit to govern themselves.[1] [Wadsworth's italics]

Reading instruction was designed to teach children to read the Bible and catechism. Other subjects, too, had their religious justifications. Grammar and rhetoric, said the New England clergyman Cotton Mather, were useful in persuading others and oneself to the service of the Lord. Logic helped in disputing with the Devil. Astronomy led to a better knowledge of Heaven. Geography prepared a man to wisely use the earth.

Much of the teaching done in early America was by exhortation. This was primarily a matter of leading the child in repetitious exercises. A good reader was one who recited well. The limitations of this method, however, were clearly recognized by the more astute observers of the educational process. Cotton Mather complained that children should do more than memorize and repeat by rote. Said Mather:

> Be not satisfied with Hearing the *Children* patter out by Rote the words of the *Catechism* like Parrots; but be Inquisitive how far their *Understandings* do take in the Things of God.[2] [Mather's italics]

Reading and spelling were the most important subjects; writing and arithmetic less so. Above all, teachers were to be morally pure. Academic preparation for teaching was minimal. Often a community considered itself fortunate to have a teacher whose penmanship was clear and whose competency in arithmetic extended to the "rule of three" (proportions). At the secondary level more was expected. The Latin grammar school was the standard college-preparatory institution. Students attending such schools received instruction in Latin grammar, literature, and composition.

The lack of good preparation for teaching was not the major concern it was by the mid 19th century. There were, however, a few who thought that "knowing" a subject did not guarantee that one could teach it. John Clarke, a provincial schoolmaster in England, published "An Essay Upon the Education of Youth in Grammar-Schools" (1730) in which he outlined a plan for the reform of "secondary" education in the Latin grammar school. Clarke tried to modernize the teaching of the classical subjects. He also observed the need for greater attention to the quality of teaching. "It is not every Stripling from the University, tho' of a sober, regular Behavior, that can or ought to be looked upon, as well enough fitted for the important charge of educating youth," said Clarke.[3] Issac Watts was another Englishman who wrote on the need for the reform of teaching and education. He also made a point of

FOR REFLECTION 9.1

As you review the history of teaching presented in this chapter, one of the recurring debates that you will observe is the importance of academics versus the importance of effective teaching methods. Clarke and Watts were not the first to recognize this dilemma. They were, however, ahead of most teachers of their time. You will experience this dilemma many times in the course of your teacher education program. In fact, it is very likely you will argue with others over what the proper academic/professional balance should be. In discussing what the balance should be, it might be worthwhile to consider two concepts: (1) necessary and (2) sufficient. For example, pose the question in this manner:

> What are the *necessary* and *sufficient* conditions for bringing about effective teaching?

First, consider what you believe to be *necessary* to effective teaching. Second, consider what is *sufficient* for it to occur. Use these concepts in asking, What is the proper balance between academic and professional preparation? Clarke and Watts raised this question very early in our educational history when they questioned the prevalent attitude that all that was needed to teach was the knowledge of a content area.

the sometimes great discrepancy between scholarship and ability to teach. Said Watts: "it is not every one who is a great scholar, that always becomes the happiest teacher."[4] It was necessary, said Watts, to fit the method of instruction and the delivery of information to the student.

The transition from the colonial period to the founding of a new nation was important educationally as well as politically. Gradually, the burden of instruction shifted from the family, church, and community to the school. It must be understood, however, that this shift did not eliminate education outside the school. It was a gradual and subtle shift at first, but eventually the school became the major institution for transmitting basic skills. Just as important was the fact that the school became the primary institution for citizenship education. Thus, in the 19th century, the school became a major institution for moral, civic, and basic-skill education.

AN EMERGING NATION

■ In 1798 Samuel Harrison Smith spoke of establishing the "right to educate and acknowledge the duty of having educated, all children."[5] Smith's words were from a prize-winning essay submitted to the American Philosophical Society, and his concern was addressed by many political leaders of the late 18th and early 19th centuries in the United States. Stabilizing the government and society of the newly formed republic called the United States was a high priority. The message was carried through educational reform movements of the 19th century. Thomas Jefferson was also well known for his concern with the education of future political leaders and his proposal for establishing a free public school system in his own state of Virginia. In 1801 James Monroe also observed that "in a government founded on the sovereignty of the people the education of youth is an object of the first importance." "In such a government," said Monroe, "knowledge should be diffused throughout the whole society, and for that purpose the means of acquiring it made not only practicable but easy to every citizen."[6]

To reconcile the promise of freedom with the necessity for a stable government was a problem that some founding fathers hoped to resolve through education. The task was both a moral and political one. Early 19th century educational leaders, says Kaestle, hoped that "a sound education would prepare men to vote intelligently and prepare women to train their sons properly."[7] They sought to convince politicians, newspaper editors, and any public-spirited citizens who would listen that American citizens needed an education in basic literacy. For Noah Webster, author of the famous *Blue-Backed Speller,* citizens needed to learn about ethics, law, commerce, and government as well.[8] Webster worked tirelessly for spelling reform and uniformity of language in hope that a "national language" would create national union.

BASIC EDUCATION

■ In the various attempts to provide instruction for the new citizens of the American republic we see the foundation of many recurring themes that have both inspired and troubled teachers to the present time. It was clear to early American educators, for example, that education should serve a moral purpose and be useful in a practical

FOR REFLECTION 9.2

It should be apparent that citizenship education in a broad sense was part of the purpose of publicly supported schooling. Although the emphases have varied over time, good citizenship has remained a central purpose of public schooling in America. On the surface, this part of the public school mission seems to raise few questions. After all, good citizens are necessary to the maintenance of good government. Every government, moreover, must have some means for teaching the values accompanying good citizenship.

We should, however, take a second look at this major purpose of public schooling. We should first ask, What definition of citizenship are we speaking of when we speak of good citizenship? As with any definition we should ask, What is the standard of reference? Is it political, economic, or social, for example? It is extremely important to decide this before going ahead with a discussion of good citizenship.

If we are speaking of citizenship in a political sense, we must ask questions about what citizens need to know to participate intelligently in their own governance. If the standard of reference is economic, then we need to ask questions about a person's contribution to the overall economic well-being of a society. If we use the term citizenship in a very broad way, then we must be aware that our definition may cover so much that it becomes meaningless. Part of the problem with defining any term is to give it a specific and clear meaning. This requires a specific standard of reference and a decision about how to use the term. In reading these chapters on the history of teaching, you should ask how the standard of reference for a term like citizenship has changed and what is the most accurate and meaningful use of the term today.

sense at the same time. They did not consider the two incompatible. A moral citizen was a good citizen. Even from an economic standpoint, morality was an asset, especially when making honest bargains and contracts.

Education for practical skills, however, was a different issue. Public schools and community-based subscription schools (schools to which parents "subscribed" for their children) did not usually offer what we think of as practical skills. Apprenticeship and special schools, such as writing schools, and some academies served the purpose of vocational instruction.

Public school instruction in the early 19th century was generally confined to teaching the basics of reading, spelling, writing, and some arithmetic. Geography and grammar were also included if the teacher had adequate preparation. The objective of this instruction was the achievement of basic literacy and was justified primarily on political and moral grounds. The teacher was both a moral agent and a teacher of basic skills.

Religious teaching was seldom absent from early 19th century schools and was closely related to the teaching of other subjects. Such teaching was generally nondenominational unless the school was run by a particular religious sect. Nonetheless, the viewpoint of religious instruction was generally Protestant. In fact, it built upon the well-established tradition of colonial days when the primary goal of instruction was to teach Bible literacy.

The method of reading instruction was ritualistic and repetitious and fit well with its religious and moral purpose. The measure of reading achievement was a child's ability to recite aloud. In practice, oration was as important as comprehension. Reading was serious business because 19th century educators strongly believed in the moral effect of knowledge. They likewise took steps to safeguard the moral character of teachers. They did this by issuing certificates of good moral character and by making public announcements about the necessity of hiring teachers with unblemished moral records. Later in the 19th century Horace Mann put this concern well when he said the teacher must be "clothed in virtue."

SCIENCE AND MENTAL DEVELOPMENT

■ At the opening of the 19th century, the impact of science and scientific thinking on education was noticeable although not popularly acknowledged. The lyceum movement eventually helped to popularize science in all its applications. In the latter 18th century, many leaders

School apparatus

Advertisement for Holbrook School Apparatus, *American Journal of Education,* vol. 1 (1855–56).

of American intellectual life enthusiastically embraced the idea of progressive science. The American attitude toward scientific progress was clearly practical. Improvements in agriculture and mechanics received a great deal of attention. The scientific approach to broader social issues, including education, was also in evidence, however.

A scientific attitude toward education did not mean an experimental attitude in the sense of that term today. It did mean, however, a rational, systematic, and objective attitude. It meant, for some educational reformers, a willingness to reevaluate methods of instruction in light of new findings about the nature of children and the nature of the mind.

The faith in the power of man's intellect was expressed well by James Cutbush in 1812. Cutbush saw education as improving unfavorable social conditions, particularly poverty. His faith in the power of intellect to improve the lot of the poor and to lead man toward a better system of government was characteristic of the period. Cutbush based much of his argument on John Locke's theory of sense learning. Said Cutbush: "It is obvious . . . that the *exercise of the senses,* must evidently be the direct way to improve the intellect [Cutbush's italics]." In a wonderful analogy to the practical field of mechanics and the laws of motion, Cutbush reasoned that the "velocity of the mind is to the velocity of the senses, as the circumference of the mind, is to the circumference of the objects." "The *action* of genius," he continued, depended "on the quickness of the sensations . . . exactly in the same ratio as power is gained in the wheel and axle [Cutbush's italics]." This theory held out the possibility of basing instruction on the cultivation of the senses. It helped open the way to a clearer explanation of the link between a child's physical and emotional development and his intellectual development.[9]

By the fourth decade of the 19th century the importance of a theory of sensation to the improvement of instruction was widely recognized by educational reformers. It was commonly thought that the link between language development and sensation was the key to all intellectual development. In her essay dealing with education as a natural science, Addicks explained that language made it possible for man to transform raw sensation into rational thinking. She concluded that "with his first thought man must have uttered his first word." It followed that "the first step to civilization must have been the improvement of language."[10]

The immediate practical significance of a theory of sensation to language development was seen by European educators first and then spread to America. In his *Pestalozzian Primer* (1827) John M. Keagy observed that our thoughts "consist of a recurrence to our minds of *what we have seen, heard, tasted, smelled, or felt, and mental combinations and judgments concerning those things.*" Our minds, continued Keagy, repeat these sensations to form an idea. It followed, he said, that the education of the senses is basic to the education of the mind.[11]

Keagy's method of teaching young children to read was based on the "cultivation of the senses." It emphasized reading with understanding, not mere pronunciation. Although his own primer fell short of the ideal, Keagy advocated a method of teaching reading called the "whole word" or analytical method. The child first learned to think through oral expression and then moved on to the study of whole words. Next came the study of sentences, through oral reading. What Keagy wished to avoid was the learning of the ABC's as the *first step* in the reading process.

Keagy was only one of many who, between 1825 and 1840, sought alternatives to the traditional ABC approach to teaching reading. Throughout the decades between 1830 and 1860 controversy increased over how to teach reading. "Whole word" advocates debated ABC'ers over the effectiveness of their methods. This debate continues today in moderated form.

By 1840 a third strategy had been added to the debate. This was the phonetic method using the phonetic alphabet. Advocates like Charles Royce were "ready to prove, that a child can be taught to read and spell the Romanic print much quicker, and at the same time will become a much better reader and speller, by first learning to read the Phonetic print."[12] By the time of the Civil War all three alternatives were considered legitimate, but not necessarily exclusive of one another. Thus compromises and combinations of the three were made in actual practice.

BEING A GOOD TEACHER

■ Advice was plentiful on how to be a good teacher in the early 19th century. No single book, however, probably had more influence on teaching than Samuel Hall's *Lectures on School-Keeping,* published in 1829. Hall's book was influential for the next 40 years.

Like others interested in the improvement of education during this period, Hall was concerned with the quality of persons entering teaching. He deplored both the motivations and the qualifications of teachers who were only looking for something a little more respectable than manual labor. Many of these had only elementary schooling themselves. Teachers were often transient and left their schools after only a few months. Others, whose nature was greedy, "kept" private schools only for financial reward and probably overcharged for what they taught.

One of the most difficult problems for teachers was the unwillingness of many school districts to pay well those teachers who were qualified and talented. Merchants were overstocked with clerks, and professors of law and medicine had more than enough students. Yet few were willing to enter teaching. The reason, thought Hall, was inadequate pay. Clerks were often paid three times the monthly wages of teachers in rural district schools. Thus, for example, the average female teacher in a rural district in 1841 made about $10.00 a month while an experienced clerk, depending on need, could make about $30.00. Male teachers fared somewhat better at $16.50 a month.[13]

Following this distressing portrait of teacher quality and public disinterest, Hall explained the general characteristics desirable in teachers. These included common sense, uniformity of temper, a capacity to understand and discriminate among indidivuals, decisiveness, affection, and moral sensibility. As for the subjects that every teacher should master, Hall explained that no teacher could be considered qualified without a thorough knowledge of subjects taught in the common school. These included reading, writing, grammar, arithmetic, geography, and occasionally history of the United States. These were minimum standards, Hall observed. A thorough preparation included intellectual arithmetic (derivation of the rules of mathematics), the constitutions of the United States and the teacher's state of residence, rhetoric, natural philosophy, chemistry, and moral philosophy. These subjects, together with the basics, supposedly gave the teacher the capability to educate children in logical and abstract thought. They were also to give them an understanding of their political freedoms and obligations, and the moral foundations of their actions.

Hall encouraged prospective teachers to familiarize themselves with day-to-day realities of the school. Observe children closely and talk to experienced teachers, Hall suggested. To teach is to "communicate ideas," said Hall. It was imperative to use language that students understood. If the illustration used to make a point is no clearer than the point you are making, you will not gain much, observed Hall. Affection for pupils, patience, and insistence on respect were necessary to good teaching. Good order and punctuality made teaching easier and inspired confidence in the teacher, said Hall, who urged teachers to be systematic but pleasant. Governing oneself would help in governing the classroom, Hall continued.

Hall urged his readers to "consider your scholars as reasonable and intelligent beings." The teacher, said Hall, should assume that pupils are capable of knowing the difference between right and wrong and are happier when they do right. Hall then proceeded to establish certain guidelines for punishment. These included (1) *"Never be in haste to believe that a pupil has done wrong"*; (2) "Be not *in haste to punish* when a fault is committed"; (3) "Decide on such a mode [of punishment] as will be most likely to benefit the scholar, and *prevent a repetition* of the crime"; and (4) "Always make the punishment *effectual.*"[14] [Hall's italics]

Near the end of his manual, Hall recommended several ways to motivate students. Teachers should appeal to the practical rewards of study such as greater respectability and usefulness. Admiration and praise by friends was also a reward that students could expect. This was the baser side of motivation, but there was the love of learning also. To communicate a "love of learning for its own sake" was a powerful long-range stimulus to further study, said Hall. Finally, in a statement characteristic of the time for its appeal to conscience and morality, Hall advised teachers to tell students of their "obligation" and "duty" to study. This was a duty that, if fulfilled, would add to

Recitation

Lyman Cobb, *New Juvenile Reader, No. 1* (Cincinnati: B. Davenport, 1848).

their happiness and, if ignored, would lead to a guilty conscience.[15]

It should be obvious to the contemporary reader that much of Hall's advice was common sense. Certain traditional values expressed by Hall were characteristic of the age in which he lived. Yet his approach to teaching was also forward-looking. His practical approach to the problems of motivation, classroom management, communication, and mastery was designed to cut through the heavy rhetoric of longer treatises on how to teach children. His work, moreover, pointed toward the eventful preoccupation of teachers with the technology (methodology) of teaching in the last half of the 19th century.

☐ **Establishing a Teaching Force**

During the late 1830s and the decade of the 1840s many issues dealing with how to teach children coalesced in a movement toward special training for teachers. This "normal school" movement, as it was called,

FOR REFLECTION 9.3

The work of Samuel Hall reminds us of the great variety of things expected from a teacher. The teacher is a transmitter of basic skills, a developer of logical and abstract thought, and a preserver of political and moral values. The task of the teacher seems broad indeed. In fact, it may be so broad as to be impossible to achieve. Hall's manual illustrates well the persistent problem of defining what it is a teacher should and can do. Many times the purposes of schooling are so broad that one despairs of ever defining the major responsibilities of the teacher.

We are faced with a twofold problem. The first is that of sorting out whether or not the many tasks of teaching are compatible with each other. In other words, do the various demands and expectations for teachers mesh together? Many times they do not. Thus, for example, to expect that a teacher will teach acceptable political attitudes and values may be inconsistent with the commitment to teach logical thinking. In this case, we are faced with the problem of choosing which expectation to fulfill. If we think both are worthy of teaching, then we are faced with a second problem: Which one has priority? In other words, where do they stand in order of importance?

The problem of priorities is a common one in teaching. Each day, the teacher is faced with decisions about priorities. These decisions are less burdensome if a teacher has spent some time reflecting on what the purposes and outcomes of teaching should be. If such reflection has not taken place, the teacher has little recourse but to follow what others say or to simply go whichever way the wind blows.

It is important to remember that priorities are extensions of what one values and believes to be true or right. These are difficult questions to get at, but in the long run they can offer a guide to choosing among various possible priorities. The teacher must be introspective to begin the sorting out process of deciding where he or she stands. This need not be a haphazard process. It can be dealt with systematically and objectively. As you continue with this chapter, try to evaluate how different historical situations have influenced teacher priorities.

was a response to expanded public schooling during the period. More children attending school meant that more teachers were needed. There were too few seminaries and academies to prepare enough teachers. Moreover, these institutions were not necessarily affiliated in law or in spirit with the expectations of public school leaders of the period.

Advocates of expanded public schooling in the mid 19th century were usually zealous about the establishment of normal schools because the latter were seen as necessary to more and better public schooling. The first state-supported normal school was opened at Lexington, Massachusetts in 1839. Special classes for teachers and the establishment of a model school had preceded the first normal school. Teacher classes and a model school, for example, had begun at Ohio University in 1831 and 1837.

The enthusiasm and efforts of normal school advocates were not far short of heroic. (This does not mean that the outcomes were successful, however.) A man like Cyrus Peirce, first principal of the normal school at Lexington, was relentless in his attempts to make the school succeed. It is said he allowed himself only 4 hours sleep, thus leaving the necessary time to prepare lessons, carry water, shovel snow, stoke the fires, and do all the other janitorial work.[16]

In his work *Common Schools and Teachers Seminaries* (1839) Calvin Stowe, an Ohio school reformer, outlined a plan for the education of teachers. Stowe's purpose was to professionalize the training of teachers. He assumed that before professional study, however, students would be well grounded in the studies they would have to teach in their schools. Stowe believed that a teacher preparation curriculum should include a "scientific and demonstrative" study of those subjects taught in the common schools. This study was to be accompanied by "directions at every step as to the best method of inculcating each lesson upon children of different dispositions and capacities, and various intellectual habits." In addition to this close link between subject and method, Stowe advocated courses in history of education, philosophy of the mind, the science of education, and the art of teaching.[17] Stowe was far ahead of his time in recommending this pattern for teacher education. Later movements to reform teacher education drew heavily on his ideas and reflected both their strength and weaknesses.

Cyrus Peirce was very much influenced by Stowe and attempted to implement his recommendations in the normal school at Lexington, Massachusetts. Not everyone agreed, however, that state-supported teacher training institutions were a good idea. Teachers themselves were not always supportive. Some religious groups saw these institutions as a threat to their beliefs. Taxpayers complained, and private educational institutions resented the intrusion into their domain.

For educational reformers the stakes were high. Their commitment to the ideal of the teacher as public servant saw the teacher as guardian of the pillars of democracy.[18] Horace Mann, first Secretary of the Board of Education in Massachusetts, was an eloquent spokesman for this ideal. His speech at the dedication of the new normal school building at Bridgewater, Massachusetts in 1846 expresses the great expectations for teachers in this period:

> Neither the art of printing, nor the trial by jury, nor a free press, nor free suffrage, can long exist, to any beneficial and salutary purpose, without schools for the training of teachers.[19]

Other states also moved rapidly in this period to establish normal school systems. By 1844 New York had moved to a normal school system and in 1850 it devised a plan for the direct subsidy of normal school students.

In Connecticut, Henry Barnard, Yale graduate and lawyer, became the leader for public school reform and the establishment of a normal school system. The normal school founded in 1848 actually opened in 1850 with 30 pupils and Henry Barnard as their principal. His plan for a policy of selective admission and high-quality candidates tells us a great deal about what teachers were expected to be. Said Barnard:

> We beg of you as far as you can, to send us candidates for admission to the Normal School, who possess [1] purity and strength of moral and religious character, [2] good health, [3] good manners, [4] love of children, [5] a competent share of talent and information, [6] a native tact and talent for teaching and governing others, [7] a love for the occupations of the schoolroom, [8] the common-school spirit, a martyr spirit, [9] some experience in teaching.[20]

By 1875, 25 states had state normal schools.

Admission to a normal school was not difficult. Early normal schools required a minimum age of 16 to 18 years, a certificate of good moral character, and an examination on subjects taught in most district schools. These, of course, were minimums. Gradually, more and more entrants were high school graduates, reaching 26% by 1900. Many entrants into normal schools had already had experience teaching.

The curriculum of early normal schools matched the expectations for basic education in the public schools of the day. Prospective teachers were to be well grounded in the subjects taught in the common schools. Whether a teacher mastered all or part of the curriculum depended on how long he or she stayed in a normal school. Some only stayed long enough to receive a grounding in reading, writing, arithmetic, geography, grammar, spelling, and composition. For many rural district schools this was sufficient. Teachers who wished a more thorough training could take vocal music, drawing, physiology, algebra, geometry, philosophy, methods of teaching, and reading of the Scriptures.

All these subjects were dealt with in about 1½ years. To move beyond this the prospective teacher took a curriculum more characteristic of the traditional college education. Thus, in the last year and one-half of a 3-year normal school preparation, a student was expected to take advanced mathematics and natural sciences such as chemistry, physical geography, and meteorology. Also included were rhetoric, some theology, and, at his or her option, Latin, French, and German.

Despite the best efforts of normal school reformers, the pattern of teacher preparation was uneven. Teachers were required to know very little about effective ways of communicating. Teacher examinations, when administered by local boards of education, stressed the basics. These examinations focused on definitions, facts that could be memorized, and performance on basic skills. For example, a teacher was expected to answer questions like "How is English Grammar divided? Define each Division," "Reduce six-sevenths of a scruple to the fraction of a pound," or "Name all the political divisions of Asia."

Many times, the only requirement was testimony that the prospective hiree was of good moral character. A job was often the result of family connections or even being the only candidate. Having taken the position, the teacher's major responsibilities might only be to keep good order among the older boys, baby-sit the 4-year-olds, tend to firewood in the winter and ventilation in the summer, and hear the recitations of those who prepared their lessons. All this could be a very uninspiring livelihood. It is no wonder that teachers had difficulty in commanding respect.

By the end of the Civil War debates over the adequacy of normal school training were more frequent. The normal school could hardly be called professional because its graduates received little instruction outside the basics. Nor could it be called collegiate, since it was quite dissimilar to traditional 4-year colleges requiring a classical language. In a very real sense the normal school was an orphan struggling for respectability. Its leaders were proud and searched for ways to professionalize their institutions.

By the end of the 19th century most of the activity to develop normal schools was at the state level. Private normal schools and those operating for and by local municipal districts had gradually phased out their operations. The quality of facilities, faculty, and administration of normal schools varied widely. Libraries and equipment were below the standards of first-rate colleges and universities. Normal schools were usually small institutions and their presidents often took charge of the day-to-day mundane affairs of the schools. The performance of students was often shaped directly by the president who taught and supervised the training schools that were part of the normal institution. The quality and leadership of a president usually determined the quality of the normal school.

Teacher's certificate

Teacher's certificate, Athens Co., Ohio, Canaan Township Board of Education, Local Government Records Collection, Archives and Special Collections, Ohio University Libraries.

Like other aspects of American life in the late 19th century, teacher preparation increasingly became specialized. Types of certificates and curricula multiplied. The debate over the professional versus the academic, the technical versus the liberal, became more intense as teachers were expected to have greater technical expertise. Specialization and technical expertise were seen as the way to respectability. The price paid, however, was a widening gap between teacher training and the roots of the American collegiate tradition.

Much of the chasm between academic and normal schools was due to the divided loyalties of the normal schools themselves. The normal idea in the United States was born of a commitment to mass public schooling, but it quickly turned this commitment into a missionary zeal to uplift its parent. The ideal of service was a crucial part of this uplifting spirit. At the same time, the normal school was dependent on the traditional academic disciplines for much of its knowledge. Legitimacy within the academic world could only be awarded by the professoriate. Normal school leaders knew their position was fragile. They steered a precarious course between the charybdis of public displeasure and the scylla of academic scorn.

EXPANDING THE SYSTEM OF PUBLIC EDUCATION

☐ Patterns of Enrollment

From 1840 to 1870 school enrollments increased rapidly among children ages 6 to 14. In the North, 75% to 80% of children ages 10 to 14 were enrolled in school in 1860 and 1870. The figures were much lower for the South. During the latter part of the 19th century, superintendents, state officials, and legislators interested in education worked to stabilize and extend schooling to all children. Regional differences in enrollments diminished, but the age at which children entered school varied. In the South, school laws kept children out of school until the age of 7 or 8, whereas in the North, entry at the age of 6 or 7 was more common. By 1910, between 90% and 95% of children age 11 to 12 were in school in the East, Mid-Atlantic, and Pacific states. The figure was somewhat lower (80%) for the Southeast and South Central states.[21]

Many factors influenced whether or not a child went to school. These included ethnic background, wealth of parents, nativity, geographical region, and density of population. All helped to create wide variations in enrollments and duration of attendance. Educators remained concerned especially with the continuity of schooling. Teachers recognized the difficulties under which some children labored because of irregular attendance.[22]

In 1910 the story of teenage enrollments was quite different from that for younger children. In the Northeast industrial sector of the country, many children left school at age 14. This was also true in the Middle Atlantic states. In the West, however, a very different pattern prevailed. Here teenage youth remained in high school longer, so that a little over half of 18-year-olds were still in school. Teenage school enrollments in the South were in an intermediate position between East and West.[23]

Between 1910 and 1930, the pattern of teenage school enrollments began to change. Just as large increases in enrollments for children ages 5 to 9 characterized the period from 1890 to 1910, the most dramatic increases between 1910 and 1930 were found among teenagers. This was true in all regions, and in the South enrollments for younger children also rose rapidly. "By 1930," says John Rury, "children aged 7 to 13 were enrolled everywhere at rates of 90% or more."[24] Regional differences among teenage enrollments were still strong, but were diminishing. The United States, by 1930, was moving toward universal schooling.

Enrollment increases in public schooling between 1870 and 1930 put unprecedented pressures on teachers and administrators to reform their teaching methods. As enrollments increased so did the cultural and socioeconomic diversity of the population being served. Mass public schooling brought the problems of cultural diversity directly into the classroom. Normal school leaders responded by making their teacher preparation programs fertile ground for curricular and instructional experiments. Most of these were directed to elementary school children.

☐ A Science of Pedagogy

Following the Civil War new attempts to make normal school training respectable took place. These efforts centered on curriculum revision and closer scrutiny of teacher qualifications. Results came in the form of more standardized curricula with professional sequences and certification requirements designed to demonstrate that the teacher was an expert.

The rapid growth of normal schools with their professional studies helped to give respectability to teaching as a career. It also led to increasing criticism of the narrowness of teacher education. This criticism came largely from traditionalists who believed the language-centered liberal arts curriculum was the proper way to train a teacher.

If modified at all for teachers, the traditional curriculum might include a course in pedagogy offered in conjunction with or parallel to "academic" studies. In the post–Civil War period the debate over the relationship between academic and professional studies intensified.

As the normal school movement grew so did a "science" of pedagogy. This put increasing pressure on teachers to improve their instruction. Following the Civil War, this pressure increased to the point where it was expected that professional studies should be grounded in "scientific" findings.

The movement toward a "science" of pedagogy must be understood within the 19th century meaning of science. Experimental science in the area of what we now call the social sciences was not practiced in the mid 19th century. Nonetheless, there was a faith among normal school leaders that the "laws" of mental development could be discovered and used to improve teaching.

Generally, the "laws" of education were deduced from other known facts in physiology, psychology, ethics, sociology, and political economy. Thus the science of education was "derived" from these "parent" disciplines. This seemed a logical way to establish a science of education, but it had the misfortune of making education an applied science. From an academic point of view this made it a second-class citizen.

In attempting to solve the problem of second-class citizenship, some educational leaders advocated a more empirical approach to understanding the educational process and human learning. The result was the child study movement of the late 19th and early 20th centuries. Attempts at child study were first characterized by an accumulation of disconnected facts. Critics of the method correctly pointed out that accumulation without selection would not serve education very well.

Gradually the child study movement took advantage of theories of maturation and readiness. These became the basis for developmental psychology. In turn, this helped to guide educators (particularly elementary teachers) in planning their sequence of instruction. By 1920 theories of both developmental psychology and curriculum reform merged with theories of social reform and a new vision of democracy to form the progressive movement in education. We will turn to this in greater detail in the next chapter.

☐ Reform in Psychology and Curriculum

During the 1860s there was a resurgence of interest in the methods of Swiss educator Johann Pestalozzi. American educational reformers of the 1830s and 1840s had made the Pestalozzian child-centered, hands-on approach to teaching basic skills popular in America. These methods, however, had not been systematically taught in teacher training curricula before the Civil War.

In 1861 Edward Sheldon of the Oswego, New York normal school helped to popularize Pestalozzian methods by inviting prominent educators to view his practice school. In a few years the methods spread to other normal schools and were reported on favorably by the National Teachers Association in 1865.[25] The Oswego version of Pestalozzian methods was called the "object method."

The object method in teacher training emphasized the close relationship between child development and instruction. The method focused the teacher's attention on the child's senses and their importance to achieving higher level thinking. Familiar objects (household objects, objects from the garden, field, or farm) were shown to children. The children, in turn, were asked to describe and classify them. The purpose of this exercise was to enhance each child's observation skills. Drawings were sometimes made. A more sophisticated version of the method had children analyze stories and poems by writing or dramatizing objects that appeared in the literature.[26]

The great popularity of the object method was due to its easy application in the classroom. It was not primarily concerned with higher order mental development, but instead with its sensory foundations. For this reason, however, its application was also limited. In the hands of those who understood very little about children, the method became mechanistic and narrow-minded. It came to signify, unfortunately, the unexpansive "cookbook" approach to teacher education. What might have been the basis for large-scale reform became preoccupied with the technical aspects of teaching. Despite its shortcomings, the object method helped to break loose the fixation of teachers with formal academic disciplines. In this respect it paved the way for two later educational reform movements known as Herbartianism and progressivism.

The work of Johann Friedrich Herbart, founder of a pedagogical seminary at the University of Königsberg, was popularized by a group of young American educators who had studied in Germany during the 1880s. Among them were Frank M. McMurray, Charles McMurray, and Charles De Garmo, all of whom helped to lead the attack on traditionalism in American education.

Like Pestalozzi, Herbart emphasized the close relationship between child development and methods of instruction. American Herbartians emphasized the idea that children learn subjects best when they are presented in an interesting way and based on previous experience. They attacked lifeless textbooks and memorization of material of interest primarily to adults. Instead, Herbartians emphasized the importance of the child's interest and experience. Herbartians adhered rigorously to what they called the five formal steps of teaching and learning. These included preparation, presentation, association, generalization, and application.[27]

With Illinois State Normal University taking the lead, teacher training institutions rapidly embraced Herbartianism during the 1890s. More than any other educational reform movement prior to progressivism, the Herbartian view of the educational process helped to convey the importance of method. In fact, it helped to redefine the relationship between content and method.

Herbartians took the position that the content of collegiate academic courses for teachers should be selected on the basis of "(1) the degree to which material fostered the development of moral character, and (2) the extent to which the material would challenge the interest of the student." This method of selection differed from the traditional approach of choosing content on the basis of what was recognized as important to the academic disciplines themselves. History and literature were favored by the Herbartians but, as Borrowman observes, the method of selecting materials from these disciplines often ignored what was considered good history.[28]

The 1895 *Report of the Committee of Fifteen on Elementary Education* of the National Educational Association helped educators focus on the close relationship between curriculum development, child study, and culture. The Committee of Fifteen's subcommittee on the "correlation of studies" emphasized the close relationship between child development and curriculum. The natural progress of the child was an important standard of reference for designing a course of study. Level of study was to correspond to "maturity" of the student. Their recommendation that studies be correlated with the "civilization into which the child was born" reflected a common expectation for schools and a responsibility to be carried out by teachers.[29]

The influence of the child study movement and the scientific findings about child development were applied primarily at the elementary school level. At the secondary school level, tradition weighed heavily in the time-honored boundaries of the academic disciplines. The logic of the academic disciplines themselves generally determined the sequence and manner of instruction. Thus, when the *Report of the Committee of Ten on Secondary School Studies* of the National Educational Association was published in 1893, the influence of child development theory was minimal.

FOR REFLECTION 9.4

In the 19th century, we have seen instances of educational reform that attempted to place instruction on a scientific basis. These included, first, those inspired by Swiss educator Johann Pestalozzi in the early 19th century. Later the object method and the movement known as Herbartianism continued this trend. In the 20th century also this was followed by the child study movement and progressivism. Today, it is common to appeal to scientific (experimental) findings as a basis for the reform of instruction. It would appear that science has gradually come to have a powerful grip on the minds of American educators. We should ask, then, why has this been the case and what is the source of the power of science?

One way of answering this question is to look at the meanings and use of the word "science" in our culture. By analyzing what the term represents we can better understand its influence on education.

First of all, science is a term that represents a certain type of inquiry characterized by objectivity and experiment. This inquiry is carried out in public and the results should be there for all to see. The foundation for this inquiry is our senses. If we have a scientific approach to inquiry, we record our observations accurately and completely. Others can then repeat our experiments to see if we are accurate.

This open, nonsecretive way of inquiry is extremely important to our acceptance of scientific findings. Part of what makes scientific findings acceptable is that they are there for all to see. They are legitimate because they belong to everyone. The idea that scientific facts or scientific evidence is open also helps to *convey* the idea that these facts really represent what is true. They can be tested and retested so that we do not have to take the word of one person only. Presumably, if enough people agree that the facts are true, then they must be true unless contradictory evidence comes to light.

Whether or not truth by majority rule is a good way of inquiry is open to question, of course. It is very possible for the majority of scientists to commit the same error over and over again. Although it is common to hear the phrase, "The facts speak for themselves," they do not. People not only define what is and what is not a fact, but they also speak for the facts.

Finally, the idea of science is a kind of metaphor for progress itself. There is a tremendous faith in science by many who use it. We saw this expressed clearly in the late 18th century. In this metaphor, science is not simply "true facts"; it is a body of facts that leads to some improvement of our situation. Science is seen as useful because it leads to the improvement of mankind's situation. Were it not for this faith, it is likely that science would not have the power over our minds that it does.

In the previous paragraphs, we have looked briefly at the historical significance of science in educational matters. We have gone beyond that however, by examining the meanings we attach to and the use we make of the term itself. This process of analyzing a term for its hidden and perhaps alternative meanings is an important tool in critically understanding the subject matter with which we are dealing. In education, and in other areas in which science is a powerful tool, we must look beyond the facts and ask: To what purpose are the facts being put and how does that purpose influence the meaning(s) we attach to facts?

Among the more notable features of the report was the continued prominence of intellectual discipline as the leading idea underlying secondary school studies. There was considerable confusion over the content and duration of secondary school studies at the turn of the century. The task faced by the Committee of Ten was to "make order out of the widespread chaos in secondary education."[30]

The Latin grammar school and the academy were major college preparatory institutions in the 19th century. Very few students attended Latin grammar schools, the purpose of which was mainly college preparatory. Academies, however, often offered a more practical curriculum than that found in the Latin grammar schools. Thus, academies provided an important alternative for those who did not wish to go to college. Academies, however, also offered a college preparatory course of study that included the classical languages. Courses such as navigation and surveying could be as much a part of the academy curriculum as courses in the "dead" languages. The report of the Committee of Ten attempted to select the best from the traditions of the academy and the Latin grammar school.

The classical, Latin-scientific, modern languages, and English were the tracks of study outlined by the Committee. These were not as dissimilar as they sound, however. The Committee was wary of abandoning what it felt were core studies and warned against early specialization: "The wisest teacher, or the most observant parent, can hardly predict with confidence a boy's gift for a subject which he has never touched."[31]

Those recommending the reform of secondary education in late 19th century America were faced with the problem of deciding whom the secondary school should serve. There were too few students who had college aspirations to make its purpose exclusively college preparatory. The Committee warned that "the secondary schools of the United States, taken as a whole, do not exist for the purpose of preparing boys and girls for colleges." Thus, the Committee concluded that in order for secondary education to be national in scope it must serve students who expected the high school degree to be terminal.[32]

From the historians' point of view, the obvious question that should be asked about this intense reform activity of the late 19th century is, "Why did it occur in this period?" A full-scale response would be very complex, but several points can be highlighted. First, the great strides made in public education in Germany during the 19th century created a body of educational theory that could not be ignored by those seriously interested in American education.

Second, American educational reformers saw similarities between the German and American experience. Both had tried to make elementary schooling universal. The political systems of the two countries were different, but each was committed to the idea that education should be a tool for citizenship and nation building. Thus, American educators were willing to learn from the European experience despite their different cultures and political systems.

Third, *mass* elementary schooling forced the redesign of curriculum and instruction. The population of elementary school children was culturally and socioeconomically diverse. This diversity had begun to spread to the early years of secondary schooling as well. With diversity came problems of management and educational opportunity. The first was a practical matter for daily classroom activities. The second was more a matter of commitment to a democratic ideal of educational opportunity for each child. What educators seemed to need was a theory and a strategy for dealing with the problems of cultural diversity. This need led to a fourth reason for the great interest in the object method and Herbartianism.

The child development theory on which the object method and Herbartianism were based was recognized as a way to achieve stability amid diversity. It was also a way to preserve educational opportunity. The "nature" of the child and the way in which that nature unfolded (development) were seen as common to all children within the normal range of intelligence. Thus, it made sense to attack the problems of curriculum and management from a common ground.

Child development theory seemed both neutral and fair. Because child development theory seemed to transcend cultural bounds, it was assumed to be culturally unbiased. All children, no matter what their heritage, could be given a fair opportunity to achieve within a curriculum based on child development theory. It did not pretend to alter the social aims of education. Yet it could be used to accomplish a variety of the social aims of education. The grounding of child development theory in experiment and observation also gave it legitimacy in a scientific sense.

The fifth reason for the popularity of theories of educational reform based on child development theory was their potential for application in management problems. In the latter 19th century, schools became increasingly bureaucratic and complex in their operation. People working in large urban school systems became specialists and were certified according to their special expertise. This was a parallel development to the specialization of labor that occurred in American industry and financial institutions.

Administrators of schools became more and more managers of people and materials. Likewise, they became more and more interested in the efficient operation of their schools. The mentality of the manager gradually became part of the teaching mentality as teachers were forced to contend with large, culturally diverse groups of students. Theories of child development offered a systematic approach to instruction, the foundations for which lay in the nature and growth of children themselves.

Increasingly, techniques associated with a particular theory such as Herbartianism were codified in the same way as the object method had been in previous decades. Caught up in the pressures of increased enrollments and administrative insistence on greater efficiency, teachers turned to technical solutions to their problems of managing a classroom. The result was to push them further away from the roots of method and toward the easily codified techniques used to manage day-to-day classroom problems. Thus the technical and the academic continued to diverge despite the theoretical link forged by the Herbartians and other child development theorists.

CHAPTER SUMMARY

■ As we look back on the practices that characterized teaching in colonial America and 19th century United States, we can identify several fundamental themes. First, the values communicated by teachers were extensions of the moral life of their communities. As these communities became gradually secularized so did the purposes of schooling. By the late 19th century, the economic benefits of schooling and literacy were beginning to receive at least equal attention with the moral benefits. Second, by the mid 19th century, educational reformers were urging teachers to approach their tasks in a more scientific way. In doing this, they drew heavily from European educators and theorists. Third, by the 1880s teacher preparation was more specialized. This specialization, moreover, was accompanied by a widening gap between the technical and the liberal in teacher preparation. Finally, by the mid 19th century, school became the major institution for inducting children into literate culture. As a result, teachers and teacher-educators were confronted more and more by problems stemming from increased enrollments. They thus turned their attention increasingly to technical problems such as classroom management. More and more the technology of teaching became associated with the professionalization of teaching.

FOR DISCUSSION

1. What differences would you expect to find in educational outcomes when education is controlled by (a) the family, (b) the church, and (c) the government?

2. What differences in learning would you expect to find as a result of different formats of instruction such as (a) ritualistic, (b) group-oriented, and (c) competitive?

3. Reflect on your own experience with school discipline and compare them with Samuel Hall's advice in the 19th century.

4. Trace and compare the differences in the purposes of public schooling from the late 18th century to the late 19th century.

5. Do you believe that teaching is a science or an art? Explain your position.

6. How do you think our commitment to mass schooling in the United States has affected the quality of education?

IN THE SCHOOL/IN THE CLASSROOM

1. We saw in this chapter that the school has historically served as an extension of the moral, political, and social life of the community. It will be remembered that teachers were asked to represent the community to their students. This role became gradually more complicated as teachers sought to improve education through the application of "scientific" findings about children. As you talk to teachers about their classrooms and the children they teach, ask the following questions:
   a. In what ways do they try to represent the basic moral beliefs of the community to their students?
   b. Do they see part of their job as promoting good citizenship?
   c. When "managing" their classrooms, do their actions teach certain values that are not part of the formal curriculum?
   d. Based on the answers to the previous questions, can you make some comparisons with teachers' behaviors in the past?
   e. To what extent do they try to apply current research findings about learning and teaching to their classrooms?
   f. Do they believe that the "scientific" study of children has led to improvements in the way that they teach?
   g. Do they see conflicts arising between what research "says" and what their experience tells them about how to teach children? If so, how do they resolve these conflicts?

SUGGESTED READINGS

Bailyn, Bernard. *Education in the Forming of American Society.* New York: Random House, Vintage Books, 1960. This short work had a tremendous impact on how historians viewed the shaping of American society through colonial developments in education. Bailyn highlights the way in which education both responded to and accelerated rapid social change.

Church, Robert, and Michael Sedlak. *Education in the United States: An Interpretive History.* New York: Free Press, 1976. The major contribution of this work is the reinterpretation of nineteenth-century public school movement in light of the findings of the so-called revisionist historians.

Cremin, Lawrence. *American Education: The National Experience, 1783–1876.* New York: Harper & Row, 1980. This is one of a multi-volume, comprehensive history by the best known historian of American education. Cremin's work is required reading for those who wish to understand the connections among American culture, major intellectual currents, and educational history.

Elson, Ruth. *Guardians of Tradition: American Schoolbooks of the Nineteenth Century.* Lincoln: University of Nebraska Press, 1964. Elson's work is a comprehensive historical treatment of the way in which cultural values permeate textbooks. It will provide important insights for students who wish to understand the ways in which textbooks reflect dominant social, religious, and moral beliefs of a given historical period.

Katz, Michael B. *The Irony of Early School Reform.* Cambridge: Harvard University Press, 1968. Katz's award-winning work was a major revisionist challenge to the mainstream, liberal interpretation of America's educational history. His work also set a new precedent for the use of quantitative techniques to shed new light on how educational decisions are made.

CHAPTER REFERENCES

1. Benjamin Wadsworth, "The Well-Ordered Family: or, Relative Duties," in *Theories of Education in Early America,* ed. Wilson Smith (Indianapolis: Bobbs-Merrill, 1973), p. 49.
2. Cotton Mather, "Cares about the Nurseries. Two Brief Discourses. (1702)," in *Theories of Education in Early America,* ed. Wilson Smith (Indianapolis: Bobbs-Merrill, 1973), pp. 16–17.
3. John Clarke, "An Essay upon the Education of Youth in Grammar Schools," in *Theories of Education in Early America,* ed. Wilson Smith (Indianapolis: Bobbs-Merrill, 1973), p. 95.
4. Issac Watts, "The Improvement of the Mind To Which is Added, A Discourse on the Education of Children and Youth. (1751)," in *Theories of Education in Early America,* ed. Wilson Smith (Indianapolis: Bobbs-Merrill, 1973), p. 107.
5. Samuel Harrison Smith, "Remarks on Education," essay presented to the

American Philosophical Society, 1798, *Early American Imprints,* no. 34558, p. 66.

6. S. M. Hamilton (ed.), *Writings of James Monroe,* vol. 3, 6 Dec. 1801, pp. 306–307; quoted in Harry Ammon, *James Monroe's The Quest for National Identity* (New York, 1971), p. 177.

7. Carl F. Kaestle, *Pillars of the Republic: Common Schools and American Society,* 1780–1860 (New York: Hill and Wang, 1983), p. 5.

8. Ibid.

9. James Cutbush, "An Oration on Education." Delivered November 7, 1811 (Philadelphia: Society for the Promotion of a Rational System of Education, 1812), pp. 12, 15.

10. Mrs. Barbara O'Sullivan Addicks, "Essay on Education . . ." (Philadelphia, 1831), pp. 18–19.

11. John M. Keagy, *The Pestalozzian Primer* (Harrisburg, Pa., 1827), p. 5.

12. Charles Royce, "Instruction in Phonetics," *Ohio Journal of Education* 2 (1853): 351–352.

13. Samuel R. Hall, *Lectures on School-Keeping* (1829; reprint, New York: Arno Press, 1969), p. 28

14. Ibid., pp. 69–71.

15. Ibid., p. 113.

16. Charles A. Harper, *A Century of Public Teacher Education* (Washington, D.C.: Hugh Birch–Horace Mann Fund, 1939), p. 26.

17. Merle L.. Borrowman, *The Liberal and Technical in Teacher Education* (New York: Teachers College Press, 1956), p. 54.

18. Kaestle, *Pillars of the Republic.*

19. Harper, *A Century of Public Teacher Education,* p. 21.

20. Ibid., p. 53.

21. John Rury, "American School Enrollment in the Progressive Era," *History of Education* 14 (1985): 52–53.

22. Lee Soltow and Edward Stevens, *The Rise of Literacy and the Common School in the United States* (Chicago: University of Chicago Press, 1981), p. 122.

23. Rury, "American School Enrollment in the Progressive Era," pp. 54–58.

24. Ibid, p. 65.

25. Harper, *A Century of Public Teacher Education,* p. 122.

26. Church, Robert, and Michael Sedlak, *Education in the United States: An Interpretive History* (New York: Free Press, 1976), pp. 108–111.

27. R. Freeman Butts, Lawrence A. Cremin, *A History of Education in American Culture* (New York: Holt, Rinehart and Winston, 1953), p. 382.

28. Borrowman, *The Liberal and Technical in Teacher Education,* p. 149.

29. National Educational Association of the United States, *Report of the Committees of Fifteen on Elementary Education* (New York: American Book Co., 1895), pp. 40–42.

30. Theodore R. Sizer, *Secondary Schools at the Turn of the Century* (New Haven: Yale University Press, 1964), p. xi.

31. National Educational Association, *Report of the Committee of Ten on Secondary School Studies* (New York: American Book Co., 1893), p. 46–47.

32. Ibid., p. 51.

10

New Contexts for Being a Teacher: The Twentieth Century

A SCENARIO: COMPETING AGENDAS

■ Each year thousands of high school students decide, usually with the help of a computer, on a schedule of classes. When they receive their computer printouts in the mail or show up for the first day of classes, they often find that the teachers assigned to them are the ones they didn't want. Likewise, the schedule they wanted wasn't possible because teachers weren't available for the courses they wanted at the time they requested. This scenario is made to order for generating frustration, ill will, and feelings of alienation from an unresponsive school system that compels students to spend a large part of their waking hours studying some courses they like, but many they do not.

The roots of this somewhat depressing scenario are found in the historical development of public schooling in America. It is part of the continuing struggle of public school teachers and administrators (managers) to offer an education that they believe will benefit all students. It is an outgrowth of attempts to control the behaviors and future prospects of teenagers who attend school.

This somewhat Orwellean scene does not necessarily make everyone unhappy. Good intentions abound, and sensitive people are numerous in the system. Within a rigid bureaucracy, people find time for other people. There are lighthearted moments, and rewards are given to those who excel academically, or in important extracurricular activities. Yet the basic structure of the system is highly restrictive. There are numerous punitive mechanisms for dealing with deviant behaviors. Ironically these are all justified by appealing to the good intentions of those who run the school.

Choosing and scheduling courses is frequently preceded by conversations among students, teachers, parents, counselors, and administrators. Advice is given and plans are made, all of which are directed toward "helping" the student choose the "right" course of study. Much of the advice given by those who have authority is in the form, "You should take. . . ." The expectations of each of these parties may be different. The teacher often looks at past performance, potential for success as measured by standardized tests, and the attitude of the student toward school or particular subjects. The counselor, from an interview or completed preference questionnaires, advises the student on the basis of future college or vocational plans. These judgments are coupled with an evaluation of standardized test scores and past performance. The parent tries to advise the student by reviewing college requirements at "good," "medium," or "last hope" colleges, while at the same time taking account of his child's interests.

The student often comes to the conclusion that no one else (excepting a best friend perhaps) really understands what he or she wants. Moreover, the student may assert that most of the courses are not "relevant" to what he or she wants to do. Knowing that there are requirements to be met and other people to be satisfied, the student adopts a fatalistic attitude and decides to wait it out for better things to come. Sometimes a special plea may get authorities to change their minds ("give in" to the student's interests) or at least compromise. At the same time, authorities feel bound to say that the student's choices are not in his or her own best interests and may limit future opportunities, by which is meant economic opportunities. By the time the process is finished, everyone is glad it's over.

"Mark, you're fitted for a career in retailing, dentistry, or engineering. You probably don't have an opinion, do you?"

Why is this scenario repeated so often? Is it that no one learns from the past, or that everyone is obstinate, or that no one cares? It is unlikely that addressing the problem this way can give many answers. It is more likely, however, that everyone cares so much and believes so strongly in what he or she is saying and doing that many avenues to communication are closed. What should be a rational decision-making process instead pits divergent commitments against one another. The decision becomes a matter of who will prevail.

The reasons for confrontation are not too difficult to find. They are located in the structure and purposes of schooling itself. Administrators are driven by a managerial point of view that stresses efficiency of operation and accountability to the public purse. Scheduling is something to be done in a cost-effective way, in a way that gets the most "bang for the buck." Counselors are, of course, sensitive to students' interests, but their function is often vocational guidance. Thus they stress how the choice of courses will affect the student's career possibilities. The central question is, "What do you want to do?", by which is meant "What career do you want when you grow up?" Seldom is the question asked, "What do you like?" Teachers are apt to think primarily of scholastic aptitude, of underachieving and overachieving. Much of parental advice is predicated on hope. Children are the bearers of dreams, but often parents must correspondingly compromise their expectations with the realities of their child's interests and abilities.

Students are at the center of this flux of expectations. They are the objects of continuous attention, but when all is said and done, they have relatively little input into the decision. The table is set, the menu offered, and the dinner served. There are a few substitutions, but the limitations are greater than the choices.

THE EARLY TWENTIETH CENTURY AND ITS LEGACY

■ The reality of this scenario has been shaped by numerous historical precedents and guided by certain philosophic assumptions underlying public schooling in America. In this chapter, we look at five major developments in the 20th century that helped to shape curriculum and instruction in public schooling. These were (1) the emergence of educational administration as a specialized field of study, (2) the development of standardized tests of intellectual ability and academic performance, (3) the continued professionalization of teaching, (4) the restructuring of secondary education and curriculum reform, and (5) the use of the schools to achieve social reform through equal educational opportunity.

◻ **Managing the School**

The growth of large urban school systems in the latter half of the 19th century set the stage for educational administration as a special field of study. By the opening of the 20th century urban schooling had become a full-fledged bureaucracy. Regulation, specialization of labor, and a complex system of governance came to characterize large urban school systems. Authority became centralized as building principals and district superintendents gained greater control of the schooling process. More and more it became apparent that the bureaucratic structure of schooling was designed for one-way communication (from the top down). Shared decision making, if it ever existed, had even less chance to survive in the hierarchy of power that characterized urban schools. In the span of a few years, school boards with ward representation gave way to smaller boards, the members of which were elected at large. Correspondingly, representation on these boards became narrower so that they tended to represent only the professional and big-business interests of the cities.

In the early 20th century the work of Frederick W. Taylor, published in his book *The Principles of Scientific Management,* was a powerful influence on educational administrators. Taylor's time studies of labor and production were designed to increase the efficiency of industrial production. Each job was divided and studied in discrete units to see how efficiency could be improved. Those in charge of the production process (managers) then used the information from time studies to make certain that workers performed their tasks in the least amount of time with the greatest profit to the company. School administrators quickly saw the advantage of applying similar methods to education.

The impact of the efficiency movement in public schools led to a greater specialization within school organization itself. Educational administrators took seriously the ideas of John Franklin Bobbitt, an influential professor of educational administration, who observed that "education is a shaping process as much as the manufacture of steel rails."[1] The school was conceived more and more as a workplace to be managed efficiently. Standardized tests of intelligence and achievement worked well within this model, also.

The efficiency craze in education shaped the behaviors of students, teachers, and administrators. Rating forms helped to measure the efficiency of all three. The student efficiency test, for example, was designed to assess how students spent their time and to spot inefficiency in their behaviors. One such Student Efficiency Test printed in the *American School Board Journal* in 1915 asked students 30 questions about their attitudes toward various activities and the

Efficiency and accountability in the early twentieth century.

WHEN STARTING OUT TO BUY!

School Board Journal, 51 (July 1915).

percentage of time they spent on them. Sample questions included: "Do you take joy in your school work?", "Do you study by a good light from behind or over your left shoulder?", and "Do you read good books?"[2]

Similar rating forms for principals and teachers appeared. The one for principals asked teachers to rate their principals in four general categories, including personal traits, social and professional traits, management, and supervisory abilities. The form for teachers included similar categories. The 46 questions shown in the list below is a good summary of the principal's expectations for teachers. In fact, such a list could easily be turned into a list of objectives for teacher training. The outcome would be a very mechanistic formula for teacher preparation, not unlike some recent proposals for testing teacher competencies.

Efficiency record[3]

Detailed Rating......	Very Poor	Poor	Medium	Good	Excellent

	1. General appearance
	2. Health
	3. Voice
	4. Intellectual capacity
	5. Initiative and self-reliance
	6. Adaptability and resourcefulness
	7. Accuracy
I. Personal	8. Industry
Equipment—	9. Enthusiasm and Optimism
	10. Integrity and sincerity
	11. Self-control
	12. Promptness
	13. Tact
	14. Sense of justice
	15. Academic preparation
	16. Professional preparation
	17. Grasp of subject-matter
	18. Understanding of children
	19. Interest in the life of the school
	20. Interest in the life of the community
II. Social and	21. Ability to meet and interest patrons
Professional	22. Interest in lives of pupils
Equipment—	23. Co-operation and loyalty
	24. Professional interest and growth
	25. Daily preparation
	26. Use of English
	27. Care of light, heat, and ventilation
	28. Neatness of room
III. School	29. Care of routine
Management—	30. Discipline (governing skill)
	31. Definiteness and clearness of aim
	32. Skill in habit formation
	33. Skill in stimulating thought
	34. Skill in teaching how to study
	35. Skill in questioning

IV. Technique of Teaching—	36. Choice in questioning
	37. Choice of subject-matter
	38. Organization of subject-matter
	39. Skill and care in assignment
	40. Skill in motivating work
	41. Attention to individual needs
	42. Attention and response of the class
	43. Growth of pupils in subject matter
V. Results—	44. General development of pupils
	45. Stimulation of community
	46. Moral influence

School buildings themselves were supposed to meet the high standards of efficiency. Efficiency formulas were developed that measured the efficiency of a school system by calculating the yearly progress of students. Teacher/student ratios and time spent on subject matter were also important ingredients in the efficiency formula. In many cases the standard of efficiency demanded increased class size. This was true especially in lecture classes, in which the transmission of information was the only goal. Administrators attempted to calculate optimal class size. Choices about what to include in the curriculum were dictated more and more by "numbers."

Measuring the quality of schools by standards of efficiency also affected the role of the teacher. More and more the student was seen as a technical expert. Increasingly, however, this meant the loss of control over teaching. Grouping of students, choice of textbooks, class size, and academic content itself became less and less the prerogatives of the teacher. This tendency has been labeled today as "teacher proofing." Recent calls for school reform in the late 1970s and 1980s continue this trend. For the most part the recommendations are to improve teachers' methods, and to apply them to a curriculum prescribed by others.

□ **Classifying Students:**
The Standardized Test

"Counting and measurement, quantification, seemed to attract educators almost as a candle attracts moths," say Button and Provenzo in their *History of Education and Culture in America*.[4] Classifying students through the use of standardized tests became more and more common in the early 20th century. Over a hundred achievement tests, many developed by Edward Thorndike, the author of *Theory of Mental and Social Measurements* (1904), were in use by the 1920s.[5]

Achievement tests were put to many uses, including ability-level grouping of students and the measurement of teacher effectiveness. It was the intelligence test, however, that captured the imaginations of educational reformers. Binet and Simon saw the development of the intelligence quotient (I.Q.) test as a way to deal with "mentally defective" children.[6] They published their test in 1905 and educators in the United States during the next two decades saw its potential for classifying all children. It was seen by many as the solution to the problem of ability grouping within a diversified student body. It was thus a practical way to bring human diversity under the control of a new science of measurement and statistics.

The setting for Binet and Simon's famous study of intelligence was the school. Binet reported a "remarkable correlation" between level of intelligence and scholastic achievement. He carefully avoided a "parallelism" between intelligence and achievement. He thought, however, their close relationship was support for the "truth" that "the first in school are likely to be the first in life."[7]

In *The Measurement of Intelligence* (1916) Lewis Terman noted that reforms such as individualized instruction, new promotion methods, and greater attention to children's health had been unsuccessful in dealing with school failure. "A large proportion of children in the schools are acquiring the habit of failure," said Terman. "The remedy," he continued, "is to measure out the work for each child in proportion to his mental ability." Terman recommended that "every child who fails in his school work or is in danger of failing should be given a mental examination."[8]

The broad social significance of applying intelligence testing was also recognized by Terman. Like others, he was impressed by the seeming evidence that linked criminality to mental weakness. The explanation, thought Terman, was very straightforward. Morality depended on "the ability to foresee" and judge the possible consequences of one's behavior and on "the willingness and capacity to exercise self-restraint. . . . All feebleminded are at least potential criminals," said Terman, and "every feebleminded woman is a potential prostitute."[9]

Terman was equally concerned about the identification and development of the gifted. To waste the talent of these children, he argued, was to threaten the "welfare of the country." He was concerned, moreover, that the "handicapping influences of poverty, social neglect, physical defects, or educational maladjustments" prevented the discovery of talents. Both teacher awareness and intelligence testing, it was thought, could aid in the discovery of the gifted.[10]

Terman and others were enthusiastic about using intelligence tests for grade promotion, "vocational fitness," and the organization of instruction. He thought the problem of great differences in intelligence among children of the same approximate age could be solved, in part, by testing. Teachers could group students homogeneously on the basis of a determination of mental age. Prediction of a child's "later mental development" could be based on the I.Q. itself. Thus teachers, with the aid of guidance counselors, could group students to attain the greatest efficiency of instruction. The concept of a differentiated curriculum (a different curriculum for different intellectual abilities and different career goals) had important implications for the organization of instruction.[11]

Vocational guidance itself was in its infancy, but it was seen by many educators as a solution to the problem of failure. Advocates of intelligence testing believed vocations could be selected for a child "well within the range" of his intelligence. "The child's natural interests and practical considerations would help make the final choice." For all practical purposes this could be done by the child's fifth or sixth school year.[12]

Terman's fundamental social concern was the "conservation of talent." The teacher, Terman explained, occupied a "strategic position" in making sure that the nation's "intellectual assets" were used efficiently. To do this, it was "her duty to foster in a pupil the highest ambitions which are consonant with his intellectual endowment."[13]

In 1917 the United States Army piloted intelligence tests in anticipation of their aiding in the classification of recruits and the sorting out of the mentally incompetent. Robert Yerkes lectured on the results of this testing and announced that the results far exceeded the original expectations. Those of superior intelligence as well as the feebleminded could be identified. Mental testing also helped to select personnel for further education and allowed men to "receive instruction suited to [their] ability to learn."[14]

Yerkes also envisioned intelligence testing as a "partial basis for grading, promotion and vocational advice." Schoolchildren could be divided into three groups A, B, and C, which corresponded to high, medium, and low levels of intelligence. These, in turn, corresponded roughly to occupational/vocational classifications, including professional, industrial, and manual. The broader social and economic implications of intelligence testing were of immense interest to Yerkes as they were to Terman. Testing, he believed, led to intelligence specifications for jobs, which, in turn, allowed better matching of employees with jobs.[15]

Yerkes knew that some eduators would view his plan as undemocratic. But, he argued, educators were "seriously discriminating against individuals because of [their] failure to take their characteristics and needs into account." "Equality of opportunity in our schools," he continued, "necessitated classification in accordance with ability, individualized treatment, recognition of limitations and of practical limits of educability, differentiation of courses, and vocational direction and training."[16]

After World War I, testing became a major tool to engineer instruction and manage the classroom. It fit nicely with the emphasis on efficiency. The presumed positive relationship between intelligence and moral worth made intelligence testing one more weapon to use in the fight against moral degeneracy. National prosperity itself was seemingly served by the widespread use of intelligence testing. The need for efficiency in the use of human resources had been demonstrated in the armed forces, and the intelligence test had proven itself valuable for that purpose. To apply the same method to American schoolchildren seemed logical in dealing with the mass education of a diversified student body.

FOR REFLECTION 10.1

Intelligence testing has always been controversial since its wholesale adoption in public education. Its use is supported because it is a good predictor of success in school. For this reason it is useful in guidance and in grouping children. Opponents point to the undemocratic results of intelligence testing, namely, that it separates students by mental ability and thereby denies equal opportunity. They also point to the "determinism" of intelligence testing. Results of the testing, they say, help determine a child's life chances because it is assumed that intelligence itself is fixed and unchanging.

At the core of the debate about intelligence testing is an argument over the nature of intelligence itself. It is common to hear people speak of intelligence as a *thing* or an innate, fixed capacity. Indeed, there are those who explicitly relate intelligence to features of the brain. Others see intelligence as behavior or a set of behaviors that people use to solve problems.

The first of these views often uses the I.Q., or intelligence quotient (mental age/chronological age × 100) to identify level of intelligence. This point on a scale is seen as representing some capacity in the person. When intelligence is seen as a behavior, then a set of behaviors (ability to adapt or logical thinking, for example) is defined as intelligence because it helps a person deal with problematic situations.

Both views of intelligence assume a *standard of reference* for defining what intelligence is. Although a standard of reference is always necessary when defining a term or concept, it is these very standards that are suspect in this case. When a point on a test scale is taken to represent some capacity in a person to act intelligently, we have to ask, "How good is the representation?" Performance on a test is basically a matter of achievement. Thus, we must ask, "Does this achievement represent some kind of natural capacity?" There is really no sound evidence to suppose it does. Rather, it simply tells us what the person has achieved to that point. The question immediately follows, "How accurately can we predict future achievement from the test?" If we are speaking of school achievement, the prediction is quite good. If we are speaking of achievement in the sense of success after school, then the prediction is quite poor. What we must realize in either case is that a test score has a certain standard of reference (items on the test) and represents a certain level of achievement. To claim any more for it is speculative and without substantial evidence.

In the second case of viewing intelligence as behavior, we are also faced with the problem of a *standard of reference.* In this case, however, it is not a matter of asking, "What does a test score represent?" Rather, it is a question of determining the criteria for deciding whether behavior is intelligent or not. Much of the behavior called intelligent has to do with abstract, formal thinking. Problems that require that kind of thinking are the standards of reference for determining intelligent behavior. But, of course, there are many behaviors that aid in solving serious problems, but do not require abstract thinking.

Finally, we must recognize that the term intelligence has a moral quality about it. People think of being or acting intelligently as a good thing. In so doing, they are implicitly making judgments about the importance and value of those behaviors in certain situations. For example, if solving technical problems associated with a space shuttle requires intelligent behavior, then it is assumed that solving such problems is a good thing. This doesn't mean that one has to like space shuttles. It does mean, however, that one implicitly places a value on solving such technical problems. The kinds of knowledge and skills that are needed to solve the problems are also valued, so we often view them as intelligent responses to the problem.

In the discussion of the concept of intelligence we have stressed the importance of determining the standard of reference for the concept and what the concept represents. These are important determinations to be made when probing the meaning of any complex idea such as that of intelligence.

A New Structure and New Expectations for the Secondary School

The restructuring of secondary schooling took place as demands for greater efficiency grew in public education. We have seen in the previous chapter that the Committee of Ten issued a compromise report in an attempt to deal with an increasingly diversified student body attending secondary schools. The dual function of secondary school—college preparatory and terminal degree—pressured educators toward greater curriculum reform. It also highlighted the issue of vocationalism versus academics in education.

In the two decades preceding World War I, American educators became increasingly distressed with the academic versus vocational split in secondary education. Clarence Kingsley and others spoke to this issue in a 1911 report issued by the *National Education Association*. This was called the *Report of the Committee of Nine on the Articulation of High School and College*.[17]

The Committee of Nine's report was only one expression of many about the direction in which secondary education ought to move. Most of these concerns were about what type of curriculum was best for those who wished a high school diploma but did not intend to go to college. The dual purpose of the high school left it vulnerable to critics who claimed that its objectives were ill-defined. Increasingly, teachers were asked to explain the relevancy of their teaching in terms of larger social objectives. No longer were traditional subjects honored for their own sakes.

Relevancy, like so many other demands placed on the teacher, grew out of the diversity in the student population with which the teacher had to deal. More and more the teacher had to take the audience into consideration rather than simply the subject. Once again, educational reformers looked to science for a solution to the problem.

David Snedden, Commissioner of Education in Massachusetts, argued that a scientific approach to education would help educators formulate objectives and measure their achievement. In particular, Snedden advocated the use of sociology to establish objectives scientifically for schools. He pointed out, for example, that the social value of a subject such as algebra was suspect. For a very few, it might be a "professional tool," but for most its purpose was vague. Efficiency was the key concept for Snedden. "Efficient living" in relation to personal culture, citizenship, and vocational efficiency was a key goal of schooling. Snedden's position was that even traditional subjects such as history and literature should prove their worth in terms of productive citizenship.[18]

The concerns of the Committee of Nine and the work of David Snedden reflect the widespread discussion of vocational education during the period. Efforts like those of the Committee of Ten in the 1890s had not solved the curriculum problem for those students who left school directly for employment. Pressure for increased vocational relevancy in public schooling was spearheaded by groups outside the public education mainstream. These included the National Association of Manufacturers (NAM) and the National Society for the Promotion of Industrial Education (NSPIE). The latter group was especially influential in pressuring schools to pay more attention to vocational education. The overriding question in the first decade of the 20th

The world of work: economic citizenship.

century was whether or not to establish a dual system similar to the German system or to make vocational guidance and vocational education part of the public school system. As the latter position gained support and triumphed, the issue of vocational education versus academic studies moved into the public schools with ever greater intensity.[19]

The final report of the NEA Committee on Vocational Education and Vocational Guidance (1916) helped to set the pattern for vocational education in the junior and senior high school. Vocational guidance became a standard feature of the comprehensive high school. Its rationale rested squarely on the efficient use of human resources. The theme of efficiency in all aspects of living dominated the report. Meyer Bloomfield, one of the authors of the report, summed up the great expectations for vocational guidance and vocational education:

> Vocational guidance aims to lay down the specifications for a life career, vocational education to supply the best methods for working them out; and if the messages of these enterprises is heeded in the occupations, we may expect employment to be a period of consummating the labors of the school.[20]

Thus were schooling, business, and industry tied together, in a symbiotic relationship.

The longest lasting and most influential report issued as a result of reevaluating the purposes and objectives of secondary education in the early 20th century was the *Report of the Commission on the Reorganization of Secondary Education* (1918). This is commonly called the "Cardinal Principles" report. The report used the general idea of citizenship to redefine the mission of public secondary schooling.[21]

The Cardinal Principles report laid a broad foundation for its recommendations, including the rapid economic, social, and demographic changes occurring in American society. The Commission explicitly recognized the contributions of educational psychology to the understanding of child development, individual differences, and the organization of subject matter. The laws of learning rather than the inherent logic of a discipline were important in the case of the last mentioned.

The cardinal principles (the main objectives) of education were defined in terms of a democractic ideal. Individual and society, said the report, were to "find fulfillment each in the other." Efficiency in education was important to the attainment of democratic ideas. From the individual's membership in family and civic polity came the goals of worthy home membership, vocation, and citizenship. From the "cultivation of personal and social interests" came the goal of worthy use of leisure time. Health was an objective derived from the necessity to maintain the "vitality of the race" and the "defense of the Nation." The thorough teaching of the basics and the formation of ethical character were seen by the Commission as useful in attaining these fundamental objectives.[22]

To implement the seven major objectives (health, command of fundamental processes, worthy home-membership, vocation, citizenship, worthy use of leisure time, and ethical character), the Commission made recommendations dealing with curriculum reform and the reorganization of the schooling process itself. Teaching of the basics was to continue in secondary school as part of the standard high-school subjects. The social studies took on an important role. These studies, said the Commission, "should deal with the home as a fundamental social institution and clarify its relation to the wider interests outside." The "household arts" (commonly referred to today as home economics or domestic science) were to receive greater attention by those whose major lifelong role would be homemaking. Vocational education in general became more important.[23]

The comprehensive high school was recommended as the "standard" type of schooling at the secondary level. The Commission's arguments in favor of the comprehensive high school included its flexibility in allowing students access to a variety of curricula and its unifying function in allowing a mix of students having different values and goals. The innovation called the "home room" was intended to accomplish the latter. Overall, the school was intended to be a "prototype" of a democracy. In short, the comprehensive high school was seen as the best way to accommodate the fact of cultural diversity and the ideal of consensus.[24]

TEACHER PREPARATION AND CURRICULUM REFORM: THE FIRST PHASE

☐ **Preparing Teachers: A New Approach**

The increasing number of teachers in teacher preparation programs and the advance of the psychological and sociological sciences produced increased debate over how teachers should be educated. Borrowman has observed that debates over curriculum in higher education focused on four problems: (1) what skills should be taught, (2) the breadth of preparation and the relations among all knowledge,

(3) the effect(s) of technical knowledge on the "liberalizing quality" of the programs, and (4) providing a common background for all members of society.[25] Concerns about these problems were even greater among professional educators because of the strained relationship between professional skills and the liberal arts and sciences.

In the early 20th century, conservatives in education believed that the product of higher education should be a well-rounded gentleman. He should be liberated from tendencies to narrow vocationalism and disciplined by the logic of academic studies. The tendency was strong in this view to see academic studies as a means of disciplining the mind. The focus of the college, including teacher preparation and the act of teaching, was on intellectual development. In this conservative view, the teacher who emerged from such studies was a master of subject matter and a transmitter of information. By inference, the classroom was teacher-centered and subject-centered. Most classroom activities focused on the mastery of content.[26]

Leaders in the field of teacher education (educationists) in the early 20th century generally supported an integrated curriculum of general and professional studies. They backed away from the common position held by 19th century educators that all academic training should be completed before professional study began.

The gradual shift toward an integrated curriculum was accompanied by new expectations for teachers. The growth of knowledge in the area of the social sciences affected curriculum content in general and helped to redefine the role of the teacher. It was clear to many by the opening of the 20th century that the purposes of public schooling should be a response to the rapid social change of the period.

Intellectual advancement in the social and physical sciences was accompanied by advances in technology. Both grew within the context of increased urbanization, "new" immigration from southern and eastern Europe, and a shift in the economy from small businesses to large corporations. In turn, the teacher was asked to understand and communicate broad social changes to his or her students.

Social reconstructionists, like George S. Counts, urged teachers to use the public school as a means to social change and to act as agents of fundamental social change themselves. Accordingly, they argued that teachers should become politically active to achieve social democracy. More moderate reformers such as John Dewey relied on individual reform efforts rather than collective political activism in attempting to right the wrongs of social injustice.

Both the activism of Counts and the moderate reformist position of Dewey pushed teachers toward greater interest in and a desire to be involved in school policy itself. This was not to be, however. The new cadre of professional administrators succeeded in capturing the domain of policy making for themselves. They were self-appointed experts in management and they derived increased status as graduates of professional programs of study in graduate schools of education. Efforts by teachers to enter into the policy-making process were resisted as a matter of professional prerogative by school administrators. Thus, teacher gains in this area were small. It was not until the post–World War II period that teachers began to enter significantly into policy decisions in education.

☐ Discontent and Progressivism

By 1920 there was widespread discontent in the northern and midwestern states with the inefficient management of public education. Among the complaints were the ineffectual responses on the part of teachers and administrators to students coming from ethnic minorities and lower socioeconomic groups. We should not misinterpret this as a renewed interest in equal educational opportunity, however. Rather, it was often seen as a management problem. New knowledge in the biological, psychological, and social sciences seemed to offer fresh hope for dealing with the increasing diversity of the student population. Educators and those advocating the reform of education responded in two distinct but related ways.

One way emphasized the need for greater efficiency in the management of pupils and curriculum. This was done through more sophisticated student classification and classroom management techniques. The aim was to create uniform and standard ways of dealing with diversity. In short, it emphasized a scientific, rational, and technical approach to managing human and material resources. The second way also drew on science, yet moved in a different direction. It did not attempt to impose a uniform, standard solution to the problem of diversity. Instead, it emphasized the importance of flexibility and alternative solutions. In short, it accepted diversity and met diversity with diversity.

The emphasis on greater efficiency was typified in the two activities of classroom management and activity analysis. The first was represented by William Bagley's work, *Classroom Management* (1907); the second by John Franklin Bobbitt's curriculum reform called "activity analysis."

Though he is sometimes seen as a progressive, Bagley's work on classroom management represented a conservative view of the teacher as disciplinarian and protector of morality. For him, the teacher was "an efficient classroom manager who produced in students the virtues of industry, accuracy, carefulness, steadfastness, patriotism, culture, cleanliness, truth, self-sacrifice, social service, and personal honor." His popular book on classroom management pictured the efficient school and classroom as one that "goes like a machine." To accomplish this, the teacher was to exercise his or her authority in a commanding way. For example, the command "attention" should result in students' sitting upright, "eyes toward the teacher," hands folded, "feet flat on the floor," and complete attention given to the teacher. The outstanding characteristics of the classroom were order and routine.[27]

In his work titled *How to Make a Curriculum* (1924) Bobbitt helped lay the foundation for an engineering approach to curriculum development. The teacher-manager pictured by Bobbitt engaged in an exhaustive analysis of all those tasks demanded of students by a particular curriculum. Much of the process of analysis was simply a matter of counting and listing the components or items to be mastered in a particular task. Thus, for example, Leonard P. Ayres "tabulated 23,629 words in business and personal letters and identified the 542 most commonly used ones" "to design a spelling curriculum." Bobbitt and his associates tabulated "1,243 traits of good citizenship" to identify the components of citizenship education.[28]

Progressivism
Much of the activity in education between 1918 and 1930 has been called "progressive." This, however, has been an elusive concept to interpret because there were many variations of progressivism in education. In teaching it meant, generally, a child-centered rather than a teacher-centered approach to instruction. It also tended to mean a distaste for restraints like fixed seats and activities confined only to the classroom. Progressive educators advocated movable furniture, abundant classroom materials to allow for more student selection, student-directed learning, and activities that allowed more student-community interaction. The traditional and the progressive was contrasted by one educator as seen in Focus 10.1.

If we interpret progressivism to mean "inspired by progress," then the name applies quite well to a host of activities. Progressives were mindful of the new classroom management techniques. Yet their attempts to reform education have generally been characterized by historians as more expansive and imaginative than those striving for efficiency. In matters relating to curriculum, classroom management, and instructional techniques, progressives laid the

FOCUS 10.1 The Two Extremes

By Helen Hay Heyl, Supervisor,
University of the State of New York, Albany

This chart does not represent the teaching of any school of thought, but merely indicates the two extremes in practice.[a]

TRADITIONAL SCHOOL	PROGRESSIVE SCHOOL
Child is *sent* to school which is *kept* until four o'clock, after which he "explodes into freedom!"	Child goes to school and cannot get there early enough, he lingers in shops, laboratories, yards, and libraries until dusk or urgent parents drag him homeward.
This is a school for *listening*.	This is a school for *working*.
Children are pigeon-holed in long rows of desks.	Children are seated in groups at light tables in comfortable chairs.
Children sit quietly, studying their lessons.	Children sit working at projects, asking questions as needs arise. They "learn by doing" under wise teacher-guidance.
Movement means marching in rows at signal, teacher-directed and teacher-controlled.	Movement means purposeful activity, with consideration for the rights of others, and leads to self-direction and self-control.
Child learns unquestioning obedience to authority.	Child learns obedience through participation.
Keynotes are *memorize, recite, pay attention*.	Keynote: *Experiences leading to growth*.
Child's mind is submitted to the grindstone of an educational discipline which dwarfs his capacity to think for himself.	Child is taught to think, to develop tolerant understanding, to question critically, to evaluate.
AIM: Mental discipline which it is believed will produce good citizens.	*AIM: Growth and tolerant understanding* which it is believed will produce good citizens and the improvement of the social order.

[a] Principal credit for these ideas is ascribed by Miss Heyl to Rugg's "The Child Centered School." *Journal of Education,* 115 (Nov. 7, 1932), 602. This chart is cited in David Tyack, Robert Lowe, and Elisabeth Hansot, *Public Schools in Hard Times* (Cambridge: Harvard University Press, 1984), p. 151.

groundwork for the next 50 years. Terms like readiness, motivation, simulation, self-concept, interdisciplinary study, and cooperative learning became part of the everyday jargon of educators. Teachers, moreover, were expected to know about and use these concepts in planning instruction.

Many "progressive" ideas were direct outgrowths of studies in developmental psychology. G. Stanley Hall and Arnold Gesell helped to popularize the concepts of maturation, readiness, and motivation among educators. More and more, elementary education teachers in particular revised the sequence of instruction to take account of what researchers had discovered about readiness to learn and physical and intellectual maturation. Motivation, too, was studied from both developmental and behaviorist perspectives. Teachers were asked to create and held responsible for providing a learning environment that motivated children.

Educators sensitive to the rapid expansion of knowledge in the social sciences saw quickly that knowledge could no longer be contained by the boundaries of the traditional formal academic disciplines. In his work *American Life and the School Curriculum* (1936), Harold Rugg commented that "nothing short of genius on the part of a student could create an ordered understanding of modern life from such a compartmentalized arrangement of materials."[29] Thus, progressive educators searched for ways to cross these boundaries and integrate new knowledge with the old.

Interdisciplinary study showed great promise for new types of inquiry and the reorganization of curriculum. The social studies made inroads into the traditional curriculum. Men like Harold Rugg of Teachers College, Columbia University, combined the disciplines of history, geography, sociology, economics, and political science into a program of studies. From this synthesis of the disciplines they believed students would better understand the events that transformed modern civilization. The starting points for curriculum organization, Rugg thought, were "real" issues in the social, political, and economic life of a civilization. The new curriculum of the social sciences, said Rugg, should be "organized into 'units of work' instead of into the conventional 'subjects'."[30]

Experiments with curriculum abounded and many were inspired by an interdisciplinary approach to inquiry. The curriculum of Lincoln School at Teachers College was one of the most famous. Here an entire elementary and secondary curriculum was built around "units of work." It included such themes as community life, transportation, food production, and environment. Students did projects on these and drew their materials from the study of geography, economics, literature, and other traditional disciplines.

FOR REFLECTION 10.2

In the latter 19th and early 20th centuries, educational reformers and those interested in the scientific study of children developed a body of theory that they thought could be put to use in instruction. They believed that instruction would be better if it were founded on scientific evidence about how children develop physically and mentally. They made the assumption that findings about the psychology of children could be transferred to teaching. In general, then, they made assumptions about the relationship(s) between learning and teaching.

We should reflect on whether or not, or to what extent, knowledge about learning can be transferred to teaching. It is common for educators to confuse these two terms: learning and teaching. We often assume that teaching is the cause of learning or that learning is the necessary result of teaching. Sometimes we even hear educators talk about the goals of teaching as if they were the goals of learning. We should look at this relationship more closely if we are going to analyze the role of the teacher.

First of all, there is no *necessary* causal relationship between teaching and learning. One can learn without being taught and one can teach without the student learning. Whether teaching results in learning seems to depend on whether the teacher has created a set of conditions that result in or produce learning. But let us remember that even here it is the student who is doing the learning. (Teachers, of course, learn, but when we speak of the teacher's learning we are actually looking at the teacher as a student.)

The basic question we must ask is: "What conditions can a teacher create that will result in student learning?" Subsequent questions follow: "Will a knowledge of learning theory help?" "Will a knowledge of subject matter help?" "Will a knowledge of the purposes of schooling help?" We could extend the list. The point is that we are asking in general, "What does a teacher have to *know* to produce learning?" A second general question would follow: "What does a teacher have to *do* to produce learning?" And then a third general question would follow: "What is the relationship between what a teacher *knows* and what a teacher *does* and how does that relationship affect learning?"

These basic questions were asked in different ways earlier in this book. The point of returning to them, however, is to illustrate that the relationship between teaching and learning is not simple and not merely a matter of "common sense." It is a relationship that deserves to be probed deeply and reflectively.

New ways of organizing knowledge demanded a great deal of the teacher, as did attempts to relate that knowledge to child development. The spirit that guided these attempts was expansive. It rested on new knowledge in the psychological and social sciences and asked teachers to reject traditional subject matter boundaries.

The skills demanded of teachers went beyond mastery of subject matter. Teachers were asked to integrate knowledge to form units of study. Moreover, study activities were not confined to the classroom. The entire school "plant" was used, as were community resources. The teacher was obviously more than a subject matter specialist. He or she was a master and manager of the total educational environment. This was a task unfortunately for which few teachers and schools were prepared.

The extent to which public school teachers implemented progressive techniques of instruction has always been problematic. Even the Denver school system with Jesse Newlon, a superintendent with a commitment to progressive ideas, had only a few classes that could be called truly progressive.

Where the commitment was present, teachers taught in an interdisciplinary way. They also planned lessons *with* students and listened to the expressed needs of students. Punishment was replaced by motivation. Overall, however, most instruction and classroom activities at the secondary level were initiated by the teacher. At the elementary school level, there was more student-centered instruction.

REACTIONS TO PROGRESSIVISM

■ Reforms in teacher preparation and curriculum and the increasing sensitivity of teachers to the developmental needs of youth placed pressures on traditionalists in education to change their ways. Progressives and life-adjustment educators dominated the thought if not the practice of public education. Yet allegiance to traditional studies

Child-centered education.

remained. Gradually these educational conservatives mounted a coun-
terattack that erupted in the 1950s.

The academic versus professional issue had a direct bearing on
teacher education and the expectations for teachers in public schools.
By the early 1950s educational conservatives became outspoken critics
of what they considered to be the "anti-intellectual" excesses of
progressive educators. They were particularly critical of those who
advocated life-adjustment education.

The life-adjustment education movement was an amalgam of
concern over what skills and attitudes should be taught to the majority
of students who were enrolled in neither college preparatory, nor
vocational education programs. In general, its advocates stressed such
things as democratic living and economic citizenship.[30] There were
many who criticized these aims as vague and anti-intellectual, but it
was Arthur Bestor who was the intellectual leader of the reaction
against progressivism.

Bestor's *Educational Wastelands* (1953) brought educational conservatism and the liberal arts to the forefront of educational debate. In
his attack on anti-intellectualism and "life adjustment" education,
Bestor blamed professional educationists for the poor quality of American public schooling. Bestor believed that schooling should teach
students to think. The curriculum of the schools should emphasize
intellectual discipline. Bestor argued that calls for relevancy and
meeting current needs were misguided because they misconstrued the
real nature of a liberal education. A liberal education, said Bestor, laid
the foundations for further intellectual development.[31]

Bestor warned against viewing education as a handout. Schooling
was an investment and therefore schools should be held accountable
for their payoff. He was particularly concerned that no priorities were
set for public schooling. As a result, both teachers and students
suffered from the lack of direction. In his own list of five priorities,
intellectual training in the fundamental disciplines was first. The
training for occupational opportunities in the community was fifth.
The other priorities were "special opportunities for the exceptionally
able," "remedial programs for the lowest third, slow learners," and
"provision of a program of physical education for all children."[32]

Bestor's ideas marked the return of the teacher as disciplinarian.
Content was the most important weapon in the arsenal of instruction.
As with the recent "back to basics" movement, the basic skills were
seen as ways of disciplining the mind and shaping the morality of
students. The teacher-centered classroom was the heart of this new
conservatism. Teachers and administrators of public schools were
asked to be more rigorous with their studies. Lest the nation become
morally, militarily, and intellectually second-rate, teachers were pres-

sured to restore the foundations of our intellectual heritage. The pressure was on the teacher to be "tough" and intellectually demanding.

The educational reform of the 1950s was linked in spirit and chronology to the Cold War politics of the period. Attention focused on the cultivation of the intellectually gifted as America competed for technological supremacy in the space race with the Soviet Union. The report prepared by Admiral Hyman G. Rickover in 1959 for the House Committee on Appropriations focused on talent. This was published subsequently in 1963 as *American Education—A National Failure*. Public schooling had "no clear-cut educational philosophy with firm objectives," said Rickover. This resulted in low scholastic achievement. Local committees, he continued, needed a national "yardstick" by which to measure their own effectiveness.[33]

When it came to basic education, American children fared poorly, according to Rickover. The child-centered philosophy of progressivism and life-adjustment education, according to Rickover, had resulted in a deterioration of the basics. At the secondary level of education, said Rickover, the best minds of American youth went uncultivated.

There was no moral issue here, thought Rickover. Rather it was a practical matter of finding the means to administer to different levels of intellectual ability. Rickover advocated separate secondary schools beginning at age 11. This would "encourage maximum development of the nation's best minds." "Bright young people must be gotten ready to enter productive careers no later than their mid-twenties," he said.[34]

With the publication of James Conant's *The American High School Today* (1959) more moderate opinions began to balance the harsh rhetoric of the conservative backlash. Conant defended the comprehensive high school, but he also was concerned with the weaknesses of programs for the academically gifted. The central question of Conant's now famous *American High School Today* was stated by him as follows:

> Can a school at one and the same time provide a good general education for *all* the pupils as future citizens of a democracy, provide elective programs for the majority to develop useful skills, and educate adequately those with a talent for handling advanced academic subjects—particularly foreign languages and advanced mathematics?[35]

Conant's study resulted in 21 recommendations for the improvement of secondary education. He observed that as a rule the talented student "is not being sufficiently challenged, does not work hard enough, and his program of academic subjects is not of sufficient range." To correct the latter problem, Conant concluded that "the number of small high schools must be drastically reduced through district reorganization."[36]

Among the recommendations, most attention focused on eliminating college preparatory, vocational, and commercial tracks, using ability grouping, providing a core program of the basic disciplines, spending more time on English composition, offering elective programs for the academically talented, requiring science courses, providing for third- and fourth-year language study, and offering a course in social studies in the 12th year.

FOR REFLECTION 10.3

The differentiated curriculum is a common feature of the public high school in the United States. It has been attacked by its opponents as undemocratic and a denial of equal educational opportunity. Its advocates defend it as necessary to the efficiency of instruction. They also say that it results in better articulation of instruction with the work-force needs of society. It should be obvious that this issue arises because the public school is a multipurpose institution. It serves many constituencies at local, state, and national levels. The question must be posed, then: Which constituency is more important and whose priorities take precedence?

To probe this question more deeply, we should identify certain assumptions underlying public schooling in the United States. Some of these are (1) that public schooling is open to all children, (2) that it is supported primarily by public funds, and (3) that its policies reflect the values and priorities of its constituencies. It is the last of these that creates most controversy.

American culture is pluralistic. Even at the local level, American schooling is usually governed by more interests than it can serve. Although the local school board is elected to represent the people of the community, it often finds that an election does not free it from conflicting interests in the community. Very often these interests are drawn along socioeconomic lines. Sometimes religious and racial differences compound the problem. These different interests are, in turn, translated into differing priorities for public schooling.

What we must realize when discussing the purposes of public schooling is that legitimate differences of opinion do exist. A discussion that assumes that there can be *one* legitimate purpose for schooling is doomed to a monologue. As long as the school is governed by the public, supported by public monies, and open to all children it would be naive to expect a lack of controversy over its purposes. To resolve such differences it is necessary to understand their origins. This is one of the major purposes of this chapter. From there, one can proceed to search for a common ground for dialogue. This does not necessarily mean that all problems will be resolved. It does, however, lay the foundation for resolution.

Conant's recommendations for the reform of secondary education were taken seriously by public school administrators. A flurry of activity followed, and the comprehensive school succeeded in warding off its critics. Yet the problems that were indigenous to the American tracking system did not go away. Many recent reform reports assume that tracking is necessary to the efficient operation of schools. Moreover, it is assumed that only through a differentiated curriculum can students be selected and sorted to best meet the work-force demands of a high-tech society. Others, however, challenge this assumption, arguing that tracking is inherently elitist and hence undemocratic. Basic to this controversy is the role of the school in a democratic society.

EQUAL OPPORTUNITY

■ The concept of equal opportunity as we usually think of it had its foundation in the 17th and 18th centuries. At that time, the so-called liberal ideal emerged as a challenge to inherited wealth and status. As part of this challenge, there was a concern that inequalities of wealth not be perpetuated from generation to generation. This was based partly on the assumption that talent and ability are widely distributed and do not belong only to a privileged class.

Today we associate equal opportunity with economic opportunity rather than political opportunity. Before the late 18th century, however, most educators did not stress the economic benefits of schooling. With the coming of the industrial revolution and the parallel decline in importance of the family as the primary economic (production) unit there was greater concern with the relationship between schooling and opportunity. The possibility for greater occupational mobility was present with the growth of major economic (employing) institutions outside of the family. At the same time political and educational leaders sought to convince parents that mass schooling was in the national interest.

Part of the challenge for 19th century school reformers in the United States was to provide children of the poor better opportunity for improved economic status. Common school reformers, as they were called, were sensitive to the plight of the poor. They were also committed to basic capitalist values and a capitalist system of production. The mass schooling they advocated was seen as both a way to combat poverty and to teach the young the virtues of capitalism. Equal opportunity thus had both a moral and an economic dimension to it. Equal access to schooling, they thought, would facilitate development along both dimensions. The burden for taking advantage of the opportunity was on the child and family. With the passing of compulsory attendance laws in the late 19th century, legislators sought to guarantee that all children would be exposed to the teachings of the "common" school.

Education expanded rapidly at the secondary level in the early 20th century and created a new dilemma for educators. Most children did not go on to college, yet the curriculum of the secondary school remained oriented toward college-bound students. Although there was much opposition from traditionalists in education, the movement toward a differentiated curriculum gained momentum because the traditional liberal arts and language-oriented curriculum of 19th century secondary schools was not relevant for large numbers of children. Children from different socioeconomic backgrounds were expected to have different occupational futures. Thus equality of opportunity required providing different curricula for different types of students. Educators argued that equal educational opportunity did not mean the *same* opportunity. Rather, it meant opportunity geared to the students' needs, abilities, and probable adult occupations.

The issue of racial equality and the *Brown* decision by the United States Supreme Court in 1954 forced educators and legislators to take a new view of what it meant to have equal educational opportunity. The "separate but equal" doctrine (different but comparable schools for different races) was overruled. Before the *Brown* decision the "inputs" (resources) of schooling available to children had been considered the primary measure of equal educational opportunity. Rethinking of the concept of equal educational opportunity led educators to consider the effects ("outputs") of schooling. Teachers, program quality, and facilities remained important. But the "output" view demanded that educators focus on the actual skills and knowledge acquired and demonstrated by students at the end of their schooling. Critics of the quality of public schooling demanded evidence that schools were in fact achieving what they said they were.

By the 1960s educators and social scientists were focusing their research on the relationship between education and race. Civil rights abuses took front stage in the political arena at the same time that judicial intervention increased in the schooling process. To understand the recent history of the concept of equal educational opportunity (EEO) we must place it within the historical context of racism in America.

Racism in America has a long history. Its effects have led to deep social divisions and political irresponsibility. The presence of large numbers of blacks in the South had historically been a threat to the political process controlled by whites. For years, literacy tests, poll taxes, white primaries, and grandfather clauses disenfranchised blacks. Segregated schooling or no schooling at all was the educational equivalent of political disenfranchisement.

In its decision *Brown* v. *Board of Education of Topeka* (1954), the United States Supreme Court faced the task of determining the psychological effects of racial segregation. As part of its decision, the Court concluded that children who were segregated by race were deprived of equal educational opportunity. Racial segregation by race, the Court observed, "generates a feeling of inferiority as to their status in the community that may affect their hearts and minds in a way unlikely ever to be undone."[37]

After the passage of the 1964 Civil Rights Act, attacks on segregated schools were renewed. As the Department of Justice and the Department of Health, Education and Welfare (HEW) proceeded with the task of integration they were met with resistance by many local school districts who could not demonstrate an acceptable racial mix in their schools. In large urban areas, both South and North, traditional patterns of segregated housing and loyalties to neighbor-

Is there equal opportunity?

hood schools made racial integration very difficult. Busing, as it turned out, aroused deep-seated racial prejudice so that Americans were forced to consider to what extent they wished schools to provide equal educational opportunity. School officials, parents, and courts had to consider whether equal and fair opportunity could be reconciled with freedom of choice and community values. Historically the public school has been seen by many to be an extension of family and community values. Yet public schooling has also been seen as an institution committed to fair play. The issue of busing brought community values and fair play on a collision course.

Since the civil rights movement of the 1950s and 1960s, the ideal of equal educational opportunity has been extended to areas other than racial discrimination. These include bilingual education, education for the handicapped, equal opportunity for women, and demands for equitable funding of public schooling. These cannot be dealt with here, but they do have common elements that are worth mentioning.

They assume that all children and adults deserve a *fair chance* to compete for the rewards that society offers. All assume that public education is an important institution through which children learn the skills, values, and knowledge that help them to be economically and socially successful. Finally they do not challenge the *fact* of inequalities, nor that inequalities will continue to exist. In other words, they do not expect everyone to be the same. Rather, they insist that *unfair* or *discriminatory* treatment be eliminated within our major political, educational, and economic institutions. They insist that *compensatory measures* be taken to assure all children the same *chance* to compete for society's rewards.

Demands for equal educational opportunity have had a direct impact on how teachers teach and grade. The grouping and tracking of students has been challenged repeatedly on the basis of unfair treatment. The structure of the classroom has been held up for review. Of all the changes resulting from the civil rights movement and the new emphasis on equal educational opportunity perhaps the raising of consciousness that took place among teachers and school officials reached the farthest. Teachers and administrators were forced to reexamine their expectations for and treatment of children from minority groups. School systems were threatened with litigation if the grouping of children was shown to be inherently discriminatory. Teachers had to reevaluate the extent to which they let prejudice or a "self-fulfilling prophecy" determine the way they treated children. In short, teachers were expected to bring their methods into line with the larger vision of equal educational opportunity for all children.

The concept of equal educational opportunity brings us full circle from the problems of the recent past to the major current educational

FOR REFLECTION 10.4

The issue of equal educational opportunity forces us to reconsider in a new light some of the major topics already posed. These include the practices of grouping and testing, the purposes of education in a democratic society, and the relationship(s) between learning and teaching. The concept of equal educational opportunity (EEO) encompasses so much that it affects virtually every other issue studied so far. Moreover, it is a good example of a concept that is used in an ideological way. That is, it is used as a tool (weapon) to persuade others that one set of values is superior to another. It is such a powerful tool and is related to so many other concepts, we should examine more closely why this is the case.

First of all, EEO is a concept that is difficult to define because it is composed of more than one element. There are such obvious questions as, "What do we mean by 'equal'?" and "What kind of 'opportunity' are we talking about?" Second, the concept has more than one dimension. It is difficult to understand it without reference to other concepts such as "fairness," "justice," and "merit." This is easily illustrated by noting the use of the term in the following sentence: Equal educational opportunity is a policy that attempts to achieve justice by providing everyone with a fair chance to be rewarded on the basis of merit. It should be evident from this sentence that there are other terms that need to be explained before the meaning of EEO can be clarified.

Educators, philosophers, and policy makers have written many volumes trying to clarify and specify the meaning of EEO. It is a concept that has a hold on the public mind, but it is also susceptible to varied meanings. This is both its strength and its weakness. EEO is not the only concept that has this problem. It does, however, remind us of several important steps we must take when discussing such complex ideas. These include (1) defining the context for usage, (2) defining other concepts or ideas that are related, and (3) making sure we understand the alternative meanings open to us. Following these steps will help us engage in a more meaningful dialogue about controversial topics.

reforms now underway. Equal educational opportunity is so basic to the mission of public schooling that it touches on how we decide what subjects to teach, how to manage our classes, how students are grouped, and what program of study is best suited for a particular student. It also affects our educational priorities and our decisions about how to spend public money.

The reason for equal educational opportunity's significance is its effects on the life chances of every child attending a public school. In American society, the public school is the only institution responsible for the education of all children. It is also the major institution for transmitting the basic knowledge that most people believe necessary for political and economic citizenship. How and to whom it transmits that knowledge thus will help determine the quality of life these students enjoy as adults. The teacher's influence in this scenario of success or failure is sometimes very great, at least for the individual student. The quality of the teacher's role will be very much determined by how well he or she understands how schooling is linked to both the welfare of the public and the individual.

CHAPTER SUMMARY

■ The story of teaching in the 20th century is the story of a developing teaching technology and its use in attempting to solve the problems of equality of educational opportunity and functional literacy. Both of these issues received national attention and marked the emergence of the public school as a major focal point for social policy. The ideal of efficiency and new, more "scientific" ways of classifying students had a major impact on how teachers interacted with their students. The differentiated curriculum and the tracking of students became a standard feature of public schooling in the 20th century. Standardized testing and the grouping of students increasingly helped to determine teacher expectations for students.

Most debates about public education in the 20th century prior to World War II pitted the progressives and social reconstructionists against the educational conservatives. The child-centered philosophy of the progressives and the philosophy of teacher activism promoted by the social reconstructionists met with stiff resistance by the back-to-basics conservatives. Strong criticism of teacher preparation programs by conservative apologists for liberal studies were combined with attacks by concerned laypersons. In the long run, however, teacher preparation programs were strengthened by having to defend their programs. As the periods of civil rights reform and increasing concern with educational equity began to impact on public schooling, teachers themselves were reintroduced to the central place of public schooling in American democracy.

FOR DISCUSSION

1. How high a priority should we place on the level of classroom efficiency? What other priorities might this conflict with?

2. How important is the ability grouping of students to classroom efficiency? Are there alternative ways to achieve the same efficiency?

3. Compare the claims of progressives and conservatives with respect to the purposes of public education.

4. Compare democracy as a political concept to democracy as an educational concept.

5. What are the points of conflict and the points of agreement between the ideals of equal educational opportunity and democracy?

IN THE SCHOOL/IN THE CLASSROOM

1. In this chapter we traced the historical relationships among the modern testing movement, efficiency in the management of schooling, and equal educational opportunity in American public schooling. The pressure to test and classify students is still heavy today. In fact, it may be increasing. In your visits to schools, find out what standardized tests are used, and ask the following questions:
   a. What is the nature of each test (norm-referenced, essay, etc.) and what do the tests claim to measure?
   b. How do teachers use the results of standardized tests?
   c. To whom are the tests results reported?
   d. Do teachers and administrators believe standardized tests help achieve the goal of equal educational opportunity?
   e. What goals do teachers and administrators have in mind when they "group" students?

SUGGESTED READINGS

Burns, Edward. *The Development, Use, and Abuse of Educational Tests.* Springfield, Ill.: Charles C Thomas, 1979. This is a sobering and forthright demystification of testing. The author explains and interprets test-making, including the norming of tests and much of the basic vocabulary of testmakers.

Callahan, Raymond. *Education and the Cult of Efficiency.* Chicago: University of Chicago Press, 1962. Callahan's work on the efficiency movement in education from the early twentieth century to the 1960s demonstrates the influence of a business mentality on education. The student will be able to trace many current management practices to their roots in the cult of efficiency.

de Lone, Richard H., *Small Futures*. New York: Harcourt Brace Jovanovich, 1979. This book helps to demythologize the ideology of equal educational opportunity. The author re-examines the problem of poverty and its relationship to education. De Lone challenges some of our most cherished beliefs about school reform and the American dream of "getting ahead."

Lazerson, Marvin, Judith McLaughlin, Bruce McPherson, and Stephen Baily, *An Education of Value: The Purposes and Practices of Schools*. Cambridge: Cambridge University Press, 1985. These authors examine both the changing and recurring priorities and purposes of schooling. Throughout, they explain and illustrate the tension between excellence in schooling and equal educational opportunity. In their final section to the book they deal with the issues raised by the use of computers for teaching and learning.

Spring, Joel. *The Sorting Machine: National Educational Policy Since 1945*. New York: David McKay, 1976. This work shows how national economic priorities are translated into political and educational policies. Of special interest are the ways in which the cold war, manpower sorting, and military needs influenced educational legislation at the national level.

CHAPTER REFERENCES

1. John Franklin Bobbitt, as in Raymond E. Callahan, *Education and the Cult of Efficiency* (Chicago: University of Chicago Press, 1962), p. 81.
2. Ibid., p. 109.
3. Adapted from Callahan, *Cult of Efficiency*, p. 106.
4. H. Warren Button and Eugene F. Provenzo, Jr., *History of Education and Culture in America* (Englewood Cliffs, N.J.: Prentice-Hall, 1983), p. 242.
5. Ibid., pp. 242–243.
6. Alfred Binet and Théodore Simon, "New Methods for the Diagnosis of the Intellectual Level of Subnormals," *L'Année Psychologique* 12 (1905). In *The Development of Intelligence in Children,* Publications of the Training School at Vineland, New Jersey, No. 11, May, 1916, trans. Elizabeth S. Kite (Baltimore: Williams and Wilkins, 1916), p. 37.
7. Alfred Binet and Théodore Simon, "New Investigation Upon the Measure of the Intellectual Level Among School Children," *L'Année Psychologique* (1911). In *The Development of Intelligence in Children,* trans. Elizabeth S. Kite, p. 291.
8. Lewis M. Terman, *The Measurement of Intelligence* (Boston: Houghton Mifflin, 1916), pp. 4–5.
9. Ibid., p. 11.

10. Ibid., p. 12.
11. Ibid., pp. 16–17.
12. Lewis M. Terman, *The Intelligence of School Children* (Boston: Houghton Mifflin, 1919), pp. 269, 271.
13. Ibid., p. 289.
14. Clarence S. Yoakum and Robert M. Yerkes, *Army Mental Tests* (New York: Henry Holt and Co., 1920), p. xiii.
15. Ibid., pp. 191–192.
16. Ibid., p. 193.
17. Edward A. Krug, *The Shaping of the American High School* (New York: Harper & Row, 1964), p. 298.
18. David Snedden, *What's Wrong with American Education?* (Philadelphia: J.B. Lippincott, 1927), pp. 36–40; Snedden, *Problems of Secondary Education* (Boston: Houghton Mifflin, 1917), pp. 169–205, 220–230.
19. Arthur G. Wirth, *Education in the Technological Society, The Vocational–Liberal Studies Controversy in the Early Twentieth Century* (Scranton, Pa.: Intext Educational Publishers, 1972), pp. 82–88.
20. Ibid., p. 124.
21. National Education Association, Commission on the Reorganization of Secondary Education, *Cardinal Principles of Secondary Education* (U.S. Bureau of Education, Bulletin No. 35 [Washington, D.C.: GPO, 1918]).
22. Ibid., pp. 9–10.
23. Ibid., p. 12.
24. Ibid., pp. 24–27.
25. Merle L. Borrowman, *The Liberal and Technical in Teacher Education* (New York: Teachers College Press, 1956), p. 131.
26. Ibid., pp. 131–134.
27. William Chandler Bagley, *Classroom Management, Its Principles and Techniques* (New York: The Macmillan Co., 1907), pp. 36, 39.
28. Button and Provenzo, *History of Education*, p. 255.
29. Harold Rugg, *American Life and the School Curriculum* (Boston: Ginn and Co., 1936), p. 332.
30. Ibid., p. 333.
31. Arthur Bestor, *Educational Wastelands, The Retreat from Learning in Our Public Schools* (Urbana: University of Illinois Press, 1985), passim.
32. Arthur Bestor, *The Restoration of Learning* (New York: Alfred A. Knopf, 1956), p. 365.
33. Hyman G. Rickover, *American Education—A National Failure* (New York: E.P. Dutton, 1963), p. 3.
34. Ibid., p. 91.
35. James B. Conant, *The American High School Today* (New York: McGraw-Hill, 1959), p. 15.
36. Ibid., p. 40.
37. *Brown* v. *The Board of Education of Topeka* (1954), 74 Sup. Ct. Rep. 691.

IV

The Science and Art of Teaching

To this point you have been introduced to the field of education, the general communication tools available to you in the classroom, and the teacher's role in the school as a social institution. We now turn our attention to the actual planning and teaching that you will do in Chapters 11, 12, and 13.

Chapter 11 is concerned with the planning of your teaching. Good teaching does not just happen. Rather, good teaching is planned for carefully by the classroom teacher. We are not suggesting that all good teaching is the result of careful planning; sometimes spontaneous events are the most educational. However, it is only the prepared teacher who can take advantage of the many opportunities each class session provides.

After planning, we move on to the actual practice of teaching, or pedagogy. Pedagogy, taken from the Greek, means the art or science of teaching. Here we take it to mean both art and science. You will be introduced to different teaching approaches (the science) and the ways in which teachers choose among them to best meet the needs of their students (the art).

Chapter 13 concludes the text with a question, "Can You Teach?" In it we ask you to reflect on yourself: who you are, and what kind of teacher you would like to become. You will be confronted directly with the challenge of deciding whether or not teaching is for you. If you decide it is not, we explore some career alternatives that could be of interest to you as a person who wants to work with people. If you decide teaching is for you, we encourage you to explore the next steps you need to take on your path to becoming a teacher.

11

Teachers and Planning

■ For several weeks Melissa had been observing Mrs. Hernandez. As the term progressed, Melissa had become more active in the classroom. Mrs. Hernandez involved Melissa in paper grading, preparing materials, and working with groups of students in various ways. She involved Melissa in most phases of instruction—like asking questions and leading activities—and she even used Melissa's ideas when planning lessons. While Melissa enjoyed her classroom observation experience, in some ways she felt inferior and intimidated because Mrs. Hernandez was so good at teaching. Melissa never thought she could equal Mrs. Hernandez's competence.

Somehow Mrs. Hernandez was able to take unexpected "emergencies" and classroom interruptions in stride and sometimes even find a way to use the interruptions in her teaching. Melissa knew with experience she could probably learn to do the same. But she wasn't so sure about other matters. Take planning for instance. While Melissa was concerned about what to do during the next 10 minutes, Mrs. Hernandez was able to see a bigger picture—to look beyond the immediate "crisis." She *knew* what to do—what was important to teach, what the kids liked, the best way to motivate them, the best questions to ask, and what to say or do in reply to unexpected answers. Mrs. Hernandez seemed always to know what kinds of materials to use and the best places to find them. She seemed able to know most things students would do before they actually did them.

Things that Melissa knew seemed more understandable when Mrs. Hernandez taught them; she used examples and made connections between ideas that Melissa somehow could not see. And another thing, Mrs. Hernandez was always well planned but did not always follow what she had written down. If Melissa changed her plans the lesson usually would falter and she became aware of waning student interest. But not Mrs. Hernandez. Her lessons seemed to improve. But how? What made the difference?

311

INTRODUCTION

■ How do teachers decide what to teach and how to teach? Certainly teachers make their decisions on the basis of what is important for students to learn, but how do they go about making these decisions? How do teachers decide on a way to organize themselves and the classroom atmosphere, and how do they involve children during instruction so that they will learn? All these questions implicate the importance of teacher planning. Planning is organized thinking about teaching and putting thoughts into action. But what kinds of things do teachers have to plan? And what is the best way to plan? Questions such as these help form the framework for this chapter. Fundamentally the purpose of the chapter is to (1) investigate why teachers plan and (2) examine how teachers may plan.

WHY DO TEACHERS PLAN?

☐ Why Are Plans Important?

In teaching, planning causes the setting for learning to be prepared. Good planning is a key to successful and effective teaching. In fact, poor planning has ruined many lessons, has discouraged pupils as well as their teachers, and has been described as the most common cause of pupils not learning. On the other hand, well-conceived plans may contribute to a desired classroom atmosphere; pupil participation; pupil positive self-images and healthy attitudes toward school; lessons that have clear purposes; pleasant learning environments; and lessons that generally flow, devoid of wasted time and motion. Not even the experienced teacher can "... teach well for long without planning well."[1]

Teachers transform the curriculum while planning. Curriculum usually refers to a set of courses approved by the school. Teachers often add or delete information, make changes in the sequence of topics, choose areas of instruction to emphasize or on which to allot more time. Teachers decide whether to work with individual pupils, groups, or entire classes and often have freedom to interpret the curriculum, to modify it to their own tastes, and to insert some of their own personalities. Sometimes school arrangements also require that teachers plan collectively as part of a team-teaching approach. This means that planning decisions are not made independently by one individual without regard for the activities of other teachers and pupils.

☐ What Are the Reasons for Planning?

Reasons given for planning usually speak of better teaching and of serving pupil needs. Clark and Yinger report three reasons that teachers say are important for them to plan.[2] The first reason is personal to teachers; planning helps teachers meet their immediate needs. For example, a plan can help to reduce the uncertainty a teacher has about facing a classroom full of expectant pupils. Anxiety and uncertainty can also be reduced because the teacher has a clearer sense of direction about what to do and feels more secure having made and recorded these decisions.

In terms of actual teaching, a plan can provide a pathway to the desired outcome of instruction—a means to an end. This second reason means that the process of planning causes teachers to think through

Lesson planning contributes to effective teaching.

what they believe pupils should learn. Decisions about how best to learn are indicated in the plan and are identified as the method(s) for learning.

For the third reason, a plan can serve a direct function during instruction. A plan helps teachers remember how to organize students or get an activity started, and it may provide a framework for teaching a lesson or evaluating pupils.

Additionally, McCutcheon reports that teachers may plan because they have to meet an administrative requirement.[3] In other words, their principal requires it and checks to see that planning books are up-to-date each week. A teacher may also write special plans to help a substitute teacher when the regular teacher has to be absent from school.

☐ What Are the Benefits of Planning?

What teachers decide to do can exert a powerful influence over what actually happens during teaching. For example, several studies indicate that a positive relationship between planning and teaching has been found; that is, teachers tend to closely follow what they planned to do.[4] (Of course if a teacher planned nothing we could probably expect little organization in his or her teaching!) Also, a positive relationship has been found between the *planned* teaching methods and teacher behavior, and *actual* methods and teacher behavior observed during teaching.[5] So, it seems that we could expect teachers who plan enterprising activities or creative approaches to instruction to do what they *planned* to do, just as those who plan routine forms of instruction teach in a routine manner.

You may assume that well-planned teachers can have considerable influence over pupils. Indeed there is broad support for your assumption. Teachers who carefully plan instruction for improving student achievement, thinking, and attitudes stand a good chance of being successful. Students can benefit from instruction that is planned to emphasize particular types of thinking and assist mental development. Measures of achievement probably will improve and pupils' attitudes toward their teacher and school can increase in a positive direction when instruction is clearly planned.[6]

Combine the possibilities mentioned above with the psychic reward teachers reap from planning—through increased confidence and reduced uncertainty—and you have a strong case for some type of planning activity.

HOW DO TEACHERS PLAN?

☐ What Types of Planning Must Teachers Do?

Daily lesson plans usually come to mind when persons think of preparing for teaching. Daily plans, in their simplest form, consist of deciding what to teach and how to teach each subject or group of students. Although most common, experienced teachers do not regard daily lesson plans as their most important type of planning.

For example, Clark and Yinger tell us that unit planning is cited most often by teachers as the most important type of planning they have to do. Weekly and daily planning follow in order of importance and only 7% of the teachers in Clark and Yinger's study listed individual lesson planning among their three most important types of planning.[7]

Planning for a unit of study, activities for the week, for an entire day, or for individual lessons—these types of planning should come as no surprise. However, what cannot be overlooked is the need teachers identify for long-range, short-range, term (like 6- or 9-week grading periods or a semester), and yearly planning.

By now you probably get the idea that teachers may devote enormous amounts of energy and time to planning, and you are right. Whether to cope or survive, researchers have found that teachers develop routines for handling matters of planning.[8] Routines are sets of procedures that are developed for both the teacher and students to follow so all behavior is controlled and coordinated—and time spent is both efficient and effective.[9] Teacher routines represent responses to the demands placed on their time. These routines become the mechanisms that teachers use to simplify their duties and use time more efficiently while handling paperwork, preparing materials, organizing the classroom, managing students, and so on. Time spent efficiently on these matters allows more time for instruction.

Teacher planning is a nested process (see Figure 11.1). Teachers use curriculum guides, textbooks, and other instructional materials to set goals for the year. These goals concern the academic, personal, and skill growth targets for the pupils and provide a framework teachers use to organize what otherwise would be an unorganized collection of discrete facts and learning exercises for pupils. The planning framework is filled out by term plans, unit plans, weekly lesson plans, and daily lesson plans. The nested nature of teacher planning helps to assure that connections are made between concepts and lessons for students, that personal needs are met, and that lower skills evolve into higher skills.

FIGURE 11.1 Planning is a nested process. A planning framework consists of small plans fit into larger plans.

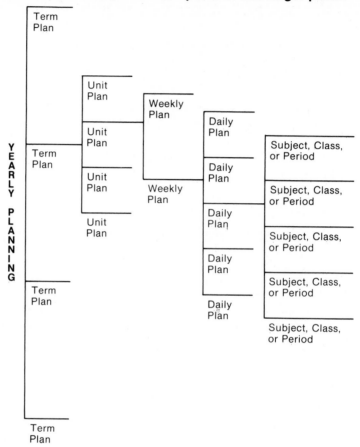

Exemplary teachers have a long-range vision of their teaching mission and plan accordingly. Their planning transcends the hour-by-hour, one-day-at-a-time type of thinking more common to novice teachers who are mostly concerned with getting through the day successfully. Experienced teachers often are recognized for their synergetic planning and teaching. Their plans guide the moment-by-moment instruction and decision-making as they fit questions and responses into a framework for learning. Present pupil learning tasks are related to those of the past and teachers help students make important mental connections so that the facts, skills, and experiences of individual lessons add up to a sum greater than the independent parts. How can teachers do this? How can they keep all these

"I haven't decided definitely on a career yet, but I certainly don't want something that requires a lot of preparation."
Phi Delta Kappan, January 1984.

responsibilities in mind while teaching? Perhaps a teacher's approach to planning helps.

☐ A Planning Approach

What is the best way to plan? It is not clear if one approach to planning is superior to another and we can expect almost as many ways to plan lessons as there are teachers to teach lessons. But certainly this does not answer the question. Here is where Clark and Peterson's review of the research on planning can help.[10] They conclude that an inexperienced person—a prospective teacher, perhaps like you—can improve planning if a linear and rational format is used. Four primary steps are recommended and usually follow this sequence of questions:

1. What does the teacher expect to accomplish and expect students to do?
2. What learning experiences and materials are needed?
3. How should the lesson be organized?
4. How can you determine what students have learned?

There are many options for planning and teaching lessons.

Actually the questions posed above tend to oversimplify teacher planning. The four steps of a linear planning approach do not represent all that needs to be considered and planned and certainly does not guarantee that the synergy between ideas, concepts, and lessons will be accomplished. Indeed, other features may be included in teacher plans. Each added feature contributes to a plan's usefulness and it is the precise combination and arrangement of a plan's components that represent the planning style of the teacher. Versions of linear and rational planning can provide a good foundation for developing a personal planning style that is compatible with a teacher's own characteristics; the mental, physical, and emotional needs of pupils; the character of the subject area; and the conditions of classrooms.

RESEARCH NOTES 11.1

The research on teacher planning is critiqued for its narrow comparisons and has been encouraged to focus more broadly on what teachers accomplish in the time they devote to planning. Aside from this point several generalizations may be gleaned from the research:

- Experienced teachers engage in a full range of planning activity throughout the school year with term, unit, weekly, and daily planning having priority over specific lessons.
- Teacher beliefs and values are important because teachers make many decisions that transform the curriculum and allot time to content, groups, and individual pupils.
- Several studies suggest that teacher planning does influence pupils' opportunities to learn, the content that is covered, the types of grouping used for instruction, and the teacher's general approach to teaching.
- Planning provides psychic rewards for teachers, in part because uncertainty is reduced and confidence about teaching is boosted.
- Planning cannot eliminate all the uncertainties of teacher-student interactions because of the complexity of human relations and interruptions to teaching as a result of surprises, unscheduled events, and classroom digressions.
- Lesson planning in itself is not regarded by experienced teachers with a high priority partly because they
  - Do not plan in such detail as instructed in teacher preparation courses.
  - Do considerable mental planning with nearly half of it occurring while actually teaching. This is justified because the finer details of teaching are unpredictable and cannot be adequately planned.
- The mental plans of experienced teachers are supplemented and cued by notes and lists of important points that teachers want to remember. Even so, once interactive teaching begins, teacher plans are moved aside to make room for interactive decision-making.
- A linear planning approach does not represent how experienced teachers plan but it is recommended as an approach for training beginning teachers because of the foundation provided for developing a personal planning style as experience is gained.

Compiled from Christopher M. Clark and Penelope L. Peterson, "Teachers' Thought Processes," in *Handbook of Research on Teaching*, 3rd ed., ed. Merlin C. Wittrock (New York: Macmillan, 1986).

PLANNING LESSONS

■ Often students in education programs spend a part of their first course visiting classrooms and observing teachers much like Melissa did in our chapter scenario. Let us suppose you are doing the same, your teacher expresses confidence in you, and he or she gives you the opportunity to plan and teach a brief lesson. Where do you start?

You might begin by putting yourself in the position of a new teacher in the school. You have been hired to teach, your contract has been signed, and you are pleased that you have been assigned to teach your preferred grade or subject(s). The start of a new school year is just a few days away, you are new to the community, and there is much to do. "Now, where do I begin?" you ask yourself as you start to plan those first days of lessons.

A simple answer to the questions above would be to open the textbook and begin with the first chapter, plan to cover the material, then proceed to the next chapter, and so on. Sound simple? Of course, but is that all there is to teaching? Hardly. At this point it is useful to remember the importance of the larger picture of planning.

There are several things you would need to do; for instance, find out about the school, the community, the pupils, and state, district, and school requirements or goals. This is part of the pre-lesson planning activity necessary for actual lesson planning and teaching. While teaching, you probably would find it necessary to modify your plans— to change your expectations or revise your pace. Some type of post-lesson planning is helpful for evaluating the outcomes of the present lesson and for planning or adjusting the next class or lesson. The broad view of planning consists of three levels of consideration, and none of your planning takes place without regard for your students.

The three levels of planning mentioned above help make up the larger picture of teacher lesson planning and are shown in Figure 11.2. We explore each level further, with a particular focus on planning lessons using a version of the linear approach. Our purpose is to introduce the tasks required for planning. Details of teacher planning are best left to other teacher preparation courses where ample time is provided for your mastery.

☐ Level 1: Pre-Lesson Planning

Several factors must be considered before the actual plan is written. Teachers must make decisions about goals, subject matter to be learned, the kinds of proper learning experiences to be provided, and

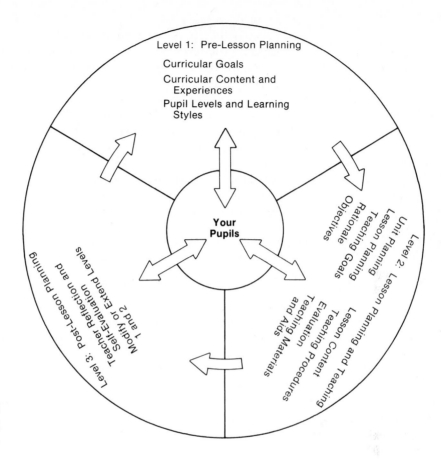

Level 1: Pre-Lesson Planning

Curricular Goals

Curricular Content and Experiences

Pupil Levels and Learning Styles

Your Pupils

Level 2: Lesson Planning and Teaching

Unit Planning

Lesson Planning

Teaching Goals

Rationale

Objectives

Lesson Content

Teaching Procedures

Evaluation

Teaching Aids and Materials

Level 3: Post-Lesson Planning

Teacher Reflection and Self-Evaluation

Modify or Extend Levels 1 and 2

**FIGURE 11.2
Teacher planning
levels.**

the capabilities of their pupils. Most of this concerns developing an answer to the first planning question: What does the teacher expect to accomplish and expect students to do? This question is partly answered by setting goals.

Setting Goals

Goals are statements that describe major outcomes of teaching. These may represent the intentions of the state, school board, curriculum committee, school, department, or teacher. Goals are important because they provide a target or destination to travel toward—an important aspect of any pre-lesson planning.

Goals are general and may be expressed rather abstractly; they do not provide the kind of specifics teachers require for organizing daily classroom activities, but goals do suggest the general kinds of content or teaching activities to include in a lesson. Goals are important because they make a teacher's intent clear.

Different lengths of time are required to meet different types of goals. Long-term curricular goals can span several weeks, months, or an entire year. Examples include things like "Promote physical and mental health," "To help students appreciate the value of music," and so on. Short-term goals are used to set the purpose of briefer episodes of instruction, like a day, week, or unit of study. "Students will learn what it means to observe," "To be able to tell the difference between wild and domestic animals," and "Learn how to care for a pet" could be some examples of short-term goals.

The information for setting goals can come from at least three distinct sources as suggested below. As you review these brief descriptions of goal sources see if you can identify the philosophical or theoretical foundation for each.

SUBJECT EXPERTS: ONE SOURCE   Experts in various academic disciplines may function as one source of goals. Advocates of this approach to goal setting tell us that the main purpose of schools is not to prepare pupils to ready themselves for society or to provide them with short-range skills that become quickly out-of-date. Knowledge that has stood the test of time is most important for learning, and teaching ought to focus on this basic knowledge.

SOCIETY: A SECOND SOURCE   Pupils live in an environment within a social context. Therefore, a second way to identify goals is to examine the community or larger society and determine what pupils need to function within it. Goals are formed from what pupils particularly need to effectively meet the challenges of *their* society. The value of any knowledge is determined by the extent to which it helps each individual function in the society.

THE STUDENTS: A THIRD SOURCE   Students provide another source for goals. Consider each individual taught. Student-centered schools believe that schools are for people and that the purpose of schools should be targeted on helping young people develop as fully as possible according to each person's potential. The specifics of pupil goals depend on many factors including the level of the pupil, prior and current learning experiences, and the subject content taught. Therefore, throughout all planning levels the pupils must be the central concern of any planning decisions. Pupils are affected by and exert a reciprocal effect on what is planned. Yet there are other factors to consider as well. We continue with investigating pre-lesson planning by presenting several additional factors below.

FOR REFLECTION 11.1   Setting Goals

When teachers set goals for students and for themselves, they primarily draw on three sources of information for making their planning decisions: (a) experts in the academic field, (b) the community or social environment, and (c) from the students themselves. Answer the following questions to deepen your understanding of goal setting:

1. If considered independently and in isolation, how would each source of information influence the goals the teacher sets?
2. Write three examples of short-term goals for your intended grade level or subject area. Let each example emphasize a different source of information.
3. Examine the short-term goals you have written. Does the subject matter and type of learning experience differ? Why?
4. How might a teacher's philosophy of education influence goal setting?

Subject Matter and Learning Experiences

The subject matter and pupil experiences necessary for learning may be implicated by state, district, and school goals. Both of these constitute an important part of pre-lesson planning and are a part of the answer to the question about teacher intentions and expectations for students. Subject and experience information can be found in planning documents and it provides a good (and often necessary) starting place for planning classroom instruction. The goal statements found in curriculum guides, courses of study, and textbook teacher guides help to provide a picture of the suggested scope as well as the sequence of information and experiences delegated to the curriculum; indications of predominant philosophy are also evident in addition to beliefs about how pupils learn.

These planning documents are often based on needs assessments that have been done by the school to determine the educational needs of local pupils. Priorities for teaching are identified from the assessments. Some of these priorities may be addressed through textbooks, commercial or custom-designed curricula, suggestions provided by the opinions of experts, or a variety of supplemental print and media materials.

Pupil Level

What pupils already know, the skills they already have, and their capabilities may be known from school needs assessments or formal testing programs. This information is necessary for setting realistic goals and can be found in pupil school files. The information may be

No one plan serves all students equally.

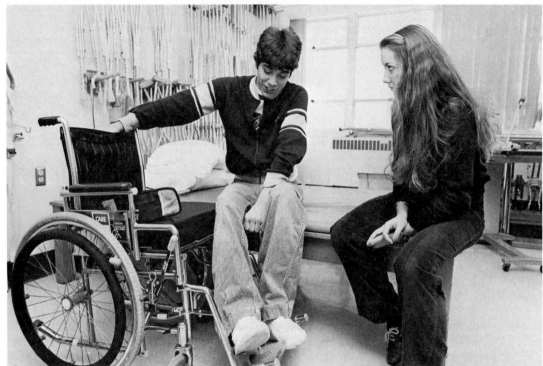

given in a form that indicates some level of ability or makes predictions about learning readiness. These factors are important to know if lessons and learning experiences are to help pupils grow. The levels at which pupils function are particularly helpful when forming learning objectives and filling in the details of lesson plans. Pupil levels are important whether the instructional goals originate from academic disciplines, society, or concerns for maximum pupil growth.

In summary, pre-lesson planning consists of knowing or developing goals, identifying relevant subject matter and pupil experiences, and considering the present capabilities of learners. We now turn to the next level of planning to look at some parts of teacher plans that are included among the details of daily lesson plans.

☐ **Level 2: Daily Lesson Planning and Teaching**

Continuing with our linear approach to planning (Figure 11.3), part of question 1—What does the teacher expect to accomplish and expect

FIGURE 11.3 Linear planning format.

TEACHING GOAL: State in broad terms what you hope to accomplish.

RATIONALE: Be specific about why it is important for you to achieve this goal or for pupils to achieve the objectives.

PUPIL OBJECTIVES: Be specific about what pupils are expected to do and state what they are to do in observable terms.

LESSON CONTENT: The most important items the lesson is to include.
  Lesson Opener: How you will motivate the pupils or start the lesson.
  Key Questions or Topic Outline: To help you to cover the most important points.
  Examples: To help you make the points clear to pupils in terms that they can understand.
  Summary Points: To help you bring closure to the lesson and a review of instruction for pupils.

TEACHING PROCEDURES OR LESSON ACTIVITIES: Select a varied approach to your teaching and involve pupils as much as possible.

TEACHING MATERIALS AND AIDS: Carefully select or develop materials or aids that help you and pupils accomplish goals and objectives; involve pupils in different types and levels of learning.

PUPIL EVALUATION: How will you determine the extent that pupils accomplish the objectives?

TEACHER EVALUATION OF THE LESSON: For the post-active level, how will you evaluate the strengths and weaknesses of the lesson? How will you decide what changes to make in tomorrow's lesson?

students to do?—is addressed in daily lesson planning along with questions 2 and 3. Expectations were made clear during pre-lesson planning. Now attention needs to be given to making decisions about learning experiences, materials needed, and how the lesson should be organized.

The thinking required for pre-lesson planning consists of setting and clarifying teacher expectations for students and leads to writing goals. Short-term goals should be selected from the sources of information already described and then arranged to fit into a framework for accomplishing long-term goals. The smaller portion of this framework consists of the daily level of instruction—the daily lesson plan.

Daily plans consist of short-term goals, a rationale for the lesson, pupil objectives, and a means for detecting how well students accomplish what teachers expect. Other factors are important as well and include the lesson opener, key questions, lesson outline, examples of the main ideas, summary of ideas, lesson activities to be used, teaching procedures to be followed, and the materials and teaching aids to be used. Daily plans essentially are descriptions of what teachers want to do with, for, or to students and they require the cooperation of pupils. Cooperation is most easily gained when students see some value in what is planned for them. The lesson rationale makes the value clear.

Rationale

"Hey teacher, why do we have to do this stuff?" is a question that could be viewed as a challenge to a teacher's authority. But is there another way to interpret this bold student's message? Perhaps a pupil could be expressing frustration with an assignment or activity because the sense or purpose of it is not clear. Some connections could be missing and, if so, pupils may not be able to see the relevance of a task, let alone agree with its value.

Teachers are responsible for making clear a rationale or reason for what pupils are asked to do. The rationale should be part of a teacher's plan. The fact that a teacher is in control and can tell pupils what to do is not a valid reason for many students. They have to believe. Better still, pupils should be able to answer the question for themselves because they can see the practicality of their learning, perhaps because it relates to prior experiences or will help them accomplish much-valued future personal goals. Realize though that an ambiguous answer like, "Because you will need to be able to do this someday" is unconvincing. You might also consider the importance of a rationale this way: if a teacher does not have a believable reason, maybe that teacher should not spend time teaching that lesson.

Objectives

So far we have covered a general idea of what to teach and why to teach it. Now let us get down to the specific level of activity. The specifics of instruction are identified by objectives. Objectives are precise descriptions of what pupils shall do and should be expressed in observable terminology. For example, how can you tell if students have "learned" or if they "know" or "appreciate" something? This cannot be observed or measured directly; rather teachers determine if students know, appreciate, or learn by making inferences. Inferences are based on measurements or observations of pupil performances on prespecified learning tasks. In other words, teacher inferences are based on details—particulars—and these particulars add up to a larger picture in which teachers can claim that students know or have learned something.

COMPONENTS OF OBJECTIVES   There are many ways to write objectives and your instructor probably has a preferred format if you are required to write examples. Performance or behavioral objectives are widely recognized and are discussed in the rest of this section. Four criteria usually are important for each objective. As such, each objective must specify the:

A.   AUDIENCE (class, group or individual) for whom the objective is intended
B.   BEHAVIOR the teacher expects from pupils
C.   CONDITIONS necessary to enable the learning to take place (like what prerequisites, prior activity, arrangements, or support materials are needed
D.   DEGREE or minimum level of performance that is acceptable to show that students have completed the objective satisfactorily.

Identifying the *audience* to be addressed by the objective is important because it helps teachers recognize the ability levels and interests of pupils, thus helping their expectations remain realistic. For many teachers who work with the same pupils, the audience may not change regularly even though growth in pupil performance is evident. However, stating objectives in terms of the *behavior* expected from pupils is important because, after all, teachers are expected to change pupils' behaviors. By this we mean that schools are held responsible for changing the mental, physical, and emotional behaviors of pupils.

Conditions under which pupils are expected to perform need to be stated insofar as it is necessary to provide all the tools for learning, as in the example, "When given a list of ten problems and several formulas. . . ." Without the problems and formulas would it be realistic to expect sixth-grade pupils to select the proper formula and correctly solve, say, seven of the ten problems? Finally, the *degree,* or expected level of accomplishment, is necessary to identify a minimal level of satisfactory performance; this is the basis for evaluating pupil progress. What is the degree shown in the example of the math problems just mentioned?

MAKE OBJECTIVES STIMULATE LEARNING   A look through the history of schooling provides some important insights about teacher objectives. The successes of pupils in American schools have been traditionally estimated by their ability to recall specific information and apply this information in the narrowest of contexts, usually while taking tests. Daniel Tanner claims that this "learning" is without any real comprehension because there

> is little opportunity for practical application and meaningful analysis, synthesis, and evaluation; [therefore] the student tends to forget rather quickly most of what he is tested for on teacher-made examinations.[11]

We can speculate that the material Tanner refers to is only useful to pupils because it helps them get grades. It certainly does not stimulate critical thought or nurture creativity if the material simply requires lower levels of thinking.

Phi Delta Kappan, September 1983.

Material limited to lower thinking levels tends to require rather mechanical pupil behavior, it is often repetitive and boring, and it can contribute to the development of pupils' poor attitudes toward learning and school. Also, learning at any level is not independent of the realities of the pupils' lives; their attitudes, interests, values, and development of skills are related to cognition if for no other than the simple reason that all neural stimuli are processed in the brain. But there is more for us to be concerned about than human physiology. Knowledge simply does not exist apart from the emotions and physical activity of the learner. Yet many teachers persist in limiting objectives to tasks that measure pupil achievement only in terms of mental "knowledge." Typically little attention is given to the emotional and physical attributes of pupils.

DOMAINS   Objectives can and should span the mental, emotional, and physical dimensions of pupils. Educators often refer to this as "teaching the whole pupil," in which no important dimension of the learner is overlooked. Educational researchers have developed domains that represent these important aspects of the learner. These are known as the *cognitive, affective,* and *psychomotor* domains and each domain is represented by a taxonomy consisting of discrete levels. It is not our purpose to present these taxonomies in detail here because they are usually studied in depth in courses on teaching methods. But the brief descriptions of the domains below should familiarize you with the concept of domains and help you think about how teachers plan lessons.

Cognitive Domain. The cognitive domain focuses on the transmission of information and development of mental skills. Some educators estimate that 80% to 90% of the pupils' time in classrooms is devoted to instruction in this domain.[12] Evidence for this claim is seen in the types of teaching strategies used, kinds of materials used, and the types of tests given. We can think of the cognitive domain as being concerned with rational, analytical, and critical thinking.

Typically the cognitive domain is thought of as being represented by two areas: one that represents information and knowledge, and the other that is concerned with the ways that information is processed in the human mind and assists in the development of an individual's knowledge base. Benjamin Bloom and his associates developed a universal taxonomy that illustrates six different levels of cognitive thinking.[13] These levels implicate the different levels of instruction and represent the complexities of thinking that can be stimulated with astute teacher planning.

As the levels increase so does the mental rigor required of pupils. The lowest level of cognition, according to Bloom, is *knowledge*; this level requires memorization and repetition of facts. The *comprehension* level requires that pupils remember facts and be able to express information in their own words by translating, interpreting, or predicting. *Application* means that pupils must be able to use or apply something like a rule, method, or principle to solve a new problem that they have not experienced previously. If pupils can *analyze* they are able to demonstrate that they can break the whole down into its many parts. If pupils can design or create an original product or solution, this shows that they can *synthesize.* Pupils *evaluate* when they make judgments, decisions, and choices *and* provide reasons or supportive evidence.

All higher levels of the taxonomy require that pupils are able to use the mental skills implied by the previous levels. In fact we can think of the lower levels of the taxonomy as tools that help promote thinking at the higher levels, so it seems prudent that a teacher plans instruction at a variety of mental levels. In some cases sequencing instruction becomes critical if pupils are going to be able to think and perform tasks that require higher levels of reasoning.

Affective Domain. To be sure, not all teachers or classrooms can be cast in the "mind only mold," and the fact that much of schooling is devoted to the cognitive domain really does not prove that the affective and psychomotor domains are unimportant. For example, let us consider the affective domain for a moment. Parents of school-age children were surveyed in a Gallup Poll about schooling and their child's teachers.[14] In one particular item parents were asked what qualities they would look for if they were able to select their child's teachers. The most mentioned qualities were teachers' abilities to communicate, understand, relate to, inspire, and motivate students. These are qualities associated with the affective side of learning.

The affective domain is primarily concerned with helping children develop attitudes and values and in helping them deal with their feelings, likes, and dislikes. Usually the affective part of learning is an implicit rather than an explicit part of teacher planning. Consider that almost every teacher wants students to leave class with positive feelings and attitudes about their learning and you have justification for affective objectives. Emphasis on the cognitive domain alone will not accomplish these implicit goals of teaching, and we cannot overlook the importance that parents place on teacher qualities that lend themselves to positive communication. Therefore what is planned for the cognitive domain must be complemented by the affective domain. Teachers cannot afford to overlook what it takes to promote positive pupil attitudes and values.

Attitudes are connected with how we feel about things in our environment, what we like or dislike, as in "I love math!" or "I hate school!" Values, on the other hand, are more global and do not refer to specific objects; they represent ways we lead our lives (or believe we ought to) and are much more abstract than the feelings we share with others and use to reveal our attitudes. Things that we value are viewed in terms of their relative importance and are not usually simply accepted or rejected. For example, which do you value: self-respect or open-mindedness? If you are like most people you probably value both, not one *or* the other, yet you may value one *more than* the other.

Attitudes and values are related to experiences. Attitudes are learned, and values are adjusted in order of importance through experiences. The role of experience is important because teachers are in a place to influence the experiences pupils have in school; hence they can influence student attitudes and values. This places an important responsibility on teachers for the attitudes that students have about school and how much or how little youth value their education. As with cognitive development, teachers must consider how they will deal with pupil attitudes and values; this has important implications for planning.

Psychomotor Domain. The psychomotor domain concerns the development of muscular strength and motor coordination. Of the three domains, it receives the least emphasis in most classrooms. But the amount of psychomotor emphasis depends on the age level of pupils and the subject area. For example, young children often lack eye-hand coordination and sensorimotor skills, so teachers plan experiences to emphasize these factors and assist in their development. Art, dance, music, physical education, and many areas of vocational or technical education require specific physical skills and levels of muscular coordination. Teachers include in their plans for students experiences to develop psychomotor skills that are necessary for productive learning. Given the importance of determining objectives that encourage more wholistic learning experiences, we now turn to the portion of lesson planning that is concerned with selecting appropriate content.

Content

Teachers cannot develop performance objectives for pupils without considering what will be taught, specifically a lesson's content. An outline or brief description of lesson content is helpful to teachers and many choose to include it in their plans. Specific details and lengthy paragraph descriptions of content can make it difficult to locate a particular point when teachers are in a rush. Something more moderate and less specific, like definitions, lists of key words, or important questions, are usually helpful.

Another important thing teachers have to consider is the arrangement or sequence of content. "Knowing my students, what is the best sequence for them?" "What will make the most sense to them?" If you have analyzed the material beforehand, while developing goals and writing objectives, most of this thinking about sequence has probably been done. When you have to plan try not to skip over this matter of sequencing, though, because some type of hierarchical analysis will help you identify lower level skills and information that have to be learned before pupils can successfully approach higher levels of learning. Also, attention to this type of detail eliminates unnecessary replication of teaching. Repetition contributes to boredom, just as failure to establish a foundation for learning creates pupil anxiety and sets them up for possible failure.

Teaching Procedures

Content represents *what* teachers will teach, while procedures concern *how* teachers teach. This can be viewed globally in the sense that we can envision an overall approach to teaching a lesson. Called teaching methods or strategies, some examples include lecture/recitation, class discussion, deductive or inductive teaching, and inquiry, among several possible approaches.

Teaching methods provide teachers with a type of road map they can use to navigate their way through a lesson. Teachers have many options to choose from while teaching. Appropriate selections will be suggested by the pupil activity stated in the lesson's objectives. For example, if teachers want students to recite, they select a method that places them in a teacher-structured atmosphere to encourage this behavior. On the other hand, if teachers want pupils to solve problems creatively they need to select a teaching approach that stimulates creative thinking and nurtures problem-solving skills, probably with limited teacher structure and perhaps with student groups or teams supported by an appropriate classroom atmosphere.

Aside from a general approach to teaching lessons, procedures can also be concerned with the step-by-step details necessary for presenting a classroom or laboratory demonstration or complex physical maneuver as in gymnastics. Whether general or specific, what is important is that the procedures be effective in helping pupils achieve the objectives. Some generic elements of effective teaching procedures include to: (1) help pupils focus on the lesson; (2) use specific procedures to provide for different pupil learning styles and to capitalize on strengths; (3) check pupil progress during the lesson—don't wait until the end of the lesson to find out about difficulties; (4) insure an appropriate level of participation; and (5) bring closure to the lesson with a summary or emphasis of important points.

Evaluation

How can you determine what students have learned? Although teachers check progress during each lesson, the time comes when they want to see how pupils perform on more than one objective at a time. Known as summative evaluation, it is important to determine *if* and *how well* pupils have mastered the objectives; this may be done as often as each day or after several lessons have been taught. If there are differences between what teachers intended students to learn and what they actually achieved, then the teachers have to decide what changes to make in future plans. Overall, teachers view the plan as a guide that they change if all does not proceed as intended.

The evaluation of pupil progress must be planned carefully. Evaluation procedures must complement lesson objectives and be concerned with evaluating what teachers expect students to do, not something else. For example, it would not be fair to expect pupils to perform well on a test that requires that they "synthesize" or "evaluate" if teacher instruction focuses on having them memorize. Another example is if teachers expect students to develop skills in, say, dribbling a basketball they would not give pupils a written test to find out if they can dribble.

Each lesson plan should state the appropriate means for evaluation of that day's lesson. Plans for longer spans of time should provide for several appropriate ways to evaluate pupil progress. Each objective helps to suggest what is appropriate. Beyond written tests, some other possible evaluation devices include skills checklists, anecdotal records, pupil logbooks, oral quizzes, pupil projects, teacher observation checklists, and attitude inventories.

FOR REFLECTION 11.2 Comparing Lesson Plans

A linear planning approach has been used to write the two sample lesson plans shown below (see Figure 11.3). Only Goals, Rationales, and Objectives are provided. Compare each for the following questions:

1. What expectations do the teachers have for themselves? For students?
2. What sources of information do you think helped shape the goals?
3. What learning experiences do you think each teacher will provide? What types of materials will they use?
4. Compare the goals and objectives. How will the teacher organize and teach each lesson?
5. How will each teacher determine what the students learn?
6. In your opinion, which plan is better? Why?
7. How would you improve either plan?

Lesson Plan #1—Archeology

Goal This lesson is on archeology. I would like for my students to understand what archeology is, how it is used, and why it exists. I would also like for the students to obtain an appreciation for and an interest in artifacts from this lesson. I would like for them to better understand what stories lay behind these artifacts, and how much history from ancient times has been learned from these pieces.

Rationale I feel that it is important for students to understand what archeology is, so they can know how it is used to discover how people from ancient times used to live. They need to understand that much of our knowledge we have today has been learned through the study of artifacts.

Objectives I would like for the students to be able to recognize some artifacts and know what kind of materials were used to make them. Also, to have an understanding of what can be learned from these artifacts.

Lesson Plan #2—General Science: Food Chains

Goal To explain a simple food chain and show possible problems when a food chain is modified.

Rationale Life, as we know it, is based on the energy from the sun. Energy is passed from one consumer to another consumer through a direct dependency (food chain). If a modification in the food chain occurs (i.e., pollution related or change in predator/prey relationships), an effect is felt up and down the chain. To be able to live together and appreciate all species, the science students need to understand how we, as humans, are directly dependent on these species. If we interfere with the food chain, life could stop.

Objectives After being given an introduction and lecture on food chains, the ninth-grade science student will be able to:
1. Develop in writing an accurate food chain of no more than four orders of consumers. The food chain must be 100% accurate and found in nature.
2. Identify on a test the different orders of consumers and label each with its appropriate order number. Mastery is shown by a score of 100%.
3. Define in writing ten vocabulary words, discussed in the given material, with at least 80% accuracy.
4. Diagnose the cause of an increase or decrease in a certain level of the food chain when given an essay test with stated problems. Mastery is shown by a score of 100%.

☐ **Level 3: Post-Lesson Planning**

Although evaluation was mentioned above, there is more to it than finding out how well pupils performed on objectives. Much of their performance depends directly on teachers' fulfilling the intentions of their plans. So, in many ways, how well pupils do reflects how well teachers teach. Rather than guessing about performance, teachers may set aside some time to reflect on each lesson and ask themselves some self-evaluation questions. For example: How appropriate were the objectives? Were assumptions or findings about prior learning correct or was reteaching necessary? Why? Were all prerequisite skills developed or is it necessary to develop some of them now? Did the teaching methods help pupils as intended? Did all pupils profit from the methods? If not, which learners did not benefit and why? Did the materials work as planned?

The questions above show us a few of the areas where teachers have to make many decisions. Indeed, planning can be complex and sometimes is complicated by unexpected factors like late buses, inclement weather, illnesses, classroom emergencies, school assemblies, field trips, and fire drills. We would be misleading you if you took all this to mean that all teachers plan all lessons with the amount of detail suggested above. In fact, many experienced teachers do not. Their plans may seem like simple lists, but that does not mean that experienced teachers take planning lightly.

Research shows that most experienced teachers do more planning in their heads than they may write on paper. Plans can remain firmly fixed in a teacher's mind from one year to the next, but this does not mean that teachers always memorize and use the same plan without changing it. In fact, out of all the time teachers may devote to planning, about half occurs while they actually teach![15] Consider that

> ... the finer details of classroom teaching (e.g., specific verbal behavior) are unpredictable and therefore not planned. Planning shapes the broad outline of what is possible or likely to occur while teaching and is used to manage transitions from one activity to another. But once interactive teaching begins, the teacher's plan moves to the background and interactive decision making becomes important.[16]

So it seems that lesson planning does not just happen before or after teaching a lesson. Planning is continuous with many of the important human factors planned as teachers and pupils interact. This type of planning requires an active mind and alert teacher, a teacher with a clear vision, a sense of educational purpose, and the willingness to make decisions. Decisions teachers make prior to teaching a lesson and after the lesson ends are important and represent what we think of when teacher planning is mentioned. These decisions usually emanate from a linear planning format— What should be done first? What should come next? and What should be done last?

The decisions made while teaching in the classroom, however, are probably the most important of all because this is when the actual person-to-person and situational decisions are made. There is no way to predict all occurrences or pupil reactions to what teachers write in predetermined plans. Logic and order can be helpful only to a point when teachers have to make decisions while teaching. Doing what is correct while interacting with a class full of expectant pupils is as much an art as it is a science.

CHAPTER SUMMARY

■ Planning lessons requires teachers to make many decisions, much like planning for making a journey. Where teachers want the class to arrive—their intended destination—needs to be identified. Then there are many necessary concerns over details like topics to be taught, district goals, the classroom environment, available resources, community expectations, ways to teach effectively, learning activities to select, procedures to set and follow, and pupils—their nature and learning objectives for them.

All these decisions require energy and may create uncertainty and anxiety. Teachers report that they feel better organized, more secure, and that they are clearer and able to teach better when they take time to plan for instruction. More importantly, teachers and researchers cite improvements in learning when lessons are planned well, mostly because teachers have a framework for teaching, making decisions, and evaluating pupil performance.

There are many different types of plans that teachers have to develop: daily lessons, units of instruction, weekly plans, and both short- and long-range plans for fulfilling administrative, extra-curricular, and clerical responsibilities. Routines help teachers deal with these many demands for plans. Many routines are developed through teaching experience, but where does a teacher start? A step-by-step linear planning sequence is suggested as a starting place to acquire this important experience and as a foundation for developing your own planning style. Some of these lesson planning steps include setting goals, a rationale, and objectives; selecting content, learning activities, and teaching aids; identifying procedures or methods for teaching; and determining appropriate methods for evaluating pupil performance.

FOR DISCUSSION

1. What aspects of planning do you think are most important? Why?

2. How would you plan your first lesson? What would you do?

3. What are the advantages of a highly structured and detailed lesson plan? Disadvantages?

4. What are the different kinds of plans teachers have to make? Which do you think is most important? Rank-order these plans and give a rationale for your selected order.

5. Do you support written objectives in which pupil behavior is specified and can be observed or measured? Why? What are possible limitations to this type of objectives?

6. Do you support planning lessons that provide opportunities for learning experiences that represent all the domains? Why?

7. Do you think experienced teachers should be expected to develop written lesson plans containing as much detail as is recommended for you? Why or why not?

8. How well do you think your teachers planned the lessons they taught you? Justify your answer.

IN THE SCHOOL/IN THE CLASSROOM

1. Researchers tell us that teachers have routines for meeting many responsibilities. Observe closely and list your teacher's routines. Describe the purpose(s) of these routines.

2. Closely observe a teacher. First record what you think the goal, rationale, and objectives are for a lesson, then compare your guess with the teacher's plan. Describe any differences. If different, why?

3. How does your classroom teacher plan? Examine the teacher's plans for the week and describe his or her procedures.

4. Plan to teach a brief lesson to a group of students (or a group of your peers). Use this version of the linear planning form.

TEACHING GOAL:

RATIONALE:

PUPIL OBJECTIVES:

LESSON CONTENT:

    Lesson Opener:

    Key Questions or Topic Outline:

    Examples:

    Summary Points:

TEACHING PROCEDURES OR LESSON ACTIVITIES:

TEACHING MATERIALS AND AIDS:

PUPIL EVALUATION:

TEACHER EVALUATION OF THE LESSON:

SUGGESTED READINGS

Clark, Leonard H., and Irving S. Starr. *Secondary and Middle School Teaching Methods.* New York: Macmillan, 1981. Although a secondary methods text, this book has practical examples of planning courses, units, and lessons. Chapters on diagnosis and providing for individual pupil differences are helpful for the pre-lesson level of planning and sample lesson plans offer good examples of the linear planning approach.

Jacobsen, David, Paul Egger, Donald Kauchak, and Carole Dulaney. *Methods for Teaching: A Skills Approach.* Columbus, Ohio: Charles E. Merrill Publishing Co., 1985. Planning, implementing, and evaluating instruction are represented as three essential and continual components teachers need to develop if they are to improve the quality of their instruction. Excellent coverage is given to goals, objectives, and lesson planning.

Lorber, Michael, A., and Walter D. Pierce. *Objectives, Methods, and Evaluation for Secondary Teaching.* Englewood Cliffs, N.J.: Prentice-Hall, 1983. In a time when some proponents advance the cause for precise, clear-cut teaching-learning processes, the authors of this book remind us of individual pupil differences. They suggest techniques for developing your own personal characteristics while mastering teaching skills and procedures related to good teaching, during a time of competency-based teaching emphasis. Sample plans and objectives are provided for secondary teaching.

Mercer, Cecil D., Ann R. Mercer, and Deborah A. Bott. *Self-Correcting Learning Materials for the Classroom.* Columbus, Ohio: Charles E. Merrill Publishing Co., 1984. Feedback to pupils is essential to insure learning. This book recognizes the difficulty teachers have in providing immediate correct feedback to individual pupils and illustrates methods for developing self-correcting learning materials that provide much-needed individual feedback. Most school content areas are represented.

Stephens, Thomas M., A. Carol Hartman, and Virginia H. Weas. *Teaching Children Basic Skills.* Columbus, Ohio: Charles E. Merrill Publishing Co., 1983. Focused on elementary and the special education of young children, this book uses specific academic and social skill content with behavioral applications. Planning and teaching techniques cover assessments of skills, concepts, and learner variables. The authors provide a convincing case for applying these approaches to children in regular and special class settings.

CHAPTER REFERENCES

1. Leonard H. Clark and Irving S. Starr, *Secondary and Middle School Teaching Methods* (New York: Macmillan, 1981), p. 119.
2. Christopher M. Clark and Robert J. Yinger, *Three Studies of Teacher Planning,* Research Series No. 55 (East Lansing: Michigan State University Press, 1979).
3. Gail McCutcheon, "How Do Elementary Teachers Plan? The Nature of Planning and Influences on It," *Elementary School Journal* 81 (1980): 4–23.

4. R. S. Carnahan, *The Effects of Teacher Planning on Classroom Processes,* Technical Report No. 51 (Madison: Wisconsin R&D Center for Individualized Schooling, 1980).

5. P. L. Peterson, R. W. Marx, and C. M. Clark, "Teacher Planning, Teacher Behavior, and Student Achievement," *American Educational Research Journal* 15 (1978): 417–432.

6. See for example the February 1987 issue of *Phi Delta Kappan* and the April and May 1986 issues of *Educational Leadership.* Additionally refer to William W. Wilen, *Questioning Skills for Teachers* (Washington, D.C.: National Education Association, 1986).

7. Clark and Yinger, *Three Studies of Teacher Planning.*

8. Robert J. Yinger, *A Study of Teacher Planning: Description and Theory Development Using Ethnographic and Information Processing Methods* (Ph.D. dissertation, Michigan State University, East Lansing, 1977); see also R. Bromme, "How to Analyze Routines in Teachers' Thinking Processes During Lesson Planning" (Paper presented at the annual meeting of the American Educational Research Association, New York, March 1982); and B. P. M. Creemers and K. Westerhof, *Routinization of Instructive and Management Behavior of Teachers,* paper pub (Haren, the Netherlands: Educational Research Institute in the North, 1982).

9. Yinger, *A Study of Teacher Planning.*

10. Christopher M. Clark and Penelope L. Peterson, "Teachers' Thought Processes," in *Handbook of Research on Teaching,* ed. Merlin C. Wittrock (New York: Macmillan Publishing Co., 1986).

11. Daniel Tanner, *Secondary Education* (New York: Macmillan, 1972), p. 182.

12. David Jacobsen, Paul Eggen, Donald Kauchak, and Carole Dulaney, *Methods for Teaching: A Skills Approach* (Columbus, Ohio: Charles E. Merrill Publishing Co., 1985).

13. Benjamin S. Bloom, ed., *Taxonomy of Educational Objectives, Handbook 1: Cognitive Domain* (New York: Longman, 1956).

14. George H. Gallup, "The 15th Annual Gallup Poll of the Public's Attitudes Toward the Public Schools," *Phi Delta Kappan,* September 1983, pp. 33–47.

15. M. A. McLeod, *The Identification of Intended Learning Outcomes by Early Childhood Teachers: An Exploratory Study* (Ph.D. dissertation, University of Alberta, Edmonton, Canada, 1981).

16. Clark and Peterson, *op. cit.,* 1986, p. 267.

12

Teachers and Teaching

INTRODUCTION

■ How did your teachers teach? What did they do? Do you remember specific approaches and predictable routines? Do you remember variety, spontaneity, and activity? What teaching approaches did your teachers use that appealed most to you? Which of their approaches seemed to help you learn best? Now that we have you thinking about how teachers teach, what approaches do you believe are most effective? The purpose of this chapter is to help you: (1) explore some ways that teachers may teach, (2) examine some of the possible effects of teaching approaches, and (3) improve your ability to identify and use what are perhaps the universal tools of teaching—questions.

There can be considerable art, creativity, and intuition that influence the outcome of teaching. Let's take a moment to visit Mrs. Sexton's class. As you visit her class, try to list the different ways she teaches and the reasons for her choices.

A CLASSROOM SCENARIO*

■ In Lockport, Illinois, a ninth-grade earth science class is just beginning a new unit on local geology, glaciology in particular. As the students walk into the classroom, they notice that Mrs. Sexton has pictures of different kinds of buildings hanging around the room. She has books and magazines open to pages showing buildings. Once settled in their seats, Mrs. Sexton begins to show some slides of other buildings from around the world.

"Good afternoon, people. I'd like you to sit back and take a look at some slides I have for you today." After showing about five or six slides of different buildings, Mrs. Sexton asks the class, "Would you all agree that these buildings look very different from one another?" A chorus of "yesses" is emitted from the class.

* The authors thank Colleen Sexton for this classroom scenario.

"What would you say unites all of these buildings?" Her question is met with a long pause before she says, "In other words, what do these buildings, or any buildings for that matter, have in common?"

The class is very quiet for a few minutes. Mrs. Sexton continues to wait; she repeats the question slowly. Finally Kevin raises his hand and hesitantly ventures, "They're all tall?"

"Well, the ones in the slides were, but are all buildings?" asks Mrs. Sexton. "Think about houses as well. What do different looking houses have in common?" inquires Mrs. Sexton. "You need plans before you can build them," Sam adds.

"Now we're on the right track! Having a plan indicates some sort of organization or structure. All of these buildings are alike in that they're all structured in a particular fashion. If you had to build a building, where would you start?" "I'd build a foundation first," says Anne. "Very good. Do you all agree that you should start from the bottom up?" Again the "yesses" have it. "Well class, I'd like you to keep in mind this idea of structures and the building of a foundation first as we begin to look at our local geology."

"Before we begin this new topic, let's try to relax for a minute. I heard some of you earlier in the week express your fears of starting this new topic. Just take a deep breath, exhale, try that again. This time think of pleasant things like spring break, the start of baseball season, no more snow. Tense those muscles, release, tense again, release." Mrs. Sexton looks around the room scanning for visible signs of tension. Confident none exist, she starts the new topic.

"Now, what I'd like you to do for me is to close your eyes and imagine yourself traveling back through time, back to 1837." While Mrs. Sexton tells the class this she projects a slide on the screen to show a section of a contour map with Lockport pointed out. She scatters some rocks in front of her (collected from the local area) and dresses in old pants, shirt, suspenders, boots, and hat; she rests on a pickaxe, and pretends to smoke a pipe. As the students return their attention to class they are a bit confused, amused, but very attentive. What Mrs. Sexton has done is transform herself and the classroom back to 1837. Now she role-plays Shamos O'Toole, an Irish immigrant hired to help dig the Illinois and Michigan Canal. She begins her slide presentation talking as Shamos would about life in Lockport when it was first settled; Shamos tells the story of local geology through his experience of digging the canal through the many layers of rocks.

The last slide shows grave markers in a local cemetery; Shamos adds, "You know, human beings have taken so much from the Earth; it's a pity this is all we're putting back." Then he walks off. Some students begin to clap, some laugh, others start asking questions about the local areas or start to tell Mrs. Sexton about different types of rocks they have seen around their neighborhoods. As this goes on, Mrs. Sexton removes her props, gets the overhead projector set up, compliments the students on the importance of their questions, and asks them to save the rest of their questions for a few moments because the lab they are about to begin should help the class answer several questions for themselves.

Mrs. Sexton asks the students to get out some paper so they can jot down some of the questions being asked. She lists these questions on the overhead projector and then when the class runs out of questions she adds some of her own. Mrs. Sexton matches the questions asked with the students' learning objectives, outlines the objectives for the class, then divides the class into smaller working groups and starts them on their way deciding what lab materials they will need, reference books, and so on, and just where they will work on the school grounds during school hours and where around town (after school) they will collect their information. Mrs. Sexton reminds the class that since today is a Friday, they will all have ample time to run around town over the weekend to collect ideas and think about possible answers to their questions. Each group is to be ready to go outside on Monday. Class ends when Mrs. Sexton asks the groups to turn in their materials lists so she can have everything ready for Monday. The students are reminded to dress appropriately for outdoor study and to be ready to get dirty!

After 2 or 3 days of collecting data, Mrs. Sexton allows the student groups one class period to come to a consensus on how to interpret their data and to answer the questions asked during the first class period. The next class meeting is spent discussing the results with the entire class, getting back to the initial idea of structure and foundation. Summary questions such as, "How important is the idea of structure in our area?" or "What effects have glaciers had on this idea of structure?" are finally asked.

With about 10 minutes of class left, Mrs. Sexton leaves the students with an ethical question that demands that the students think critically and put their creativity to work. "Please think back to last Friday when Shamos O'Toole was visiting with us," Mrs. Sexton asks. "I'd like each of you to reflect on Shamos's last statement. Remember you were looking at a slide of a cemetery and Shamos stated 'human beings have taken so much from the Earth; it's a pity this is all we're putting back.' Try to place yourself in the position of the Earth. Make it more personal, think about sites you've seen around town this past week as we came to know our local geology. Imagine yourself being one of these sites. Think of how you feel as humans continue to alter your appearance, expose you to the forces of weathering and erosion, and change your basic structure. Keep in mind that mankind needs things from you to build roads, houses, and so on. How many of these changes to you are necessary? What kinds of problems do you think are caused for the future generations? How do you think you can help mankind become responsible for its actions?" Mrs. Sexton leaves the students with this assignment, confident that the next time they meet the students will come back eager to share their ideas.

HOW DO TEACHERS TEACH?

■ Let's look to Mrs. Sexton as a possible answer to this question. As a teacher, Mrs. Sexton is both an artist and a scientist (we don't refer to her as a scientist just because she happens to teach science!). She knows a lot about teaching—what works and what doesn't—and what she knows is based on the systematic work and reports of researchers as well as her own classroom experimentation. Mrs. Sexton has built up a storehouse of knowledge over the years and she values keeping current in her profession as well as her subject matter. What makes Mrs. Sexton special is her tendency to use her creative talents in unique ways. She is thoughtful; she takes the hard core findings of others, extracts portions, and mixes a special blend of instruction for her classes. This blending combines the best from what she knows about teaching and learning and allows her to use her own personality in ways that helps her bring her teaching to life. As a teacher she is both an artist and scientist out of necessity.

Mrs. Sexton realizes that the classroom climate is vital to learning and she spends considerable time trying to develop just the right teaching approaches for her pupils. This brings us back to the questions we asked you to think about before we visited Mrs. Sexton's classroom. How did Mrs. Sexton teach? What methods were you able to identify? And, why do you believe Mrs. Sexton decided to teach as she did?

Do you have anything on your list aside from some lecture, questioning, recitation, group work, and lab work? We realize you couldn't see all that happened so we asked Mrs. Sexton the same questions. She mentioned that she used all of these methods:

1. Advance organizers to introduce and focus her students' attention on the new topic
2. Desensitization techniques to help students overcome anxieties that might interfere with their ability to learn about the new topic

3. Memorization techniques to help students learn materials that must be recalled for later use
4. Inquiry to stimulate active learning through critical thinking and problem solving
5. Discussion so students can benefit from alternative viewpoints
6. Synectics—the creative use of analogies—to help stimulate creative thinking.

Mrs. Sexton believes that her pupils are basically inquisitive, and eager to learn new information and receive her praise. Her decisions about how she should teach are influenced by how she sees her pupils and how she sees her responsibilities as a teacher.

Mrs. Sexton sees her teacher responsibilities as including: (1) helping students' personal growth, (2) preparing students to be good citizens, (3) helping students master academic subjects, and (4) helping students learn to discipline their own thinking through organized inquiry. She realizes that several of these responsibilities fall outside of traditional teaching practices and she believes that a successful teacher must take care to develop and maintain a positive climate for learning; she believes that teachers must use a wide repertoire of teaching methods.

Mrs. Sexton believes that it is possible to take the individual methods of teaching, use aspects of several and combine them into unique, effective teaching approaches that can relate to each of the responsibilities she sees for herself. She agrees with the importance of having a solid foundation of subject knowledge in her teaching fields; she understands the important concepts of human growth and development, particularly for her teaching assignment; she is familiar with several principles of learning; she understands the purposes and importance of lesson planning and curriculum development; and she understands and uses several diagnostic procedures and classroom evaluation techniques for making teaching decisions and tracking the progress of her pupils.[1]

Mrs. Sexton is a competent consumer of current research in education who believes that *how* she teaches is just as important as *what* she teaches. She is able to extract what is important and essential to her mission from scientific research and published reports on effective teaching. Mrs. Sexton keeps herself informed. She knows the valued goals of education and is able to organize instruction for her students with grace. Mrs. Sexton is an artist in her own way. She is like the artist who mixes the colors on her palette to produce a precise effect in her painted portrait; she is like the gifted conductor who organizes the different musicians in her orchestra who play different instruments at different times. Mrs. Sexton is regarded by her col-

Research shows that students benefit from manipulating concrete learning materials.

leagues as a superior teacher, but she was not "born" a superior teacher. Her training and experience help make essential contributions to her superior teaching abilities. She became what she is; she became and remains a superior teacher with considerable effort and by using her professional judgment.

☐ What Types of Teaching Approaches Do Teachers Use?

Books are written on teaching approaches and we just don't have enough space to detail them here. But in this section we want you to realize that how teachers choose to teach offers important implications for the effects of their teaching.

In his book, *The Teaching and Learning Process,* Terry Blue describes two broad classifications of teaching approaches: teacher-centered and student-centered.[2]

Teacher-Centered Approaches
Teacher-centered approaches place the teacher at the center of classroom activity. Teacher-centered approaches are also known by other names. One common name is direct instruction. Direct instruction

Teacher-centered teaching: The teacher is the main actor with students playing a less active role.

relies primarily on the teacher to direct the students' thinking and participation and relies heavily on a structured content emphasis. Some research also refers to this approach as *explicit teaching*. Several examples include review, drill and practice, brief lectures, and student recitations.

TEACHING EXPLICITLY   Explicit teaching is a particular approach of teaching that consists of presenting material in small, systematic steps with calculated pauses to check for student understanding. This approach is particularly useful for teaching a specialized body of knowledge in which specific facts or well-defined skills exist. For example, teaching science or social studies facts, map skills, grammar rules and concepts, foreign language vocabulary, math computations, reading decoding, and distinguishing fact from opinion are some appropriate examples where explicit teaching approaches may be most useful.

An explicit teaching approach consists of teaching in small steps with an emphasis on student practice after each step. The teacher's role is to present material, guide students through initial practice sessions, and provide all students with frequent and high levels of practice. Barak Rosenshine reports the specific steps of explicit teaching. He writes that when effective teachers teach information, concepts, and skills explicitly, they should:

1. Begin a lesson with a short statement of goals
2. Begin a lesson with a short review of previous, prerequisite learning
3. Present new material in small steps, with student practice after each step
4. Give clear and detailed instructions and explanations
5. Provide active practice for all students
6. Ask many questions, check for student understanding, and obtain responses from all students
7. Guide students during initial practice
8. Provide systematic feedback and corrections
9. Provide explicit instruction and practice for seatwork exercises and, where necessary, monitor students during seatwork
10. Continue practice until students are independent and confident.[3]

Be aware that the procedures of explicit teaching do not apply equally to all learners all the time. For example, younger, slower, or less capable students benefit from the small steps of explicit teaching and most learners seem to benefit when they encounter new material, difficult material, or hierarchical tasks. Brief teacher presentations followed by student practice sessions are suggested in these instances. Larger steps are recommended when the learners are older, more capable, brighter, or when in the middle of a teaching unit. Under these circumstances, teachers usually have to spend less time with guided practice or in checking student progress and understanding.

Results on using the techniques of explicit teaching confirm that when teachers teach more systematically student achievement improves, often accompanied by gains in students' attitudes toward learning and in improvements in their self-esteem.[4] Even so,

> these findings are less relevant for teaching in areas that are less well-structured, that is, where the skills do not follow explicit steps or the concepts are fuzzier and entangled.[5]

Also, explicit approaches are not particularly useful when less structured material is to be learned, ideas developed, or when skills do not follow explicit or sequential steps.[6]

Student-Centered Approaches
Student-centered teaching approaches may be more suitable when information cannot be effectively transmitted by teacher-centered

FOCUS 12.1   What Are the Differences Between Student-Centered and Teacher-Centered Methods of Teaching?

Student-Centered Methods	Teacher-Centered Methods
1. Much student participation	1. Much teacher participation
2. Student-to-student interaction	2. Interaction is teacher-to-student
3. Teacher acceptance and use of student ideas	3. Teacher may criticize, correct, or reject student ideas
4. Student group decides how to proceed with learning task	4. Teacher makes decisions and decides learning activities
5. Discussion of personal experiences is encouraged	5. Discussion is focused on course content
6. Tests and grades are not the major product of learning	6. Tests and grades are traditionally used as the major products of learning
7. Students share a role and responsibility in evaluation	7. Teacher is solely responsible for evaluation
8. Teacher acknowledges and interprets student feelings and ideas when necessary to maintain class progress	8. Student feelings are not acknowledged
9. Teacher also emphasizes attitude changes	9. Emphasis is on intellectual changes
10. Students are involved in setting class goals	10. Goals are determined by the teacher
11. Attempts are made to establish class cohesiveness	11. No attempts to establish class cohesiveness

Based on Terry Blue's comparison in *The Teaching and Learning Process* (Washington, D.C.: National Education Association, 1981), p. 54.

approaches and when goals include creative as well as critical thinking skills to be developed. Instruction in student-centered classrooms is usually less explicit. Concerning student-centered teaching approaches, Blue writes that

> the purpose of student-centered approaches is to break away from the traditional teacher-dominated classroom and to encourage greater student responsibility and participation.[7]

A teacher who uses student-centered approaches does not turn over control to the pupils and let them do what they wish, although student-centered approaches are less direct or explicit. The teacher retains authority and delegates quite a bit of responsibility to the students. The usual role of authoritarian is surrendered; instead the teacher is authoritative, choosing to delegate a portion of the authority to students instead of centering the power in himself or herself.

When compared with teacher-centered forms of teaching, student-centered teaching fares well. Student-centered approaches have been found to be superior in developing pupil abilities in applying concepts and in developing positive attitudes, fostering motivation, developing personal growth, and in encouraging appropriate group social skills. These student-centered classrooms also show evidence of more cognitive growth at higher levels, yet they are suspected of being inferior in helping students achieve at tasks that require lower levels of thinking.[8]

Student-centered approaches may also be called indirect methods of teaching partly because more responsibility for learning is placed on students, and teachers function in less direct roles. Some examples may include exploration, inquiry and discovery learning, and some forms of discussion. Some examples of less explicit lessons include analyzing trends in history, literature, documents, or practical problems, the discussion and speculation of solutions for social issues, teaching composition, and writing term papers. These learning requirements may be better accomplished with *less explicit* methods of teaching.

TEACHING LESS EXPLICITLY   Less explicit methods of teaching tend to contrast with explicit teaching by having teachers encourage the building of each "student's personal capacity for independent learning and [in] attempts to develop self-concept as well as concepts about academic subjects."[9] Teachers who teach in less explicit ways tend to show pupils how the material to be learned relates to their own lives and purposes. Less explicit methods of teaching may be patterned after the non-direct teaching model developed by Carl Rogers,[10] the indirect methods of teaching described by Ned Flanders,[11] or any of the many discovery and problem-solving models of teaching and learning described by Bruce Joyce and Marshal Weil.[12]

What all these less explicit methods of teaching have in common is a requirement for "teachers to shift from their traditional roles as lecture-demonstrators to a role that demands new skills in planning and facilitating student work" and in the development of self-reliance as well as potent intellectual skills.[13] In short, the emphasis is on helping students *learn how to learn*. The central mission of less

Student-centered teaching: Students play a central role in their own learning.

explicit teaching methods usually consists of creating and arranging a classroom atmosphere in which students can interact with the teacher and other students.

The role of the teacher, in other words exactly what the teacher does while teaching less explicitly, is critical. The very least that is required is that teachers must be well versed in the subjects they are teaching; each teacher must examine the structure of the discipline, identify the important concepts, and select or develop experiences that are meaningful to the students and that will offer students opportunities to explore and discover what the teacher wants them to learn.[14]

Selecting an Approach

Explicit and less explicit approaches to teaching have merit and it would be shortsighted to adopt either approach totally and ignore the other one completely. Like so many methods of teaching, each can have a specialized use and, as a method, help a teacher produce superior classroom results. Changes in student behavior, particularly increases in student mental growth, are accepted by the public as evidence that students are learning. A teacher's knowledge of the students' frames of reference and understanding of the material to be learned is basic to teaching. One task of teaching is to bring the material within each student's frame of reference. In this sense, instruction must be adapted to each learner. How to do this can be approached systematically, but success almost invariably requires the creative and artistic talents of each teacher. Probably the most potent tool within the teacher's repertoire for accomplishing this awesome task is the question. Both explicit and less explicit methods of teaching rely on questioning. We turn our attention to this most useful tool in the next section and then provide examples of questions that may be used with a variety of general teaching methods at the end of the chapter.

USING QUESTIONS TO TEACH

☐ Why Are Questions Important?

What Is a Question?
William Wilen gives us a useful definition in his book, *Questioning Skills, for Teachers*. According to Wilen, a question consists of any sentence that has an interrogative purpose.[15] We use questions to find out what someone else knows, like a teacher who asks a student a question to find out what has been learned, or like a student who feels free to ask the teacher a question to find out what needs to be learned. But is that the only way teachers use questions?

How Can Questions Be Used in Teaching?
Norris Sanders helps us answer this question. In his book, *Classroom Questions: What Kinds?*, Sanders shows us that questions have uses far beyond the simple back-and-forth question and answer technique described above.[16] Obviously questions can help teachers instruct, and questions can provide a teacher with an immediate evaluation of what students seem to remember, know, understand, or what is unclear or confusing. What other ways do you think teachers can use questions?

Teachers can use rhetorical questions—questions to which *no answer is expected* from the class. Rhetorical questions function as verbal cues about the importance of information or instructions soon to follow in a lesson. Teachers can organize entire lessons around questions by identifying the important concepts, forming deliberate questions, and using these questions to form the framework of a lesson. Therefore, lesson planning is deliberate because the instruction tries to provide answers for specific questions.

Questions also come in different types and can be used to promote the forms of thinking appropriate for students in any class. While teaching, questions can help students form guideposts for determining the development of specific skills, or questions may function as mental anchors for stabilizing thinking as information and ideas are linked to form new concepts.

Specific types of questions can assure the development of particular forms of thinking that otherwise might be neglected. Specific, narrow questions can cause students to examine and analyze a situation or even construct their own information. Broad, open-ended questions can motivate creative thinking, original solutions to problems, or help stimulate unique student projects. Questions that ask for choices to be made and for the choices to be justified or explained can encourage evaluative thinking. Questions specifically designed and sequenced can be useful to teachers who attempt to accomplish long-range plans with a conscious consideration and emphasis on developing student thinking. Consider Meredith Gall's observation:

> Teachers' questions that require students to think independently and those that require recall of information are both useful but serve different purposes. The challenge for teachers is to use each type to its best advantage.[17]

What Types of Questions?
What do the following questions have in common and how are they different?

1. Who led the charge up San Juan Hill?
2. Is this painting by Picasso?
3. Would someone please repeat what was just said?
4. Jimmy! What are you doing?
5. How can alcohol be used in this experiment?
6. What do you think would happen if the lake water rose by 10 meters?
7. Should Junction City build a dam? Why?

Certainly two things these questions have in common is that they are all questions and each requests a response from students. But how are they different? Let's compare them. The first question requires the student to remember some information and the second question requires a choice, in this case a selection of yes or no. The third question could be answered with a yes or no, just like the second, but actually implies a direction to no particular student. Question 4 holds Jimmy accountable for his behavior and suggests that he should change it. The fifth asks a narrow question about how something can be used. The sixth question is quite broad in that it asks for an individual's own thoughts on the subject of the question. And, while the last question is similar to the second in that it asks for a choice, it is different because a reason for the choice is requested. Perhaps you detected some other differences as well.

The question is probably the most powerful tool a teacher has. This power becomes evident when you consider that questions come in different types, require different kinds of responses, and have potential for stimulating different levels of student thinking. This is why it is important to know how to identify different types of questions and decide when they should be used.

Questions can be classified in several ways. The four-category classification system given below appeals to us because of its simplicity and its similarity to some aspects of Bloom's taxonomy mentioned in the previous chapter. This is Aschner and Gallagher's classification system for examining questions in teacher and student classroom interactions. If teachers have some knowledge of question types and have skills in classifying questions, they can use these to examine the types and amounts of student thinking stimulated by their teaching. In turn, they are in a position to judge if their goals are met and if their teaching methods have the desired impact. A brief description of Aschner and Gallagher's classification system follows.[18] See Figure 12.1 for examples of mental processes required, key concepts represented by the question types, and samples of questions in each of the four categories, which are described as follows:

1. *Cognitive Memory Questions*—require students to recall facts, formulas, procedures, and other information; this is similar to Bloom's Knowledge and Comprehension levels.
2. *Convergent Thinking Questions*—require students to apply information and analyze factors; doing this requires that cognitive memory types of information have been previously developed.
3. *Divergent Thinking Questions*—students are given little structure or prior information and are expected to independently develop their own information by original thinking and combining ideas into a new plan, solution, or product; it requires synthesis thinking.
4. *Evaluative Thinking Questions*—require students to judge, value, choose, criticize, defend, or justify.

FIGURE 12.1   Selecting the right questions.

Question Category	Intended Mental Activity	Key Concepts	Sample Question Phrases
Evaluative Thinking	Choose Criticize Value Judge Defend Justify	Choices Solutions Judgments Appraisals Evaluation Assessments Defend Justify	Why do you favor . . . ? What is your feeling about . . . ? What is your reason for . . . ?
Divergent Thinking	Develop own information Originate ideas Integrate ideas or information Plan Construct or reconstruct	Infer Reconstruct Predict Hypothesize Problem-solve Design Invent	What do you think . . . ? What could you do if . . . ? How can you design . . . ? What do you think will happen if . . . ?
Convergent Thinking	Memorization Application Analysis Use of logic Deductive and inductive reasoning	Solution application Use of logic State relationships Problem-solve Explanations Compare and contrast Express in another mode	If "A", then what will happen to "B" . . . ? Which are facts, opinions, and inferences? What is the author's purpose? What is the relationship of "x" to "y"?
Cognitive Memory	Recognition Rote memorization Selective recall of facts, formulas, procedures and information	Memory Yes-no responses Information Repetition Description Explanation Comparison Name, identify illustration	What is the definition of . . . ? What are the three steps in . . . ? Who discovered . . . ? In your own words, what is the meaning of . . . ?

INTENDED MENTAL ACTIVITY   KEY CONCEPTS

☐ **What Does the Research Say
About Teacher Questioning?**

So far we have described the different types of questions and the ways questions can be used to accomplish a variety of teaching tasks. Questions appear to be universally useful and to have potential for stimulating different kinds of learning—to assist development of different types of thinking. Of the different types of questions teachers can ask, what types are asked most often and why?, and what effects can a teacher's use of questions have on students?

What Types of Questions Do Teachers Use?
Since there are many different types of questions, you may believe teachers use a variety of questions while teaching. Is this assumption true? Apparently not.

Several status studies have been done to find out how many and what types of questions teachers seem to use. As early as 1912,

DENNIS THE MENACE

"TEACHER DOESN'T KNOW MUCH. SHE ASKS ME A LOT OF QUESTIONS. I GUESS THAT'S WHY SHE'S ONLY TEACHIN' KIDDIGARTEN."

Dennis the Menace® used by permission of Hank Ketcham and © by News America Syndicate.

Romiett Stevens estimated that 80% of school time was devoted to teachers' asking and students' answering questions, that is, lecture-recitation.[19] Fifty years later, Ambrose Clegg found that a sample of high school teachers used an average of 395 questions daily.[20] In 1968, Amelia Melnik found that some teachers asked as many as 150 questions per hour,[21] and in 1970, Meredith Gall reported several studies in which elementary teachers used questions anywhere from 64 to 180 times in one class period; the average found was 348 questions per day.[22] In fact, out of all the questions asked in the classroom, teachers seem to ask about 93% of them and leave little opportunity for students to ask their own.[23]

The amount of time teachers devote to questioning should encourage a variety of questions to be asked. But is this what happens? No. For example, Floyd discovered that teachers asked 42% of their questions on the memory level and only 6% required a high level of thinking.[24] H. C. Haynes found that 77% of teachers' questions required facts as answers and 17% were satisfied by thoughtful responses.[25] Corey found that 71% of the questions observed in his study were factual types, whereas 29% required a higher level of thought.[26] Meredith Gall analyzed eight studies that occurred between 1912 and 1967 and concluded that the teacher questioning practices described above showed little change during more than 50 years.[27] The conclusion is that teachers, by and large, rely mostly on questions that require lower levels of thought and this pattern has changed little from grade levels and between subject areas.[28]

How Do Teachers Use Questions?

How teachers regularly use questions gives us a look at how they view students, instruction, and curriculum. In many ways,

> the kinds of questions teachers ask and the techniques they employ to interact with students imply their philosophy of instruction. Most decisions teachers make about questioning in the classroom are intuitive and are therefore based primarily on experience. But effective teaching reflects effective decision making; . . . teachers need to give careful consideration to the questions asked and the interaction patterns to be developed in order to facilitate student achievement of learning outcomes.[29]

Teachers can use questions to determine how well students understand what is taught and to encourage critical and creative thinking. But questions have more uses than these. Some teachers use questions:

1. To stimulate student participation in class
2. To review previously studied material
3. To begin a discussion on a topic, issue, or problem
4. To involve students in thinking creatively
5. To determine student abilities and difficulties, in other words, for diagnostic purposes
6. To evaluate student readiness for a learning task
7. To determine how much and how well objectives have been accomplished
8. To motivate or arouse interest
9. To control student misbehavior
10. To reinforce and support student participation.

How widely do you suppose these options for questions are used? Pate and Bremer questioned nearly 200 elementary teachers to find out what they believe were the important functions of questions. According to the teachers, the three most important functions included: (1) 86% used questions to check on pupil learning; (2) 54% used questions for diagnosis; and (3) 10% used questions to require students to apply facts in generalizing and making inferences. Pate and Bremer concluded that teachers do not consider a major purpose of questioning to be the stimulation of higher levels of thinking and that teachers tend to use questions for limited purposes.[30]

Why, then, do teachers use so many low-level questions? There can be justification for this practice. First, students need facts to help them with higher levels of questions. Second, there is much emphasis on learning information and considerable emphasis placed on teaching techniques for doing so. Many teachers have had little exposure to alternatives for learning facts and teaching them. Another reason for using so many low-level questions could be that teachers have no way to keep track of the types of questions they do use. Simple and reliable question classification systems are more recent developments that can help teachers determine the effects their questions have on students' learning.

What Influences Do Questions Have on Students?
Students' attitudes toward their learning, students' thinking, and students' achievements are three important areas in which researchers have investigated the influences of questions.

STUDENT ATTITUDES   This is an aspect of teaching and questioning receiving more recent attention. Researchers and teachers realize that student attitudes influence thinking, achievement, and behavior. Students who display positive attitudes or preferences tend to behave favorably toward a school subject, teaching method, or questioning technique. Students who display negative attitudes or preferences tend to resist and perform poorly because of their negative perceptions toward a subject, teacher, method, or type of question. William Wilen gives us a view of how a teacher's use of questions influences student attitudes:

> Several studies have investigated the influence of the discussion method on student attitudes, and student preferences for the cognitive levels of teacher questions. Fisher found that reading literature changed fifth graders' attitudes toward the topic (Indians), and involving students in a discussion after reading significantly increased attitude change more than reading alone. Gall and others also found a relationship between questions and the positive attitudes of sixth graders. Using six attitude measures, these researchers found written and discussion questions equally effective in stimulating positive attitudes toward the topic (ecology) and toward discussion as an instructional method. They also found that higher cognitive questions did not affect student attitudes.[31]

Wilen investigated student preferences for different levels of teachers' verbal questions and test score gains. He concluded that "students must develop positive attitudes toward higher-level questioning if instructional approaches such as inquiry are to be effective."[32]

STUDENT THINKING   Logic suggests a positive relationship between the level of teacher questions and the level of student thinking. For example, if you want students to think critically, ask them questions that require them to think critically. Does this logic hold true?

Hilda Taba studied the effects of a specially designed elementary curriculum on student thinking skills. The curriculum relied heavily on teaching strategies that emphasized different types of questioning. Taba found that teaching strategies that relied extensively on questioning influenced the students' thinking most. She postulated that the questions that teachers asked set the limits and influenced the progression of the class; teachers expected students to think at a certain level and they did![33] Similarly Gallagher and Aschner investigated the responses of gifted secondary school students to the various levels of questions used. They found that a mere 5% increase in teachers' asking divergent questions encouraged as much as a 40% increase in divergent responses from students. These researchers concluded that the teacher controls the thought levels of the students.[34] Other researchers have also found that question levels significantly affect student response levels.[35] Hunkins researched the effects of analysis and evaluation questions in elementary social studies class-

Proper use of questions can improve students' attitudes, thinking, and achievement.

rooms and found that high levels of questions helped students to evaluate better and improved their understanding of lower level facts.[36]

Not all studies support the belief that higher levels of teacher questions will generate higher levels of student thinking. Some studies show that higher levels of questions are not answered by high-thought-level responses.[37] What should we make of these exceptions? Winne and Marx provide a method for interpreting the inconsistency in the research findings. They suggest that students' perceptions of the type of thinking required by teacher questions may be different than the teacher intends. The result can be that students provide a response at a level lower than required by the teacher's question.[38] Of prime importance here may be how long a teacher waits after asking a question.

How long a teacher waits, called *wait time,* is critical for complex questions that require considerable thought. In cases where students did not immediately respond, Mary Budd Rowe found that teachers waited about 1 second after asking a question before redirecting the question to another student, rephrasing the question, or answering the question themselves. She noted that when teachers were trained to increase this wait time to just 3 to 5 seconds several benefits occurred: (1) student responses increased, (2) appropriate, unsolicited responses increased, (3) failure to respond decreased, (4) student confidence increased, (5) speculative and divergent thinking increased, (6) teacher-centered teaching decreased, (7) students provided more evidence for inference statements, (8) student questions increased, (9) slower students contributed more, and (10) more variety in student responses increased. Rowe speculates that several of these benefits are caused by greater teacher flexibility, differences in the number and types of questions teachers use, and that teachers tend to wait longer for responses even from capable students.[39]

Three distinct steps are urged for teachers who wish to extend wait time. The first step consists of teacher preparation; establish a routine for using wait time by silently counting up to 5 seconds after asking questions. Step 2 must be made along with step 1; prepare the students for an extended wait time by telling them what you are doing. The third step consists of how to get started for optimum results; begin slowly and plan to use wait time during a specific part of a lesson, especially when questions using higher levels of thinking are planned.[40]

STUDENT ACHIEVEMENT The American public seems most concerned about one primary factor—are students learning? Despite the importance of other factors associated with schooling, the pulic is most concerned that students demonstrate increases in achievement. Do different types of questions influence achievement? If so, to what extent? And what types of questions seem best to use under particular conditions? Some tentative conclusions are available to answer these questions and come from recent research efforts that reveal that the studies on questioning are incomplete, but not totally inconclusive.

Earlier studies sought to answer the question of whether teacher oral questions produced achievement superior to teacher written questions. The studies here are limited but indicate that a teacher's oral questions lead to student achievement superior to that produced by written questions in class textbooks or individual seatwork materials.[41]

The frequency of teachers' questions has also been investigated for its influence on student achievement. Barak Rosenshine found a positive and significant relationship between a high frequency of teacher interaction through questions and student achievement. His conclusions support the frequent use of factual single-answer questions during explicit teaching to produce superior achievement in learning basic skills. Rosenshine did not find that frequent higher level questions produced achievement gains superior to lower levels of questions for basic skills or learning factual information.[42] Rosenshine especially found that "open-ended questions, questions about personal experience, and questions about opinions were negatively correlated with achievement" especially in primary grades for low socioeconomic status students in learning mathematics and reading.[43]

In general, Rosenshine's conclusions seem to hold up for elementary, middle/junior high, and high school students' achievement. It appears that when facts or well-defined bodies of information are to be learned, frequent use of lower-cognitive-level questions with factual single answers is superior to more general, open-ended questions even when the questions are posed at a higher cognitive level. Thomas Good and Jere Brophy suggest three reasons for this outcome: (1) in general, teachers who use a high frequency of low level questions tend to teach directly and are well planned, well organized, and have fewer classroom discipline problems; (2) when these teachers spend more class time on instructional tasks they heavily involve their students in achievement-oriented activities, and give students little time to get involved in nonacademic tasks; and (3) these teachers probably spend more time being explicit and interact with students by involving them in a wide variety of academically oriented oral-participation activities.[44]

Is the direct approach and a complementary use of lower cognitive questions the best approach to teaching? No. Earlier in this chapter we investigated the use of explicit and less explicit methods of teaching. We discovered that all that is important for students to learn cannot be learned best by any single method. The same can be concluded about using low or high levels of questions to cause superior gains in achievement. This conclusion is supported by the research on questioning.

Several studies have found that higher levels of questions, when asked by teachers during instruction, lead to greater gains in achievement than lower levels of questions. These studies seem to be mostly conducted at the middle and high school grades, but some report positive effects on elementary pupils as well.[45] Many of these studies investigated the effects of question levels on achievement during inquiry lessons. As a method of teaching, inquiry is less explicit than a teacher-centered approach like teacher lecture and student recitation. Higher levels of questions appropriate for inquiry methods were found to produce significant gains in student achievement. Students receiving instruction with a greater proportion of higher-inquiry questions achieved greater on achievement tests consisting of high- and low-inquiry questions than students who received instruction with a greater proportion of low-inquiry questions.[46] When students are expected to think critically and respond to critical-thinking questions, higher levels of questions oriented to this level will contribute to achievement gains that are greater than critical achievement tasks whose instruction is provided by questions that require students to recall information.[47]

FOCUS 12.2 Questioning

By William J. Bennett

RESEARCH FINDING: Student achievement rises when teachers ask questions that require students to apply, analyze, synthesize, and evaluate information in addition to simply recalling facts.

COMMENT: Even before Socrates, questioning was one of teaching's most common and most effective techniques. Some teachers ask hundreds of questions, especially when teaching science, geography, history, or literature.

But questions take different forms and place different demands on students. Some questions require only factual recall and do not provoke analysis. For example, of more than 61,000 questions found in the teacher guides, student workbooks, and tests for 9 history textbooks, more than 95 percent were devoted to factual recall. This is not to say that questions meant to elicit facts are unimportant. Students need basic information to engage in higher level thinking processes and discussions. Such questions also promote class participation and provide a high success rate in answering questions correctly.

The difference between factual and thought-provoking questions is the difference between asking: "When did Lincoln deliver the Gettysburg Address?" and asking "Why was Lincoln's Gettysburg Address an important speech?" Each kind of question has its place, but the second one intends that the student analyze the speech in terms of the issues of the Civil War.

Although both kinds of questions are important, students achieve more when teachers ask thought-provoking questions and insist on thoughtful answers. Students' answers may also improve if teachers wait longer for a response, giving students more time to think.

From William J. Bennett, Secretary of Education, *What Works* (Washington, D.C.: U.S. Department of Education, 1986), p. 38.

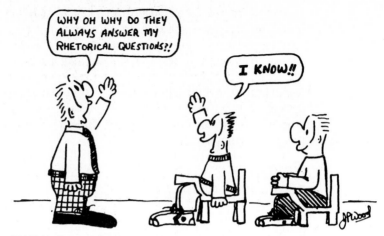

Phi Delta Kappan, October 1984.

FOR REFLECTION 12.1   Questions on Questions

Considerable research has been done on teachers' uses of questions and effects on students. Conduct some of your own research on questioning by observing several teachers ask different type of questions or by looking into published material to help you answer the following questions:

1. On whom do you think the teacher calls more frequently, the low or high achiever? Why?
2. To whose response is the teacher more likely to react—the low or high achiever? What kind of response does the teacher usually provide?
3. To whom is the teacher more likely to afford more time to answer a question—the low or high achiever? Why?
4. In a traditional classroom consisting of rows of desks, is questioning related to where a student sits? Explain your answer.
5. What effect(s), if any, do you think students' sexes and ethnicities have on a teacher's questioning process? Give a reason for your answer.

☐ Summary on Questions

When used properly, questions can have a tremendous effect on the classroom environment, the level of student thinking, and the extent of student achievement. More than 60 years of research on classroom questions tend to suggest that questioning is a universal teaching strategy in itself and is probably the most important tool that teachers have. We know that systematic uses of questions can improve student learning and we know that teachers can classify their questions, determine the level at which their classes can work, and plan accordingly to improve instruction and learning. Systematic questioning can be used to diagnose the entry level of individuals and whole classes of students in virtually any subject area during any grade of schooling. Many questioning options are open to teachers and no one type of question is superior or applicable to all teaching methods or classroom situations.

GENERAL METHODS OF TEACHING

■ We have discussed two key concepts in this chapter: (1) there are distinctly different teaching approaches available to teachers, and (2) teachers have different types of questions they use while teaching. In each case we concluded that teaching approaches and questioning can exert different effects on students and are chosen for their desired outcomes.

Teachers may combine approaches with other techniques, like questioning, to create unique methods of teaching similar to those used by Mrs. Sexton in the chapter scenario. As part of your introduction to teaching, we owe it to you to highlight some of the specific methods available to teachers. Teaching methods will be studied in depth in other teacher preparation courses so we only summarize them here to assist you in looking at teaching.

Table 12.1 provides a general description of several methods of teaching. Explore this table and try to categorize each method in terms of the responsibilities required of teachers and students, the intent of the methods, and the probable outcome of each. You may wish to discuss the uses of these methods with your instructor or classroom teacher to learn more about them. If your course provides an opportunity to observe in classrooms, you may wish to arrange some brief practice teaching opportunities so you can experiment with each as you begin to develop your own style of teaching. But remember, it takes teachers a long time to perfect their teaching styles and no one teaching method is best all of the time. Consider the classroom atmosphere you wish to establish and what you expect students to accomplish, then select the teaching approach and specific tools to help meet your expectations.

CHAPTER SUMMARY

■ This chapter focused on three aspects of teaching. First we explored two conceptual approaches to teaching. We discovered that the explicit

TABLE 12.1   Summary of Predominant Teaching Methods

Method	What It Is	How Used?	Main Types of Questions	Advantages	Disadvantages
Lecture and Student Recitation	Teacher explains, demonstrates, presents, asks questions, and students answer.	Teacher uses direct delivery to help students acquire information; questions to elicit responses from students. Student responses provide a basis for judging amount and level of learning.	Cog. Memory Convergent Evaluative Rhetorical	Time-efficient way to transmit information. Helps to clarify and build a frame of reference. Good for introducing, summarizing, and constructing concepts. Effective approach for fundamentals. Can provide eclectic and interesting coverage of material.	Relies on students' abilities to focus attention, think purposefully, identify important ideas, and take notes. Best students can retain only half of what they hear. Teacher has most responsibility; students have little responsibility. Majority of communication is one-way.
Deduction	A reasoning approach from whole to part or general to particular, or from the universal to the individual.	Teacher organizes lesson to present the abstract, clarify key terms, provide examples and provide students with practice and application.	Cog. Memory Convergent Evaluative	Time-efficient way to organize thinking. Information is conveyed efficiently. Several subordinate ideas linked together. Teacher provides abundant concrete examples to make abstract ideas clear. An explicit framework for learning. Emphasis on logic.	Teacher may dominate while students are mentally inactive. Possible overemphasis on low levels of thought and questions. Students may rely on teacher to think for them.

TEACHER-CENTERED

MORE EXPLICIT ←

LESS EXPLICIT →

Method	Description		Thinking	Advantages	Disadvantages
Discussion	A question or problem is considered as possibilities are sifted in order to reach a conclusion or to convince. Class setting may be formal or informal with the teacher having a dominant to nondominant role.	Multiple opinions shared; everyone examines and responds. Questions stimulate and focus thinking. Multiple points of view are encouraged. May be teacher-led, student-led, or leaderless.	Divergent Convergent Evaluative	Students exposed to wide range of thoughts. Wide student participation is encouraged. Can promote positive attitudes and reduce anxiety. Can improve student self-concepts. Addresses relevant problems or social issues. Can help students develop intellect and social skills.	Outcome is unpredictable. Can be an exchange of ignorance. Can lack organization, focus, and closure. Closed minds can prevent exchange of viewpoints.
Induction	A reasoning approach from part to whole or particulars to generals or from the individual to the universal.	Students use firsthand experiences to learn concepts. Lesson progresses from observations to generalizations. Teacher guides students in investigating, inferencing, and problem solving with variable class formats.	Evaluative Divergent Convergent Cog. Memory	Specific experiences used to form concepts. Emphasis on learning how to think; thinking evolves. Active student participation (mental, physical, emotional). Multiple learning opportunities. Students evaluate own thinking. Superior retention.	Control of class must be eased. Individual and direct involvement may be difficult with large classes. Takes time.
Inquiry	Teachers and students cooperatively search for solutions by gaining experiences, processing information, and constructing solutions.	Problems are solved systematically by (1) exploring to gather facts, (2) identifying problem and hypothesizing a solution, (3) testing hypotheses, and (4) revising or concluding with a solution.	Evaluative Divergent Convergent Cog. Memory	Apply learned information. Students learn how to learn and how to problem-solve. A concrete foundation for abstract learning. Gain new experiences. Make discoveries. Cause and effect reasoning. Emphasis on high levels of thinking. Responsibility for learning. Critical and creative thinking emphasized.	Not suited to all subjects. Students must be willing and able to be self-directed. Time-inefficient method. Teacher must be creative and well prepared. Variety of teaching materials needed. Flexible classroom management needed.

teaching methods of the teacher-centered approach are superior for directly teaching discrete information and building definite skills. But there are limitations to this approach. In instances in which learning experiences need to be more exploratory, a student-centered approach that is less explicit works best in developing higher levels of student thinking and in stimulating suitable class interaction.

The functions and effects of questions was the second aspect of teaching we investigated. Although research studies conflict in providing clear answers to certain questions about the uses and effects of questions, we feel confident in concluding that questions promise to be teaching tools of universal value. Particular types of questions can elicit specific levels of student responses: factual questions stimulate factual thinking, and higher levels of questions encourage various higher levels of student thinking.

Question types and usage patterns are essential to the success of some methods of teaching. We summarized five general methods of teaching that ranged from those that are more explicit and less student-centered to those methods that are less explicit and more student-centered. Each method has its own advantages and disadvantages as well as its proper occasions for use.

These aspects of teaching—type of approach, use of questions, and method of teaching—were presented to you as part of the belief that teaching is both a science and an art. Teaching can be scientific in the sense that considerable scientific research is used in developing and in selecting an approach, its questions and its methods. It is possible to apply an approach and use questions and teaching methods in a step-by-step fashion, knowing that there is considerable pedagogical support. But teaching consists of interactions between human beings, not machines. Human beings do not always respond the same way to the same stimuli. Humans have an accumulation of different experiences, thoughts, and needs. Creativity, sensitivity, sensibility, and diversity are some things that humans thrive on—some things that they need. Therefore, teachers' artistic talents are important for creating entire classroom atmospheres where selections from the scientific side of teaching can flourish and have maximum effects because they have creatively tailored them to their specific students and teaching situation. Our next chapter asks you to consider all that you have read, discussed, and experienced and to venture an answer to that most important question, "Can you teach?"

FOR DISCUSSION

1. What do you see as advantages and disadvantages to a teacher-centered approach? A student-centered approach?

2. If you could use any teaching approaches and methods you wanted to teach the subject of your choice, what would you teach and how would you teach it?

3. A *heterogeneous* group or class consists of students of different abilities and possibly different ages. A *homogeneous* group or class is made up of students who are approximately the same in ability and age. What approaches to teaching and what teaching methods do you believe are appropriate for these types of groups or classes? Why?

4. Why do you suppose teachers tend to wait such a short time after asking students questions?

5. Can a wait time of less than 2 seconds be justified? Explain.

6. What is your view on the importance of questioning? Why would you use questions?

IN THE SCHOOL/IN THE CLASSROOM

Two options are presented for applying the ideas in this chapter. The first option consists of your observing a classroom teacher and discussing the results of particular approaches or methods of teaching and the effects of different types of questions. The second option encourages you to teach a topic and then investigate the results of your efforts using similar questions to those presented for the first option.

Option 1

Arrange to observe a classroom teacher with the assistance of your course instructor. Interview the teacher before and after several lessons. First, ask the teacher about planning and teaching so you can estimate the teacher's expectations. Then, develop a list of interview questions so you can examine the reasons for the teacher's methods as well as the teacher's impressions of the lesson's outcome—did the students perform as expected? Consider the following questions to help you develop an analysis of your observations and interviews.

1. Did the teacher actually teach what was planned and use the intended method(s)? If not, why not?

2. In your opinion, were the lesson's objectives realistic? Did new objectives emerge during the teaching of the lesson? If new objectives emerged, how did the teacher handle them?

3. Were the students able to perform as expected?

4. What teaching approach was used? What teaching methods were used? Why were these methods selected?

5. Did the method(s) work as intended? If not, why not?

6. What types of feedback did the teacher use to make decisions about the lesson's outcome?

7. What types of questions did the teacher use? Did the students respond with answers on the appropriate level? If not, why not?

8. What did you observe about the teacher's wait time for questions?

9. In your opinion, was wait time adequate? How can you tell?

10. What type of follow-up did the teacher plan for the lesson? What effects were intended by the follow-up activities? Did the activities succeed as planned? If not, why not?

Option 2

Plan to teach a lesson as assigned by your instructor. The lesson can be taught in a regular classroom under the supervision of a teacher and arranged with your instructor, or you can arrange to teach a lesson to a group of your peers from your education class. Plan the lesson, identify the teaching approach and method you will use and the kinds of questions, and then analyze the outcome of your efforts. Arrange to audiotape or videotape your teaching so you can review it and answer the following questions.

1. Did you actually teach what you planned and did you use the methods you selected? If not, why not?

2. Were your objectives realistic? Did the need for new objectives become evident as the lesson progressed? If yes, what were they and how did you handle these new objectives?

3. Did your students perform as you intended?

4. What teaching approach and method(s) did you use? Why did you select these methods?

5. Did the teaching method(s) work as you intended? If not, why not?

6. What types of feedback did you use to decide about the outcome of your teaching?

7. What types of questions did you use while teaching?

8. How long was your wait time? What did you notice about your wait time as the lesson progressed?

9. Was your amount of wait time adequate for your questions? What information do you base your answer on?

10. Did you plan a follow-up activity for your lesson? If yes, what was it? What did you want it to accomplish? Did it succeed? If not, why didn't it succeed?

SUGGESTED READINGS

Carin, Arthur, and Robert Sund. *Creative Questioning and Sensitive Listening Techniques*. Columbus, Ohio: Charles E. Merrill Publishing Co., 1978. This book provides many examples of different types of questions and how they can be used in different types of teaching methods. Chapters deal with topics like developing better classroom communication, stimulating student creativity, constructing inquiry activities, writing questions for developing and clarifying student values, writing appropriate cognitive domain questions, and for analyzing and modifying your own questioning techniques.

Duck, Lloyd. *Teaching with Charisma*. Boston: Allyn & Bacon, 1981. Duck describes vivid examples of classroom teaching and putting your views on teaching to work. The role models presented in the chapters can help you to see how the strengths of any teaching method can be maximally used and how the weaknesses can be avoided or compensations found. This book is useful to teachers at any level of school.

Friedman, Paul G. *Listening Processes: Attention, Understanding, Evaluation*. Washington, D.C.: National Education Association, 1983. This booklet is one of several practical and highly useful publications in the What

Research Says to the Teacher series by NEA. Questioning is an important skill that is only successful insofar as teachers can listen for the cues provided by students. This brief, easy to read book will help you to learn the techniques of better listening and to think about how you can apply these techniques to any teaching method.

Hoover, Kenneth H. *The Professional Teacher's Handbook*. Boston: Allyn & Bacon, 1982. This book can be used as a guide for improving your teaching in middle and high schools. The examples cover a broad range of secondary school settings and include specific content area examples on planning, methods of teaching, and techniques for evaluating what students learn.

Jacobsen, David, Paul Eggen, Donald Kauchak, and Carol Dulaney. *Methods For Teaching: A Skills Approach*. Columbus, Ohio: Charles E. Merrill Publishing Co., 1985. Questioning skills and teaching strategies are two useful chapters. A systematic skills approach is used to present the ideas and help you apply the book's concepts to various teaching situations.

Kohl, Herbert. *Growing Minds: On Becoming A Teacher*. New York: Harper & Row, 1984. Kohl's book is based on his extensive experiences, is sensibly written, and promises to touch every reader who was ever taught or has taught. Part II—The Craft Of Teaching—is particularly useful to this chapter. Kohl's chapter titled "The Teacher as Trickster," gives us a keen view of his exemplary teaching.

Orlich, Donald C., and Ian C. Armitage. *Teaching Strategies*. Lexington, Mass.: D. C. Heath and Co., 1980. This book covers a wide range of teacher decisions about teaching. Its chapters on planning and methods are very detailed and peppered by examples drawn from all levels of school. This is an excellent book to keep as a reference for years as a teacher.

Wilen, William W. *Questioning Skills, for Teachers*. Washington, D.C.: National Education Association, 1986. We used Wilen's book extensively in preparing the chapter section on using questions. This book also comes from the What Research Says to the Teacher series published by the NEA and is a good starting point for learning more about using questions while teaching.

Young, Robert E., guest ed. *Fostering Critical Thinking*. San Francisco, Calif.: Jossey-Bass, 1980. This book probes deeply into the need and methods for helping students to think more critically. Chapters cover topics like strategies for solving problems and exploring issues in the classroom.

CHAPTER REFERENCES

1. Philip L. Hosford, "The Art of Applying the Science of Education," in *Using What We Know About Teaching*, ed. P. L. Hosford (Washington, D.C.: Association for Supervision and Curriculum Development, 1984).

2. Terry W. Blue, *The Teaching and Learning Process* (Washington, D.C.: National Education Association, 1981).

3. Barak V. Rosenshine, "Synthesis of Research on Explicit Teaching," *Educational Leadership,* 56 (April 1986), pp. 60–69.

4. Ibid, p. 69.

5. Ibid, p. 60.

6. Ibid, pp. 60–69.

7. Blue, *The Teaching and Learning Process,* 1981, p. 54.

8. Rosenshine, "Synthesis of Research on Explicit Teaching," 1986, p. 60.

9. Thomas L. Good and Jere E. Brophy, *Looking in Classrooms* (New York: Harper & Row, 1984), p. 320.

10. Carl Rogers, *Freedom to Learn* (Columbus, Ohio: Charles E. Merrill Publishing Co., 1969).

11. Edmund J. Amidon and Ned A. Flanders, *The Role of the Teacher in the Classroom* (St. Paul, Minn.: Association for Productive Teaching, 1971).

12. Bruce Joyce and Marsha Weil, *Models of Teaching* (Englewood Cliffs, N.J.: Prentice-Hall, 1986).

13. Martin A. Simon, "The Teacher's Role in Increasing Student Understanding of Mathematics," *Educational Leadership,* April 1986, pp. 40–43.

14. D. C. Phillips and Jonas Soltis, *Perspectives On Learning* (New York: Teachers College Press, 1985).

15. William W. Wilen, *Questioning Skills, for Teachers* (Washington, D.C.: National Education Association, 1986).

16. Norris M. Sanders, *Classroom Questions: What Kinds?* (New York: Harper & Row, 1966).

17. Meredith Gall, "Synthesis of Research on Teachers' Questioning," *Educational Leadership* 42 (April 1984): 41.

18. J. J. Gallagher and M. J. Aschner, "A Preliminary Report on Analyses of Classroom Interaction," *Merrill-Palmer Quarterly* 9 (1963): 183–194.

19. Romiett Stevens, *The Question as a Measure of Efficiency in Instruction: A Critical Study of Classroom Practice* (New York: Teachers College, Columbia University, 1912).

20. Ambrose Clegg, Jr., "Classroom Questions," in *The Encyclopedia of Education,* vol. 2 (New York: Macmillan Publishing Company, 1971).

21. Amelia Melnik, "Questions: An Instructional-Diagnostic Tool," *Journal of Reading,* no. 11, 1968, pp. 509–512.

22. Meredith D. Gall, "The Use of Questions in Teaching," *Review of Educational Research* 40 (1970): 707–721.

23. W. D. Floyd, "An Analysis of the Oral Questioning Activity in Selected Colorado Primary Classrooms" (Ph.D. dissertation, Colorado State University, 1960).

24. Ibid., passim.

25. H. C. Haynes, "The Relation of Teacher Intelligence, Experience, and Type of School to Type of Questions" (Ph.D. dissertation, George Peabody College for Teachers, Nashville, 1935).

26. Stephen M. Corey, "The Teachers Out-Talk the Pupils," *The School Review* 48 (1940): 745–752.

27. Meredith Gall, "The Use of Questions in Teaching," p. 707–721.

28. Wilen, *Questioning Skills, for Teachers,* passim.

29. Ibid., pp. 7–8.

30. R. T. Pate and N. H. Bremer, "Guiding Learning Through Skillful Questioning," *Elementary School Journal* 67 (1962): 417–422.

31. Wilen, *Questioning Skills, for Teachers,* p. 22.

32. Ibid., p. 21.

33. Hilda Taba, S. Levine, and F. F. Elzey, *Thinking in Elementary School Children,* U.S. Office of Education Cooperative Research Project No. 1574 (San Francisco: San Francisco State College, 1964).

34. Gallagher and Aschner, *A Preliminary Report on Analyses of Classroom Interaction,* pp. 183–194.

35. D. S. Arnold, R. K. Atwood, and U. M. Rogers, "An Investigation of the Relationships Among Question Level, Response Level, and Lapse Time," *School Science and Mathematics* 73 (October 1973): 591–594.

36. Francis P. Hunkins, "Analysis and Evaluation Questions: Their Effects Upon Critical Thinking," *Educational Leadership* 27 (1970): 697–705.

37. Wilen, *Questioning Skills, for Teachers,* p. 17.

38. P. H. Winne and R. W. Marx, "Experiments Relating to Teachers' Use of Higher Cognitive Questions to Student Achievement," *Review of Educational Research* 49 (Winter 1979): 13–50.

39. Mary Budd Rowe, "Wait-Time and Reward as Instructional Variables, Their Influence on Language, Logic, and Fate Control: Part One—Wait Time," *Journal of Research on Science Teaching* 11 (1974): 81–94.

40. Wilen, *Questioning Skills, for Teachers,* p. 19.

41. E. Z. Rothkopf, "Variable Adjunct Question Schedules, Interpersonal Interaction, and Incidental Learning from Written Material," *Journal of Educational Psychology* 63 (April 1972): 87–92; and O. D. Hargie, "The Importance of Teacher Questions in the Classroom," *Educational Research* 20 (February 1978): 99–102.

42. Barak Rosenshine, "Classroom Instruction," in *The Psychology of Teaching Methods,* ed. W. L. Gage (Chicago: University of Chicago Press, 1976).

43. Barak Rosenshine, "Content, Time, and Direct Instruction," in *Research on Teaching: Concepts, Findings, and Implications,* ed. Penelope L. Peterson and Herbert L. Walberg (Berkeley, Calif.: McCutcheon, 1979).

44. T. Good and J. Brophy, *Looking in Classrooms* (New York: Harper & Row, 1987), passim.

45. G. Kleinman, "Teachers' Questions and Student Understanding of Science," *Journal of Research in Science Teaching* 3 (December 1965): 307–317; G. T. Ladd, "Determining the Level of Inquiry in Teachers' Questions" (Ph.D. dissertation, Indiana University, 1969); and L. J. Buggey, "A Study of the Relationship of Classroom Questions and Social Studies Achievement of Second Grade Children" (Ph.D. dissertation, University of Washington, 1971).

46. G. T. Ladd, "Determining the Level of Inquiry in Teachers' Questions" (Ph.D. dissertation, University of Washington, 1969), passim.

47. Wilen, *Questioning Skills, for Teachers,* p. 18.

13

Can You Teach?

■ Jessica Becker and Jonathan Renner had known each other for years. The two had known each other during high school but had not grown fond of one another until after going to separate colleges. They planned to marry and their career choices seemed logical. Both found merits and conveniences in becoming teachers. However, what was logical didn't always feel quite right.

"Jon, do you ever worry about student teaching? You don't seem to say much about it. I mean, you talk about the work, the kids, and other teachers, but you don't say much about how *you* feel about becoming a teacher and teaching for maybe the next 30 years. Is anything wrong?"

"Oh, I don't know, Jess. There's a lot of work to do, you know. Why do you ask?"

"Well, I guess I'm asking because of the way I feel. Here I am already into my second professional education course and I'm wondering about a lot of things. Last semester gave me a lot to think about. And sometimes I wonder if I'm cut out to be a teacher."

"Jessi, are you saying that you don't want to teach? You know that would really mess up our plans about vacations, traveling, and graduate school after we're married! And what about having children? What other kind of job can you get that makes it so easy to take time off and start back to work?"

"Hey, look, I'm just being honest, Jonathan. I didn't say I don't *want* to teach. I just don't know if I *can* teach. But you really didn't answer my question. How do you actually *feel* about teaching? You didn't have contact with teachers, schools, and kids during your earlier courses like my college's program requires. How did you find out about your teaching philosophy and develop your ideas about classroom management and instruction before student teaching? Wasn't that a problem for you?"

Jonathan took a deep breath and let out that characteristic slow

375

deliberate sigh like he always did before letting down his defenses with Jessica.

"Yeah, it's a problem. You remember what the very first course was I ever took at college? Speech. Yes, speech at 8:00 A.M. And who do you think was the first one called on that first day of class to give a 2-minute impromptu speech? Me, and I wondered then what business I had in wanting to become a teacher. I mean, I thought each day would be like giving speeches all day long. I thought then that I could overcome the jitters with some practice. Yet the thought of me facing dozens of expectant faces turned my stomach. But actually that wasn't a problem I had to face until now. My other education courses insulated me from it. They were useful courses, though, and I believe I learned a lot.

"Well, maybe it's too soon and things will get better," Jonathan continued, "but I just don't know. I kind of feel trapped. Look, I'll graduate soon and hope to get a teaching job so we can follow through with our plans after you finish school. You know I can't afford to change my major now and get another degree. Where would I get the money? And besides, what about our future? I guess I have no choice but to stick with it and hope I feel better about teaching. But it seems you have a choice, Jessica. You can change your mind. I believe you can teach, but it's not too late for you to change your mind if you have doubts about wanting to teach."

INTRODUCTION

■   It seems that several important questions are raised in the opening scenario. How well do you know yourself? might be one question Jonathan and Jessica should consider. Knowing about your personal preferences and characteristics, how you feel about other people, how you feel about young children, teenagers, community expectations, teacher responsibilities, the things young people talk about, knowing what you believe and value, knowing how you believe teachers should teach and how students learn—all of these factors and others are related to your own self-image; your thoughts on all these factors represent part of who you are. Who are you? The first part of this chapter is devoted to exercises designed to help you answer this question.

Are you capable of teaching? Do you know what conditions limit your performance or bring out the best in you? The second part of this chapter focuses on these questions.

What about this business about feeling trapped—that there is nothing else you can do if you choose not to teach? Is this true? Could you really be wasting your time in this course if you don't decide to become a teacher? These are important questions we explore in the last portion of this chapter.

WHO ARE YOU?

■ From the standpoint of being a teacher, knowing what you believe about teaching, having reasons to back up your beliefs, and being able to put your beliefs into action provide the broad areas to examine in answering this question of who you are. Sure, when asked the question you can provide your name, address, brief description of family lineage, and chart some of your family history, but have you ever had to come to grips with the important questions about who you are in terms of what you expect of others, and how you prefer to function within the profession of teaching?

Exploring teaching as a career requires that you begin a continuing quest. As a prospective teacher or as a person who is only casually exploring teaching, your task is to pinpoint your philosophy of education, develop it, and use it. The quest is continual because there is never a singular, universally correct answer to the question of philosophy. Instead, there are many plausible and correct answers to the question, at least in American schools. By now, you have already explored some of the diversity in education and you have come to understand the origin of some of its roots by reading and reflecting on previous chapters. What sense have you made of all this?

What are your ideas about the purpose of education and why we have places called schools and persons called teachers and administrators? We know students can learn in a variety of different ways. How do you believe students learn? What definition do you think of when you hear the terms "teaching" and "learning"? What particular values do you have that you think are worthy of passing on to students? Must students value the same things as you and in the same way? What is your image of the ideal student and the ideal citizen? How would you describe an educated person? As already suggested, what you believe affects how you answer these questions and your answers reflect you as a person who potentially may become a teacher. Your answers are personal since they reflect aspects of your personality, give clues about your beliefs, provide insight into your values, and help to form your identity as a teacher.

Are you at a loss for some of the answers? If so, perhaps the following exercises should help you to focus your thoughts, make your vision more acute, and come to grips with some answers to the questions posed above. We begin with exercises that help you explore the roles of teachers that you believe are important. Next, we investigate your beliefs about the context of teaching and your preferred approach to it. Part of this investigation emphasizes types of content you believe are worth teaching and the ultimate purposes of instruction. Using an inductive approach, we help you move from a look at the specifics of teaching toward the larger, general ideas that undergird it. We start with your examination of teacher roles, the context of teaching, teaching styles, your personality, the types of content you favor, and your beliefs about teaching. Finally, your philosophical views are explored at the end of this section of the chapter.

☐ Teacher Roles

As you already know, teachers have simultaneous roles to play. Some roles are essential to the profession, while some roles are only ancillary to the job of teaching. No one role entirely sums up what teachers must do. Complete the activity in Exercise 13.1 by rating each role relative to how much or how little emphasis *you believe* the role should have. This activity should help you analyze your personal characteristics, beliefs, and values about teaching and look into the unique combination of roles that may constitute your teacher identity.

EXERCISE 13.1   Teaching Roles

Directions: Read each of the following role descriptions and consider how important each is to the function of teaching. Circle the number that best represents your belief about the role's importance.

I believe a teacher should be:	Little Emphasis				Much Emphasis
1. A guide and lead students, not force them, to learn things they are not interested in.	1	2	3	4	5
2. A person who teaches directly by helping students learn things they don't understand.	1	2	3	4	5
3. Modern and contemporary; provide experiences that have meaning to the students and help students translate experiences into meaningful terms.	1	2	3	4	5
4. A model citizen and is an example for students to emulate.	1	2	3	4	5

I believe a teacher should be:	Little Emphasis				Much Emphasis
5. Known as a searcher; one who constantly seeks meaning; one who tries to understand what he or she doesn't know.	1	2	3	4	5
6. A counselor who is as a friend and confidant of students.	1	2	3	4	5
7. A creator who is capable of demonstrating an understanding of the creative process.	1	2	3	4	5
8. An authority figure who knows more than students and wants to share this knowledge with them through a journey of learning.	1	2	3	4	5
9. An inspiration; one who has vision and inspires each student to develop fully and release what he or she is capable of doing.	1	2	3	4	5
10. A master of routine; one who is able to efficiently attend to all necessary tasks.	1	2	3	4	5
11. An explorer who helps students leave behind the old in order to experience the new and previously unknown.	1	2	3	4	5
12. A storyteller who uses suspense and intrigue to bring learning to life.	1	2	3	4	5
13. An actor or actress who performs dynamically in the classroom, yet with the intent of sharing an accurate, artistic interpretation of reality.	1	2	3	4	5
14. A scene designer who can create a setting and mood appropriate for the learning task.	1	2	3	4	5

I believe a teacher should be:	Little Emphasis				Much Emphasis
15. A builder of community and collegiality; one who works with people of the community for the betterment of the community.	1	2	3	4	5
16. A learner who grows along with each class of students.	1	2	3	4	5
17. A realist who accepts students as they are, with their respective strengths and weaknesses, and who works with these attributes to place them into proper perspective.	1	2	3	4	5
18. An emancipator who works to free the students from the shackles of their poor self-images, from their ignorance, and from their feelings of rejection and inferiority.	1	2	3	4	5
19. An evaluator who constantly calculates the progress and directions of students' learning and the effects of teaching.	1	2	3	4	5
20. A conserver of energy who helps students develop patience with less important situations so they can be more effective in more important situations.	1	2	3	4	5
21. A culminator who can bring into focus the process of learning, who can provide a sense of summary, a sense of completion and achievement.	1	2	3	4	5
22. A real person without false pretenses who shows human qualities of success, failure, disappointment, enthusiasm, satisfaction, and continued growth as a human being.	1	2	3	4	5

Adapted from Terry W. Blue, *The Teaching and Learning Process* (Washington, D.C.: National Education Association, 1981), pp. 33–34.

Take a look over your responses to Exercise 13.1. Try to summarize your beliefs about the roles of teachers, what teachers should do. Do you see consistency in your responses? Are there any beliefs you have that could be inconsistent or even in conflict? If so, how do you explain this? What do your responses reveal regarding your beliefs about teaching?

Perhaps after reflecting on your responses to the exercise you agree that teachers do have many different, and sometimes potentially conflicting, roles to play. Teachers at times may have to be advisors to students. Teachers may have to function as guides or facilitators on some occasions, be managers of instruction at times, be disciplinarians, academicians, and evaluators on other occasions, perhaps even fill all of these roles in a single day. Some teachers maintain an experimental approach to their profession and constantly look for better ways to complete their duties and to make their teaching have more meaning for students. Consequently, teachers may develop a large repertoire of teaching approaches that help them fulfill their roles.

A teacher must comfort, guide, mediate, and counsel as well as teach.

□ The Context of Teaching

The different roles of teaching may require different teaching approaches. Roles are linked to goals; different roles are the means through which teachers accomplish different ends—the goals of instruction. According to Bruce Joyce and Marsha Weil, some goals may prompt teachers to teach in ways that promote *social interaction* by emphasizing the relationships between the individual and society. Teacher roles would favor approaches that give priority to improving the individual student's ability to relate to others in class. There is also concern for teaching in a way that encourages the democratic process, improvement of a society, and development of the mental capacity of the learner.[1]

Teachers who favor roles that emphasize students' abilities to *process information* use approaches to teaching that focus on information and a student's ability to master it. *Personal approaches* favor teacher roles that promote the development of the individual student's ability and self-perception. The emotional aspects of the learner and development of a unique sense of reality are areas of teacher concern. Teacher approaches that emphasize *behavior modification* techniques use control over the environment and behavioral reinforcement strategies. All these families of approaches to teaching favor teacher roles that specifically support the beliefs, theories, and philosophies that undergird the teaching methods. Teachers commonly combine roles to achieve specific effects as well as to get specific results. Even

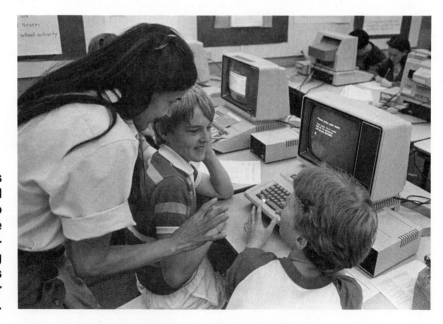

Some teachers prefer automated classrooms to provide more time for developing strong human relations with their students.

"The principal would like another look at your diploma."
Phi Delta Kappan, March 1985.

so, each approach taken by any teacher has a common factor. This common factor is the context within which teaching takes place. This context largely consists of an established atmosphere and provides another glimpse into a teacher's views on teaching.

The classroom atmosphere is within the control of the teacher. If you become a teacher, your classroom atmosphere will be a variable of teaching that you control. You will decide what factors are important and what type of classroom you prefer. This atmosphere should complement your teaching roles and approaches to instruction. What types of atmospheres do you favor? Berquist and Phillips provide ideas useful in developing a framework for classifying several types of classrooms.[2] Read the classifications below, think about the styles, then complete Exercise 13.2 to show how much time you believe is important to give to each style.

1. *Student-oriented classrooms* use techniques like independent study, learning packets, contracts, and facilities of nonclassroom settings. Students may study and learn in their homes, outdoor learning labs, libraries, museums, school lounges, and student study areas.
2. *Teacher-oriented classrooms* consist of traditional classroom arrangements wherein individual student seats usually face

EXERCISE 13.2   What Type of Education Atmosphere Do You Prefer?

How much time do you believe should be devoted to each type of classroom atmosphere? Draw a circle around the number that best shows your belief.

Type of Classroom Atmosphere	No Time	Little Time				Much Time
1. Student-oriented atmosphere	0	1	2	3	4	5
2. Teacher-oriented atmosphere	0	1	2	3	4	5
3. Interaction-oriented atmosphere	0	1	2	3	4	5
4. Automated atmosphere	0	1	2	3	4	5
5. Sheltered experience atmosphere	0	1	2	3	4	5
6. Experience-oriented atmosphere	0	1	2	3	4	5

the front of the room or some central point where teacher-led instruction takes place. Sometimes these seats may be permanently fixed, even bolted to the floor making them immovable.

3. *Interaction-oriented classrooms* are arranged so students and teachers can face each other. The setting can be informal, seminar-like, where chairs can be arranged in a circle or around a table to promote interactive learning and idea sharing.

4. *Automated classrooms* make use of instructional technology like audiovisual equipment, programmed instruction materials, computer instruction systems, educational television, and microwave interactive television systems. Room arrangement is important and is designed to support the type of automation.

5. *Sheltered-experience-oriented classes* make use of learning aids like simulations, educational games, role-playing, laboratory experiences, apprenticeships, workshops, and practica.

6. *Experience-oriented classes* make use of on-the-job learning opportunities, school work-study programs, field experiences, internships, and credit-for-life experiences. Formal school classrooms may not be needed.

Do you favor more than one type of atmosphere? What types? Why? Do you favor several atmospheres much of the time? A few a little of the time? What rationale can you give for your choices? How consistent are your choices of atmosphere with your beliefs about the roles of teachers? What inconsistencies, if any, do you notice and why do you have them? Do you believe it is important to reconcile any inconsistency? Why? What kind of teacher do you think you are? What kind of teacher do you think you can become?

Teaching Styles

What you believe about teacher roles and what kinds of classroom atmospheres you prefer give an indication of the styles of teaching you favor. Teachers can and do develop distinct styles of teaching. After all, each teacher is a different person who is subject to differences in values and beliefs about what is and what is not important to teaching and learning. Teachers are not automatons programed to teach in precisely the same way as all other teachers. Exercise 13.3 summarizes several different teaching styles and asks you to identify characteristics that are most like your own style of teaching.

☐ Your Personality

Your teaching style makes a difference because it influences how you teach and what students learn. Do you suppose your teaching style matches with how students prefer to learn? The ways students learn are explored later in this chapter. But for now, let us focus on a factor related to students and teachers—personality. Research on the influence of personality is not entirely conclusive, yet there is evidence that supports the conclusion that a teacher's personality, particularly the behavior that accompanies personality, makes a difference in student learning.[3]

What are some teacher behaviors that have an influence? Personal factors like commitment and responsibility in lesson preparation have a positive correlation with student learning. A teacher's ability to present information and state instructions clearly are other factors. Ability to communicate effectively, ability to select and ask appropriate questions, and use of listening skills and techniques of motivation also play important roles in learning. The personal approach, tone of voice, temperament, and unbiased treatment of students—the personality dimension—show clearly when a teacher communicates with students.

Other personal behaviors of teachers are believed important, but they show less of a clear relationship to gains in student achievement. Behaviors like enthusiasm, warmth, sensitivity, flexibility, and other types of attitudinal factors represent the human relations skills of the teachers—skills involved with one human interacting with other human beings. While these personality factors are important, no research is conclusive enough to prescribe precisely how every teacher

EXERCISE 13.3   What Is Your Teaching Style?

Six descriptions of common teaching styles are given below. Rate each style by circling the number closest to how much you believe it is or is not like you. If you have not taught enough to identify a style, rate each style in terms of how much it appeals to you or how much you would like to teach like the description.

Teaching Style	Is Not Like Me					Is Like Me
1. *Subject Matter Expert:* I take pride in knowing my subject(s) and see my role as being mostly an information giver. I am respected for what I know and can do. I want students to be in my classes because they want to learn from me.	0	1	2	3	4	5
2. *Formal Authority:* I expect students to be punctual, turn work in on time, and in the format I require. Students are expected to follow the class rules that I make up—that is part of my responsibility as a teacher. I am in control and conduct myself as a model. We all have to conform to rules throughout our lives and students must learn to follow school rules so they can follow society's rules as independent citizens.	0	1	2	3	4	5
3. *Socializing Agent:* I am constantly looking for talented students and will do what I can for those who are interested and wish to pursue higher levels of education. I feel great when students follow in my footsteps, so I function sort of like a recruiter and gatekeeper for my field.	0	1	2	3	4	5
4. *Facilitator:* Even though students and I have different goals and interests, my responsibility is to respond to the goals and interests of my students. I don't be-						

lieve I should particularly tell students what they should learn because there is so much to learn and no one can ever know everything about everything. I do a lot of listening and question-asking because I believe in meeting students on their own terms and I want to be able to help them learn what they want to learn.

0   1   2   3   4   5

5. *Ego Ideal:* Students look up to me as a model adult, not just for my areas of learning specialty, but for my good wholesome living as well. I have energy and enthusiasm for what I do; I have a zest for life. Students may not remember everything I teach; in fact they don't have to, because when my class is over they will be inspired to find out more, to find out what is mentally liberating and exciting for them, just as teaching is for me.

0   1   2   3   4   5

6. *Personal:* Students learn from me, but I learn as much from them. Teaching is dynamic, it is part of a social system, and teachers and students should learn from each other. Why do I teach? Because I value personal growth, mine and the growth of my students. My classroom atmosphere tries to maintain a climate of trust and openness. I am not reluctant to share my own feelings and uncertainties, both personal and academic. I want students to see me as a person both in and outside the classroom.

0   1   2   3   4   5

Based on Terry W. Blue, *The Teaching and Learning Process* (Washington, D.C.: National Education Association, 1981), pp. 37–38.

should behave and treat students. Aside from the logic in not expecting, nor in finding it reasonable to expect any teacher to conform his or her personality to a prescribed style, what type of personality do you believe teachers should have? Furthermore, how would you describe your own personality? How well suited is your personality for teaching? For Reflection 13.1 should help you investigate the nature and importance of your personality.

FOR REFLECTION 13.1   Describe Your Personality

Personality and attitude are important factors of teaching. While we know there is no one particular combination of knowledge, skills, attitudes, and personal factors required of teachers, some combinations are clearly more desirable and more effective than others. Each teacher has a responsibility for developing an effective combination of knowledge, skills, attitudes, beliefs, and other personal factors. Each teacher is responsible for identifying the factors important for this combination and in experimenting to find out what combinations work best for him or her, the students, and the community's expectations.

Answer the following questions to determine the relationship between your own personality and teaching.

1. What personal factors do you believe teachers must have and use to teach as effectively as they possibly can?

2. Describe your personality.

3. What strengths does your personality have? How can you exploit these strengths and use them for teaching effectively?

4. What shortcomings for teaching do you see in your own personality? How can you overcome these shortcomings?

5. Personality is important, but is limited in terms of its influence on learning. What nonpersonality factors are important for a teacher to have and use?

☐ **What Types of Content Do You Favor?**

In Chapter 11 you studied several types of content areas that could be emphasized in planning lessons. More than 25 years ago Benjamin Bloom and several other researchers developed a taxonomy for instruction. Broadly referred to as "domains" of learning, three important areas of teaching and learning were developed: (1) the cognitive domain; (2) the affective domain; and (3) the psychomotor domain. Your views on teaching probably influence what you believe is important to teach. In Exercise 13.4 we ask you to consider what these domains represent and to make some decisions about how much emphasis you believe ought to be given to each while teaching.

EXERCISE 13.4 What Types of Content Do You Favor?

Brief descriptions are given for three domains of learning. Consider what could be taught within each domain and make a decision about how much emphasis you believe should be given to each. Circle the number closest to the emphasis you believe should be given. You might want to refer to Chapter 11 for additional descriptions.

Domains	Little or No Emphasis				Much Emphasis
1. *Cognitive Domain:* Information is emphasized in this domain. Students must acquire new information or organize existing information. Information is usually obtained through lecture, discussion, reading, television, computerized instruction, or packaged types of media materials. Learning is determined often by using written papers, objective tests, essays, or oral examinations.	0	1	2	3	4	5
2. *Affective Domain:* People's emotions, attitudes, values, self-images, and beliefs are included in topics of study. There is an emphasis on increasing understanding and/or in increasing control over some aspects of students' lives. The affective content of teaching may be conveyed						

Domains	Little or No Emphasis					Much Emphasis

through involvement exercises, personal experiences, and group simulations. Learning can be planned as well as unplanned or even spontaneous. Evaluation of what is learned is difficult to determine and relies on more subjective approaches like divergent questioning, open-ended interviews, open-ended essays, and personal diaries.

0   1   2   3   4   5

3. *Psychomotor Domain:* Physical skills that students learn to perform represent this domain. Content may be taught through lecturing, modeling, demonstrations, practice, and personal feedback. Evaluation of learning focuses on skills acquired and is measured directly through performance tests. Factors like speed, accuracy, endurance, and consistency are considered.

0   1   2   3   4   5

☐ What Do You Really Believe About Teaching?

So far we have asked you to think about teacher roles, class atmosphere, your preferred teaching style(s), the influence of your personality on your teaching, and the types of content you believe ought to be emphasized during teaching. These small parts fit into a larger framework and your decisions about the parts of teaching we have already asked you to think about are based on certain assumptions about students, the purposes of schools, the tasks of teachers, and expectations or actual needs of a society.

Your assumptions may not be uppermost in your mind as you make the decisions necessary for teaching. Nevertheless you do make assumptions. Do you believe teachers make the same decisions about teaching if they make different assumptions? If they have different views on how students learn? If they have different views on what needs to be learned?

If you can identify the roots of your viewpoints, your decision making can become easier. Identification can add a rationale to your decisions and help you investigate any inconsistencies in your thinking. Identification can also add a degree of prescription to your decision making. The roots of your ideas can clear your vision of education; you may be able to see the desired end and the means for accomplishing this end easier. The roots of your ideas can recommend alternatives for the dilemmas and decisions that you face. What are the great ideas of education that provide the roots of your viewpoints? The next exercise, Exercise 13.5, asks you to complete a viewpoints inventory and then identify the roots of your views.

EXERCISE 13.5 Contemporary Educational Viewpoints Inventory

Directions: Mark the response that best explains your reactions to each statement. Mark SA if you strongly agree, A if you moderately agree, U if you are undecided, D if you moderately disagree, and SD if you strongly disagree.

	SA	A	U	D	SD
1. Despite differing atmospheres, human nature remains the same everywhere; hence education should be the same for everyone.	___	___	___	___	___
2. It is the educator's task to impart knowledge of eternal truth.	___	___	___	___	___
3. Education is not an imitation of life, but a preparation for it.	___	___	___	___	___
4. Students should study the great works of literature, philosophy, history, and science in which humans through the ages have revealed their greatest aspirations and achievements.	___	___	___	___	___
5. Learning, of its very nature, involves hard work and often unwilling application.	___	___	___	___	___
6. The initiative in education should be with the teacher rather than the pupil.	___	___	___	___	___
7. The heart of the educational process is the assimilation of prescribed subject matter.	___	___	___	___	___

	SA	A	U	D	SD
8. The school should retain traditional methods of mental discipline.	—	—	—	—	—
9. Education is always in the process of development and must be ready to modify methods and policies in light of new knowledge and changes in the atmosphere.	—	—	—	—	—
10. Education should be life itself, not a preparation for living.	—	—	—	—	—
11. Learning should be directly related to the interests of the child.	—	—	—	—	—
12. Learning through problem solving should take precedence over inculcating subject matter.	—	—	—	—	—
13. The teacher's role is not to direct, but to advise.	—	—	—	—	—
14. Education must commit itself to a new social order that will fulfill the basic values of our culture and at the same time harmonize with the underlying social and economic forces of the modern world.	—	—	—	—	—
15. The child, the school, and education itself are conditioned inexorably by social and cultural forces.	—	—	—	—	—
16. The means and ends of education must be completely refashioned to meet the demands of the present cultural crisis and to accord with the findings of the behavioral sciences.	—	—	—	—	—
17. Education should emphasize deep personal reflection of one's commitments and choices.	—	—	—	—	—
18. By the choices we make, we create a personal definition. We					

	SA	A	U	D	SD
are what we choose to be. Education should allow and support this.	___	___	___	___	___
19. While we live in a world of physical realities and while we have developed useful and scientific knowledge about these realities, the most significant aspects of our lives are personal and nonscientific.	___	___	___	___	___
20. Teaching methods should focus on a questioning process aimed at encouraging self-definition.	___	___	___	___	___

Terry W. Blue, *The Teaching and Learning Process* (Washington, D.C.: National Education Association, 1981), pp. 49–50.

What do your responses to Exercise 13.5 mean? Each of five rather common and traditional classifications of educational philosophy are represented by the statements above. See how strongly you agree or disagree with these statements and determine which philosophy(ies) you seem to favor.

The first four statements represent beliefs that are consistent with a Perennialist viewpoint of schools. For the perennialist, a premium is placed on permanence; change is avoided. This is because the main aim of perennialist educators is to pass along the knowledge of eternal truths of past generations to new generations. The great works of history, literature, and philosophy are particularly useful in helping the teacher cultivate each student's rational ability. Motivation for learning is provided through external discipline and control. The teacher is a central authority figure and the end product is a corps of educated elite.

The next four statements, 5–8, help to provide us with a summary of Essentialist beliefs about school. Essentialist educators strive to conserve our cultural heritage and are concerned with transmitting knowledge of our physical world. Teaching tends to emphasize a traditional approach to prescribed subject matter. Emphasis is on learning systematically and by using traditional methods of mental discipline. Led by the teacher who has great authority, students strive to learn essential knowledge and skills to help them function in a contemporary world. Essentialist viewpoints have several similarities with perennial views, but differ mainly by less emphasis being placed on intellectual elitism and on the goals of education being cast in the present instead of the past.

And now, Miss Miller, would you just briefly tell me your methods for teaching reading, your philosophy of education, your views on testing, your ideas on discipline in the classroom, your opinions about homework, where you think education is heading in this country and how you would upgrade math skills in our school should you be hired?

Sipeess

Learning, January 1982.

Statements 9–13 give us an indication of Progressive viewpoints. Progressive teachers view education as constantly changing and in need of a dynamic approach that favors contemporary needs. Teachers function less as authoritarians and more as guides or leaders. Progressive teachers favor real or lifelike learning experiences with an emphasis on problem solving and other skill-acquiring strategies. Cooperation is stressed instead of competition among learners and students have some degree of choice in what they learn. Progressives believe that students will learn because they want to learn, not because they are told what and how to learn.

The next three statements, 14–16, help to summarize Social-reconstructionist points of view. Social-reconstructionists use progressive teaching methods to make use of the school's place for empowering students and in helping them build new and equitable social orders. Democratic principles are highly valued and are used to help students inspect the conditions of their communities. Teachers urge students to consider the democratic political process in developing solutions to urgent and valid social problems.

The last four statements, 17–20, provide us with an Existential viewpoint. Existentialism is more of a systematic method for examining life in a personal way than it is an educational philosophy.

Existentialists have a high regard for the individual and are concerned with each individual's control over his or her destiny. Existential teachers favor experiences and topics that lend themselves to philosophical discussions. Teachers emphasize analysis of real problems with real choices and compel students to make thoughtful decisions. While "teaching," the existentialist teacher plays a nondirective role that appears diametrically opposed to that of the perennialist and the essentialist teacher.

What philosophy or philosophies do you favor? Do you find yourself completely attached to one over the others? Or do you find that aspects of several philosophies appeal to you? If this latter condition applies to you, you will find that you have a lot of company. The question, "Which philosophy is best?" is actually a loaded question. Each person can have a different answer for the question and each philosophy has been found to work when properly used.

CAN YOU TEACH?

■ "Can you teach?" Ahh, a simple question that defies a simple answer. At the very least, you are probably aware that teaching is not as incredibly simple as many believe it is. There are so many things to do, to know, and so many options to use. The decision about whether or not a teacher can or cannot teach is often left to someone else, like a principal or supervisor. This in itself may not be bad and it is always helpful to receive a valid point of view. But the question here as we intend to use it has personal meaning. We believe you must delve into teaching, examine it deeply, and weigh what is demanded of teachers against your interests and capabilities.

Can you teach? How do you know? Try now to synthesize all of the experiences you have gained in this course, the readings of this book and others, and the personal information you have provided. What kind of a match do you find between what teaching is, who you are, and what you can do?

As you do this, remember that teaching is a people activity. Your personal evaluation should not overlook your clients—the students. Let us now turn our attention once again to the people we must work with, the students, before tying this course all together and making those final decisions we have been urging you to make.

☐ Student Differences

Sections II and III of this book gave us several opportunities to look closely at students. This was important because the habitat of teachers consists largely of interactions with students, or at least coexisting with them. Before you declare yourself capable of teaching and pronounce your philosophy of education, consider for one last time the people you are hired to work with—the students.

Students differ in interests, maturation, readiness, motivation, culture, and nurturance. They have different personalities and different purposes for being in school because they *are* different. A preschooler may be in school because working parents need quality day-care or they wish to provide an enriched life for their child. Youngsters in the primary grades may be eager to go to school because of the excitement of its new experiences. Intermediate youngsters may have an emerging mental expansion that defies restraint; they may be stimulated or bored beyond description. The middle or junior high school students are well known for their "moody" pendulum swings of childish zest for life at one moment and mature detachment from activity at other moments. High school youth could be biding time until released from the shackles of school, could relish the opportunities for peer socialization, or show earnest preparation for continued education or careers. Beyond these superficial descriptions of student differences, what do you know about the differences in student characteristics at these different levels of schooling? What do these similarities and differences imply for teaching and learning? What age or grade levels of students do you feel most comfortable with and which might you prefer to teach?

We ask you to examine the age-level similarities and the differences in characteristics between age levels in Table 13.1. Be aware that these characteristics could be oversimplifications and that they are based on relatively small samples of children. Treat these characteristics as predictions or guiding ideas and do not use them to label individuals or to generalize all students of a given age. Bear in mind that the purpose of this text and of this categorization is not to provide a broad and deep investigation into child and adolescent development or educational psychology. Courses like these often are taken separately and about the same time as this course. Do the exercise in For Reflection 13.2 to heighten your awareness of the importance of student similarities and differences and to recognize that child and adolescent development results from the interaction of two major factors: maturation and learning.

Maturation is affected by heredity and environment and may be relatively independent of education. The learning factor is a combination of experience and environment. We know that students change more from what they learn as they become older and change less from maturational influences. It seems that teachers can play a key role in these learned similarities and differences. Although changes become

TABLE 13.1   Age-Level Characteristics

Preschool and Kindergarten, 3–5 Years
Children learn to play cooperatively between ages 2 and 5.
Adults tend to encourage girls to become dependent on other persons.
Young children tend to follow their own language rules.

Primary School, 6–9 Years
Children have difficulty focusing their eyes on small print.
Children rigidly interpret rules of games or the classroom.
Teachers must avoid criticism and must use praise to encourage pupil industry.

Intermediate Elementary Grades, 9–12 Years
Girls are usually taller than boys during ages 11–14.
Boys have greater strength and endurance after their growth spurt.
Delinquent students usually have few friends and may be antagonistic; they may do poorly in school and lack
   self-confidence.
Girls generally show verbal abilities that are superior to boys.
Boys often show math and spatial abilities that are superior to girls.
Reflective thinkers concentrate on details and impulsive thinkers tend to look at the big picture.
All students show differences in distractibility, categorization, divergence, memorization, and evaluation.

Middle/Junior High School Grades, 12–15 Years
Late maturing boys may act in ways to seek attention.
Late maturing girls may appear popular and carefree.
Early maturing boys are likely to draw favorable responses and attention to their actions.
Many teenagers experience depression.
Student thinking becomes more abstract, students become more knowledgeable, and thinking becomes less
   influenced by authoritative sources.

High School Grades, 15–18 Years
Students are expected to be interested in sex.
Students are likely to be peer motivated to engage in sexual relationships and may feel guilty about premarital
   sex.
Parents exert influence over future plans; peers influence immediate social status.
Girls are generally anxious about friendships.
Girls are likely to experience depression because of learned helplessness.
Depression may be caused by a sense of loss.

Based on Ronald F. Biehler and Jack Snowman, *Psychology Applied To Teaching* (Boston: Houghton Mifflin, 1986).

less predictable as students become older, it is important for teachers to speculate about what these changes imply for teaching and learning. What age or grade levels do you believe you can best teach? Why? What do the similarities among students of the same ages and differences among and between age groups of students mean for your teaching?

FOR REFLECTION 13.2 What Level of Students Do You Prefer to Teach?

Think about the age-level characteristics shown in Table 13.1 as you answer the following questions.

   1. How much do you prefer to teach students who are in the following grades?

Grade/Age	Not at All					Quite a Lot
Preschool-Kindergarten, ages 3–6	0	1	2	3	4	5
Primary, ages 6–9	0	1	2	3	4	5
Intermediate, ages 9–12	0	1	2	3	4	5
Middle/Junior High, ages 12–15	0	1	2	3	4	5
High School, ages 15–18	0	1	2	3	4	5

   2. What personal characteristics do you have that makes you a good match as a teacher for these students?

   3. What personal characteristics do you have that might hinder your teaching of these students?

   4. How do you believe these students learn best? Why?

   5. How do you believe these students should be taught? Why?

☐ **Student Learning Styles**

Take a close look at certain philosophies of education and you will see that particular assumptions have been made about how students should learn. Historically, schools in the United States functioned for a long time (and many still do) according to the policy that schools must mold children; they used techniques of conformity to prepare them to fit into society. Viewed this way, education is seen as an undertaking that is well defined and has specific boundaries; education is a body of information, attitudes, and skills that exist, and which must be acquired by each student. This viewpoint believes that students must "adapt themselves to the school and its conventions, needs, and interests. Those who were unable or unwilling to do so were considered uneducable."[4]

Within the last 50 years or so, schools and teachers have viewed their roles differently. In many places there is an emphasis on teaching all students. Not all students are expected to conform to a standard curriculum. Neither is it believed that all students learn the same things in exactly the same ways and under the same conditions.

We know that students vary respective to several factors: heredity, environment, and socioeconomic status. Students have different levels of intelligence and aptitudes; they differ by gender and have different personalities. Students differ from their peers just as you differ from yours. These factors also do not include differences in previous experiences, knowledge, different needs (physical, social, emotional, and mental), attitudes, learning rates, amounts and types of motivation, and levels of maturation. Still other students may differ from their age mates in ways not mentioned above. These children may be known as "exceptional students" and can range from those who have tremendous gifts and talents to those who have problems learning because they are mentally retarded, physically or emotionally handicapped, or learning disabled. All of these factors may interact and influence the style in which any individual student prefers to learn. We may define learning style as a set of distinctive behaviors that serve as indicators of how any person learns.

Many researchers have investigated teaching approaches that appear best suited for students with particular learning needs and preferences. Barbara Fischer and Louis Fischer have developed a rather comprehensive list of learning styles from classroom observations and interviews with teachers. Consider the summary of these styles shown in Exercise 13.6 and rate your level of comfort with each style. When you finish, look over the summary and identify those student learning styles you feel comfortable with and those you do not. Every student in your classroom deserves an equal opportunity to learn. How will you provide them with these opportunities?

Students display different age-level characteristics. What ages do you prefer?

☐ **What Is Your Philosophy of Education?**

The word "philosophy" has several aspects to its definition. The parts that apply here are concerned with an analysis of the concepts that express your fundamental beliefs about teaching and education. These beliefs consist of theories that underlie the activity of teaching and your attitudes as well as your approach to teaching.

EXERCISE 13.6   Student Learning Styles

How comfortable would you feel with students who learn in the following ways? Read each learning style summary and rate your level of comfort with it.

Learning Style	Not Comfortable					Very Comfortable
1. *Incremental Learners:* learn in step-by-step fashion; put bits and pieces together to learn.	0	1	2	3	4	5
2. *Intuitive Learners:* have sudden insights and gather information unsystematically while learning.	0	1	2	3	4	5
3. *Special Senses:* usually rely on visual or auditory senses to learn.	0	1	2	3	4	5
4. *General Senses:* make full use of all senses to gather information and learn.	0	1	2	3	4	5
5. *Emotional Involvement:* prefer environment where emotions add color to the classroom climate and where there are opportunities to share emotions.	0	1	2	3	4	5
6. *Neutral Emotions:* prefer a low-key level of emotional involvement in class.	0	1	2	3	4	5
7. *Explicit Structure:* profit from clear and precise teacher instructions and information delivery.	0	1	2	3	4	5
8. *Open-Ended Structure:* prefer lack of structure and opportunities to explore options.	0	1	2	3	4	5
9. *Damaged Learners:* have damaged self-concepts, are sensitive to own failures and the successes of others; may develop negative learning styles.	0	1	2	3	4	5

(Continued)

10. *Eclectic Learners:* use several learning styles, may have a dominant beneficial style, but can adapt to and benefit from others.   0   1   2   3   4   5

Based on Barbara Fischer and Louis Fischer, "Styles in Teaching and Learning," *Educational Leadership* 36, no. 4 (January 1979): 245–254.

Beneath the day-to-day activities of teachers and schools lies an entire system of ideas, operating principles, and beliefs that influence what and how teachers teach. Every lesson plan, objective, textbook, discipline policy, rule, and every other teaching action draws from philosophy. At first glance this may be difficult to see. Seldom does a school have its philosophy directly visible for observers to see and you will not normally hear teachers discuss philosophy openly. Yet it is still there serving its purpose—influencing daily decisions that define education.

You may think of philosophy as a teaching style—the sum of your beliefs, decisions, and teaching actions. Analyzing the teaching styles of other teachers is a good way to identify and refine your own style. The many questions we have asked throughout this book and particularly this chapter are directed toward urging your own analysis of other teachers in an attempt to make decisions about yourself. In the previous exercises of this chapter we placed a premium on your making choices and encouraged you to continue to look back on these choices, to examine them for consistency or any inconsistency. For

"His school seems to be emphasizing a classical education."
Phi Delta Kappan, January 1984.

Reflection 13.3 asks you to summarize these beliefs. Please take the time to reflect on the key questions again and try to reconcile any differences in your previous choices. You may find it helpful to refer back to the previous exercises again as you evaluate your choices and synthesize your style or philosophy.

FOR REFLECTION 13.3   What Is Your Philosophy of Education?

The exercises and reflections given in this book have encouraged you to develop your perceptions of teaching by analyzing the ideas and issues of education and by looking closely at the classroom settings and teaching of other teachers. Now is the time to apply your ideas and impressions to yourself. The questions below segment teaching into three primary areas for decision making: the curriculum and teaching process, learning theory, and philosophy of education. The first two areas represent the action of teaching. Let's take several more steps toward your quest by providing personal answers to the questions below.

Curriculum and Teaching Process
1. What are your roles as a teacher? What kind of relationship do you wish to have with your students? What kind of a word or metaphor describes your most desired function and relationship with your class?

2. What role will your students have? What do you expect of them and within what limits will they have to function? What kind of a word or metaphor describes what you wish your students to be? How does your vision of your students' role compare with your own role?

3. How will you interact with your students? What is the basic flow of communication like? Two-way, one-way, or multiple directions? Open-ended, preplanned, structured? How much time will be given for interaction? From where does the lesson content originate and what form does it take? What happens to the lesson content during class interaction?

4. What kinds of routines or rituals will be significant for conducting class business? How will students enter and leave? How will you take care of tasks like students going to the restroom? Going to the library? Getting a drink of water? Sharpening pencils, etc.? Will visitors be welcome to your classroom? If yes, how will you greet them? What will you provide for your visitors? How will you prefer to start your school day? End your school day?

5. What kind of learning climate do you prefer? Describe it. Will it be quiet, active, friendly, oriented toward individual students, teacher-structured, almost unstructured? What will your personality be like? What would an observer see: enthusiasm, even pace, variable tempo, or what other observations? What words would best describe your atmosphere: rigorous, friendly, fearful, mutual respect, personal growth, or what other qualities?

6. Draw a picture of your classroom and ask a friend to describe it. What would you expect that friend to say about you, your students, and the class climate based on the picture?

Learning Theory

1. How do you believe children learn? What do you believe is your function in teaching them?

2. What are your thoughts on motivation? What is your role in motivating students to learn? What is a student's role in becoming motivated for learning? Will you rely on a reward system? If so, what is its purpose and how will it function? How could it interfere with learning? How could you minimize any interference?

3. How will you "discipline" your class? What is your role? What are the roles and responsibilities of individual students, student groups, and the entire class? How will you handle individual problems? How will you handle large class problems? What kinds of counterproductive side effects could your methods have? How could the methods distract you or the class from learning? How could you avoid or overcome these distractions?

4. How will you evaluate your students' work? What kinds of evaluation information will you need? How will you manage the information? How will you know how each student progresses? How will you inform students of their progress? What limitations or undesirable side effects could your evaluation method have? How can you avoid or overcome these side effects?

Philosophy of Education

1. How do you view the world and what image of the world will you represent for your students?

2. What is your image of humans? How do you picture the ideal student who is a product of your teaching? How will your teaching help students to arrive at your ideal? What relationship will your teaching have with other social or community institutions, with the students' churches or temples, with the students' families?

3. What makes truth? You will deal with information at least some of the time; how will you and your students know what is true? What procedures will you teach students so that they know what is true?

4. What is your value system? What do you value? What should your students value? How should your values affect your students? Will you teach your values to them? Will you teach students to find or choose their own values? Why? How?

5. What do you believe is the purpose of education? The purpose of teachers? How will your classroom demonstrate your beliefs? What will you try to accomplish as a teacher? Why will you teach? What is your ultimate educational mission? What is your ultimate personal mission?

☐ Developing Your Philosophy

Perhaps you have several clear answers to many of the questions we have asked, but you are unsure about some of your answers. What can you do to overcome your uncertainties and what can be done to continue the development of your philosophy? What can you do to determine if you *can* teach? Here are some suggestions.

1. *Read authors who support a particular style of education.* Most authors are highly committed to their views and present them persuasively. As you read their points of view, try to read critically and analyze their viewpoints much as you would analyze the teaching of another teacher. Compare one author with another, contrast their viewpoints, and identify similarities and differences. How do they account for similarities and justify differences? Use the authors; use their writings as forums for comparing your own views and sharpening your own commitments. The following books represent the basic educational philosophies mentioned earlier in this chapter.

Arthur Bestor, *Educational Wastelands* (perennialist)

The National Commission for Excellence in Education, *A Nation At Risk* (essentialist)

Eliot Wigginton, *Sometimes A Shining Moment* (progressivist)

Paulo Freire, *Pedagogy of the Oppressed* (social-reconstructionist)

Carl Rogers, *Freedom To Learn* (existentialist)

2. *Serve as a teaching assistant.* Volunteer in a local school to serve on a weekly basis as a teacher's aide and teaching assistant. Perhaps 1 day a week is enough to examine teaching more closely and to get to know more about students. Try to spend time with ages or grade levels in different types of schools with different teachers. The variety of experiences will help you gauge the effects of particular combinations of teaching styles, help you to make some of your own decisions about teaching, and help you determine if you can teach.

3. *Try to arrange a variety of classroom observations.* Perhaps in association with your classwork, arrange to make several observations in different schools. Try to observe all levels of education and sample classes taught in structured and unstructured schools, schools with depressed economies and schools that are well-off, schools with racial and cultural mixes of students and teachers like your own as well as different from your own. Also visit rural, suburban, and urban schools, public schools and private schools. Select those schools known for a particular philosophy and fully committed to its practice. Evaluate your own reactions to the different philosophies at work and your reactions to the factors that make the schools special.

4. *Keep an educational journal.* Make this a simple personal dialogue that chronicles your observations and feelings. Make a note of important ideas that arise from class discussions, and from talking with friends, teachers, and students. Be sure to record your personal feelings and thoughts and keep coming back to the questions: "What is my personal style of teaching? Can I teach? How do I know if I can?" Bits and pieces of information will start to come together and you will eventually form a comprehensive view of what it means to teach and who you are. Soon you will have the framework of a philosophy of education formed, your teaching will start to be defined, and you will approach the classroom with confidence. Over time, this framework will fill itself in and your view of teaching and learning will become more comprehensive. You will know who you are, what you can (or should) do, and what results you can expect from your efforts.

☐ **Inventory and Prescription**

Now that you have taken a long, difficult look at yourself, tackle that question we used as the chapter title. Can you teach? The personal inventory you have taken should help you to do several things at this point. List your strengths—make this your personal inventory of what you know is good, true, and worthy of commitment. Use your strengths to help you meet the challenges of teaching, to form a durable teaching style. But know that there are several problems that can be inherent to forming your own style.

Permanence Can Be One Problem
Do not believe we have encouraged you to form a style of teaching so you can lock yourself into it and teach that way permanently. This should not happen. Throughout this entire book we have encouraged you to reflect on teaching by thinking about intents, actions, and consequences. We believe the more you reflect, the more you will sense the power of realism. You will see your strengths, weaknesses, accuracies, and inefficiencies. You will be in a position to change, to capitalize on your strengths and overcome your limitations. Your reflection should be a first step in a long journey toward personal perfection.

Inflexibility Can Be Another Problem
Can you compromise? Should you? Be aware that your teaching style may not complement the variety of teaching styles your students need. Inner city schools, suburban schools, rural schools, and variances in student socioeconomic statuses will require that different needs be met. If your preferences, values, and beliefs are inconsistent with what is needed, what will you do? Will you be able to compromise and provide what is needed? If you prefer traditional teaching approaches and a school where you wish to teach expects progressive teaching approaches, what should you do? Be aware that the employment interview has two sides and find out what qualities the school prefers its teachers to have. If you find that the school's expectations and your own are incompatible, should you seek a compromise or look for a position in another school?

Inconsistency Can Be Still Another Problem
We have encouraged you to look at numerous issues in this book and to explore alternatives in teaching approaches. This amounts to encouraging you to form an eclectic teaching style. Were you able to decide that students benefit from one "best" teaching style? Is one "best" classroom environment appropriate for all children? Don't be alarmed if you say no. If you find opportunities to use several of the ideas discovered in this course on education, so much the better. We are not attempting to peddle a particular pedagogy. Realize though, that if various ideas about education appeal to you, it is likely that you

will have a classroom that demonstrates these different ideas—you will have an eclectic curriculum and teaching style, an eclectic view on learning, and an eclectic philosophy. If eclecticism describes you, be alert for the possibility of combining several underlying beliefs that are inconsistent with each other. Some ideas do not fit well together, just like Ford parts do not fit Volkswagens. After all, an existential perennialist is difficult to imagine, let alone demonstrate!

☐ Are You Up to the Challenge?

Certainly, to teach well is a difficult challenge to accomplish, but many teachers do just that. Some seem like they were born to teach and appear to accomplish what seems like great feats with little support and against incredible odds. But you can easily bet that these teachers don't see teaching as a 7:30 to 3:30 job. They work at it because they believe in what they are doing and trust in their approaches.

Outstanding teachers work hard at what they do. They continually think and are not docile about their profession. Some things get easier with time and experience, but you have to start somewhere, so start where you are. Set goals for yourself and work toward them. Keep track of your progress and identify the causes of your setbacks. Start now. This book is probably used in one of your first courses in preparing to teach. Look ahead to other courses. Determine what you need to work on now and turn these needs into expectations for yourself and the instruction in those other courses. And don't just limit yourself to education courses; take these expectations to courses in other departments as well. We believe that what you learn in additional courses should be treated similar to the teaching interview mentioned earlier—it works both ways. Speak up and seek what you

"I'm thinking of leaving teaching and getting myself a nice, easy, 12-hour-a-day, six-day-a-week job!"
Phi Delta Kappan, September 1982.

know you need. Another word of caution: don't be like William James's image of teachers. While delivering his well-known series of lectures to teachers at Cambridge during the late 1800s, James, a renowned professor at Harvard, privately confided in a colleague at Stanford:

> Experience has taught me that teachers have less freedom of intellect than any class of people I know. . . . A teacher wrings his very soul out to understand you, and if he does ever understand anything you say, he lies down on it with his whole weight like a cow on a doorstep so that you can neither get out or in with him. He never forgets it or can reconcile anything else you say with it and carries it to the grave.[5]

Not a very flattering image of teachers, but James did try to get teachers to break away from their docility. We encourage you to do the same. You can start now in other ways, too. The following activities can help you continue your quest for self-understanding and personal perfection.

1. Talk to students. Interview them, ask lots of questions. Ask them what they like best and the least about school. Ask them about their teachers and ask for reasons for their feelings. Try to identify the dominant teaching philosophy used by the teachers of these students and try to figure out why students are or are not satisfied. Speculate about what could be done differently to improve satisfaction.

2. Look closely at the textbooks and learning materials used by teachers; become familiar with what publishers are selling. What assumptions about teaching and learning seem to be apparent and what philosophies are favored?

3. Examine the student learning activities encouraged by the textbooks. What differences do you see within and between academic subjects? What potential difficulties do you see?

4. Examine the teaching of your college professors. What philosophies are they using? How do you think the professors would answer the questions raised in this chapter?

5. Look beyond the niche in schools you may have identified for yourself. Acquaint yourself with the broad picture. What skills are taught to students in other grades and subjects, or to disadvantaged children? What do you think should be taught and why?

6. Find out how teachers who subscribe to the different philosophies mentioned in this chapter would teach basic subjects like reading, writing, or arithmetic.

7. Take several audiotaped or videotaped samples of your own teaching and examine them. Work with a teacher or classmate and analyze what you do. Do you get the kinds of interactions with

students you expect? Are you happy with the student responses? Do you play the teacher roles you wanted? Is your teaching consistent with your preferred style, your philosophy? Think back to previous chapters. What can you say about your communication and human relations skills? Do you choose only certain students to participate? Do you feel free to operate free from personal bias, or at least aware of them? Do you see yourself showing any discriminatory treatment toward any one group of students? Do you permit equal opportunities for all students? Is your classroom a place students enjoy and in which they find valuable experiences? What do you need to work on and what will you do to improve before you get your first teaching position?

☐ What If I Don't Want to Teach?

Obviously, we believe teaching is a necessary and noble profession. We assume many people who consider teaching will feel the same way about it after they take a close look. Well, what if you don't feel the same way? Have you wasted your time? Are you trapped like Jonathan felt in the scenario at the beginning of this chapter? No.

Preparing for teaching and then deciding that teaching is not what you want to do still leaves you with many good options. Teaching is a people activity that depends on one person, usually an authority figure, interacting with others who want to benefit from the interaction. If you decide you do not want to teach in public or private schools you can still do other kinds of teaching and you can do so many other things.

For starters, corporations need teachers, people with leadership qualities who are self-starters and who can communicate well with other employees. Management training is a big business you might find attractive. Personnel and business systems management positions also benefit from those who have capabilities for and training in teaching, as do other positions in banks, insurance companies, and so on.

People who are prepared in teaching have another common denominator—the ability to organize and analyze material and use language well (native or foreign). Commercial and free-lance publishing businesses need people with these skills as do public relations firms and writers for local, state, or national government officials. In fact, why not consider a career in politics? Our country always needs politicians who are intelligent, skilled in information usage, and who care about serving the needs of our citizens.

Don't overlook the academic and nonacademic needs of university

'Teachers'
have many
career
options.

campuses. Careers are possible in libraries, media resource centers, research and computing centers, administrative positions, student services, university publications, fund raising, and alumni relations. All of these occupations depend on skills and talents similar to those needed by teachers.

Many helping professions and public service occupations rely on persons with the same kinds of characteristics. As our population expands and continues to age, social service agencies need many persons who have several of the talents good teachers require. Medicine has an obvious teaching side to it, but so do several of the dietary and technical positions affiliated with medicine. The military operates extensive education programs—an option for you perhaps? Sales managers relish having a former teacher or someone who has preparation for teaching; sales positions have many uses for teacher types. And professions heavily dependent on those who can master academics like computers, electronics, science, mathematics, languages, political science, and so on need people with the skills possessed by teachers. In fact, corporations sometimes raid schools for their outstanding teachers and tempt them away with large salaries.

Certainly our list is not complete. More information on alternative careers for teachers is available in your career library. What are some other options you can think of?

A CLOSING COMMENT

■ As you read historical accounts of education in the United States, you soon become aware that a particular kind of cycle seems to repeat itself. Of course, the details change and the reasons vary, but the similarity of the present to the past is still there as strong as ever. Sooner or later someone discovers that all is not well in schools and that students are not performing equal to their counterparts from the good old days. A flurry of activity then takes place. Speeches are given, interviews granted, mandates made, and publications written about what is wrong with schools and who is to blame. Teachers seem always to get the blame and every good citizen, merchant, or politician has a plan for fixing the schools. Attention and sometimes extra money seem to fix the problem and all is well again, at least for a while, until the cycle repeats itself.

We don't mean to sound sarcastic here. We do want you to understand that these kinds of things do happen and if you decide to teach you will have to grow a pretty thick skin to keep from taking all of this personally. Please don't become complacent knowing that you

Can you teach?

can ignore the cycle because it soon goes away. Ignorance and neglect do not fix the problem. Complacency, or better yet docility, is probably what feeds this cycle. Teachers are guilty; teachers are victims, too, because many people have a responsibility for assuring quality in education. Accept the distinct possibility of this cycle, anticipate it, and do your part to keep it from happening so often. Learn to accept the saber-rattling, but do your own part of the rattling. Accept this as part of the responsibility in teaching.

Knowing all of this, do you still want to teach? If you say YES!, you must be destined to become a member of one of the most unique corps ever established. Henry Adams once wrote: "A teacher affects eternity. He can never tell where his influence stops."[6] Let the influence be positive. But maybe one of our own students expressed his feeling about teaching just as well:

> This experience has opened my eyes as to what teaching is really about. It has shown me that teaching isn't as easy as it looks, but also that it can be more rewarding than most people tend to think. My desire to become a teacher is stronger now than ever before. I just can't wait to get through the rest of school so I can begin. . . . What have I learned about the role of teachers? I have learned that

teachers have to put up with a lot more crap than I previously believed. They have to please everyone . . . and simultaneously teach and do all of the teacher "chores." My main reaction is that it's not as easy as it looks from the outside. And I guess that's why I still want to become a teacher. I like the challenge.[7]

Are you worthy of the challenge? Can *you* teach?

CHAPTER REFERENCES

1. Bruce Joyce and Marsha Weil, *Models of Teaching* (Englewood Cliffs, N.J.: Prentice-Hall, 1986).
2. William H. Berquist and Steven R. Phillips, *A Handbook for Faculty Development* (Washington, D.C.: Council for the Advancement of Small Colleges, 1975).
3. Madan Mohan and Ronald E. Hull, *Teaching Effectiveness: Its Meaning, Assessment, and Improvement* (Englewood Cliffs, N.J.: Educational Testing Publications, 1975).
4. Terry W. Blue, *The Teaching and Learning Process* (Washington, D.C.: National Education Association, 1981), p. 26.
5. William James, as quoted in Philip W. Jackson, *The Practice of Teaching* (New York: Teachers College Press, 1986), pp. 34–35
6. Henry Adams, as quoted in Jackson, *The Practice of Teaching,* p. 53.
7. Written by Douglas Barber, a student, in an introduction to teaching class: Analysis of Teacher Characteristics and Teaching Tasks, March 1986.

Index

Cohen, David, 59, 62
Combs, Arthur, 166n, 200, 201n
Conant, James, 298–299
Corey, Stephen M., 357
Counts, George S., 290
Cremin, Lawrence A., 267n
Cunningham, Luvern L., 220n, 227n
Curran, Jay, 166n
Cusick, Philip, 59
Cutbush, James, 253–254

D

D'Alessandro, John, 19n
Darling-Hammond, Linda, 35–36
De Garmo, Charles, 266
Dewey, John, 99, 114, 138, 290
Douglas, Barbara, 414n
Doyle, W., 13n
Dreikers, Rudolf, 202–204, 205
Duckworth, Eleanor, 62
Duke, Daniel L., 34n, 192, 193n, 195, 199n
Dulaney, Carole, 328n
Dustin, Dick, 166n

E

Eder, D., 15n
Eggen, Paul, 328n
Eisenhower, Dwight, 55
Elkind, David, 130, 131n, 133–134, 137n
Elliot, P. G., 103n
Elzey, F. F., 359n

F

Farrar, Eleanor, 59
Feistritzer, Emily, 35n, 36n, 122n
Fischer, Barbara, 399, 401–402n
Fischer, Louis, 399, 401–402n
Flanders, Ned, 146n, 350

Floyd, W. D., 357n,
Foxley, Cecelia H., 174
Frazier, Nancy, 157, 158n, 175
Freire, Paulo, 204n, 205
Freud, Sigmund, 133

G

Gall, Meredith, 353, 357
Gallagher, J. J., 354, 359
Galloway, Charles, 149, 151
Gallup, Alec M., 34n, 35n, 36n, 188
Gallup, George H., 329n
Garcia, Ricardo L., 173
George, Richy L., 165
Gesell, Arnold, 294
Gips, Crystal, 215
Glasser, William, 200
Glazer-Waldman, Hilda, 165
Good, Thomas L., 15, 152, 154, 155, 168–169, 350n, 362
Good, Weinstein, 15n
Goodlad, John, 13, 35, 59, 62, 63, 67, 80, 147, 153, 155
Grant, Carl, 98n, 99–100
Grubb, W. Norton, 76

H

Hall, G. Stanley, 294
Hall, Samuel, 255–257, 258
Hamilton, S. M., 250n
Hargie, O. D., 361n
Harper, Charles A., 259n, 260n
Hasford, Philip L., 345n
Haynes, H. C., 357
Health, Douglas, 20, 22n
Hentges, Joseph, 220n
Herbart, Johann Friedrich, 266–267
Heyl, Helen Hay, 292–293
Holt, John, 56
Hoy, Wayne K., 232n
Hull, Ronald E., 387n
Hunkins, Francis P., 359–360

Hyman, I. A., 19n, 208n
Hyman, Ronald, 162n

J

Jackson, P., 87–88, 89, 145
Jacobsen, Daid, 328n
Jacobson, Lenore, 152
James, William, 409
Jefferson, Thomas, 67, 250
John, Kenneth E., 125n
Johnson, D. W., 171n
Johnson, David, 170n
Johnson, Lyndon, 58
Johnson, Roger, 171n
Johnston, Lloyd, 124n
Jones, Louise S., 195n, 196
Jones, Vernon F., 195n, 196, 199n
Joyce, Bruce, 350, 382

K

Kaestle, Carl F., 250, 251n, 259n,
    260n
Kagan, Spencer, 171n
Kallen, Horace M., 172n
Kauchak, Donald, 328n
Keagy, John M., 254
Kennedy, Robert, 58
Kiebard, Herbert, 162n
King, Martin Luther, 58
Kingsley, Clarence, 286
Kleinman, G., 362n
Knezevich, Stephen J., 228n
Koerner, James D., 55n
Kozol, Jonathan, 56–57
Krafsky, Marie, 17–20

L

Ladd, G. T., 362n, 363n
Lamberth, John, 208n
Lauer, Jeannette, 122n
Lauer, Robert, 122n
Lazarowitz, Rachel Hertz, 171n

Lazerson, Marvin, 76
Leerhsen, Charles, 122n
Levine, S., 359n
Lieb-Brilhart, Barbara, 144n
Lieberman, Ann, 42n, 45n, 47n,
    48n
Lightfoot, Sara Lawrence, 59, 76,
    171
Lipka, Richard P., 168
Locke, John, 254
Lucking, Robert, 147–149

M

Mann, Horace, 259
Mann, James, 122n
Marshall, H. H., 16n
Maruyama, Geoffrey, 171n
Marx, R. W., 314n, 360
Mather, Cotton, 248
McCutcheon, Gail, 314
McGinnis, Alan Loy, 23n
McLeod, M. A., 335n
McMurray, Charles, 266
McMurray, Frank M., 266
Meckel, Adrienne, 192, 193n, 195
Melnik, Amelia, 357
Mertz, Norma, 227n
Middlestadt, Susan, 153n
Miller, Lynn, 42n, 45n, 47n, 48n
Miller, Patrick, 149
Minez, Robin, 157n
Miskel, Cecil G., 232n
Mohan, Madan, 387n
Monroe, James, 250

N

Nelson, Deborah, 171n
Newlon, Jesse, 296
Nixon, Richard, 58
Nystrand, Raphael O., 227n

O

Oakes, Jeannie, 154, 155–156, 171
Olson, Lynn, 115n

P

Pate, R. T., 358
Peirce, Cyrus, 259
Pestalozzi, Johann, 264, 266,
    267–268
Peterson, Penelope L., 314*n,* 317,
    319*n,* 335*n*
Phillips, D. C., 351*n*
Phillips, Steven R., 383
Pinnell, Gay Su, 308–309
Plisko, Vilema, 116*n*
Postman, Neil, 130, 131*n*
Powell, Arthur G., 59
Provenzo, Eugene F., Jr., 281*n*

R

Ravitch, Diane, 59
Raywid, Mary Ann, 55, 59, 78*n*
Reagan, Ronald, 60, 185
Reimer, Everett, 56*n*
Rickover, Hyman, 55, 298
Rogers, Carl, 350, 406
Rogers, U. M., 359*n*
Rogus, Joseph, 200
Rosenshine, Barak, 347–348, 350*n,*
    361–362
Rosenthal, Robert, 152
Rothkopf, E. Z., 361*n*
Rowe, Mary Budd, 361
Royce, Charles, 255
Rubinstein, Robert E., 197–199
Rugg, Harold, 295
Rury, John, 263*n,* 264

S

Sadker, David, 156*n*
Sadker, Myra, 156*n,* 157, 158*n,* 175
Sanders, Norris, 352
Scherman, Tony, 17–20
Schlechty, Phillip C., 34*n*
Schmuck, Richard, 171*n*
Schuelke, L. David, 144*n*
Schuler, Viola A., 42, 43–44

Sedlak, Michael, 266*n*
Seiler, William J., 144*n*
Sexton, Colleen, 341–344, 345–346
Shanker, Albert, 36
Sharan, Shlomo, 171*n*
Shaw, George Bernard, 151
Sheldon, Edward, 266
Shon, Linda, 171*n*
Silberman, Charles, 56
Simon, Martin A., 350*n*
Simon, Thédore, 282
Sirotnik, Ken, 58, 147*n*
Sizer, Theodore, 59, 62, 63*n,* 269*n*
Slavin, Robert, 171*n,* 173
Slyfield, Diane, 111
Smaley, Marlowe H., 167
Smith, Frank, 162*n*
Smith, Samuel Harrison, 250
Smith, Wilson, 248
Snedden, David, 286
Snowman, Jack, 397*n*
Soltis, Jonas, 351*n*
Soltow, Lee, 264*n*
Stern, Joyce, 116*n*
Stevens, Edward, 264*n*
Stevens, Romiett, 356–357
Stolbery, Arnold L., 122*n*
Stowe, Calvin, 259
Strother, Deborah Burnett, 123*n*

T

Taba, Hilda, 359
Tamminen, Armas W., 167
Tanner, Daniel, 327
Taylor, Frederick W., 278
Terman, Louis, 282–283
Tesconi, Charles, 59, 60, 78*n*
Thorndike, Edward, 281
Toby, Jackson, 19*n*
Tom, Alan, 99
Truth, Sojourner, 175

U

Ulich, Ivan, 56*n*
Usdan, Michael, 227*n*

V

Valverde, Leonard L., 228*n*
Vance, Victor S., 34*n*
Veenman, S., 93*n*
Venditti, Frederick, 227*n*

W

Wadsworth, Benjamin, 248
Warren, Donald R., 59, 78*n*
Watts, Isaac, 249–250
Wayson, William W., 207
Weber, Max, 221*n*
Webster, Noah, 251
Weil, Marshal, 350, 382
Weinaul, Bernard, 185*n*
Weinstein, R. S., 16*n*

Weinstein, Rhona, 15, 153*n*
Welsh, Clark, 171*n*
West, Anne Grant, 158*n*
Wigginton, Eliot, 138*n*, 173*n*, 406
Wilen, William, 314*n*, 352, 359, 360, 361*n*, 363*n*
Winn, Marie, 128, 130
Winne, P. H., 360
Wirtenberg, Jeana, 157*n*
Wirth, Arthur G., 288*n*
Wise, James H., 208*n*

Y

Yerkes, Robert, 283
Yinger, Robert J., 313*n*, 315
Yoakum, Clarence S., 283

SUBJECT

■ **A**

Ability grouping, 64
Academic ability, of teachers, 33–35
Academic skills, focus of public education on, 74–75
Action for Excellence, 61
Activity analysis, 291–292
Additive reform, in public education, 76–77
Administration. *See* School administration
Advance organizers, 344
Affective domain, 329–330, 389–390
Age, of teachers, 33
Alcohol use
  in schools, 185, 190
  by youth, 73, 124, 131
American Philosophical Society, 250
Arbitrary rules, and self-discipline, 209
Assertive discipline, 194

advantages of, 194–195
disadvantages of, 195
Automated classrooms, 384

B

Back-to-the basics movement, 67, 297–298
Behavior management, 185
Behavior modification, 193–194, 382
  advantages/disadvantages to, 196–197
  assertive discipline, 194–195
Bilingual education, 69
Black nonstandard English, 172–173
Blacks, textbook treatment of, 156–157
Brown v. *Board of Education of Topeka, Kansas,* 68–69, 301, 302

Business-Higher Education Forum, 59

C

"Cardinal Principles" report, 288–289
Child abuse, 73, 122–123
Child development theory, 270
Children. *See also* Students
  disappearance of, 131–134
  pressures on
    as challenge to teachers, 135–138
    to grow up, 130–134
  social construction of, 130–131
Child study movement, 265, 268
Civil rights movement, 303
Class discrimination, 158–159
Classroom atmosphere, 183–185
  and classroom management, 192–199
  comprehensive, 201–207
  discipline in, 185–191
  and logical consequences model, 202–204
  and self-discipline, 199–200, 201, 207–209
  and social literacy, 204–205
Classroom communication
  barriers to, 145–160
  channels of effective, 161–176
  human relations skills in, 165–168
  opening up lines of, 144
  organizing speech in, 162–164
  overcoming stereotypes in, 171–176
  and positive expectations, 168–171
  praise in, 162
  teachers' verbal and nonverbal messages to students, 146–151
Classroom environment, characteristics of, 13, 15

Classroom interaction, and multicultural education, 173–174
Classroom management, role of teachers in, 94
Classroom routines, estalishment of, 9
Cognitive domain, 328–329, 389
Cognitive-memory questions, 354
Commitment, importance of, 20
Committee of Correspondence on the Future of Public Education, 59
Communication. *See* Classroom communication
Complacency, 413
Confrontation, 167
  negative, 167
  positive, 167–168
Convergent thinking questions, 354
Cooperative classrooms, 170–171
Corporal punishment, 208
Council for Basic Education, 55, 60
Crime, and schools, 185
Cultural discrimination, 159
Culture, and multicultural education, 173
Curriculum, 312
Curriculum reform, 265–271

D

Deduction teaching method, 366
Democracy, role of public education in solving problems of, 67–72
Desensitization techniques, 344
Differentiated curriculum, 299–300
Direct instruction, 346–347
Discipline. *See also* Punishment
  image versus reality in, 185–191
  proper amount of, 197–199
  public perceptions of, 186–189
  realities of, 190–191
  teacher perceptions of, 189–190
Discrimination
  class, 158–159

cultural, 159
and negative expectations,
    158–160
racial, 159
sex, 159–160
Discussion, 345, 367
Discussion teaching method, 367
Divergent thinking questions,
    354
Diversity, in teaching, 45–46
Divorce, 121
Domain, 328
    affective, 329–330, 389–390
    cognitive, 328–329, 389
    psychomotor, 330, 390
Dropping out, issue of, 116
Drug use
    in schools, 185, 190
    by youth, 73, 124–125, 131
Due-process requirements, 235

E

*Educating Americans for the 21st
    Century,* 61
Education, scientific attitude to-
    ward, 253
Educational Amendments of 1966,
    58
Educational Amendments of 1967,
    58
Educational Amendments of 1972,
    58, 70
Educational atmosphere, 384
Educational philosophy, 400,
    402–405
    development of personal,
        405–406
    impact of, on teaching, 20–21
Educational reform, 294–295
Education Commission of the
    States (ECS), 59, 61
Education for All Handicapped
    Children Act of 1975 (PL
    94-142), 71–72
Education for work and defense
    movement, 61–62, 67

Educators
    contextual challenge to, 75–77
    and the search for purpose,
        77–80
Elementary and Secondary Educa-
    tion Act (1965), 58
Empathic understanding, 166
Employment, role of education in
    providing vocational skills,
    72
Equal educational opportunity
    (EEO), 303–304
Equal opportunity, concept of,
    300–305
Equal Rights Amendment (ERA),
    70
Equality, and schooling, 62–64, 67
Essentialist viewpoint of schools,
    393
Evaluative thinking questions, 354
Existential viewpoint of schools,
    394–395
Expectations, communicating,
    151–156
Experience, of teachers, 33
Experience-oriented classes, 384
Explicit teaching, 347–348

F

Family, 120–121
    structure of, 121–123
Federal government, responsibility
    of, for education, 223, 225
First-grade studies, on student
    group placement, 15
First-year teachers, and reality
    shock, 93
Foxfire folk life project, 138, 173

G

Gender, of teachers, 32
Gifted, identification and develop-
    ment of, 282

H

Handicapped, education of, 70–72
Herbartianism, 266–267, 270, 271
Hidden curriculum, 153–154
High School: A Report on Secondary Education in America, 62
Hispanic Americans, textbook treatment of, 156
Home room, 289
Humanistic critique, of education, 56, 58
Human relations skills, in classroom communications, 165–168

I

Induction teaching method, 367
Inquiry, as teaching method, 345, 367
Instrumental reason, 75
    schooling and, 76–77
Intelligence quotient (I.Q.) testing controversy over, 284–285
    development of, 282
Interaction-oriented classrooms, 384

J

Jewish Americans, textbook treatment of, 156
Job advancement, in teaching, 39–40
Job security, in teaching, 40

L

Labeling, of students, 155–156
Language
    and bilingual education, 69
    and multicultural education, 172–173
Language development, significance of sensation theory to, 254–255

Latchkey children, 123
Latin grammar school, 269
Learning
    relation between teaching and, 294–295
    role of teachers in facilitating, 94
Lecture teaching method, 366
Lesson plans, 320–321. *See also* Teaching plans
    comparing, 333–334
    content, 330–331
    daily lesson planning and teaching, 324–334
    domains in, 328–330
    evaluation, 331, 333
    goal setting in, 321–323
    learning experiences, 323
    objectives in, 325–328
    post-lesson planning, 334–336
    pre-lesson planning, 321–324
    priority of, 319
    pupil level in, 323–324
    rationale in, 325
    subject matter in, 323
    teaching procedures, 331
Life-adjustment education movement, 297, 298
Lincoln School at Teachers College, 295
Linear planning approach, 318, 319
    format for, 332
Local community, responsibility of, for education, 223, 225–226
Logical consequences model, 202–204
Lyseum movement, 252–253

M

Mainstream, expansion of, and treatment of the handicapped, 70–72
Making the Grade, 61
Media, and American youth, 126–129
Memorization techniques, 345

Men
    in leadership roles, 226–228
    in teaching, 32
Metaphorical representations of
        schools, 233–234
Minorities
    educational rights of, 68–69
    representation of, in textbooks,
        156–157
    in teaching, 33
Multicultural education, 172
    and classroom interaction,
        173–174
    language in, 172–173
    use of cultures in, 173

N

National Assessment of
        Educational Progress
        (NAEP), 115
National Association of Manufac-
        turers (NAM), 286
National Coalition of Advocates for
        Children, 157
National Commission on Excel-
        lence in Education, 59,
        60–61
National Council for Accreditation
        of Teacher Education
        (NCATE), 36
National Defense Education Act
        (NDEA), 55–56
National Education Association
        (NEA)
    Committee on Vocational Educa-
        tion and Vocational Guid-
        ance, 288
    survey on discipline, 190
National Science Board, 61
National Science Board Commis-
        sion on Precollege Education
        in Mathematics, 59
National Science Foundation
        (NSF), 55
National Society for the Promotion

of Industrial Education
        (NSPIE), 286
Nation at Risk, A, 60–61
Native Americans, textbook treat-
        ment of, 156
Nonsexist education, 174
    and classroom activities,
        175–176
    and classroom materials, 175
    and student actions, 175
    and teacher actions, 174–175
    and teacher attitudes, 174
Nonverbal communication,
        149–151
Nonverbal praise, 162
Normal school movement, 257–
        260
    admission to, 260
    curriculum of, 260–261
    growth of schools in, 264–265
    and teacher preparation, 261

O

Object method, in teacher training,
        265–266, 270, 271
Organizational structure of schools,
        221–222
    See also School administration

P

Parent-teacher conference, 245–
        246
Pay structure, in teaching, 39–40
Pedagogy, 264–265, 309
Peer pressures, 124
    and alcohol use, 124
    and drug use, 124–125
    and prevalence of sex, 125–126
Pennsylvania Chapter of the Na-
        tional Association of
        Retarded Children (PARC),
        70–71
Perennialist viewpoint of schools,
        393

Pestalozzian methods, 265–266
Phonetics, 255
Place Called School, A, 62
Positive expectations, in classroom
    communications, 168–171
Post-lesson planning, 334–336
Pregnancy, 73
Prescribed curriculum, in public
    education, 76–77
Principals, measuring efficiency of,
    279–281
Professional decision-making by
    teachers, 94–95
Progressive viewpoint of schools,
    394
Progressivism, 292–296, 298
  reactions to, 296–299
Psychomotor domain, 330, 390
Public, perceptions of, of discipline,
    186–189
Public debate, over quality of pub-
    lic education, 54–67
Public education
  continuing debate on, 54–67
  and curriculum reform, 265–271
  humanistic critique of, 56, 58
  impact of *Sputnik* on, 55–56
  and instrumental reason, 76–77
  meeting challenges in, 104
  multiple roles of, 67–75
  patterns of enrollment in,
    263–264
  pedagogy in, 264–265
  public support for, 77
  reports on quality of, 58–67
Public support, for education, 77
Punishment. *See also* Discipline
  corporal, 208
  replacement with motivation, 296
Puritans, influence of, on educa-
    tion, 247–250
"Pygmalion effect," 152

Q

Questions
  definition of, 352

reasons for importance of,
    352–355
research on use of, 356–364
types of, 353–355
use of, in teaching, 352–353

R

Race, of teachers, 33
Racial discrimination, 159
Racism, history of, 301–305
Reading instruction, 248–249, 252
Reality shock, 93
Reflection
  definition of, 99–100
  prerequisites for, 100–101
  process of, 101–103
Reform movements, in public edu-
    cation, 76–77
Religious instruction, 248, 252
Report of the Commission on the
    Reorganization of Secondary
    Education, 288–289
Report of the Committee of Fifteen
    on Elementary Education of
    the National Educational
    Association, 267
Report of the Committee of Nine
    on the Articulation of High
    School and College, 286
Report of the Committee of Ten on
    Secondary School Studies of
    the National Educational
    Association, 268–269, 285,
    286
Rhetorical questions, 352
Risk taking, and teaching, 22–23
Runaways, 122–123

S

School(s). *See also* Public educa-
    tion; Teachers; Teaching
  academic programs in, 226
  differences in, 228–234

and equality, 62–64, 67

financial dependence of, on local community, 228–229

governmental responsibility for, 223–226

integration of organizational structure and individual impact, 233

male dominance in leadership roles in, 226–228

metaphorical representations of, 233–234

organizational structure of, 221–222

similarities in, 221–228

School administration

bureaucracies in, 222

efficiency ratings for, 278–281

and government responsibility for, 223–226

male dominance in, 226–228

reactions of students to, 112–113

similaries of, 221–222

School boards, 219, 224

School buildings, measuring efficiency of, 281

School districts, number of, 225–226

School rules, development of, 234–235, 238–239

School superintendents, 224

typical, 219–220

Scientific attitude, toward education, 253

Self-discipline

and arbitrary rules, 209

barriers to developing, 207–209

and corporal punishment, 208

definition of, 199

and locus of control, 200

positive, 201

and suspension, 208–209

teaching of, 200–201

Self-disclosure, 166–167

Self-image, of teacher, 10

Self-perception, positive, 201

Sense learning, theory of, 254

Sex, prevalence of, among America's youth, 125–126

Sex discrimination, in education, 70, 159–160

Sheltered-experience-oriented classes, 384

Single mothers, 121–122

Social interaction, 382

Social literacy approach, 204–205

Social reconstructionism, 290–291, 394

Social skills, focus of public education on, 74

Special education programs, 160

Spelling instruction, 249, 251

Sputnik era, 55–56

Standardized tests, 281–285

use of, for teachers, 37–38

State, responsibility of, for education, 223, 224, 225

Stereotypes

communicating, 156–158, 160

overcoming, in classroom communication, 171–176

in treatment, 158, 160

Student(s). *See also* Children

age-level characteristics of, 397

classification of, through standardized tests, 281–285

effect of teacher expectations on, 15

grouping and tracking of, 153–156

involvement of, in classroom activities, 191

learning styles of, 399, 401–402

reactions of, to administrators, 112–113

reactions of, to teachers, 111–112

role of public education in solving personal problems, 72–73

Student academic performances, 114–115

drop out ratio, 116

and falling test scores, 115–116

measurement of, 115–116

and teacher perceptions, 116–120

Student-centered teaching approaches, 348–351
Student Efficiency Test, 278–279
Student group placement, first-grade studies on, 15
Student movements, direction of, 9
Student-oriented classrooms, 383
Student recitation teaching method, 366
Subject matter, interest in, and decision to teach, 45
Substance abuse. *See* Alcohol use; Drug use
Suspension, 208–209
Synectics, 345

T

Teacher(s). *See also* Teaching
  academic ability of, 33–35
  age and experience of, 33
  certification requirements for, 31
  characteristics of, 31–33
  competence issue, 31, 223
  complex roles of, 234–239
  and decision making, 95–97
  expectations of, 12–13
    bring out the best in students, 23–24
    communicating negative, 153
    effect of, on student treatment, 95–96
    personal, 95–96
  of the future, 35–38
  gender of, 32
  measuring efficiency of, 279–281
  and nonsexist education, 174–176
  openmindedness of, 100
  perceptions of
    on discipline, 189–190
    on student achievement, 116–120
  personal development of, 102–103
  personal responsibilities of, 88–90, 92

  pressures on children as challenge to, 135–138
  race of, 33
  reactions of students to, 111–112
  reasons for becoming, 38–46
  roles of, 297–298, 378–381
  self-image of, 10
  sense of responsibility of, 100
  verbal and nonverbal messages of, to students, 146–151
  wholeheartedness of, 100–101
Teacher-centered approaches to teaching, 346–348
Teacher-oriented classrooms, 383–384
Teacher perceptions, and student academic performance, 116–120
Teacher rapes, 190
Teacher routines, 315
Teacher-student relationships, quality of, 16–17
Teacher training
  and Herbartianism, 266–267
  new approach to, 289–296
  object method of, 265–266
  quality of, 36–38
Teaching. *See also* Teachers
  accepting tasks of, 92–95
  avoiding handicaps of, 20–23
  and bringing out the best in self and others, 23–24
  deciding not to, 410, 412
  exploring, as a career, 1–2, 85–95, 377–378
  extrinsic rewards of, 39–40
  joy in, 40–45
  meeting challenges in, 104
  and the normal school movement, 257–263
  perceptions about, 3–7, 9–13, 15–20
  reflections on, 22, 97–104
  relation between learning and, 294–295
  strategies of, 22
  style of, 387–395

Teaching ability, determination of, 406–412
Teaching context, 382–385
  of basic skills, 251–252
  and being a good teacher, 255–263
  colonial precedents in, 247–251
  in the early 20th century, 277–289
  and equal opportunity, 300–305
  and expansion of public education, 263–271
  reactions to progressivism, 296–300
  science and mental development, 252–255
  teacher preparation and curriculum reform, 289–296
  teaching styles, 385–387
Teaching materials, 9–10
Teaching methods, 344–346
  deduction, 366
  discussion, 367
  induction, 367
  inquiry, 367
  lecture and student recitation, 366
  questions in, 352–365
  student-centered approaches, 348–352
  teacher-centered approaches, 346–348
Teaching objectives, 325–326
  components of, 326–327
  use of, to stimulate learning, 327–328
Teaching plans. *See also* Lesson plans
  benefits of using, 314
  importance of, 312
  reasons for, 313–314
  as nested process, 315
  research on, 319
  setting goals in, 323
  types of, 315–319
Team teaching, 312
Test scores, phenomenon of falling, 115–116

Textbooks, 9–10
  and nonsexist education, 175
  stereotyping in, 156–157
  women in, 157–158
Title IX, 70
"Toyota problem," 62
Tracking, of students, 153–156
Twentieth Century Fund Task Force on Federal Elementary and Secondary Education Policy, 59, 61

U

United States Army, use of intelligence tests by, 283
U.S. Commission on Civil Rights, 157
User-friendly environment, creation of, 78–80

V

Vacation time, in teaching, 40
Verbal praise, 162
Vocational education, 72
Vocational guidance, 283

W

Wait time, 361
Women
  educational rights of, 70
  in teaching, 32
  textbook treatment of, 157–158
Women on Words and Images project, 157–158

Y

Youth clubs, 137–138
Youth culture, 120
  family in, 120–123
  media in, 126–129
  peer pressure in, 124–128